9/18

THE ENCYCLOPEDIA
OF MISINFORMATION

THE
ENCYCLOPEDIA
OF MISINFORMATION

A COMPENDIUM OF IMITATIONS, SPOOFS, DELUSIONS, SIMULATIONS, COUNTERFEITS, IMPOSTORS, ILLUSIONS, CONFABULATIONS, SKULLDUGGERY, FRAUDS, PSEUDOSCIENCE, PROPAGANDA, HOAXES, FLIMFLAM, PRANKS, HORNSWOGGLE, CONSPIRACIES & MISCELLANEOUS FAKERY

REX SORGATZ

ABRAMS, NEW YORK

FOR MICHELLE,
WHO IS THE OPPOSITE OF THIS BOOK

◀◉◎◉◉◉ ◀◀◀◀ CONTENTS ▶▶▶▶ ◉◉◉◉◎▶

"Facts are stubborn things."
— **JOHN ADAMS**

"Facts are stupid things."
— **RONALD REAGAN**

"Facts are lonely things."
— **DON DELILLO,** *Libra*

★ ★ ★

"I don't know where the artificial
stops and the real starts."
— **ANDY WARHOL**

"Reality is that which, when you
stop believing in it, doesn't go away."
— **PHILIP K. DICK**

"Humankind cannot bear very much reality."
— **T. S. ELIOT,** *Four Quartets*

★ ★ ★

"Encyclopedia.
Laugh at it pityingly for being
quaint and old-fashioned.
Even so: thunder against it."
— **GUSTAVE FLAUBERT,**
Dictionary of Accepted Ideas

INTRODUCTION

Several months before this book was published, a curious advertisement started to appear on the streets and subways of New York City. In the shape of a poster, the ad presented a simple apple, and below that, a caption that waxed rhapsodically, like a childhood fable:

This is an apple.
Some people might try to
tell you that it's a banana.
They might scream
banana, banana, banana.
Or put banana in all caps.
You might even start to believe
that this is a banana.
But it's not.
This is an apple.
FACTS FIRST

At the bottom—below the fruit, past the winsome prose poem and the earnest slogan—appeared the logo for the product being promoted: CNN. If something can be both *sorta genius* and *kinda dumb* at the same time, it might be this ad campaign.

Undoubtedly, the message was crafted for its political moment. Under ceaseless partisan and economic assault, the mainstream media had been showing signs of duress for decades. But the presidential administration had been particularly relentless, not only rebuking specific news outlets and denigrating reporters by name, but screaming "fake news!"

to every exurban cul-de-sac that would repeat the signal. Facing the spread of misinformation, some marketer at CNN probably conjured the zany scheme to defend the media against the raiding barbarians with—*presto!*—an advertising campaign. Given the state of the media industry, and the public battle being waged over basic facts, it was easy to sympathize with their plight. Until, that is, you realized the crux of the message behind the campaign: *some people think apples are bananas.*[1]

Yes, it's true, the framing of the message accidentally exposed an implicit media elitism (*they* see bananas, but not *you*), and sure, the campaign seemed to imply that a dire epistemological meltdown could be resolved with the same crafty sloganeering that engineered *Think Different* or *Just Do It!* But behind all the convoluted rhetoric about the ownership of truth, a deeper concern stewed. Whether consciously or not, the campaign recalled another iconic image/text juxtaposition:

Ceci n'est pas une pipe.

Long before cable news declared *this is an apple*, the surrealist painter René Magritte cut a more counterintuitive message with the dictum *this is not a pipe*. Images, for Magritte, are not what they appear,

---

1   The advertisement also appeared online, taking shape as a YouTube video and, of course, a hashtag: #FactsFirst. The campaign also resembled the *Washington Post*'s new alliterative motto, "Democracy Dies in Darkness," a crafty bit of ominous archetyping that forebodes evil-doing like nothing this side of Joseph Campbell.

or at the very least, words and pictures are out of sync. The very title of the painting, THE TREACHERY OF IMAGES, is unequivocal on its attitude toward representation. Though separated from modern mass media by nearly a century, the painting still whispers to us today: *Images are elusive, language is fragmentary, the news is an imperfect simulation, and the media ranks presentation over information, entertainment over data.* Maybe the apple really is a banana.

During politically polarized moments, contrasting these images can be precarious. Facts are a contested battleground, now more than ever. This book will not pretend to resolve the stalemate, but it will, hopefully, outline its vector through history and provide some space to consider how deception, manipulation, and subterfuge function in our society. We will try to separate apples from bananas, but any pomegranates discovered along the way will be joyfully devoured.

Inside this compendium you will find nearly 300 encyclopedic entries, many of which could—with some brusque editing—appear in one of those hefty reference tomes produced by prestigious university lexicographers. But this is not exactly that kind of anthology.

The example above, in which an iconic surrealist painting marinates with a recent advertising campaign, is a decent sample of the contents herein. Plainspoken descriptions of dense subject matter can be found here, but this is not precisely a technical manual. This reference book is less interested in imposing strict definitions than in investigating how misinformation vexes and confounds. These pages contain blips of ideas of a more ambiguous nature, with tables, charts, and illustrations that provoke as much as elucidate. Interspersed throughout are dozens of thought experiments, a slew of aphorisms, a few puzzles, some secret messages, and footnotes up the wazoo. There are two short stories,

a few imagined interviews, a play, a product review, and an obituary. The Platonic dialogue at the end (ZENO'S PARADOX) reads like a desperate ploy to sell a *Rick and Morty* spec script. (Can you hear me now, Dan Harmon?)

Why the kitchen-sink treatment? Because, let's face it, normal reference books are usually kinda boring. But more significantly, when the subject is misinformation, one needs a little subterfuge to knead the mental dough. This is a wily subject, cutting through the distant past and the very modern present, science and society, history and philosophy. Circumnavigating the misinformation globe from diverse angles might help us discover new lands.

In that spirit, another narrative contrivance will now be tested: the author interview. If this were the internet, we might imitate a Reddit AMA, but because you dished out 20 frogskins for this regal tome, a more classy rendering is due. Let us pretend, momentarily, that Terry Gross has extended an invitation into her radio studio to discuss this compendium.

Welcome to the show.
Delighted to be here. It is a dream come true to be on *Fresh Air*.

You call this an *encyclopedia*. Is it really a reference book?
Dang, Terry. Throwing shade already?

It's true, this book is a deception, or at least a contradiction. Encyclopedias are collections of information, but this is a collection of its opposite: deception, propaganda, and bad data.

Who should read this book?
I would say this book will appeal to skeptical people: Those who are predisposed to distrust conventional wisdom, but are reasonable enough to avoid ensnarement in conspiratorial traps. They find FLAT EARTH

THEORY and the MOON LANDING HOAX as goofy as Coen brothers plots, but they adore the kooky adherents of such mega-schemes like quixotic Christopher Guest characters.

Those gruff sophisticates who believe themselves right on all matters will find little comfort in this compendium. But those who enjoy CRYPTIDS will totally will dig it.

Could this reference book be read as a how-to manual for mental manipulation?
Sure, it's *The Anarchist Cookbook* of the mind. Go crazy, and please, tell everyone that.

How do you define *misinformation*?
Broadly, to the point of ridiculousness.

Constructing a specialized compendium usually involves demarcating boundaries; *these topics fit within our scope of study*. But when the scope is literally all of experienced reality, drawing the borders resembles stabbing a pencil into the night sky.

The social sciences have supplied worthy definitions for *misinformation* (inaccurate info), *disinformation* (inaccurate info spread malevolently), and *malinformation* (accurate info spread malevolently). Each of these topics are absorbed here, and a whole lot more. Some astute social researcher will undoubtedly stumble upon this book and become perturbed to find no entries on subjects like *apophenia* or *motivated reasoning*.[2]

By its very nature, this compendium will be unable to satisfy the compulsive academic who craves exhaustive comprehensiveness. Instead, like many of the first dictionaries and encyclopedias, this compilation meanders around its subject, poking at it with a divining rod and a scrying mirror to see which strain of ectoplasm oozes out.

With a wide aperture, the lens of this anthology also absorbs squishier topics, including authenticity, identity, cognition, and artistic fakery. All the fun stuff of life.

Is that why terms like COSPLAY, DARK ENERGY, and ESPERANTO are included?
When used academically, *misinformation* is an evaluative term—a judgment, a condemnation. Misinformation is the stuff to be examined and eradicated. The work of social scientists is laudable and heavily referenced herein, but as someone raised on the fatberg of television and the internet, I see society through slightly different goggles: Not as some *homo economicus* who can be sliced into nifty segments for analysis, but as mysterious creatures who act in stupendously irrational ways.

In advocating a more global use of terms, this book happily absorbs acts of cultural manipulation like SLASHFIC, LARPS, and A MODEST PROPOSAL. I realize that appropriation, performance, and satire do not traditionally fall within this rubric, but their ironic relationship to society might move us closer to a universal theory of obfuscation.[3]

Also, taking FAKE SHEMPS seriously is super fun.

Are people naturally deceptive?
Deception—especially self-deception, plus whatever convoluted psychological mechanism asks that others lie to us—seems one of our few innate traits. Misdirection and subterfuge are not the anomaly, but the norm. Manipulation is not the exhaust fume of history, but rather its fuel.

---

2   Tricked you already! *Apophenia* is covered in PAREIDOLIA; *motivated reasoning* gets its due in COGNITIVE DISSONANCE.

3   To see why irony demands inclusion in a study of misinformation, look no further than the alt-right revolt emanating from the hate-filled corners of 4chan and Reddit. A founding principle of the movement involves resisting explicit endorsement of its own racist memes, claiming their sarcastic absurdity merely arouses sclerotic minds into action. Irony is essentially the "alt" in alt-right. Remove the internet-enabled sarcasm, and dime-store national fascism festers beneath.

Even a quick glance at the culture we humans produce reveals how trickery is celebrated, especially in the fields of comedy, politics, visual arts, and even technology. I intend no value judgment in assigning acts of playful artifice to a book about misinformation, other than to suggest that the universe can be pretty goddamn complicated. (I'm not crazy about reality either, but as Groucho Marx said, it's the only place to get a decent meal.)

That is how you ended up holding a book that engulfs 3D PRINTING, CELEBRITY SEX TAPES, CHILEAN SEA BASS, LAUGH TRACKS, and the TURING TEST into its purview.

So *how* should I read this book?
Whatever you do, *do not* start at the beginning. Those first few entries are terribly disappointing. I hear the P's are great—start there!

But seriously, you should read this book however you damn well please. Not that it matters, but it was composed to be read interactively. Try paging around for an engaging topic and use the **SEE ALSO** pointers at the bottom of each entry to carom through related topics. Reading this way, following a catch-if-you-can path, you might stitch together disconnected vignettes into a salient thread on how propaganda works, or how artificial intelligence can deceive, or how skulduggery functions in art and aesthetics, or how satire and parody are inherently flawed. Skip whatever bores you. Choose your own mis-adventure.

Also, read the footnotes. That's where all the good jokes are buried.[4]

There is a lot of history in here, but new technology pops up, too.
We may have finally entered that *2001: A Space Odyssey* phase of human history, when artificial intelligence starts to plot against us.

Maybe the internet was the protophase.
Well said, Terry. Everything is fucked up today because of the internet, right?

Please, this is public radio.
Sorry! Anyway, despite how disconcerting social media and reality television can be, I sometimes think they might accidentally become the utensils of choice for scraping together a larger theory of human psychology. In particular, how identity works.

As I was writing this book, one particularly insane anecdote—involving the 2016 lawsuit between Hulk Hogan and Gawker Media—lurked in the back of my mind. A refresher: The professional wrestler sued the internet tabloid for $100 million for publishing excerpts of a CELEBRITY SEX TAPE that captures him boinking his best friend's wife. (The nom de plume of the frenemy cuckold? Bubba the Love Sponge, *because obviously reality has inadvertently diverged into the porn fairy-tale dimension.*) That story is already bananas, but then it was revealed that billionaire Peter Thiel (an advisor to Donald Trump and a cofounder of PayPal) had secretly funded the lawsuit for the Hulkster. And then to every first amendment scholar's dismay, *Hogan somehow won the lawsuit.* And yet, we still have not reached peak Hulkamania. . . .

While on the stand, Hogan was asked about a radio interview he did on the Love Sponge's show in which he brags about his manhood. This courtroom testimony transpires with the Gawker attorney:

> **Attorney:** Do you have any doubt you were discussing the length of your penis?
> **Hulk:** Well, it's not mine, because mine is not the size. We were discussing Hulk Hogan's.
> **Attorney:** Seriously?
> **Hulk:** No, sir. I do not have a 10-inch penis.

---

4   A grasshopper walks into a bar, and the bartender says, "Hey, we have a drink named after you." The surprised grasshopper replies, "Really? In that case, give me a Steve!" (Hope that didn't scare you off from the footnotes.)

At this point, Hulk Hogan begins to argue that he, *as a character*, has a sizable phallus, but he, *as a person*, has a shrimpy weenie. Besides egregiously breaking KAYFABE, this might just be the most cogent illustration of just how fractured the concept of identity has become.

It's like what Richard Nixon told a reporter...
"I am myself, and I'm going to continue playing that role!" It's a good one. But I prefer the Cary Grant bit.

What did he say?
"Everyone wants to be Cary Grant. Even I want to be Cary Grant." Wouldn't you want to be Cary Grant?

No, I want to be Terry Gross.
You just blew my mind, Terry.

THE
ENCYCLOPEDIA
OF MISINFORMATION

3D PRINTING

Like their inkjet forefathers, 3D printers are machines that create facsimiles based upon a template. But instead of spewing paper, these machines create copies of full-fledged objects, everything from cell-phone cases to airplane parts. During a brief period of intense high-tech euphoria around 2009, it seemed like the 3D printer revolution might follow the same trajectory as the personal computer—leaping from obscure research vessel to ubiquitous machine. Optimistic futurists, high on their own hullabaloo, were predicting that desktop 3D printers would soon be found in every home, churning out full-size bespoke automobiles and backyard Eiffel Towers. The replicators from *Star Trek* were just around the corner.

That future still might come to fruition someday, but the personal printing revolution has mostly stalled, except for a small band of fervent enthusiasts who use their expensive desktop printers to produce fancy pencil holders in the shape of Julius Caesar's bust. But just as the personal printing revolution is petering out, the industrial 3D printing revolution shows no signs of slackening. Among the accomplishments in printing trickery that are challenging our notions of ownership, identity, labor, biology, and creativity:

- A bioprinter has been used to create ear, bone, and muscle structures out of plastic. Kidney and brain tissue has also been printed for drug trials.
- The Culinary Institute of America has used a 3D printer to invent new foods.
- About a mile east of King Tut's tomb in Egypt stands a full-size replica of the funky pharaoh's resting place.
- After a motorcycle accident, a man in Wales had the bones in his face reconstructed via 3D printing.
- The Van Gogh Museum has created exacting reproductions of several paintings, including *Sunflowers* (1884). Realistic down to the cracks in the paint, the "Relievos," as they're called, have gone on tour around the world.
- Rocket Lab, a Silicon Valley–funded start-up, launched a 3D-printed rocket into space in May 2017.
- Trying to keep pace with destruction brought about by global warming, 3D printers are creating coral reefs in the Mediterranean, the Caribbean, and the Indian Ocean around Australia.
- The caves of Lascaux have been closed to visitors

for half a century, but a 3D replica of the grotto and its paintings has been created nearby.

Despite these innovations, the most famous object to come from the 3D printing movement is likely a gun. Cody Wilson, a self-described "information anarchist" from Texas, released the blueprints for a printable firearm, which could be manufactured with any 3D printer, on the internet in 2012. Though the State Department demanded its removal, the template found its way onto illicit filesharing services. It was a killer app, but not the one the personal 3D printing movement needed.

SEE ALSO: GREEBLES; HUMAN CLONING; SHIP OF THESEUS; SYNTHETIC DIAMONDS

13TH FLOOR, THE

Some fears are more irrational than others. Falling off a jagged cliff sounds objectively terrifying, so a modest fear of heights (*acrophobia*) could be tantamount to bodily survival. Similar intense anxieties, like the fear of fire (*pyrophobia*) or of the dark (*nyctophobia*), might be hardwired into our brains, part of the atavistic circuitry of being a nervous human. Spiders (*arachnophobia*) and sharks (*galeophobia*) could—at least in theory—inflict pain, so anticipating their animalistic wrath makes some rational sense. Same goes for needles (*trypanophobia*), flying (*aerophobia*), and—sure, it's a stretch, but—zombies (*kinemortophobia*). Most fears, if not precisely logical, are at least reasonably deducible.

Other fears make no goddamn sense. The aversions to mirrors (*catoptrophobia*) and beards (*pogonopho-* *bia*) sound suspiciously like the inventions of desperate think piece scribes, thirsty to disseminate their musings on self-love and hipster hate. But not even those zeitgeisty disorders occupy the top ranks of Most Irrational Human Fears. Among the phobic contenders, the most inexplicable insecurity might be the one in which we fret over a *number*. Because every fright is bequeathed its own moniker, we have even invented a word for the dread that envelops the number thirteen—*triskaidekaphobia*. If urban architecture were the gauge of measurement, triskaidekaphobia would be a pandemic, with American skyscrapers appearing the most panic-stricken. According to a study of apartments conducted in New York City in 2015, 91 percent of Manhattan buildings have skipped numbering a floor as the thirteenth floor.[1] It is an indisputably strange superstition. A building cannot literally eliminate a floor, so the jump in stories can only be understood as a frivolous embellishment. Are we supposed to believe that everyone who lives on the fourteenth floor has somehow been duped?

But at this point, the urban legend can no longer be repealed. Fear of the thirteenth floor has been literally chiseled into our buildings—the cement and the circuitry. Just as buxom teens cannot abstain from camping in the woods of Jason Voorhees on a certain recurring Friday, real estate tycoons must persist in creating blueprints that skip an entire floor in their numbering system. The wheels of paranoia in motion, we cannot stop designing elevators without a button labeled 13. The thirteenth-floor urban legend is irretrievably embedded into that American philosophy that ranks tradition over rationality.

SEE ALSO: POTEMKIN VILLAGE; ILLEGAL PRIME NUMBER; NOT EVEN WRONG; VOMITORIUMS

---

1   The study of buildings with more than thirteen floors was performed by CityRealty. But real people seem less concerned with the number than do real estate developers. According to a 2007 Gallup poll, only 13 percent (naturally) of Americans say they would be bothered by a thirteenth-floor room assignment in a hotel.

555-2368

Who you gonna call? Within a certain supernatural comedy, the emergency phone number for reaching a squad of exterminators is 555-2368. Those digits not only dial into a Ghostbusters hotline to report a Slimer but also work within many other fictional universes, where the exact same number reaches out to the Bionic Woman, Jim Rockford, the motel room in *Memento*, the Mod Squad, Kojak (office), Howard the Duck (home), and the family of the abductee in *Close Encounters of the Third Kind*. Pretty good for four random digits that, technically, break the telecom rules.

There is an actual entity that specifies what telephone numbers should appear in movies and television. According to the North American Numbering Plan Administration (NANPA—we're back in reality now; that's a real thing), fictitious telephone numbers are supposed to fall within a preset range. There are only one hundred numerals officially reserved for fiction—those 555 digits between 0100 and 0199. Because 555-2368 falls outside that range, dialing it nowadays might lead to someone actually picking up, depending on what area code you prepend.

Using 555 as a dummy prefix started in movies of the early '60s; the 2368 extension became an inside joke in the '80s. Though they are the most popular fictitious digits, plenty of other characters and places reside within the 555 Cinematic Universe: Agent Scully (1013), the Mike and Carol Brady residence (1212), Moe's Tavern (1239), Buffy (0101), Seinfeld (2390), Kramer (3455), D. J. Tanner (8722), Alf (7787), the Peach Pit (4352), Lloyd Dobler (4312), Laverne and Shirley (9988), and the Bates Motel (9130).[2] In the *Last Action Hero*, a kid tries to convince Schwarzenegger that they are living in a movie by arguing there are only 9,999 available 555 phone numbers, not nearly enough to account for the population of Los Angeles. "That's why we have area codes," counters Schwarzenegger, handily tamping a potential cinematic universe meltdown.

During the theatrical release of *Ghostbusters*, director Ivan Reitman set up 1-800-555-2368 with a recording of Bill Murray and Dan Aykroyd in character. When it started to receive a thousand calls per hour on his bill, he shut it down. At the time of this writing, the number resolves to a Kafkaesque message for a "nonworking extension for Corporate Telecom."

SEE ALSO: DOE, JOHN; THE FOURTH WALL; ILLEGAL PRIME NUMBER; LOREM IPSUM; NULL ISLAND; TOMMY WESTPHALL UNIVERSE

---

2   That last one is found in *Psycho III*, from 1986. Of course, there's a detailed website that lists hundreds of fictional numbers, but it's an old obscure Earthlink address with tildes in its URL, so as a sign of how far we have come since the phonebook, instead try googling "555-LIST" to find it.

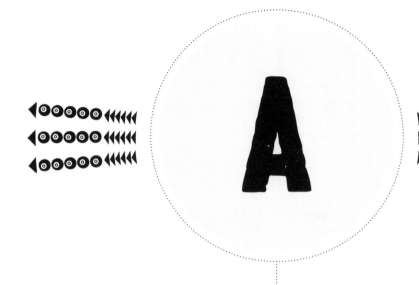

AETHER

Aether is an inert, invisible, universe-spanning substance that has been invented, refuted, and reinvented by physicists and philosophers throughout history to explain the unexplainable.

It has had a long, storied life in many forms. In Greek mythology, aether was a kind of pure essence, breathed only by gods. Aristotle granted it status as the fifth element (after earth, air, fire, and water), but it was unique from the others in being neither hot nor cold, wet nor dry. Through the Middle Ages, alchemists venerated aether as the quintessence of matter, synonymous with the PHILOSOPHER'S STONE. Newton kept the concept alive as a kluge for explaining the mechanical universe, as did nineteenth-century physicists who used *luminiferous aether* to describe the substance through which light could travel in a vacuum. Even Einstein hung onto the term *aether*, using it to depict the physical qualities of space-time within general relativity.

But by the mid-twentieth century, the fungible concept had accrued too much historical baggage. Aether eventually fell out of favor as a descriptive term, though the way that physicists now describe DARK ENERGY is not wildly dissimilar from the mysterious ingredient of millennia past. The best historical definition of aether might be *an always-changing substance that scientists speculate exists but have yet to prove.* There will always be an aether, because there will always be the next unknowable thing.

SEE ALSO: DARK ENERGY; LOREM IPSUM; PHILOSOPHER'S STONE

AGNOTOLOGY

Agnotology is the science of creating stupidity.

First coined by a history professor,[3] agnotology (from the Greek for "not knowing") is the study of

---

3   In a footnote! The term *agnotology* was first used in the footnotes of *Cancer Wars* (1995) by Stanford professor Robert N. Proctor. Always read the footnotes! (And the parentheticals.)

culturally constructed ignorance, usually manufactured by special interest groups to suppress facts and create confusion. Its specious methodologies are often deployed in complex scientific issues, by sowing the seeds of doubt with inaccurate or misleading data.

For decades, cigarette companies notoriously implemented the tactics of agnotology, ignoring any evidence that huffing a carton of Marlboros might cause harm. As millions died from lung cancer, the tobacco industry actually hired thousands of scholars to produce a mountain of research about all aspects of smoking—except its health risks. "*Doubt* is our product," said one tobacco marketing exec, "since it is the best means of competing with the body of fact that exists in the mind of the general public."

This is the insidious conceit of agnotology: It succeeds not by a lack of information but by a surfeit of it. Agnotologists inundate the citizenry with enough disinformation to cast doubt on an entire issue. Masters of the discipline have muddied countless scientific waters, formulating questions that already had answers: *Is global warming a hoax? Do football concussions create chronic brain damage? Are prescription opiates addictive? Do vaccines cause autism?*

This is the dilemma of living in the age of plentiful data. Someone out there has created the answer you want—the one that matches your preexisting beliefs. They have it down to a science.

SEE ALSO: ANTI-VAXXERS; ASTROTURFING; FILTER BUBBLE; THE RUMSFELD MATRIX; TRUTHINESS; WOOZLE EFFECT

ALIEN SPACE BATS

Alien space bats is a sarcastic rejoinder used within ALT-HISTORY communities (*rejoice! such a literary subculture exists!*) when a plot has gone off the rails of established tradition in a wildly implausible manner. When Napoleon flees to America, when Hitler is cloned, when the Cubs win the World Series—only *alien space bats* could explain such ridiculous revisionist tales. "Hitler would need alien space bats," an alternate historian might say, "for a *deus ex machina* like Operation Sea Lion to prevail."[4]

Initially a derisive term, the ASB card can now

4   In fact, that's close to what Alison Brooks actually said when coining the phrase in 1988 on Usenet (soc.history.what-if) about Operation Sea Lion—Germany's plan to invade Britain during World War II. Remarkably, a few years later, Harry Turtledove would publish one of the most beloved ALT-HISTORY novels, *Worldwar: In the Balance*, in which aliens invade earth during World War II. Even the existence of alien space bats is a case of alien space bats.

also be assigned to any plot that contains *intentional* implausibility. In HBO's *The Leftovers*, for instance, 2 percent of the world's population suddenly disappears on a random day in 2011. Why? Who knows! Must be alien space bats.

SEE ALSO: ALT-HISTORY; NOT EVEN WRONG

ALT-HISTORY

"For what if history to work," historian Stephen E. Ambrose once wondered, "there has to be a real chance that things could have turned out differently?" That whisper of speculation—the *what if*, the *could have*—has birthed an entire genre of hypothetical writing known as *alternate histories*.

Ambrose posed this theory in an alt-history compilation, *What If? The World's Foremost Military Historians Imagine What Might Have Been* (2000). In his contribution to the alt-canon, Ambrose ponders the Allies losing D-Day—one of most popular of myriad historical what-ifs. The website Uchronia.net, an online database of such revisionist works, counts more than 3,300 novels, stories, and essays of published counterfactuals. Here one can find alternate histories wherein Napoleon is vanquished during the Russian winter, Martin Luther reconciles with the Catholic Church, and innumerable versions of Nazis prevailing in World War II. (The genre even has an annual prize, the Sidewise Awards, granted to the best work of conjectural history. A diverse cast, from Michael Chabon to Philip Roth, has received the honor.) The chart on pages 24–25 contains a list of the more prominent alt-history conjectures.

SEE ALSO: ALIEN SPACE BATS; HISTORIES; SLASHFIC; PHANTOM TIME HYPOTHESIS; RETCONNING; UTOPIA

ALTERNATIVE FACTS

Alternative facts is a phrase that was accidentally coined by presidential advisor Kellyanne Conway after the 2016 presidential election. Though she was seemingly trying to express epistemological uncertainty (as in, *you have your truths, I have mine*), many people thought it a euphemism for *lying*.

The remark surfaced in a January 2017 interview on *Meet the Press*. In an exchange about false statements regarding attendance figures at Donald Trump's inauguration, Conway blithely referred to the "alternative facts" that the White House provided. "Look, alternative facts are not facts," the host, Chuck Todd, responded. "They're falsehoods."

When later confronted about the gaffe, Conway inscrutably told *New York* magazine, "Two plus two is four. Three plus one is four. Partly cloudy, partly sunny. Glass half full, glass half empty. Those are alternative facts."

Some commentators charitably characterized the flub as a kind of lawyerly jest, but many perceived a hint of Orwellian NEWSPEAK in the utterance.

SEE ALSO: CONFIRMATION BIAS; GASLIGHTING; NEWSPEAK; TRUTHINESS

ANTI-VAXXERS

There's no denying it—vaccines are curious, even paradoxical agents of medical progress. When you receive an immunization, a chemical compound known as an *antigen* is injected into your body to trick it into having an immunological reaction. These antigens are often a diluted or attenuated form of the disease itself, so it can seem perversely contradictory that millions of lives have been saved by fooling our immune systems into thinking they're under attack. Vaccines are misinformation at the cellular level.

Some people are still dubious. The anti-vaccination movement, which has gained frightening momentum over the past decade, includes a loose collective of parents who blame immunizations for a wide range of child health concerns, particularly autism and ADHD. With essentially zero support from the medical community, but armed with a cache of kooky Facebook memes, many of these zealous parents have refused to immunize their kids, taking special care to avoid the MMR (measles, mumps, rubella) vaccine. Pathologists warn this is extremely dangerous, as just one person infected with measles has the capacity to infect up to eighteen unvaccinated people. When vaccination levels fall below 95 percent of the population, epidemics can occur, as happened in a 2014 outbreak of measles at Disneyland, where ninety people were infected with a disease that was once eradicated in the United States.

Exasperatingly, most vaccine disinformation can be attributed to one person. In 1998, gastroenterologist Andrew Wakefield published a small paper in the British journal *The Lancet* that hypothesized a link between MMR and autism. The sample size for the study was just twelve children, but when online media tabloidized the findings, it spread faster than gratis wine spritzers at a mommy blogger convention. The fraudulent study was later retracted after it was shown that Wakefield had fabricated evidence, manipulated patient data, abused study subjects, and received funding from anti-vaccine litigants. Undeterred, even after his medical license was revoked, Wakefield released *Vaxxed: From Cover-Up to Catastrophe* (2016), a propaganda hit job disguised as a documentary, alleging a CDC conspiracy to manipulate scientific evidence relating autism to the MMR vaccine.

His smear campaign had the intended effect—vaccine misinformation canvased the internet. ("The University of Google is where I got my degree from!" prominent anti-vaxxer Jenny McCarthy once told Oprah.) In parts of California, the measles vaccination rate for kindergarteners in 2015 plummeted to around 60 percent. In Seattle, polio inoculation fell to just 81 percent—lower than in Rwanda and Sudan. To combat the spread of pseudoscience, the American Academy of Pediatrics produced a twenty-one-page document for doctors to share with parents, listing study after study clearly stating no link between vaccines and autism. Coupled with legislation, these information campaigns have incrementally pushed vaccination numbers back up.

To illustrate why vaccines require mass participation to prevail, immunologists have coined the term *herd immunity* to describe the protective shell that forms around vaccine-saturated communities. This term does not sit well with those rebellious folk who are suspicious of groupthink. For those who imagine their views outside the mainstream, *herd immunity* sounds an awful lot like *herd mentality*. Their defiance is what makes the anti-vaxxer cabal so vexing—seemingly smart people can be easily seduced by its rhetoric. In one astonishing example, a Brooklyn newspaper reported in 2017 that a growing number of residents had stopped vaccinating *their dogs* due to the skepticism over human immunizations.[5] Many of these people view themselves as altruistic activists, fighting against government intrusion or global corporate interests. This is why the anti-vaxxer movement cuts across political lines, and is particularly trendy in progressive circles, which have a history of distrusting the dogma of western medicine and the economics of big pharma. Green Party spoiler Jill Stein, for instance, is an ally of the anti-vaxxing crusade. (The movement has an uncanny ability to attract celebrity cranks. Billy Corgan, Alex Jones, Bill Maher, Donald Trump, RFK Jr., and Rob "Deuce

5   The report appeared on August 1, 2017, on BrooklynPaper.com. "I had a client concerned about an autistic child who didn't want to vaccinate the dog for the same reason," says one of the veterinarians quoted in the story. "We've never diagnosed autism in a dog. I don't think you could."

PROMINENT ALTERNATE HISTORIES

WHAT IF...	the Cuban Missile Crisis had escalated?
THEN...	the United States invades Cuba, leading to a nuclear war that destroys the Soviet Union, New York City, Washington, D.C., and millions of lives; Europe ascends.
ACCORDING TO...	*Resurrection Day* (1999), Brendan DuBois

WHAT IF...	Hitler had successfully invaded Russia in 1942?
THEN...	Germany calls a truce after learning the Enigma code is cracked; twenty years later, Hitler is revered as a beloved leader.
ACCORDING TO...	*Fatherland* (1992), Robert Harris

WHAT IF...	the Black Death plague had killed 99 percent of Europe?
THEN...	the lives of most people from the Middle Ages until 2045 CE kinda suck.
ACCORDING TO...	*The Years of Rice and Salt* (2002), Kim Stanley Robinson

WHAT IF...	Hitler was never born?
THEN...	a more competent (but just as ruthless) Third Reich leader arises instead, the '60s social justice movements never transpire, and America, in a Cold War with Germany, becomes icky conservative.
ACCORDING TO...	*Making History* (1996), Stephen Fry

WHAT IF...	FDR was assassinated in 1933?
THEN...	the Axis wins the war and America really, really sucks. The good news: The moon, Venus, and Mars are colonized by 1962. The bad: Slavery is back.
ACCORDING TO...	*The Man in the High Castle* (1962), Philip K. Dick

WHAT IF...	Hitler had become a writer instead of a politician?
THEN...	the Führer migrates to America in 1919 and writes pulpy sci-fi, cuz why not?
ACCORDING TO...	*The Iron Dream* (1972), Norman Spinrad

PROMINENT ALTERNATE HISTORIES

WHAT IF...	the computer was invented much sooner?
THEN...	Great Britain is more powerful in the Victorian Age; the United States is fragmented; Manhattan has a commune led by Karl Marx.
ACCORDING TO...	*The Difference Engine* (1990), William Gibson and Bruce Sterling

WHAT IF...	Russia colonized the Americas first?
THEN...	the late nineteenth century is both more advanced (airplanes, cars) and less advanced (electricity is banned); everything is confusing.
ACCORDING TO...	*Ada, or Ardor* (1969), Vladimir Nabokov

WHAT IF...	the Protestant Reformation never happened?
THEN...	Martin Luther, reconciled with the Catholic Church, becomes Pope Germanian I; Europe, ruled by the Vatican, stays medieval; a Christian/Muslim cold war pervades.
ACCORDING TO...	*The Alteration* (1976), Kingsley Amis

WHAT IF...	FDR had lost the election of 1940?
THEN...	President Charles Lindbergh pushes America to become allies with Nazis; lots of terrible fascism follows.
ACCORDING TO...	*The Plot Against America* (2004), Philip Roth

WHAT IF...	the State of Israel never materialized?
THEN...	Jews persecuted by the Nazis take sanctuary in Alaska, which becomes a vibrant Yiddish neo-Zion (and, among other things, JFK marries Marilyn Monroe).
ACCORDING TO...	*The Yiddish Policemen's Union* (2007), Michael Chabon

WHAT IF...	Woodrow Wilson had never been elected?
THEN...	the League of Nations never happens and World War II is averted.
ACCORDING TO...	*The Smithsonian Institution* (1998), Gore Vidal

Bigalow" Schneider have all thrown sympathy behind the cause.)

There are excellent selfish reasons to get your shots (*polio really sucks!* tops the list), but vaccinations are ultimately a gesture of community empathy. Many vulnerable infants cannot receive immunizations, so they need other healthy members of their herd to be inoculated. This shared responsibility situates immunization in the same category as voting, recycling, and other gestures of social compassion. At the individual level, your participation won't change the world (just as you probably won't get polio, your individual vote probably won't dictate the next president), but we perform these civic acts as part of a larger ritual of participating in a cohesive society. To show empathy, we take the needle.

SEE ALSO: AGNOTOLOGY; BIRTHERS; PAREIDOLIA

APOCRYPHA

The Apocrypha are those early religious texts that did not make the final cut into the canonical Bible but are still deemed worthy of religious scholarship. Their authorship might be in doubt, their provenance could be suspect, or they might recount events that contradict other sacred books. Something has put these texts into the scriptural version of limbo—neither completely false nor entirely holy but somewhere in between.

But one religion's apocrypha is another's canon. The famed Gutenberg Bible, for instance, contained such now-apocryphal works as the Prayer of Manasseh (located after Chronicles) and the Prayer of Solomon (after Ecclesiasticus, itself of variable canonicity) when it was published in 1455. The King James Bible, published less than a half-century later, would corral more than a dozen texts into their own section, *Books of the Apocrypha*, located between the Old and New Testaments.

Disputes over the biblical canon have been commonplace throughout history. For his part, Martin Luther attempted to reassign the books of Esther, Hebrews, James, Jude, and Revelation to apocryphal status. He was unsuccessful, but other differences ruptured between faiths. To this day, the Catholic Bible contains eight additional so-called deuterocanonical books (including 1 and 2 Maccabees, Baruch, and Tobit) that Protestants and Jews do not deem worthy, while Eastern and Oriental Orthodox Bibles likewise vary slightly on which books make the cut. In addition, more than a dozen books that have been lost to time are mentioned in the Old Testament. The lost Book of Jasher, for instance, is referenced in Joshua, 2 Samuel, and 2 Timothy; the Book of the Wars of the Lord is referenced in Numbers.

The twenty-seven books constituting the New Testament are generally static, though their order varies slightly among Christian traditions. Dozens of other gospels (particularly later gnostic works like the Gospel of Thomas, the Gospel of Mary, and the Gospel of Judas) have been judged apocrypha or pseudepigrapha (falsely attributed works) but are still occasionally used as resources by scholars. The most notorious of these might be the Infancy Gospel of Thomas, probably written around the same time as the other gospels, wherein Jesus becomes a trickster figure. And of course, Jesus is mentioned throughout the Quran, as a precursor to Muhammad.

Could a new book ever be added to the Bible? If the Book of Jasher were suddenly discovered, or if some scholarship found the Gospel of Judas to be more credible, would the canon expand to include it? The official answer is *no*, the biblical canon is closed and new books cannot be added. The more credible answer is *of course*, because the canon has always been in flux.

SEE ALSO: GOSPEL OF JESUS' WIFE; HOMER; POPE JOAN; PRESTER JOHN; SHROUD OF TURIN

THE ARCHIES

Even if it had not included *Abbey Road* and *Let It Bleed*, 1969 would still loom large in the history of popular music. It was the year, after all, that also witnessed major album releases from Bob Dylan, James Brown, Led Zeppelin, Janis Joplin, The Stooges, Marvin Gaye, Diana Ross, Neil Young, the Velvet Underground, Aretha Franklin, Elvis Presley, Joan Baez, Stevie Wonder, the Kinks, Joni Mitchell, Fleetwood Mac, the Beach Boys, Leonard Cohen, Dusty Springfield, Miles Davis, Pink Floyd, the Doors, Sly & the Family Stone, and—*phew*—Johnny Cash. And yet, somehow, none of these colossal figures produced the biggest song of the year. So, who toppled the giants?

Forget the obvious. Though chanted from every dorm room, "Give Peace a Chance," that zeitgeisty plea from John Lennon, would not top the charts. Nor would David Bowie's interstellar curio "Space Oddity," nor any of the Who's rock opera *Tommy*, nor future karaoke anthems from Neil Diamond ("Sweet Caroline") or Creedence Clearwater Revival ("Proud Mary"). What a year! Surely, the biggest song of 1969 must have been extraordinary, worthy of comparison to an "Auld Lang Syne" or a "Thriller."

Alas, the biggest single of the year was "Sugar, Sugar,"[7] a bubblegum pop tune from Archie, Reggie, Jughead, Veronica, Betty, and Hot Dog—the Archies, a fake but fun-loving band trapped inside an animated television show. The band's music director, Don Kirshner, recorded the song with the Archies (or rather, their studio musicians) after the Monkees turned it down. (A few years earlier, Kirshner had

---

7   The most common yardstick—The *Billboard* Hot 100—is the gauge of measurement here.

actually invented the Monkees, another fake but fun-loving band trapped inside a live-action television show.) When Davy Jones and crew rebuffed their svengali puppet master by refusing to record "Sugar, Sugar," which they deemed childish, Kirshner gave it to his other television band, the Archies, instead.

That is how a sham band beat Dylan, Aretha, Elvis, Jagger, Bowie, Iggy, Janis, McCartney, and Lennon for the biggest hit of 1969.

SEE ALSO: AUTOMATED DIALOGUE REPLACEMENT; THE BUGGS; THE MASKED MARAUDERS; MILLI VANILLI; KARAOKE; TRIBUTE BANDS

AREA 51

Area 51 is a highly classified military facility, remotely located in the desolate Mojave Desert of Nevada. The current purpose of the base is publicly unknown, but historically the site has been a testing facility for experimental aircraft and weapons.

The base is also, of course, where the remains of a 1947 alien spacecraft crash in Roswell, New Mexico, are being studied and reverse-engineered into highly advanced military technology. Or, perhaps, it is merely a quaint tourist trap for ufologists and other tinfoil-hatters. The highway that approaches the site, Route 375, which is littered with alien trinket shops, has been officially designated *Extraterrestrial Highway* by the state of Nevada.

The government did not even acknowledge the existence of Area 51 until a 2013 Freedom of Information Act request finally declassified documents detailing the history of the base, which was used to test the U-2 spy plane during the Cold War.

Barack Obama was the first president to publicly recognize the site. "The aliens won't let it happen," Obama deadpanned to Jimmy Kimmel, when he asked about disclosing the truth of Area 51. "You'd reveal all their secrets. They exercise strict control over us."

SEE ALSO: BEHOLD A PALE HORSE; DEEP STATE; MOON LANDING; RED MERCURY; TRAP STREETS

ASTROTURFING

Astroturfing is the practice of impersonating a grassroots movement for political gain. Tactics for disguising a dubious "from the people" message include mass letter-writing campaigns and, more recently, scripted attacks on social media. The Russian plutocracy led by Vladimir Putin, for instance, is widely believed to have implemented a vast influence campaign that astroturfs the internet with comments under disparate false names, or SOCK PUPPETS, who spread mass confusion and create the illusion of widespread support in democratic elections.[8]

AstroTurf—the artificial grass material—was first deployed in 1966 by Monsanto to provide an indoor field for the Houston Astrodome. *Astroturfing*—the scammy communications campaign—was coined in 1985 by Senator Lloyd Bentsen to denounce dodgy lobbying from the insurance industry.

Shakespeare, unsurprisingly, provides superb illustration of the backhanded technique, when Cassius divulges his insidious scheme to eliminate Caesar:

> *I will this night,*
> *In several hands, in at his windows throw,*

---

8   This is hardly contested news. In February 2016, a top Russian cyberintelligence officer told the attendees of a security conference, "I'm warning you: We are at the verge of having something in the information arena that will allow to us to talk to the Americans as equals."

> *As if they came from several citizens,*
> *Writings, all tending to the great opinion*
> *That Rome holds of his name, wherein obscurely*
> *Caesar's ambition shall be glanced at.*[9]

In this soliloquy, Cassius reveals his plot: to forge letters denouncing the unseemly ambition of Caesar, and to plop them in the inbox of Brutus, "as if they came from several citizens." (The subterfuge of "as if" makes it an astroturfing campaign.) The manufactured revolt, a sort of faux-plebiscite, convinces Brutus that, for the sake of the people, Caesar must go. The rest is history:

Et tu, astroturfed, Brute?

SEE ALSO: AGNOTOLOGY; BLACK PROPAGANDA; CRISIS ACTORS; FALSE FLAG OPERATION; FUD; GERRYMANDERING; NEWSPEAK; PUSH POLL; SOCKPUPPET

AUTO-TUNE

Auto-Tune is a simple audio effect that modulates off-key vocals into perfect pitch. Initially the software was used to correct the sour notes on a vocal track (making the intonations less irregular, more natural), but the process was quickly exploited (making voices sound less human, more artificial). Eventually, the Auto-Tuned song became its own genre, resembling the sound of a robot nervously wobbling past a tinfoil factory.

Auto-Tune's first big hit was Cher's "Believe" (1998), which cranked the pitch-correction into a cyborg cry somewhere between pain and ecstasy. (Though as Twain once snarked of Wagner, "The music is better than it sounds.") The technique spread, and backlash quickly followed—*Time* magazine named it one of the fifty worst inventions, "T-Pain can't sing" became a wildly popular YouTube comment, and Jay-Z released the diss track, "D.O.A. (Death of Auto-Tune)." Even as "Auto-Tune Sucks!" became the slogan of an overzealous authenticity death cult, a backlash to the backlash countered with adored Auto-Tune–heavy works like Kanye West's *808s & Heartbreak* and Daft Punk's "One More Time."

At its peak, trendy producers unleashed Auto-Tune on even the best technical singers, simply because it was fashionable.[10] Eventually, Auto-Tune would return to its original use, subtly correcting vocal pitch in the studio. When the cybernetic dust settled, it was clear that Auto-Tune was just another instrument—one that can be overused (like alto sax, in the '80s) or underused (like cowbell, all the time). Now the Auto-Tuned songs sound dated, like a first-generation Roomba learning to twerk.

When asked if Auto-Tune was evil, the sound engineer who invented the software responded, "Well, my wife wears makeup. Is that evil?"

Sick burn, machine-man.

SEE ALSO: AUTOMATED DIALOGUE REPLACEMENT; BACKMASKING; MIKU, HATSUNE; KARAOKE; PHOTOSHOP; TUPAC HOLOGRAM; UNCANNY VALLEY

---

9   The events transpire in act 1, scene 2 of *Julius Caesar* (1599). One of the most blatant anachronisms in literature occurs soon thereafter: While the conspirators discuss assassination plans, a clock strikes three, even though chiming clocks would not be invented in the West for another 1,400 years.

10 Mariah Carey is perhaps the best case study here. Though she is one of only two popular singers with a five-octave vocal range (Axl Rose being the other), studio producers inexplicably believed pitch correction software could improve upon diva perfection.

AUTOBIOGRAPHY OF HOWARD HUGHES

Forged diaries or biographies of the rich and famous are nothing new. What makes this bogus work so unique is that the subject of the counterfeit was still *alive*, though at the time even that was uncertain.

Clifford Irving knew a thing or two about art fraud. He was the author of *Fake!*, a 1969 biography of Elmyr de Hory, the infamous art forger exiled to Ibiza. Impressed by the forgery feats of Elmyr, Irving decided to take a crack at the counterfeiting business.

If Irving, a forger's apprentice, was the ideal artisan, then Howard Hughes, a reclusive weirdo, would be the perfect subject. The isolated billionaire, reasoned Irving, might not even stir from his Beverly Hills Hotel bungalow to denounce his fake autobiography. And despite his reclusiveness (or, more likely, because of it), the eccentric mogul still garnered immense public interest and speculation, somehow gracing the covers of magazines without ever being photographed or interviewed. Irving knew his book would be a hit.

His first step was to forge letters from Hughes, patterned on a fragment of his handwriting published in *Newsweek*. Irving then approached his publisher, McGraw-Hill, with the forged missives stating that Hughes wanted him to write a memoir addressing the lies that surrounded his life. It should be ghostwritten, wrote "Hughes," by a writer whose work he appreciated—Clifford Irving, naturally. The publishers instantly offered $765,000 (in 1971 dollars) to secure the rights to the book. Well, not quite instantly. First, they hired handwriting specialists to analyze the letters. Graphologists declared them genuine. Irving also later passed a POLYGRAPH test.

Howard Hughes—the richest man in the world at the time—was already a hugely popular subject, but in the months leading up to the book's release, the story turned ubiquitous. *60 Minutes* aired an interview with Irving immediately after the Super Bowl; *Life* and *Time* planned to excerpt the book for their cover. But then Hughes did exactly what Irving

reasoned he wouldn't do. In an arranged phone interview with seven reporters, Hughes denounced the book as a forgery, claiming he had never even met this imposter. Three weeks later, Irving confessed to the hoax. *Time* cancelled their Hughes story and replaced it with the Irving con. On the cover, under the banner "Con Man of the Year," was an image of Irving, painted by none other than Elmyr de Hory.

Irving was sentenced to two and a half years in prison for fraud, of which he served seventeen months. He would later recount the events in *The Hoax* (1981), which was made into a pretty terrible movie in 2006 starring Richard Gere. Irving, who despised the movie, called it "a hoax about a hoax." The fake autobiography of Hughes did not see the light of day until 1999, when it was published online.

The story should end here, but the most shocking consequence of the forged book would not come to light until decades later. While researching the faux-autobiography, Irving discovered that Hughes had secretly loaned Richard Nixon's brother money ($205,000)—a juicy detail included in his manuscript (inflated to $400,000). When the White House learned that this illicit loan might be made public, via galleys leaked to the FBI, they grew worried that further financial dealings between Nixon and Hughes might become public. As later recounted in memoirs by numerous Nixon insiders, including Nixon's chief of staff H. R. Haldeman, the conspiracy to burgle the DNC headquarters in the Watergate building was triggered by concern over what other damaging material the Democrats might have on Nixon.

A fake autobiography of the richest man alive may have precipitated the downfall of the most powerful man alive by creating the biggest political scandal in American history.

SEE ALSO: F FOR FAKE; HITLER DIARIES; IF I DID IT; A MILLION LITTLE PIECES; NAKED CAME THE STRANGER; TATE, NAT; UNRELIABLE NARRATOR; VAN MEEGEREN, HAN; THE WAR OF THE WORLDS

AUTOMATED DIALOGUE REPLACEMENT

In the film editing booth, where countless hours of raw footage gets spliced into real movies, directors often discover they need new audio tracks, either to reflect script changes or to improve sound quality. They can't reshoot the film, so they use *automated dialogue replacement*, or ADR, to dub the new audio. Usually, this involves an actor rerecording their dialogue, plus some fancy video software that syncs lip movements to the new voice track, so they don't look like poorly dubbed kung fu characters. But sometimes the actor is unavailable, so a voice actor who can imitate the screen actor is used. (Though not an imitation, the most famous example of dialogue replacement is probably James Earl Jones adding Darth Vader's asthmatic baritone in postproduction.)

Because the practice is increasingly common, most famous actors have an audio stunt double—a person who can imitate them closely enough to record their redubs. Julia Roberts's voice matcher, for example, is Amy Landecker, best known from *Transparent*. Christopher Walken's verbal doppelganger is renowned video game voice actor Nolan North. The impressionist Stephen Stanton is the audio double for Bruce Willis, Clive Owen, Nicolas Cage, Robert Downey Jr., Jeff Goldblum, and many others. It might not seem a naturalistic technique, but most acclaimed actors, including Meryl Streep and Marlon Brando, have relied heavily on ADR to correct diction and intonation in postproduction.

Soon, all those celebrity vocal stand-ins could be out of jobs, due to new speech software that can re-create any voice. Products such as Lyrebird and Adobe Voco, which have been dubbed "the Photoshops of voice," can create dialogue in the likeness of any person, regardless of whether that person has ever said the words. After ingesting a sample vocal track, the software will dissect the audio into a complete phonetic library of that person's voice. Then just by typing text into an input box, the software can have Tom Cruise claim, "I actually hate Scientology," or more diabolically, have Hillary Clinton seethe, "I WIPED the email server myself, you monsters." Unlike the voices of robot assistants, it sounds unmistakably human—and exactly like the emulated person.

The implications for this new type of ADR are vast. Adobe says that its customers will use Voco to fix minor edits in podcasts or audiobooks, but far more nefarious uses come to mind. When combined with human image synthesis software, which can change the facial expressions and mouth movements of real people in videos, any sort of video could be manufactured. The future of news looks increasingly fake.[11]

SEE ALSO: MIKU, HATSUNE; MILLI VANILLI; PHOTOSHOP; TEMP MUSIC

---

[11]   An alarming example, created by the podcast Radiolab, can be seen at FutureOfFakeNews.com.

B

BACKFIRE EFFECT

If you have decided to read this book (or at least, this sentence), you likely think of yourself as an open-minded person. You are willing to have your beliefs challenged, to wonder what sorts of *misinformation* you might harbor. And if given sufficient evidence, you are probably even prepared to change your mind. Despite your firm opinions, you are not ideologically strident. You have known doubt; you can be persuaded by facts. You are, after all, an evidence-based person.

The problem is, nearly everyone thinks they are an evidence-based person. And not everyone is. Let's be honest; most people aren't.

Just about any politically charged issue could test our intellectual agility, but let's use climate change as the example. Most reasonable people know that global warming is a real phenomenon, either because they have studied the evidence, or because they trust scientists, or because it aligns with their political worldview. But let's switch the issue on its head: What if incontrovertible scientific evidence were produced saying that climate change was *not* real? When confronted with updated facts, how quickly would your opinion alter? How would you feel about changing your mind? What role does the media play in maintaining or correcting your misperceptions?

Brendan Nyhan, a political science professor at Dartmouth, has become a minor academic celebrity by addressing these questions with social experiments. He and his research partner, Jason Reifler, created a study in 2006 in which subjects were shown a fake news article saying the United States had discovered WMDs in Iraq after the defeat of Saddam Hussein. After reading the article, the subjects were quickly shown a second article that debunked the first—there were no WMDs. Unsurprisingly, those who opposed the war were more likely to believe the second article; those who supported the invasion, the first one. This is not shocking—it usually takes more than one random article to overturn our deeply held beliefs. The surprise, however, came when the researchers noticed that certain people in favor of the war became *even more certain* after reading the debunking report. Not only did irrefutable evidence not change their minds, but this segment of the population became *even more adamant* in the face of contradictory facts. The correction actually made their understanding of the issue *worse*. The researchers dubbed this the *backfire effect*, or the tendency to double down on your beliefs when shown contrary evidence.

Within journalism communities, the findings of this study (and other similar ones by Nyhan, examining divisive issues like death panels, tax cuts, and BIRTHERISM) were like a dirty bomb going off. Questioning the efficacy of the media was already a cherished ritual for jaded journalists, but the backfire effect introduced difficult questions about their role in society. If the job of a reporter is to accurately relay information, how should one convey politically charged issues to a public intent on distrust? Can reporters even have an educational effect in these politically charged times?[12]

It turns out all this journalistic handwringing may have been for naught. After the discovery of the backfire effect, a series of studies from other researchers showed that corrective information might not generate the harmful effect originally reported. In one study, 8,100 people were asked about their knowledge of abortion, gun control, fracking, and dozens of other issues that elicit strong reactions.[13] These participants did *not* demonstrate a tendency to double down on their false beliefs in the face of truth. Their intransigence was not so intransigent.

The backfire effect may have backfired, but no one seems to have noticed. The internet barely recognizes the results of the second round of studies. Search for *backfire effect* today, and you will find it cited in essay after essay, with nary a mention of the follow-up research that failed to corroborate the phenomenon. The deliberate blind spot makes sense, in a way: The backfire effect is such a useful metaphor for describing that irritating person who ignores even the most basic empirical evidence. The backfire effect is the perfect totem—disguised as *science*—for the futility of convincing your dogmatic Facebook friends of established facts. Even if it's not real, the backfire effect *feels real*.

For his part, Nyhan, who coined the term, has tried to correct misperceptions. "It would be a terrible irony," he told the radio show *On the Media*, "if evidence contradicting the backfire effect provoked me into doubling down on the backfire effect."[14] Yes, and an even more terrible irony would be the media clinging to misinformation. By choosing to ignore the updated data, the media almost seems intent on reenacting the backfire study itself. *New facts? What new facts?* Even the most sincere evidence-based person can become rigidly dogmatic when common misperceptions comport with their worldview.

SEE ALSO: BARNUM EFFECT; BIRTHERS; BOGUS PIPELINE; COGNITIVE DISSONANCE; CONFIRMATION BIAS; TRUTHINESS; WOOZLE EFFECT

---

12 Of course the media is capable of discrediting widespread misinformation. A heroic example was the change in public perception regarding the dangers of smoking. It took decades of reporting, but in the face of strong opposition (heavy corporate lobbying, incessant obfuscation campaigns, ruthless AGNOTOLOGY), the media was nonetheless able to debunk the prevailing view that the dangers of tobacco were "unsettled science." Truth prevailed! Smoking, however, is not an issue attached to a specific political party, which is how most obstinate opinions become entrenched.

13 "The Elusive Backfire Effect" (2016), by Tom Wood and Ethan Porter, showed that people can heed corrective data, though other disconcerting relationships to information, like CONFIRMATION BIAS, still thrive.

14 The *On the Media* episode was "Doubt It" from July 21, 2017. The segment closes with Nyhan saying, "It's healthy for all of us to call our beliefs into question. And that's, obviously, not something that our political system, in particular, is encouraging or rewarding right now."

BACKMASKING

"Seadth rurnow memyar nyear ethifee."

That is (very approximately) the sound of John Lennon yodel-chirping the coda of the 1966 Beatles song "Rain." The syllables spool forth like a melisma of gibberish, but play it backward on a turntable, and it snaps back to sense: "If the rain comes, they run and hide their heads." Not exactly subversive content (the same lyric, forward, opens the song), but that snippet of psychedelic audio, a B-side from the *Revolver* sessions, has nonetheless accrued esoteric historical significance: It is the first instance of *backmasking*, or vocals played backward in recorded music.

Though a seemingly minor musicological innovation for sound engineers, backmasking would go on to be used by a barrage of musical acts, from Styx to Missy Elliott to Prince. At first, it was a gratuitous gesture—a reward to diehard fans who took the time to decode tracks. Attentive listeners who reversed "Empty Spaces" from Pink Floyd's 1979 album *The Wall*, which contained obvious backmasking, clearly heard Roger Waters deliver a Pavlovian treat, "Congratulations. You have just discovered the secret message." Woof.

Eventually, the aural trickery became an annoyance as crackpots became convinced that every song must contain encrypted subliminal messages. They got busy reverse engineering all popular music—twisting knobs on Queen tracks, slowing down Iron Maiden, rewinding Judas Priest, speeding up Jimi Hendrix. Forensic audio dissection became the paranoiac pastime of cranks. From the '60s through the '80s, stoned Satanists forged an unlikely alliance with zealous evangelicals, as both groups became audio gumshoes who investigated (and promoted) cases of covert occult messages. With a reverse record player, plus either some hydroponic pot or the voice of god in your ear, you can *maaaaybe* hear, "Oh, here's to my sweet Satan" burrowed away in Led Zeppelin's "Stairway to Heaven." That particular bustle in your hedgerow would be an insane place to hide a satanic

message, but logic is no virtue to the madman.

Listen closely, you can hear whatever you want.

SEE ALSO: DARK SIDE OF THE RAINBOW; MONDEGREEN; PAREIDOLIA; PAUL IS DEAD; STEGANOGRAPHY; SUBLIMINAL ADVERTISING

BACKWARDS Я

To make it look Russian, just flip the R—so goes the logic of global products like *CHEЯNOBYL DIAЯIES* (the movie) and *TETЯIS* (the video game). With their majuscule logos, the **Я** evokes a hint of the muscovite, but something is amiss.

The Russian alphabet does indeed contain a glyph that resembles our R gazing at itself in a mirror—the **Я**, the last letter of the Cyrillic alphabet. But that letter is pronounced nothing like our *r* in *red* or *rascal*; it sounds more like the *ya* in *yankee* or *yahoo*. So a Russian speaker—say, one who frantically rotates multishaped neon blocks plummeting from above into perfect horizontal lines—would have to pronounce his favorite arcade game *tetyaiz*. It's a mouth of marbles in Russian, too.

Я is not alone in its vulnerability to repatriation. Other letters look the part in faux-Cyrillic. Our rotund O can be de-Latinized into a spry **Ф**; Y, rejiggered as a hangman scaffold **Ч**; A, molded into a boxy **Д**. With these typographic cudgels, an industrial rock band can assume gothic airs on album covers—**ИИNE ИИCH ИAILS** or **LIИKIN PARK** or **KOЯN**. Or a Sacha Baron Cohen character, traipsing across Kazakhstan, can announce himself in movie posters as **BOЯДT**, which looks neat to us, but to Soviet ears would make a noisy clang—something like *Vowyadt*.

On the path to anglicization, other languages must also endure tortured typefaces. *My Big Fat GRΣΣK Wedding*, using Σ (sigma), would sound *grssk* to both an Athenian and a Spartan. And fraternity culture, known for stretching the limits of acceptable language, has spawned a mouthy T-shirt: **DΘΣS THΦS SHΦRT MΛKΣ MΣ LΘΘK ГRΛT**? If not getting busy with swans, Zeus would be hurling lightning bolts from Olympus at such cacophony.

But a Cold War lament, starring Sean Connery in a submarine, sets the standard for transliterated blather. **7HΣ HUИГ FOЯ RΣD OCTOBΣЯ**, as it has appeared in advertisements on television, contains letters from *three* alphabets. This impressive clamor—a sort of Tower of Babel razed for parts—somehow reads instinctively to us but would require years of college to pronounce.

The most cryptic **Я** might be the most renowned. It's anyone's guess why a knife-wielding boy scrawls **REDЯUM** on a door in *The Shining*, but when reflected in the bathroom mirror, his mother later recognizes it as **MURDER** spelled backwards. Or technically, it says **MURDЭЯ**, so who knows, maybe the boy's red lipstick etching is some sort of reverse commentary on Mother Russia.

Like the heävy mëtal ümlaut, **Я** evinces a touch of Slavic exoticism. The ersatz typography might screech like a caterwauling obscenity to native ears, but it looks strangely appealing to us. Sorry Russians, your **Я** just looks cool in our posters.

SEE ALSO: ESPERANTO; FOREIGN BRANDING; LOREM IPSUM

BANANADINE

1. *Obtain 15 lb of ripe yellow bananas.*
2. *Peel the bananas and eat the fruit. Save the skins.*

Those are the first two steps in *The Anarchist Cookbook*'s recipe for the psychoactive drug bananadine. The final three steps involve scraping, boiling, and baking the plantain skins into a smokable "fine black powder." The complete formula can easily be found on the internet, but unless you are trying to trick a hippie into a headache, preparing the recipe is not recommended. This concoction will get you about as high as snorting a papaya.

Bananadine's curious history began during the Summer of Love, 1967, when an underground newspaper, the *Berkeley Barb*, wrote a story about the drug, intended as a prank. When British folk-rocker Donovan released the hit "Mellow Yellow," popular druggy culture—never known for casting light upon the nuances of farce and fact—interpreted the "electrical banana" in the song as a secret coded message about the hallucinogenic qualities of banana peels.[15] By the time *Newsweek* and *Time* picked up the story, bananadine was already appearing in head shops across the country. *The New York Times* even described a "be-in" in Central Park where "beatniks and students chanted 'banana-banana'" while hoisting a large wooden yellow phallus into the sky. (The '60s. You had to be there.)

Eventually, the FDA announced an investigation into "the possible hallucinogenic effects of banana

---

15 The operative lyrics from the chill-out tune: "Electrical banana/Is gonna be a sudden craze/Electrical banana/Is bound to be the very next phase." Donovan later asserted that the inspiration for the "electrical banana" was not, as popularly interpreted, an alchemical plantain, but rather was a new popular mail-order yellow vibrator. The real progenitor of the bananadine hoax appears to have been a completely different band—Country Joe and the Fish, a psychedelic jug band from Berkeley, probably most renowned for performing "The Fuck Cheer" at Woodstock. Their manager, ED Denson, penned the *Berkeley Barb* story.

peels." In a study titled "The Great Banana Hoax," published in the *American Journal of Psychiatry*, NYU researchers reported no evidence of intoxicating chemicals in bananas. As the abstract suggests, any psychotropic reactions were likely the result of a PLACEBO:

> The recent practice of smoking dried banana scrapings to achieve a "psychedelic experience" led the authors to investigate the hallucinogenic properties of bananadine, or "mellow yellow." They conclude that the "active ingredient" in bananadine is the psychic suggestibility of the user in the proper setting.

None of this stopped *The Anarchist Cookbook* from printing the "official" recipe in 1971, preserving the bananadine craze for future generations of nihilists. Much of the controversial information contained in the cookbook (including instructions for making everything from TNT to LSD) was viewed as dangerous to public safety. Bananadine, however, was the opposite—a harmless concoction that distracted the counterculture from any true personal revelation or political insurrection.

SEE ALSO: EXPLODING POP ROCKS; JENKEM; PLACEBO EFFECT; SNIPE HUNT

BARNUM EFFECT

You pride yourself on being an independent thinker. At times, you have doubts about whether you handled a situation correctly. You want others to admire you, yet you tend to be self-critical. Sometimes you are extroverted, while at other times you are introverted. You have so much unlocked potential.

It sounds a lot like you, right? Sorry, but it sounds a lot like everyone.

These sorts of blanket characterizations are some-times called *Barnum statements*, in reference to P. T. Barnum's egalitarian claim, "We have something for everyone." Studies show that when people are given those statements after bogus personality tests, they tend to believe the excessively broad results, regardless of what they answered on the actual test. And technically, the statements are true. But they are true for nearly everyone.

The Barnum effect—the propensity to derive personal meaning from statements that could apply to many people—helps explain why certain individuals can become susceptible to hokum peddlers. Astrologists, palm readers, psychics, graphologists, and HR managers all thrive on the Barnum effect. So, at your next tarot reading, tell your clairvoyant that you really admire her *independent thinking* and *unlocked potential*. She might fall for her own trick.

SEE ALSO: CLICKBAIT; CONFIDENCE GAME; COGNITIVE DISSONANCE; DREAM ARGUMENT; HUMBUGGERY; PLACEBO EFFECT; TRUTHINESS

BARRON, JOHN

John Barron (aka John Miller) was Donald Trump's spokesperson, representing the real estate tycoon and human tabloid blotter for decades. Except John Barron was as real as George Washington's cherry tree. Trump, who would later become the forty-fifth president of the United States, completely made him up.

Starting around 1980, Trump would assume the name "John Barron" when calling gossip publications to promote his projects and boast about his celebrity dalliances. (Madonna, Kim Basinger, and Carla Bruni were all subjects in the rumors he spread about himself.) City desk editors from that era describe calls from Barron as being so common that they became a recurring joke. While tabloids winked along with the narcissistic ruse, mainstream news publications unknowingly fell for the CATFISH. Quotes from John Barron, identified variously as a "spokesman" or "executive" or "representative" for Trump, tunneled their way into the pages of the *New York Times*, the *Washington Post*, *New York* magazine, and *Newsweek*. Long before he claimed to revile such balderdash, Trump hustled his own fake news.

The huckster was forced to confess his alter ego in 1990, during a lawsuit involving his employment of undocumented migrant workers. "I believe on occasion I used that name," Trump admitted under oath. When asked later about the pseudonym, he told reporters outside the courtroom, "Lots of people use pen names. Ernest Hemingway used one."

That day, John Barron disappeared. But a new head on the hydra, John Miller, instantly sprouted in his place.

A reporter from *People* contacted Trump's office in 1991, seeking quotes about his recent divorce from Ivana. John Miller got on the line, extolling his boss's virtues as a husband. Suspecting that "John Miller" was Trump, the reporter played the recorded conversation for various associates, including his second wife, Marla Maples. Everyone immediately confirmed that Miller was Trump. (Judge for yourself on the website for the *Washington Post*, which published the audio.)[16]

Trump now avoids the topic whenever possible. When *Washington Post* reporters brought up John Miller during a 2016 phone interview with the presidential candidate, he hung up. In 2006, Trump bestowed upon his (very real) third son the name Barron, presumably in honor of his (very fake) publicist.

SEE ALSO: AGNOTOLOGY; CATFISH; CLAQUE; CONFIDENCE GAME; CRISIS ACTORS; SOCK PUPPET; TRUTHINESS

BEANIE BABY BUBBLE

An economy fabricated from thin air, the Beanie Baby industry ballooned, instantly, to the market size of a small country, and then quickly burst, like a fast-forward of the macrocosm it resembled: the '90s dot-com bubble. Luau the Pig, Garcia the Bear, Dinky the Dodo Bird—those cheap pellet-packed plush rags became the symbols of economic hokum.

Their creator, Ty Warner, started with good intentions. He wanted to create a unique inexpensive toy, unlike anything else. He failed, miserably, over and over, but he kept iterating, creating countless versions of the cheap doll. Once the toys became popular, his mistakes revealed a bigger economic idea: scarcity. By limiting the batch size of each failure, Warner created a sense of depletion within the market. And so, from perceived scarcity, an enormous collectibles empire was born overnight.

At its peak in 1998, Ty Inc., Beanie Babies' parent company, raked in three billion dollars per year in sales, but that was foam peanuts compared to the online secondary market, where a single ultra-rare doll could fetch a half-million dollars. Counterfeits, of course, swamped the market—the surest sign of a bustling industry. But the knockoffs only seemed to bolster the value of "genuine" Beanie Babies.

When the inflated Beanie Baby–economy finally burst, a different company emerged from the dust as the undisputed victor of the bubble: eBay. At peak craze, Beanie Babies represented nearly 10 percent of eBay's sales. (We know this because the ecommerce company had to divulge the Beanie Baby bubble as a "risk factor" in a SEC filing for its IPO.) When suburban parents saw they could flip a five-dollar toy for fifty, they rushed to the internet, often for the first time, to hawk it on eBay. Ultimately, that is the legacy of the Beanie Baby: The legume-stuffed fad made the

---

16 "Donald Trump Masqueraded as Publicist to Brag about Himself," *Washington Post*, May 13, 2016. It is completely bananas. For more than fourteen minutes, Trump talks about himself in the third person.

internet feel safe and propelled ecommerce into the mainstream.[17]

SEE ALSO: KNOCKOFF HANDBAGS; MONEY; PONZI SCHEME; PRODUCT PLACEMENT; TOYETIC; TULIPOMANIA

BEHOLD A PALE HORSE

Though relatively obscure, *Behold a Pale Horse*, a 1991 book by mysterious ex-military man William Milton Cooper, gradually became an extremely influential compendium, by synthesizing and popularizing many of the dominant conspiratorial narratives of our time.

Like a paranoid historian reworking Stefon's *Saturday Night Live* club reviews, this labyrinthine emporium *has it all*. From a sweeping pell-mell of world events, *Behold a Pale Horse* constructs a convoluted alternate history in which the United States government has been secretly colluding with an alien race that arrived during the Truman administration. Over 500 pages, the book rambles through explanations for JFK's demise (assassinated before revealing our alien overlords), AIDS (a government plot to shrink minority populations), the international drug trade (run by the CIA to funnel money toward alien military bases), and an intricate warren of internecine subplots. At the center of the story is the New World Order, a cabal that has incorporated every imaginable organization into its skein of history: the Freemasons, the Bilderberg Group, the Nazis, the Communist Party, the Vatican, the Rockefellers, the Skull and Bones society, the RAND corporation, and FEMA. A failed attempt to turn Jupiter into a second sun (to prevent a new Ice Age) and that old shibboleth THE PROTOCOLS OF THE ELDERS OF ZION (created by the Illuminati) are among the many longeurs dragged into the mix.

Caveat lector and all that, but the book is, undeniably, an extremely entertaining journey: a helter-skelter blur of personal memoir, "secret classified documents," dime bag Nostradamus-izing, and the rococo language of paranoia. Like its Luciferian plot, fonts and formatting jump all over the place, as though someone unaccustomed to copying and pasting between Word docs rushed out the door to Kinkos before an alien probe. The evocative title refers to the spooky fourth horse of the apocalypse, named Death, who arrives with Hades in the Book of Revelation. For Cooper, who invokes religion only to augur doom, "the true nature of the Beast" is the horde of invading aliens.

"We have been taught lies. Reality is not at all what we perceive it to be," writes Cooper about history. Though it starts as a surreal romp through an alternate reality, *Behold a Pale Horse* gradually morphs into a survivalist handbook. (Having fans like Oklahoma City bomber Timothy McVeigh likely aided its transformation to anti-government user manual.) After being charged with tax evasion in 1998, Cooper was named a "major fugitive" by federal marshals. He was fatally shot in 2001 after a standoff with police outside his Arizona home.

With an estimable 4.4 rating on Amazon, *Behold a Pale Horse* has sold over a quarter-million copies.

SEE ALSO: AREA 51; DEEP STATE; MOON LANDING; PHANTOM TIME HYPOTHESIS

---

17 The definitive book on the subject, *The Great Beanie Baby Bubble* (2016), by Zac Bissonnette, delves into much greater detail about how the Beanie Baby bubble fueled the dot-com bubble.

BELLMAN'S FALLACY

According to Bellman's fallacy, any assertion that is repeated over and over—three times seems to be the magic number—will become true. The notion derives from the first stanzas of Lewis Carroll's surreal poem "The Hunting of the Snark," in which the leader of an expedition thrice exclaims, "Just the place for a Snark!" The pronouncement convinces his crewmates they have discovered an island ripe for hunting the dangerous creature:

> "Just the place for a Snark!" the Bellman cried,
> As he landed his crew with care . . .
> "Just the place for a Snark! I have said it twice:
> That alone should encourage the crew.
> Just the place for a Snark! I have said it thrice:
> What I tell you three times is true."

Accepting oft-repeated false claims as truth is a constant danger on the internet, in media trend stories, and within advertising. That's three examples, so it must be true.

SEE ALSO: AGNOTOLOGY; THE BIG LIE; JABBERWOCKY; MERE-EXPOSURE EFFECT; TRUTH CLAIM; WOOZLE EFFECT

BERENSTAIN BEARS CONSPIRACY

The night is still, but you are restless. After a long day, you have burrowed into the couch, droopy-eyed, flipping absently through television channels. In the upper reaches of the dial, you stop on an animated kids' show that shouldn't be on at this hour. It defies logic, but somehow the screen is full of anthropomorphic grizzly bears. Papa Bear is chiding his cub son for not saying "please" and "thank you." You remember watching this show as a child and loving the books

from which it sprung.

At that instant, your cell phone rings, scaring you awake. Grabbing the device, you look at the caller ID and see your own name on the screen. That's odd.

"Hello?" you answer apprehensively.

"Are you seeing what I am seeing?" says an urgent voice.

"Uh, who is this?" you ask.

"It's *you*, dummy. We need to talk."

You are bewildered, speechless. The voice on the other end of the line does indeed sound very, very familiar.

"What do you see on TV right now?" asks the voice.

"Some . . . bears?" you answer, tentatively, watching Papa Bear discipline Brother Bear for not clipping his toenails.

"Yes, dummy. What kind of bears?"

"Um, grizzlies?"

"No! What is the name of *the show*?" asks the voice.

"I believe it is *The Berenstein Bears*?" you answer.

"Exactly!" shrieks your interlocutor. "Now, here's an important question: How do you spell the family name of the bears?"

You are still shocked but feel compelled to answer. "B-E-R-E-N-S-T . . ." You pause for a moment. The family's name is on the screen, but the spelling doesn't look right. Your childhood memory conflicts with the logo.

"Do you see it?" screams the voice in the phone. "It has changed!"

It's true. You do remember this pack of animated bears as the *Berenstein* family, not the *Berenstain* family, as it says on the screen. That's odd.

"It gets worse. I have proof," says the voice that sounds like you. "Check your email."

Flipping the phone around, an email with the subject line "Crashing Memories" appears in your inbox. The sender's address is yours. *Freaky*. You check your sent items folder. The same email is there. *Really freaky*. It seems you somehow sent yourself an email.

"I am calling from an alternate universe," says the voice on the phone. "In my world, it's not just the *Berenstein Bears*. Other things are slightly different.

GLITCHES IN THE MATRIX

WHAT YOU REMEMBER	WHAT "REALLY" HAPPENED
The Berenstein Bears	The Berenstain Bears
Snow White said, "Mirror, mirror on the wall."	Snow White said, "Magic mirror on the wall."
Chinese tanks ran over a Tiananmen Square protester in 1989.	Chinese tanks did not run over a Tiananmen Square protester in 1989.
Mr. Rogers sang, "It's a beautiful day in the neighborhood."	Mr. Rogers sang, "It's a beautiful day in this neighborhood."
Darth Vader said, "Luke, I am your father."	Darth Vader said, "No, I am your father."
A peanut butter brand called Jiffy exists.	A peanut butter brand called Jif exists.
The actor Sinbad starred in a '90s movie, *Shazaam*, about a genie.	No such movie exists.
The Statue of Liberty is on Ellis Island.	The Statue of Liberty is on Liberty Island.
Sherlock Holmes said, "Elementary, my dear Watson."	Sherlock Holmes said only, "Elementary."
Eli Whitney was black.	Eli Whitney was white.
"Play it again, Sam."	"Play it once, Sam, for old times' sake."
Nelson Mandela died in prison in the 1980s.	Nelson Mandela died out of prison in 2013.

I believe these are glitches in the matrix—moments when the computer simulation we live in accidentally reveals itself with bad code."

You had no idea you could be so conspiratorial.[18]

"I sent you a chart," continues alterna-you. "It shows other glitches in the matrix. History is full of lies." You look down at your phone and see a chart, like the one on the opposite page.

It's true: You, or the person impersonating you, are right. You remember many items in the left column, and find the items on the right spurious. Could the fabric of reality have shifted? Are we oscillating between parallel universes?

"Wait a minute," you finally say. "Many of these misremembered events have easy explanations. Maybe Vader didn't say those exact words, but parodies of *Star Wars* often had him say, 'Luke, I am your father.' And maybe I confused Eli Whitney with George Washington Carver. And Shaquille O'Neal was a genie in the movie called *Kazaam.*"

The other end of the line is silent, so you continue. "We collectively believe Berenstain should be spelled -*stein* only because it fits the pattern of so many other similar names—Einstein, Frankenstein, Goldstein. That's all. The confabulation is no cover-up. My life is not a lie!"

Suddenly, the phone call ends. The room seems to dim, briefly, and then return to normal. You feel a small shudder, like awaking from a nap. You're still on the couch, but maybe you nodded off? You check your inbox, but the email is gone. The TV is still on but tuned to a different channel, with a music video playing. A man with a black leather jacket and headband is singing "Born in the U.S.A." When the video ends, it says his name at the bottom of the screen: Bruce Springstain.

Everything else is exactly the same.

SEE ALSO: ALT-HISTORY; EXPLODING POP ROCKS; GASLIGHTING; MANDELA EFFECT; PHANTOM TIME HYPOTHESIS; RETCONNING; WOOZLE EFFECT; WIPING

BIG LIE, THE

Liars come in ample varieties, from those low fruit on the vine, the *jocular fibster* and the *windbag sophist*, all the way up the tree to that paragon of rascals, the *sociopathic scoundrel*. The lies they tell occupy their own unique cosmology. On good days, you might encounter only the *white lie*, or luckier still, the exalted NOBLE LIE. More often, the simple *bluff* makes an appearance at the office, maybe trying to shill Amway, while its friend, *puffery*, sidles up next to you at the bar. *Bunkum* here, *bullshitting* there—these jesters make our lives interesting, until you encounter their egregious cousins, *perjury* and *slander*, liars who spread only grief. But among this pack of lies, one deceit lords over the rest: *the Big Lie*. A monster so mendacious, it wraps itself in all the other lies.

Times being what they are, the Big Lie often takes shape as an internet meme, a demagogic quote splayed atop a photo of Adolf Hitler: "Make the lie big, make it simple, keep saying it, and eventually they will believe it." It is a foreboding image, with just one problem: It is itself a lie. Hitler never actually said those words. Nonetheless, we might call this falsehood a *half-truth*, as the quote roughly captures the propagandistic sentiment that the Führer would later espouse.[19]

In his 1925 autobiography *Mein Kampf,* Hitler put forth the theory that "in the big lie there is a force of credibility." He imagined "untruths so colossal" that

---

18 The Berenstain Bears conspiracy is a very real theory, espoused primarily on the internet. While copious evidence points toward the spelling *Berenstain* all along, photographs of (possibly dubious) books with *Berenstein* have been produced as universe-melting evidence. The subreddit /r/Glitch_in_the_Matrix/ is your bible, should you become a Berensteinite.

the public "would not believe that others could have the impudence to distort the truth so infamously." In these passages, he was accusing Jews and Marxists of using the rhetorical Big Lie to start World War I. (Accusing others of using the Big Lie is a good way to deploy the Big Lie.) But really, he was writing a guidebook that he would later follow.

It seems obvious now that when Hitler wrote, "The great masses will more easily fall victim to a Big Lie than to a small one," he was plotting a theory for implementing the Holocaust. Writing this in your autobiography might seem like tipping your hand, but it actually helps illustrate how propaganda works. Authoritarians succeed not so much by convincing people of their falsehoods as by creating confusion and disarray. Like tributaries that flow into a river, a constant stream of disinformation eventually creates a tsunami of distrust. In these shambolic moments, the masses finally throw their arms aloft and capitulate, *who knows what's true?* Here, the Big Lie can flourish, not by stealth but by opulence, by constant repetition. You can write it in huge letters in the sky, *I am lying.*

The Big Lie is deceit as spectacle.

SEE ALSO: AGNOTOLOGY; BLACK PROPAGANDA; FALSE FLAG OPERATION; FUD; HITLER DIARIES; NOBLE LIE; THE PROTOCOLS OF THE ELDERS OF ZION

BIRTHERS

The birther movement was a *manufactroversy*—a constructed conspiracy circulated during the 2008 election asserting that presidential candidate Barack Obama was not a natural born citizen of the United States. Theories alleged that his Hawaiian birth certificate was a forgery and that he was actually born in Kenya. The accusation of fakery was itself fake.

The loudest voice of the birther movement was future president Donald Trump, who foresaw political opportunity in the fashioned accusation. In April 2011, when Obama released a certified copy of his long-form birth certificate, along with birth announcements published contemporaneously in Hawaiian newspapers, Trump claimed victory in the disclosure. "I am really honored and I am really proud, that I was able to do something that nobody else could do," he said in response, taking credit for putting the controversy to rest—a controversy he promulgated more than any other person.

An August 2016 poll showed that 72 percent of registered Republicans still had doubts about president Obama's citizenship.

SEE ALSO: ALTERNATIVE FACTS; AUTOBIOGRAPHY OF HOWARD HUGHES; BACKFIRE EFFECT; BARRON, JOHN; CUNNINGHAM'S LAW; SNOPES

BLACK PROPAGANDA

If you want to turn a political foe into an ally, you might try bombarding them with misleading information about your cause. This standard method of persuasion, which often lacks nuance and fails to conceal its origin, is known as *white propaganda*, apparently due to its relative innocence. A more effective technique would be to disguise your actions so that your opponent does not even realize they have been influenced by your covert campaign. This

---

19 Another common memetic misquotation: "If you tell a lie big enough and keep repeating it, people will eventually come to believe it." That one is often attributed to Joseph Goebbels, who carried the cute title of the Reich Minister of Propaganda, but again, there is no record of him saying or writing this.

is *black propaganda*—information that purports to emanate from a source other than its true origin.

With intricate plots and perverse schemes, black propaganda operations demand subversive tactics, which can include planted evidence, forged documents, fabricated patsies, and staged media spectacles. Because the goal is often to make a political opponent look bad publicly, these campaigns sometimes incorporate tricking the media into reporting half-informed stories.

Black propaganda is an insidious force because it succeeds even when it fails. Provocateurs are difficult to identify, but even when their schemes are exposed, their existence creates an environment of suspicion. Once you suspect black propaganda, you start to see it everywhere. (Regardless of whether Russian cyberspies *did* alter American elections, the impression that they *could* sway the electoral process has been inimical to democratic ideals and has nurtured an environment of conspiracy.) More than simply spreading agitprop, the goal of the black propaganda campaign is to sow suspicion and create dissent.

SEE ALSO: ASTROTURFING; THE BIG LIE; FALSE FLAG OPERATION; PSEUDO-EVENT; PUSH POLL

BLAIR, JAYSON

As journalism scandals go, the fabulism of Jayson Blair was fairly run-of-the-mill, though it seemed calamitous at the time.

In May 2003, the young reporter was caught plagiarizing and fabricating fifty of his six hundred–plus articles for the *New York Times* over four years. The scandal precipitated a massive 7,200-word front-page apologia from the paper of record. The gist:

> He fabricated comments. He concocted scenes. He lifted material from other newspapers and wire services. He selected details from photo-

graphs to create the impression he had been somewhere or seen someone, when he had not. And he used these techniques to write falsely about emotionally charged moments in recent history.

The following year, Blair wrote a memoir (of course) with a provocative title, *Burning Down My Masters' House*, in which he dished on his undiagnosed bipolar disorder and substance abuse problems. (He had a fondness for Johnnie Walker Black and was spending $500 to $1,000 per week on cocaine.) A documentary about the scandal, *A Fragile Trust*, was made in 2014, but it is not exactly a roller-coaster thrill ride. In both works, Blair seems not interesting enough to even be called a sociopath (real sociopaths, like James Frey and STEPHEN GLASS, are at least charismatic). Fabulists are usually interesting character studies, but Blair appears more leaden than mercurial. He pinocchioed datelines from places he had never been, and from his Brooklyn bedroom, he pilfered quotes from small-town newspapers. Maybe that is clinical depression, but it could easily pass for dopey ennui.

At the time, the Blair scandal seemed a dirty bomb detonated in the journalism industry, and there was at least one casualty—the executive editor of the *New York Times*, Howell Raines, was forced to resign. A keen observer might contend that Blair's baleful deeds had less consequence than those of his colleague Judith Miller. She was never accused of plagiarism, but while Blair was busy falsifying travel expense reports, Miller's faulty reporting beat the drum that took America into a terrible war. But then one wonders if Blair would read that sentence and find some solace where none should be.

Though he would seem a precarious fount of personal advice, today Blair is a certified life coach in the Washington, D.C., area.

SEE ALSO: GLASS, STEPHEN; LEROY, JT; A MILLION LITTLE PIECES

BLAIR WITCH PROJECT, THE

Often called the first VIRAL MARKETING campaign, *The Blair Witch Project* (1999) could just as reasonably be called the first internet movie. Which is to say, it is somewhat real and somewhat artificial.

Released long before the invention of YouTube, much less Facebook and Twitter, the "true story" of the Blair Witch aligned with the aesthetic of the early web, back when secret documents on servers were discovered, not hacked. With scrawled police reports and gritty newsreel, the movie's website simulated a documentary, not a horror film. In media appearances, the producers claimed their work was "found footage," and at Cannes, MISSING posters of the actors were pasted around the film festival. Profiles on IMDB listed cast members as "presumed dead."

Clever marketing, sure, but reality itself was weaponized in its creation. To stimulate terror while filming, the cast was told the Blair Witch legend, which they only later learned was a hoax. The unknown actors were paid meager salaries and placed in situations of duress—literally shooting, writing, acting, and directing the whole movie in eight days. The original "script" contained no dialogue and scenes were improvised. (The shaky steadicam style would later cause sickness for some theatergoers.) Like ruthless METHOD coaches, or sinister reality TV directors, the producers gave actors less food each day, goading conflict in the cast.

Audiences wanted to believe, too. Only a few credulous simps actually fell for the marketing ruse, but millions participated in *the idea* of falling for it.[20] Viewers seemed to enjoy *pretending* they had succumbed to the "true story." Almost like actors themselves, moviegoers embodied their own role, the gullible audience of the grand guignol. *Blair Witch* was a movie you watched, but the whole experience—*The Project*—blurred the real world with the film. The genius wasn't that it *tricked* people (it didn't), but that it made people *pretend* they were tricked.

We lack a precise vocabulary to describe the hocus-pocus the human mind plays on itself, but Freud, who studied fantasies and lies, devised a helpful notion for this predicament. In the eyes of the fatalistic psychoanalyst, humans are instinctively driven to imagine the horrific, to propel ourselves toward the abyss. Freud called it the *death drive*. Nightmares, for him, were repackaged fantasies of self-destruction, and if he were alive today, movies, replete with armageddon and annihilation, would likely supplant dreams as his object of study.

The Blair Witch Project, however, isn't just a memento mori, another reminder of the scary end we will all reach. More than mere death wish, the movie embodies a different insatiable yearning—for the false to be true, the fake to be real. *Blair Witch Project* is a *reality drive*.

> SEE ALSO: CANNIBAL HOLOCAUST; CARDIFF GIANT; LARP; MANNING, DAVID; ROBINSON CRUSOE; SLENDERMAN; TWERKING FAIL; VIRAL MARKETING; WORK OF FICTION DISCLAIMER

BOGUS PIPELINE

A bogus pipeline is a POLYGRAPH used as a PLACEBO.

As with most psycho-economic techniques, a skillful demonstration can be found on *The Wire*. In the opening scene of the fifth season, Detective Bunk Moreland interrogates a suspect who will not confess. The detectives cuff the perp to a precinct photocopier. "The machine tells the tale," says one detective, placing the suspect's hand on its oracular surface.

Bunk begins to ask control questions, as though administering a polygraph. After each answer, the

---

20   Despite a budget of $60,000, the movie made a very real $248.6 million at the box office.

copier spits out a sheet that says TRUE or FALSE. The gag tricks the confused suspect into confessing.

The mechanics of the scene are known in the social sciences as a *bogus pipeline*—a method for reducing false answers in self-reported studies by making subjects think the examiners can detect lying. When psychologists suspect their test participants might be lying, perhaps out of a desire to appear more socially acceptable, they will sometimes connect subjects to a polygraph. The machine is fake, but studies have shown the artifice of truth-finding causes subjects to disclose more honest answers.

The machine, they fear, might outsmart them.

SEE ALSO: CUNNINGHAM'S LAW; PLACEBO; POLYGRAPH; SODIUM PENTOTHAL; VOIGHT-KAMPFF MACHINE

BONSAI KITTEN

BonsaiKitten.com was a DIY educational website that provided homemade instructions for molding a cat into a decorative ornament. Launched in December 2000, the site contained detailed instructions for growing your kitty into any shape, simply by raising it in a jar, similar to a bonsai plant taking form. "There is virtually no limit to the eventual shape of your pet!" beamed the site's creator, Dr. Michael Wong Chang from MIT.

Joke's on you. Only a monster could think it real. See the chart on the next page for some prominent internet hoaxes.

SEE ALSO: BANANADINE; THE BLAIR WITCH PROJECT; CRYPTID; SNIPE HUNT

BOTOX

Botox, medically known as *botulinum*, is the neurotoxin responsible for botulism. From the Latin for "black sausage," botulinum can block nerves, causing paralysis or death. One of the most lethal toxins on earth, a speck of botulinum, smaller than a grain of sand, can kill you. *The Journal of the American Medical Association* has said one evenly distributed gram could kill more than a million people, making it an immensely feared toxin in bioterrorism, linked to extremist groups including Al-Qaeda and Hezbollah. In 1991, at the end of the Gulf War, Saddam Hussein's government claimed it had produced 19,000 liters of the toxin, enough to kill every human on earth three times. During World War II, the United States manufactured more than a million doses of the botulinum vaccine for the D-Day landings, fearing Germany had weaponized the chemical.

Also, Botox is a $2.8 billion per year cosmetic industry, because millions of people inject it into their face to reduce wrinkles and appear younger.

SEE ALSO: CYBORG; PLASTIC SURGERY

BRAIN IN A VAT

Maybe the drugs clenched your mind in a cosmic hellbox, maybe the virtual reality orgy was too intense, maybe *The Matrix* shook your belief in a coherent world—at some point, you have probably entertained the idea that you are living inside a manufactured reality.

Like all ideas, especially those related to deception, this is not a new hypothesis. At least as far back as PLATO'S CAVE, reality was maybe all *an illusion*. (Hints of such solipsism are found in nearly every religion.) But those doctrines were ambiguous about this illusive existence compared to the extreme modern

PROMINENT INTERNET HOAXES

HOAX	PREMISE	OUTCOME
Lonelygirl15	Teen vlogger dumps her personal life on YouTube; things get crazy when she becomes the target of a cult.	After months of intrigue, the series is exposed as an elaborate interactive fiction.
Montauk Monster	A strange animal carcass washes up on the shore of Long Island in the summer of 2008.	Raccoon? Turtle? Chupacabra? Mutant? It's still a mystery.
Kaycee Nicole	After years of struggling with leukemia, a young woman with a prominent social media presence dies in 2001.	She didn't exist. SEE ALSO: MUNCHAUSEN SYNDROME
Goodtimes Virus	A much-forwarded email in 1994 warns of a virus in emails that contain the subject "Goodtimes."	It's a hoax, but in a meta twist, the warning itself spreads like a virus.
Nigerian Prince Scam	A wealthy foreigner promises a share of his fortune to help move millions of dollars from his homeland.	Versions of this email con continue to this day.
Twerker on Fire	A video of a Miley Cyrus wannabe who catches fire while twerking in her apartment goes viral.	Damn you, Jimmy Kimmel! SEE ALSO: TWERKING FAIL
Pizza Rat	A video of a rat carrying a slice of pizza through the NYC subway goes viral.	It's clever performance art. SEE ALSO: ZARDULU
Kidney Thieves in New Orleans	An email rumor spreads before Mardi Gras in 1997 that a ring of organ thieves is operating out of New Orleans.	Local police are forced to publish an official statement saying it is bogus.
Free Money from Bill Gates	Starting in 1997, a chain letter claims Microsoft is testing email forwarding; every time the email itself is forwarded, Gates gives money to charity.	The chain letter still makes the rounds today and is still, regrettably, fake.
Tourist Guy	After 9/11, a photo circulates of a tourist in the World Trade Center observation deck with a plane in the background about to strike.	The guy in the image confesses to manipulating the photo, taken in 1997. SEE ALSO: PHOTOSHOP

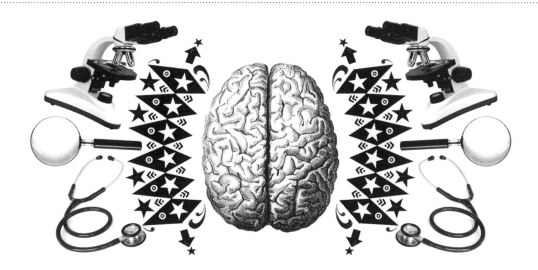

iteration: What we perceive as consciousness is actually a supercomputer simulation. Like a brain in a vat, connected to a network mainframe, your entire life has been a video game.

To embrace this fatalistic worldview, you have to believe that consciousness itself is nothing more than an enhanced digital hard drive. The idea has backers. The loudest advocate has been the philosopher Nick Bostrom, who sincerely believes we are (most likely) living inside a computer simulation. He even outlined a logical proof, which starts with a bold axiom of technology: *Digital resolution will continue to evolve toward ever higher fidelity, until simulated experiences become indistinguishable from real ones.* If that happens—if computers inevitably turn virtual reality into reality—then we have no way of knowing whether we currently inhabit a digital illusion. And if the axiom is true, Bostrom argues, only three possible outcomes exist for humanity:

1. We destroy ourselves before we reach complete virtualization. (*Maybe!*)
2. We collectively decide not to pursue that future. (*Unlikely?*)
3. We reach that point and create millions of digital simulations. (*Yay!?*)

If the third outcome occurs, which disturbingly seems both most likely and most optimistic, then our reality becomes a roll of the dice. If there are millions of simulations indistinguishable from reality, then what are the odds that *this reality*—the one where you read this sentence—is actually happening? Statistically, not good. (This theory, usually referred to as the *simulation hypothesis*, bears remarkable structural similarity to PASCAL'S WAGER, which postulated a statistical rationale for believing in god.)

As one physicist said, "Reality is merely an illusion, albeit a very persistent one." Perhaps too persistent. Those were the words of Albert Einstein, whose brain was removed postmortem and preserved in a vat of alcohol. Today, pieces of it are spread across multiple vats, or maybe, multiple universes.

SEE ALSO: ALT-HISTORY; LARP; MANDELA EFFECT; PASCAL'S WAGER; PLATO'S CAVE; THE RED PILL; SIMULISM; TOMMY WESTPHALL UNIVERSE

BUGGS, THE

Imagine being in a TRIBUTE BAND, but not knowing.

Such was the fate of the Coachmen V, an American band who in 1963 surprisingly fulfilled their dream of landing a record deal. Upon arriving at the studio in New York City, almost immediately, the quintet was handed songs to record. They quickly laid down new tracks, a mix of originals ("Big Ben Hop," "Liverpool Drag") and covers of recent hits ("I Want to Hold Your Hand," "She Loves You").

When the album dropped in February 1964, the band was instantly perplexed. Their name was absent from the album cover; in its stead was a group called the Buggs (in small print). When they played the album, titled *The Beetle Beat* (in large print), their music came from the speakers, but the cover art was four unfamiliar faces—models arranged suspiciously similar to those on the cover of *With the Beatles*, released in the UK a few months prior. The words "The Original Liverpool Sound" spanned the base of the album cover. The Coachmen V, however, were from New Jersey. Finally, they realized that they had been bamboozled into recording a Beatles knockoff.

Albums like *The Beetle Beat* were not uncommon in the '60s. At peak Beatlemania, record labels flooded the music market with soundalike productions, which, like early Beatles records, featured R&B covers mixed with Lennon-McCartney tunes. Naive consumers bought the imitations, thinking they were hearing legit Beatles music.

Despite the ruse, one very real person did emerge from the Buggs. Gary Wright, the organ player on *The Beetle Beat*, went on to record such '70s prog rock staples as "Dream Weaver," which often appears on soundtracks when a movie wants to evoke the spooky mystique of lost innocence. The song also inspired *A Nightmare on Elm Street*, according to its DVD commentary with Wes Craven.

So, *very indirectly*, you could say John Lennon created Freddy Krueger.

SEE ALSO: THE ARCHIES; KARAOKE; THE MASKED MARAUDERS; MILLI VANILLI; MOCKBUSTER; TRIBUTE BANDS

BULLSHIT

An inept reporter once asked Louis Armstrong to define jazz. "Man," replied Satchmo, "if you gotta ask, you're never gonna know." The same is true with bullshit.

Nonetheless, somebody took an enviable shot at defining the ineffable—Princeton philosopher Harry Frankfurt, who in 2005 published "On Bullshit," a monograph that will never be improved upon, so quoting it at length seems the only just way to approach the topic:

> It is impossible for someone to lie unless he thinks he knows the truth. Producing bullshit requires no such conviction. A person who lies is thereby responding to the truth, and he is to that extent respectful of it. When an honest man speaks, he says only what he believes to be true; and for the liar, it is correspondingly indispensable that he considers his statements to be false. For the bullshitter, however, all these bets are off: he is neither on the side of the true nor on the side of the false. His eye is not on the facts at all, as the eyes of the honest man and of the liar are, except insofar as they may be pertinent to his interest in getting away with what he says. He does not care whether the things he says describe reality correctly. He just picks them out, or makes them up, to suit his purpose.

SEE ALSO: CONCERN TROLLING; KAYFABE; SMARKS; SOKAL HOAX; TRUTHINESS

C

Tyrion Lannister has a spy in his cabinet. As Hand of the King, Tyrion knows that one member of King Joffrey's small council is a traitor, leaking information to his conniving sister, Queen Regent Cersei Lannister. As there are three council members, the dwarf has three suspects. He tells each potential quisling a unique piece of information, so that when Cersei confronts Tyrion about one piece of supplanted intel, he can easily identify which cowardly councilman betrayed him.

By planting *misinformation*, Tyrion has successfully deployed a canary trap.[21]

This method of exposing the source of an information leak was coined by Tom Clancy in his novel *Patriot Games*. In espionage circles (real spies use it, too), it goes by the more mouthy catchphrase "barium meal test."

Canary traps are also commonly dispatched by corporations that suspect an employee is leaking sensitive information to the press. The trap is set by sending what seems to be a mass corporate email to all employees, but each memo has slightly different information. When the missive is forwarded to and published by a reporter, the tattling tipster is easily exposed by the specific phrasing in the memo. The NBA, Apple, and Tesla are among companies caught using versions of this snitch-identification tactic.

Hollywood frequently deploys a similar technique. When movie studios need to share scripts with cast members, they will sometimes change a line or two in each version of the text. When a script is leaked, producers can track that specific copy back to its leaky source. Similarly, DVD movie screeners often contain personalized watermarks (either a name or some numeric identifier placed directly on the video) as a type of canary trap—one in which the trap itself is placed conspicuously, as a warning to filesharers.

The term itself likely derives from the bygone practice of sending canaries into coal mines, to test

21 This scenario is, of course, derived from *Game of Thrones*. On television, the scene transpires in "What Is Dead May Never Die," the third episode of the second season; in the books, in chapters 17 and 25 of *A Clash of Kings* by George R. R. Martin.

for the existence of dangerous gas. If the canary failed to return, the air was deemed unsafe.

SEE ALSO: HONEYPOT; HONEYTRAP; STEGANOGRAPHY

CANNED HEAT

Canned heat—not to be confused with the band who performed "Going up the Country" at Woodstock—is the practice of blaring pretaped crowd noise through loudspeakers at live sporting events. The term tumbles down from professional wrestling, where recordings of jubilant cheering and chthonic booing are often blasted through an arena's sound system. Like a live LAUGH TRACK, the crescendo acts as an audio cue for wrestling fans to react, which in turn helps producers direct specific storylines.

More controversially, use of canned heat has often been alleged at genuine sporting events, where a raucous crowd burst can disrupt player communication. Over the years, many professional teams—the Indianapolis Colts, the Boston Celtics, the Seattle Seahawks—have been accused of pumping fake crowd noise into their arenas and stadiums. Only the Atlanta Falcons have confessed to the practice.

Although canned heat breaks the rules, there are no regulations against manipulating the materials and structural elements of a stadium to amplify the acoustic reverberations. Canopies at CenturyLink Field in Seattle are notoriously touted as natural sonic amplifiers that can reflect crowd noise onto the playing field. The Seahawks' so-called 12th man (a sort of CYBORG composed of raucous fans plus sonic architecture) set a Guinness World Record for crowd noise, at 137.6 decibels.

SEE ALSO: CLAPTER; CLAQUE; KAYFABE; LAUGH TRACK; SMARKS

CANNIBAL HOLOCAUST

Cannibal Holocaust was the first "found footage" horror movie and by far the genre's most believable creation—and therefore its most disturbing. The 1980 film depicts anthropological documentarians in the Amazon who encounter an indigenous cannibalistic tribe. (Let your macabre mind wander from there.)

The film's style was so realistic and gruesome that its Italian director was arrested and tried on charges of murder. Despite contracts stating they would essentially disappear for one year following its release, the actors had to come out from hiding to testify on the director's behalf, swearing under oath that they had not, technically, perished in a snuff film, as depicted on-screen.

SEE ALSO: THE BLAIR WITCH PROJECT; NACIREMA; TOFURKEY; WORK OF FICTION DISCLAIMER

CAPGRAS DELUSION

Are you convinced that your husband has been replaced with a replica? If he is Harrison Ford in *Blade Runner*, then you might be onto something; otherwise, you likely suffer from the rare disorder known as Capgras delusion.

People with this affliction believe that someone close to them (usually a spouse, though occasionally a pet) is an impostor. The syndrome is sometimes associated with schizophrenia but can also afflict people who have no other mental illness.

The disorder is named after Joseph Capgras, a French psychiatrist who, in 1923, described the case of Madame M., who insisted that her family had been replaced by impostors. Though she did not suffer from paranoia (the belief that someone was "out to get her"), she surmised that her husband was eighty different doppelgangers.

Recent research has suggested that Capgras syndrome is something like the inverse of *prosopagnosia*, or the inability to recognize faces. Testing reveals that while those afflicted with prosopagnosia can't recognize people, they do show an unconscious reaction to familiar faces, measured by a galvanic skin response. So, while people with prosopagnosia *consciously* can't recognize faces but *unconsciously* can, patients with Capgras syndrome seem to suffer from the opposite: the inability to unconsciously have an emotional response to familiar faces.

Tony Rosato, a former *SNL* cast member who played Luigi in a television version of *Super Mario Bros. 3*, suffered from Capgras syndrome.

> **SEE ALSO:** COTARD DELUSION; IMPOSTOR SYNDROME; PAUL IS DEAD; ROSENHAN EFFECT; TAMAGOTCHI EFFECT; TRUMAN SYNDROME

CARDIFF GIANT

In October 1869, construction workers uncovered a ten-foot-tall "petrified man" while digging a well behind a barn in Cardiff, NY. As news spread, the owner of the land, William C. "Stub" Newell, conveniently began charging a quarter to individuals interested in seeing the giant. After two days, so many gawkers arrived that he bumped admission to a half-dollar.

Audiences were divided on whether the Cardiff Giant was a mummified man or an ancient statue. Respected paleontologists immediately dubbed it a HUMBUG, which did nothing to stem the flow of paying spectators to the farm. Recognizing its success in the country, a syndicate of men bought the giant and moved it to Syracuse, where even more gapers paid admission. With larger crowds came more debunking, but no one seemed to care. Even savvy observers became fervent fans, affectionately dubbing the giant "Old Hoaxy."

As would eventually happen to any nineteenth-century object of questionable legitimacy, the attention of P. T. Barnum was finally piqued. The human-curiosity showman offered the syndicate $60,000 for a three-month lease of the colossus. When they turned him down, Barnum made his own plaster replica, putting it on display at his American Museum in New York. His "real" Cardiff Giant drew even bigger crowds than the original.

Barnum declared the original a fake. Of course, it was a fake (it was made from gypsum by Newell's coconspirator cousin), but that did not stop its owners from suing Barnum. After a judge dismissed the case—experts assessed both giants were fraudulent—one of the annoyed owners reportedly said, "There's a sucker born every minute." It's a bizarre statement from someone peddling a counterfeit mummy, but as

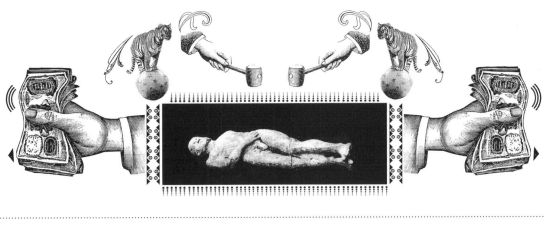

the phrase spread, Barnum reportedly grew jealous that he had not uttered it himself. And for a long time, the misquote was attributed to him, partially because he never denied saying it.

Phineas Taylor Barnum may have invented more phrases than anyone since Shakespeare. "Let's get the show on the road," "There's no such thing as bad publicity," "Throw your hat in the ring," "The greatest show on earth," and "Siamese twins" are all Barnum coinages. But he was not the first to say of his audiences "There's a sucker born every minute." Rather, somewhat ironically, it's what an exasperated foe said in reference to him.

SEE ALSO: BARNUM EFFECT; HUMBUGGERY; SMARKS

CATFISH

A *catfish* is a person who feigns an online identity, particularly in pursuit of romance. Most often, the term is used in its verb form, meaning *to lure someone into an amorous relationship by adopting a fictional internet persona*. Its eponym is a 2010 documentary that became a popular MTV series.

The show follows a formula. An episode commences with its two winsome hosts, Nev Schulman and Max Joseph, being contacted by a "hopeful"—a person who suspects their internet amour might be fake. (As detailed in a *Vulture* story, "Here's How MTV's *Catfish* Actually Works," more often than not, the catfish is actually the one who first contacts MTV.[22]) In the second act, the cybersleuths get to work on the case, digging around for clues on social media, querying Spokeo for public records, and using Google Reverse Image Search like it is an elite forensic tool

from *CSI*. When all the fishy findings are compiled—a suspicious social graph connection, a dubious profile with no followers—Nev and Max reveal their dossier to the hopeful. In the final act, everyone confronts the catfish. At the big reveal of their online sweetie, the hopeful either laughs, cries, shrugs, screams, sulks, or, least likely, swoons. (In one episode from season two, a woman believes her virtual paramour is the rapper Bow Wow, but she is very, very much mistaken.)

The show's most astonishing revelation initially seemed to be the sheer number of catfishers roaming the internet looking for prey. (A mix of motives constitute their deviousness—misplaced romantic desires, sexual identities, malevolent trolling, loneliness, revenge, and, very often, crippling body dysmorphia.) But as you continue watching episodes, a more ponderous data point emerges: the staggering number of people willing *to fall* for a catfish. In case after case, even a small bit of investigative work would have uncovered an uncouth catfish and saved the victim from undue emotional stress, but the hopefuls so often allow themselves to fall victim to the scheme. This interplay between the exploited and the exploiter, plus the moral questions that come with such imposture, is the massive subtext of the show.

SEE ALSO: HONEYTRAP; INTERNET TROLLS; SOCKPUPPET; TEOING

CELEBRITY SEX TAPES

The celebrity sex tape is a deceptive species. It can beguile through simple MIMICRY (those videos that purport to contain a celebrity but subvert with dop-

---

22 Surprisingly, no matter how many seasons of *Unreal* you watch, the secret mechanics of reality television remain somewhat guarded. But this revealing story, published in May 2014 on Vulture.com, provides a rare behind-the-scenes account of how a reality show is constructed. (Much of it is manufactured, but not necessarily the parts you would imagine.)

pelgangers) or with metaphysical mind play (if a sex tape is rumored, but no one wanks to it, did it happen?).[23] But one type of deception is more devious than all others: The tape that presents itself as a gonzo bootleg but was knowingly produced for mass distribution to make its participants famous.

The three most notorious celebrity sex tapes—those showcasing the talents of Paris Hilton, Kim Kardashian, and Pamela Anderson—have all been accused of this bodacious deceit. In all three cases, rumors persist that the celebutante was somehow implicated in the distribution of their own smut. This is not an unreasonable conclusion—the tapes do seem to be the products of narcissists who seek fame by any means. Paris Hilton's sex tape suspiciously dropped only three weeks before the premiere of her new reality show, *The Simple Life*. And if not for Kim's leaked skin flick, a "Kardashian" might today be mistaken for the name of a sandwich. However, in these three cases, subterfuge is (most likely) not at play. It appears that none of these women *intentionally* leaked their tawdry tapes, as we might be prone to believe, and all three *reportedly* tried to block the distribution of their eponymous videos.

When Paris Hilton learned that her letchy beau, Rick Salomon, was selling their sex tape, she sued for $30 million but was awarded only $400,000 by the court. She claims to have received nothing from the infamous night-vision tape that became *1 Night in Paris*, despite selling more than a million copies. Even if she did not want the tape released, Hilton appears keenly aware of an audience in the video. "You're, like, obsessed," she says in flagrante delicto. "You always film me." She seems to be speaking to you, the viewer, as much as to her scuzzy screen collaborator.

Kim Kardashian was also a minor Hollywood figure when her tape surfaced. She had made a few media appearances as the BFF/closet organizer of Hilton, but her tape with singer Ray J (filmed in Cabo on her twenty-third birthday in 2002) was a surprise when it was announced in 2007. She sued Vivid Entertainment to stop the release of *Kim Kardashian, Superstar*, but settled out of court for $5 million. Months later, E! announced its new reality series, *Keeping Up with the Kardashians*. The sex tape made more than $50 million for Vivid.

Pamela Anderson and Tommy Lee also initially tried to halt distribution of their magnum opus but reportedly signed a deal when they realized they might as well profit from what they cannot stop.[24]

Today, when the origin of a new sex tape is publicly debated, the word "leaked" is inevitably placed in ironic quotes, to suggest a furtive push by the wannabe celeb into the marketplace. Though Paris, Kim, and Pam tried to quash their sex tapes (at least initially), many D-List celebs have unabashedly created scripted porn that feigns gonzo provenance. Tom Sizemore, for instance, released his "personal archive of pure hardcore crazy fun" on DVD in 2005. A year later, Dustin Diamond dropped *Screeched: Saved by the Smell* on an unwanting public. Even Tonya Harding pushed a sex tape, which was marketed as a leaked wedding night video but was actually choreographed in costume with her husband. Shame on them all! What has the world come to when you can't trust a sex tape?

SEE ALSO: HONEYTRAP; PORNOGRAPHY; REALDOLL; STREISAND EFFECT

---

23 Practically every celebrity, from Justin Bieber to Von Miller to Lauren Conrad, has endured a rumored sex tape. No one has seen it, but we know that presidential candidate John Edwards recorded himself with his mistress Rielle Hunter, because a judge ordered the tape be destroyed.

24 They still deny involvement. According to *Rolling Stone*'s "Pam and Tommy: The Untold Story of the World's Most Infamous Sex Tape" (the most riveting 7,400 words you will ever read about a sex tape), the video made $77 million in its first year.

CHEWBACCA DEFENSE

Incredibly, the Chewbacca Defense is a legal strategy proposed by the loutish animated sitcom *South Park*.

In an episode from the second season, which aired four days after the O. J. Simpson murder trial verdict, an animated Johnnie Cochran delivers a haranguing closing argument about how it "makes no sense" that Chewbacca would live on the planet Endor "with a bunch of two-foot-tall Ewoks." Of course, he is right. (Don't be daft. Chewie is a Wookiee from Kashyyyk.) No one in the courtroom contends otherwise, but Cochran prolongs his rant, undaunted by the lack of disputation. "If Chewbacca lives on Endor, you must acquit." He finally concludes with trademark sophistry, "The defense rests."

This is the Chewbacca Defense: a mix of prevaricating filibuster, lunatic troll logic, semantic nitpicking, derailing smoke screens, and vituperative shouting—or what debate tutors call "winning." (The O. J. Simpson defense was a lucid wet dream for shitty high school debate coaches.)

The Chewbacca Defense coexists with many unique criminal defenses that originated in pop culture. Below is a collection of other examples.

SEE ALSO: AGNOTOLOGY; IF I DID IT; INTERNET TROLL; LOREM IPSUM; SOPHISTS

THE DEFENSE	USED BY	ACCUSED OF	THE RATIONALE
The Taxi Driver Defense	John Hinckley Jr.	the attempted assassination of Ronald Reagan	Jodie Foster made me do it!
The Matrix Defense	Lee Boyd Malvo	the Beltway Sniper attacks	I did it because we are trapped in the Matrix!
The Subway Diet Defense	Jared Fogle	paying for sex with minors; possessing child porn	That lousy Subway sandwich diet made me do it!
The Twinkie Defense	Dan White	murdering Harvey Milk and George Moscone	Junk food made me do it!
The King Kong Defense	Carl Lundström	infringing copyright via The Pirate Bay	A user "in the jungles of Cambodia" shared those files!
The Evil Twin Defense	Aaron Lucas	sexual assault	My twin with the same DNA did it!
The Sleepwalking Defense	Kenneth Parks (acquitted)	murdering in-laws	I was dreaming the whole time!
The Urban Survival Defense	Bernie Goetz (acquitted)	shooting four black kids on a New York subway	Those kids were trying to rob me!
The Sergeant Schultz Defense	Chris Christie (no legal charges)	closing a bridge as political retribution	"I hear nothing, I see nothing, I know nothing!"

CHILEAN SEA BASS

The Chilean sea bass might be the most successful exercise in food rebranding of all time.[25]

Until 1977, this denizen of the deep sea went by a completely different name—*toothfish*. But when a Los Angeles seafood wholesaler discovered the obscure species residing around Antarctica, he set upon devising a more palatable moniker. After considering *Pacific sea bass* and *South American sea bass*, the fishmonger decided a hyperlocal epithet would garner the most attention. Thus, the *Chilean sea bass* was hatched, despite the fish being neither particularly Chilean (only a small portion comes from Chile) nor even a bass (toothfish is a cod!). Even the "sea" portion of its moniker is a partial misnomer, as much of the stock is now raised in fisheries.

After its rebranding, the fish went mostly unnoticed until 1990, when the New York Four Seasons finally added the dish to its snooty menu next to pan-seared filet mignon and poached lobster. By 2001, the luxurious white morsel had become *Bon Appétit*'s dish of the year—an estimable accomplishment for an unremarkable cod from Antarctica.

Chilean sea bass is far from the only seafood to prosper from successful rebranding. The regal *orange roughy* once went by the ignoble name *slimehead*. And more recently, the *sea urchin* has adopted its Japanese moniker, *uni*. Below are some other tasty foods that seem historically and geographically specific but whose origins belie their savvy branding.

SEE ALSO: FOREIGN BRANDING; FRANKENFOOD; SAMPURU; TOFURKEY

THE FOOD...	SEEMS INVENTED IN...	ACTUALLY INVENTED IN...
Ciabatta	The Renaissance?	1982 in Verona, Italy
Fortune Cookies	Confucian China?	early twentieth-century California
Tiramisu	Eighteenth-century Italy?	1960s Italy; unknown until the 1980s
Vichyssoise	Nineteenth-century France?	1917 at the Ritz-Carlton in New York City
General Tso's Chicken	Qing Dynasty?	1970s New York City
Spaghetti & Meatballs	A long time ago in Italy?	1920s Little Italy, New York City
Pasta Primavera	1920s Italy?	1977 at Le Cirque in New York City
French Dip Sandwich	Nineteenth-century Paris?	1908, Los Angeles
Fajitas	Colonial Mexico?	1970s southwest America
Chicken Tikka Masala	Precolonial India?	1971 in Glasgow
Apple Pie	Colonial America?	the Middle Ages, Netherlands

25 Does water count as a food? If so, bottled water undoubtedly prevails as the biggest culinary marketing scam in history.

CHINESE ART REPRODUCTION

Depending on which authenticator is counting, there are around thirty-five extant paintings by the great seventeenth-century master of light, Johannes Vermeer. Their scarcity makes his paintings among the most coveted objects in the world—so scarce that art historians reserve a certain adjective for precisely these types of cultish obsessions, which are not exactly beyond value, but are rather, as they say, *priceless*, which is to say, without price. Because the artworks are so infrequently bought and sold, the marketplace is unable to publicly access numerative value. But the bidding would start in the hundreds of millions.

Or you can buy one online for around a hundred bucks. Through numerous websites, you can custom-order your very own Vermeer, or whatever your bon vivant heart desires, straight from China. Classic to modern, da Vinci to Duchamp, it can be purchased online. You won't even need to tread into the nefarious corners of the dark web, where assassins and ayahuasca fluctuate with bitcoin values. The worst you will have to endure is some transgressive web design, plus the queasy feeling that accompanies the shaky politics of Chinese labor production.[26]

About a month after placing your order, you will receive a high-quality painting, most likely with the return address of Dafen Village, a suburb of Shenzhen, just north of Hong Kong. This province alone employs an estimated 8,000 artists. Some painters specialize in reproducing the classics—the *Mona Lisa* or *Starry Night*. Others do portraits of American celebrities or produce the generic art found in hotels and Wal-Mart. Dafen Village is an enormous art factory, producing an estimated 60 percent of the world's oil paintings—that includes all the "real" paintings by Western artists.[27]

If buying a masterwork reproduction rings gauche to your delicate ears, you likely belong to a snooty class of aesthetes—the sort of person who would equate owning an ersatz Vermeer to finding a wife on RussianBrides.com. But consider all of the other luxury imitations that society has come to accept—costume jewelry, faux fur, artificial nails, KNOCKOFF HANDBAGS. Eventually, like those imitations, the meretricious aura of a fake Vermeer will wear off. Owning a reproduction of a masterwork (perhaps *Girl with a Pearl Earring* via 3D PRINTING) could one day become as commonplace as owning a Bob Marley poster.

SEE ALSO: FOUNTAIN; VAN MEEGEREN, HAN

CHINESE WHISPERS

Most English-speaking countries know it as *Chinese Whispers*, but in America the game is often called *Broken Telephone*, usually abridged to just *Telephone*, or if we trust oral history—and we really shouldn't, according to this very entry—other designations, such as *Grapevine*, *Gossip*, and *Operator*.

Whatever its name, the game begins when a brood of people (usually children) gathers in a circle. One person whispers a message into the ear of an adjacent person, and that person whispers what they hear to the next, and so on, until the message circumnavigates the room. When the communiqué returns to its origin, the roving message is announced aloud. Everyone chuckles at its garbled incoherence.

The game is often deployed as a life lesson, an illus-

---

26 Among your vibrant website options: ChinaOilPaintingGallery.com, OilPaintingSupplier.com, Super-Art.com, OilPaintingCentre.com, and OilPaintingsGallery.com. There are more. Many, many more.

27 About 500 miles away in Wushipu Village, in the city of Xiamen, directly across from Taiwan, another estimated 5,000 artists are employed the same way.

tration of how gossip snowballs into misinformation. The same accumulative error also produces urban legends, such as the apocryphal tale behind the song "In the Air Tonight." In a BBC interview, Phil Collins even cited Chinese Whispers as the mechanism for the legend:

> I don't know what this song is about. . . .
> I hear these stories which started many years ago, particularly in America, of someone come up to me and said, "Did you really see someone drowning?"
> I said, "No, wrong."
> And then every time I go back to America, the story gets Chinese Whispers. It gets more and more elaborate. It's so frustrating.[28]

Maybe it is frustrating, but Chinese Whispers is also a handy metaphor for reflecting on the authenticity of canonical texts. When reading Plato, for instance, you might assume the words are translated from original dialogues, but that seems unlikely. Plato was hanging at the Acropolis around the year 400 BCE, but the oldest manuscripts we have are literally medieval—from 900 CE. That's 1,300 years of transcription with no record of provenance.

Or consider HOMER. The *Iliad* was probably written (or more likely, spoken) around 700 BCE, but the earliest fully extant manuscript is from 900 CE—more than 1,600 years later. Is it possible that verbatim copies of the *Iliad* were passed down for 1,600 years? Sure. But it seems you forgot the childhood teachings of Chinese Whispers.

SEE ALSO: HOMER; MONDEGREEN; RASHOMON EFFECT; SNOPES

CHURCH OF SUBGENIUS

The Church of SubGenius is a spoof religion with vengeful extraterrestrial gods, created to satirize other religions but accidentally developing the qualities of an actual religion. (But it's not Scientology.)

According to photocopied scripture (zines), a drilling equipment salesman from the '50s, J. R. "Bob" Dobbs, is the prophet of the church. The religion is polytheistic—with deities that include aliens, mutants, and fictional characters—but the central deity is Jehovah 1, a wrathful extraterrestrial who contacted Dobbs on his self-made television.

The religion eschews absolute truth, making doctrine difficult to pin down, but a mélange of popular culture, conspiracy theories, and other religions constitutes its antidogma. The central tenet involves attaining a state of *Slack*, defined as "perfect luck, effortless achievement." Ways to attain Slack include sex and avoiding work.

The primary symbol of the religion is clipart that the church maintains is Dobbs with a pipe. The image spread as an underground phenomenon in the '80s and '90s, when truth through absurdity seemed a radical method for rejecting mainstream culture. A lot of stoned slackers kinda believed the orthodoxy of the Church of SubGenius, or played along with believing it, which might be the same thing as believing it.

SEE ALSO: OPERATION MINDFUCK; XENU

---

28 According to the legend, Phil Collins witnessed a person drowning but was too far away to help. But he also saw another person, close enough to rescue the victim, who did nothing. The fable ends climactically, years later, when the singer spots the soulless drowning-watcher at his concert. Pointing the arena searchlights into the crowd, Collins vindictively hate-sings "In the Air Tonight" at his spotlit face. The moral? If you can't swim, avoid Phil Collins concerts.

CLAPTER

Clapter is the earnest applause of a like-minded audience. Clapter is the polite laughter at a joke that matches your political taste, even if it isn't funny. Clapter is the robotic response to politically edifying humor. Clapter is the soft hum of a crowd agreeing with itself. Clapter is approval over adulation.

Clapter—a portmanteau of clapping and laughter—was coined by comedian Seth Meyers to connote political humor that reaffirms existing beliefs.

SEE ALSO: CANNED HEAT; CLAQUE; LAUGH TRACK

CLAQUE

A claque is a group of people hired to applaud a performer. The practice of orchestrated applause dates back to at least Nero, who maintained a claque of 5,000 soldiers, but the word itself derives from French for *to clap*, because *rieurs* (laughers), *pleureurs* (criers), and *bisseurs* (encore-ers) were rou-tinely hired at operas and plays in France up until the late nineteenth century.

If the claque seems an absurd conceit of the past, consider its recent resurrection in the form of Donald Trump. At his very first campaign event, the famous Trump Tower launch of his presidential campaign, actors were paid $50 each to wear campaign T-shirts and cheer as the neo-Nero descended on a gold-plated escalator.[29] The campaign also hired actors to act as "concerned citizens" on local news and regularly positioned a Greek chorus of paid staffers to holler and jeer reporters. The claque is back.

SEE ALSO: CANNED HEAT; CLAPTER; CRISIS ACTORS; LAUGH TRACK; THE METHOD; MOIROLOGIST

CLICKBAIT

Clickbait is anything on the internet that you disagree with. Or *sigh*, that is the regrettably weakened definition of a once-specific word that has suffered many rounds of semantic dilution.

---

29 This is not wild-eyed conspiracy mongering. The Federal Election Commission released documents proving he was billed $12,000 by a talent contractor for the fake audience.

Initially, clickbait was an invective cast toward a particular internet specimen, a story that preyed upon your curiosity gap with a cliffhanger headline: "...and You Won't Believe What Happens Next" or "...and You Will Never Feel the Same." These cutesy nonpareils ultimately annoyed readers who clicked through to find non-life-changing articles. Even the *Oxford English Dictionary* adopted this definition of clickbait: "content whose main purpose is to attract attention and encourage visitors to click on a link to a particular web page." But that finespun definition soon dilated to encompass much more.

In its first semantic expansion, clickbait grew to include not just misdirection but any content of trifling value. Dopamine-inducing listicles and infectious cat-based slideshows were assigned the clickbait label. Content from the website Buzzfeed was most often indicted. (Actual Buzzfeed headline: "The 25 Most Awkward Cat Sleeping Positions." It has been viewed more than 3 million times.) Soon enough, even this harmless pandering was lost in the vast sea of clickbait.

Today, the term has attenuated into near meaninglessness. Clickbait is invoked for anything on the internet that you, personally, do not enjoy. Alarming headlines like "Russians Attempt to Hack American Elections" are dubbed clickbait, even if they are simply stating a fact.

SEE ALSO: THE DRESS; FIVERR; NAKED CAME THE STRANGER; YELLOW JOURNALISM

CLIFTON, TONY

If for some reason you find yourself awake late at night, looking at the Wikipedia page for Tony Clifton, and you absently click the tab that shows its "talk" page, this declaration from user Jtpaladin will appear, just below a subtitle that reads "Tony Clifton is a real lounge singer":

> I think it's disgusting the way Andy Kaufman and his family used Tony Clifton to make money. Tony Clifton was a lounge singer in Las Vegas when Kaufman was nothing. Tony Clifton should not be associated with Kaufman other than Clifton opened some shows for Kaufman.

This comment is funny on multiple levels, perhaps most because it has led to a Wikipedia "talk" page being cited in a reference book about misinformation.[30] But more intriguingly, there are only two possible conclusions to draw from this remark: [1] Someone out there still cannot distinguish between Tony Clifton and Andy Kaufman, or [2] someone out there is still invested in conflating the two for obscure comedic effect.[31]

Kaufman's alter ego, Tony Clifton, was an obnoxious lounge act who assaulted his audience with slurred crooning and scuzzy wisecracks. People who need labels for such things called it *anticomedy*—a sleazy has-been in a polyester suit telling intentionally bad jokes. *It's funny because it's not funny*, they might say.

But that's not quite right. From nearly the beginning, everyone knew that Clifton was Kaufman, yet

---

30 Every Wikipedia entry has an associated "talk" page, which contains a blow-by-blow account of its edit-war history. Like Herodotus chronicling the Peloponnesian War, it is a highly unstable account. If you relish vociferous discord over whether Neapolitan ice cream must, *by definition*, contain the flavors chocolate, vanilla, and strawberry (*absolutely no substitutes!*), this is the place for you.

31 The other two choices—[3] they actually are different people, or [4] a sentient Andy Kaufman who still wanders the planet wrote the comment—have been dismissed as improbable.

he persisted in the illusion. The gag *seemed* like a mockery of a Vegas lounge act, but it became something else—a bit about a performance artist who refuses to break character. And actually, that's pretty funny.

Clifton landed his own gigs. Asked directly if he was Kaufman during an appearance on *Late Night with David Letterman*, Clifton sputtered that his nemesis was using his name "to get places." On *The Dinah Shore Show*, Clifton took the ruse a bit too far, pouring eggs over the terrified host's head. *Taxi* even hired Clifton, on a contract distinct from Kaufman's, to appear as Louie's brother. After fighting with the cast and crew, he either quit or was fired, depending on which story you believe. The APOCRYPHA surrounding Kaufman is vast.

To keep the gag afloat, Kaufman asked others to don the belly prosthetic, baby blue ruffles, and dark shades. The boorish curmudgeon was played by his brother, Michael, and his best friend, Bob Zmuda—both of whom are the leading proponents of the "Kaufman is still alive" theory. (His brother claimed to receive letters from Andy in 2013; Zmuda wrote an entire book in 2014, *The Truth, Finally*, which starts by making the case that Andy is alive but then veers toward the theory that he was closeted and may have died from an early undiagnosed case of AIDS.)

According to Zmuda, Kaufman, on his (possibly fake) deathbed, asked him to keep Tony Clifton alive. And so, the crass misanthrope still occasionally straps on the ruffles and dark shades for the occasional stand-up or benefit appearance, goofing on Elvis, *hey baby*.

SEE ALSO: THE MASKED MARAUDERS; SMARKS; TRUTHINESS

COGNITIVE DISSONANCE

Dorothy Martin, an eccentric housewife in suburban Chicago, received a message from outer space in early 1954, warning her that on December 21 of that year, a great flood would inundate the planet. "It is an actual fact that the world is in a mess," the aliens channeled to her, via automatic writing, in surprisingly turgid prose. "But the Supreme Being is going to clean house by sinking all of the land masses as we know them now and raising the land masses from under the sea."

As luck would have it, the aliens (called *Guardians*) were arriving from a secret planet hidden behind the moon (called *Clarion*) to evacuate true believers (called *Seekers*) from earth. (Scientology was among the many doctrines in which Martin had dabbled.) When the day of reckoning arrived, Martin had convinced around twenty people to quit college, leave their jobs, dump their spouses, relinquish their possessions, and join her cozy apocalyptic death cult. On December 20, they gathered at her home, removed all metal from their bodies (to avoid being burned from contact with the spacecraft), and waited for the extraterrestrials to arrive.

Unbeknownst to Martin, imposters were in their midst. The social psychologist Leon Festinger and two colleagues had embedded themselves among the followers. After reading about the doomsday cult in his local paper, Festinger had infiltrated the group, hoping to study how they would react to information that contradicts their eschatological doctrine. What would happen when the little green people did not arrive? How would they rationalize their fervent beliefs against unassailable reality? Would the devotees rebel against their prophet? The researchers watched and waited.

Before midnight, after singing carols for reporters who had gathered, the group retreated to the living room, to wait.[32] A clock struck midnight—yet

---

32 Martin's husband, who thought the death cult hooey, went to bed and slept soundly through the caper.

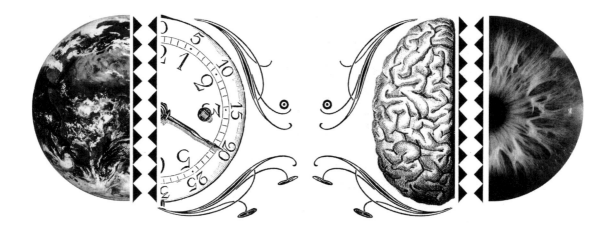

no aliens appeared. The cultists were stunned, but they waited. By 2:00 AM, the room was dead silent; everyone appeared worried. Finally, at 4:45 AM, Martin received a new prophecy from the aliens—the human race would be saved! Because the followers had impressed god with their faith, they would be spared from annihilation. How did the group respond? Surprisingly, with renewed vigor. To mitigate the mental discomfort of reality conflicting with prophecy, the group quickly updated their beliefs to fit the new circumstance. Armageddon, they reasoned, was simply postponed.

From what he witnessed, Festinger developed a psychological framework, which he called *cognitive dissonance*, to characterize the discomfort one feels when holding two contradictory beliefs. At the center of Festinger's theory is a question, *how do we change our minds?* "A man with a conviction is a hard man to change," he wrote crisply in *When Prophecy Fails* (1956). "Show him facts and figures and he questions your sources. Appeal to logic and he fails to see your point. We all have experienced the futility of trying to change a strong conviction, especially if the convinced person has some investment in their belief." And when that conviction involves imminent salvation from the heavens, "it may even be less painful

to tolerate the dissonance than to discard the belief and admit one had been wrong."

Changing your mind sucks, and no one likes to admit they are wrong. Festinger's framework showed how, when forced to change our minds, we can resolve the dissonance. Later studies, from Festinger and others, went a step further, illustrating how individuals develop coping mechanisms, not merely *to adopt* new information but *to avoid* encountering it at all. Through a decision-making rigmarole called *motivated reasoning*, people find clever ways to mitigate cognitive dissonance by never encountering it. By steering clear of potentially contradictory information, one can avoid the discomfort of changing their mind. Research shows that people actively seek out agreeable information while cunningly avoiding, ignoring, devaluing, or simply forgetting contradictory information.

Cognitive dissonance goes a long way toward explaining our current partisan media environment.

SEE ALSO: BACKFIRE EFFECT; BARNUM EFFECT; CONFIRMATION BIAS; DOUBLE THINK; FILTER BUBBLE; GASLIGHTING; MANDELA EFFECT; NEWSPEAK

COLD FUSION

In the spring of 1989, two electrochemists held a press conference in Salt Lake City to announce an incredible discovery: a new source of energy that was clean, cheap, and abundant.[33] The scientists claimed that through a simple process (requiring merely a test tube of heavy water, plus some palladium, lithium, and a jolt of electricity) they could create a small nuclear reaction. *Cold fusion*, it was called, but "cold" only by comparison to the sun, where traditional fusion occurs. This nuclear reaction, which produced no waste material, could be induced at room temperature. For an instant, it seemed the world was about to change forever.

It was an opportune time to believe in the impossible. The tantalizing promise of unlimited energy, yanked from the pages of science fiction, could not have come at a better moment. Memories of the '70s oil crisis still haunted America, while the impending meltdown of the Cold War created a vibe of utopian credulity. At first, the media loved the story, hyping it with unfettered glee ("The Race for Fusion" splashed *Newsweek* on its cover), but hopes were quickly dashed ("Fusion or Illusion?" *Time* inquired on its cover, only a month after the initial press conference). Before we could even welcome flying cars and warp drive into our lives, the thrilling vision of infinite energy was imploding.

Other scientists quickly debunked the findings of the cold fusion electrochemists. Scientific fraud, thankfully, did not appear to be the culprit; more likely, this was a simple matter of poor methodology and unchecked optimism. "Some scientist put a thermometer at one place and not another" is how one physicist denounced the faulty research. Another remarked that the mishap was the result of "incompetence and perhaps delusion."

Yes, perhaps. But just for a moment, their delusion made the most harebrained science fiction fantasies seem possible.

SEE ALSO: AETHER; DARK ENERGY; SCHRÖDINGER'S CAT; SOKAL HOAX; UTOPIA

COLEMAN, ALLEGRA

DREAM GIRL

That's what it said, in bold and shimmery letters, right there on the November 1996 cover of *Esquire*, next to a tangle of blond bed-hair tumbling to the halter top of Allegra Coleman, Hollywood's newest starlet, who had finally landed her first magazine profile. Inside, *Esquire* dished on the debutante's rocky relationship with the friendly David Schwimmer, glossed over her recent tabloid nude photos, and hinted at a new suitor, Quentin Tarantino. "She is without blind vanities," Deepak Chopra gushed. "Her nature is spongy and luminescent."

Calls immediately poured into *Esquire* from publicists and agents, hoping to sign the new It Girl. Finally, the magazine issued a confessional press release: Allegra Coleman was fake. "A parody of the celebrity journalism that's run wild in the '90s," is how *Esquire* described their spoof, but the target of such parody seemed unclear. The same issue of the magazine contained a (very real) profile of the Baldwin brothers and a (seemingly real) think-piece on "the post-gay man."

And yet, a question persisted: *Who was the woman on the cover?* Agents and publicists still wanted the face, even if the story was phony-baloney. The

---

33 The two electrochemists were Dr. Stanley Pons and Dr. Martin Fleischmann. If nerdy names were the sole determinant in producing mad scientists, these two would be ringers for inventing a new type of energy.

answer: Ali Larter, an unknown model, who instantly started to receive casting calls. With no prior acting experience, Larter landed small roles on shows like *Dawson's Creek* and *Chicago Hope*, which led to higher profile gigs, including the movies *Legally Blonde* and recurring franchise characters in *Final Destination* and *Resident Evil*, and eventually a starring role in NBC's science fiction drama *Heroes*, where she played identical triplet superheroes with dissociative identity disorder. (She would also appear, as herself, on covers of *Cosmo*, *Lucky*, *Shape*, *Allure*—and *Esquire Mexico*.)

The fake profile of an ingénue launched a very real acting career.

SEE ALSO: CELEBRITY SEX TAPES; WARHOL, ANDY

CONCERN TROLLING

A concern troll inveigles their way into discussions by posing as an ally but soon undermines the topic with their disingenuous *concerns*. They feign interest in your plight as a cover for mischief. Their chicanery can be difficult to spot, but these patronizing impostors often begin sentences like this:

- "I have just a few questions . . ."
- "I agree, but others might not see your point . . ."
- "Your position might be too extreme . . ."
- "I am worried about you . . ."
- "You are being too strident about . . ."
- "I'm with you, but . . ."
- "We could improve your argument by . . ."

After cajoling their way into a community, the concern troll uses cloying rhetoric to neuter debate.

With *just a few innocent questions*, they can steer a conversation into the ditch.

The biggest dilemma is that a concern troll can often resemble an honest critic simply trying to disrupt groupthink. This makes their conniving agitprop so insidious—they make you doubt your convictions. Are they allies or agent provocateurs? Sometimes not even the concern troll knows the answer.

SEE ALSO: CONFIDENCE GAME; FALSE FLAG OPERATION; GASLIGHTING; INTERNET TROLL

CONFIDENCE GAME

In movies, confidence games are limned with ornate plotting, layer upon layer of calculated treachery. *Who is deceiving whom?* is the baroque game of skulduggery in these capers, performed with particular elegance in *The Sting* and *The Spanish Prisoner*. Despite the knotty storylines on the screen, grifts are ultimately distillable to one very simple edict: Tell a story that persuades the victim. And to persuade, you must become a convincing actor. "A con game," said Ricky Jay in *House of Games*, "is a dramatization for an audience of one person."[34]

That one-member audience, known as *the mark*, also dictates the mechanics of the con. Some grifts exploit a mark's naiveté; in others, their opportunism blinds them to the ruse. A master con incorporates the faults of their marks.

Because the mark participates in their own undoing, the con artist is sometimes referred to as the most noble criminal. A good con man never forces you to do anything. He doesn't steal; you give. Guns and violence are prohibited in most cons. The only weapon is the story of the con itself.[35]

---

34 Ricky Jay plays a cardshark in this masterful David Mamet con man thriller from 1987, but he actually says these words as himself, in the DVD commentary of the Criterion Collection version of the movie.

CON MAN GLOSSARY

GRIFTER TERM	MEANING
Account Flash	A large sum of money briefly appearing in a mark's bank account
Basement Dealer	A card player who deals from the bottom of the deck
Big Store	Scam with a large team and elaborate sets
Blow Off	To shake the mark after a con
Cackle Bladder	When a con artist fakes his death with fake blood
Change Raising	Short con where you give less change in a transaction than it seems
Cool Off	Pacifying a victim so he does not contact the police
Crack out of Turn	When someone accidentally goes off-script and ruins the con
Curdle	When something goes wrong in a con
Earnest Money	Money given by the mark as a show of good faith
Fiddle Game	Two-person scam involving elevated pricing of a worthless object
Flight Store	Long con involving a (perceived) fixed boxing match
Fine Wirers	A good pickpocket
Gaff	Prop or gimmick used in a scam
Glim-dropper	Variation on the Fiddle Game with a one-eyed man
Jamaican Switch	Con involving money switched for worthless paper
Mark	The intended victim
Pig in a Poke	Medieval scam; a mark buys a bag with a cat inside, expecting a pig
Pigeon Drop	Scam in which the mark puts up earnest money to secure a larger sum
Play the C	The first step in a con, winning the confidence of a mark
Roper	The person who brings a mark into the scam
Salting the Mine	Making a mine look more valuable by secretly placing gold in it
Shill	An accomplice on the con
Short Con	A quick grift with low returns
Single-O	Grifter who works solo
Sliders	People on the look-out for police during a con
Slough	A universal safe word to abort the con
Spanish Prisoner	Scam where the mark is enlisted to retrieve (nonexistent) stolen money
Sting	The precise moment when the money is taken from the mark
Tell	An unconscious signal giving away a scheme

Long cons require a large cast of bamboozlers. As such, the profession—a sort of ad hoc community theater troupe—has developed a playful nomenclature around their camaraderie. (Honor among thieves, and all that.) This vernacular of the flimflam was parodied in the *Ocean*'s trilogy, in such lines as "It's actually a Lookie-Loo with a Bundle of Joy."[36] The suggestion is clear: Cons are equivalent to *tropes*, or stock narrative devices, which can be moved around from scene to scene. Like the dramatic arts, cons are composed of interchangeable blocks—a coldhearted swindle here, a conspiring pinch there. Both are art forms that demand perfect timing, shades of believability, and attention to details of stagecraft.

Because this is an encyclopedia, a compendium of vocabulary is obligatory. The glossary to the left contains some of the more savory patois used in the grifter underworld, gathered indiscriminately from across criminal history.

SEE ALSO: CRISIS ACTORS; FALSE FLAG OPERATION; HONEYTRAP; PONZI SCHEME; SNIPE HUNT

CONFIRMATION BIAS

Confirmation bias is the overwhelming tendency to seek out information that conforms with existing beliefs while ignoring facts that contradict entrenched viewpoints. The bias helps explain diverse phenomena, from why conservatives watch FOX News to how astrology can persist in an age of reason, from why Ariana Grande gets played on the radio to why cops can exhibit racial profiling prejudices.

Confirmation bias is a democratic ailment—no one consumes information with complete objectivity. (Not even you, super freethinker.) An immense amount of sociological research has gone into the phenomenon, with entire shelves of documented experimentation.

SEE ALSO: BACKFIRE EFFECT; BARNUM EFFECT; COGNITIVE DISSONANCE; FILTER BUBBLE; OVERTON WINDOW; PAREIDOLIA; WOOZLE EFFECT

COSPLAY

Cosplay is a form of interactive roleplaying for enthusiastic fans with very, very, very passionate feelings (*shut up*, not in *that way*) for a fictional character. Cosplaying involves donning a costume that embodies an adored character, usually drawn from fantasy or science fiction.[37]

The term comes from Japan, naturally, but is actually a portmanteau of two English words, *costume* and *play*. The "play" half is crucial, as it suggests a lively social activity. Enormous festivals and conventions, with judged competitions, have exploded around cosplay communities.

Cosplay costumes often require elaborate construction and accessorizing. Raw materials include wigs, metallic fabric, fake fur, hair dye, liquid latex,

---

35 *The Confidence Game* (2016) by Maria Konnikova is a stupendous review of the psychological aspects of cons.

36 The Ocean's grifts are all made up, but that line describes the con in *Ocean's Twelve*, where Julia Roberts plays herself. (To recap: That's an actress playing herself playing a grifter playing herself.) Another hustler aperçu, from *Ocean's Eleven*, exemplifies the complexity of building a grift: "Off the top of my head, I'd say you're looking at a Boesky, a Jim Brown, a Miss Daisy, two Jethros, and a Leon Spinks, not to mention the biggest Ella Fitzgerald ever!"

37 Popular subjects include characters from "universes" like Harry Potter, Marvel Comics, Doctor Who, The Legend of Zelda, My Little Pony, Star Wars, Star Trek, Mortal Kombat, The Elder Scrolls, and Final Fantasy.

contact lenses, body paint, facial cosmetics, costume jewelry, tassels, and prop weapons. As in life, the simulacrum engenders a delicate balance. Each cosplayer weighs authenticity against aesthetics, strict precision versus personal style, in assembling their costume. "The role of expression," as sociologist Erving Goffman once wrote, "is conveying impressions of self."[38]

Generally considered harmless fun by its enthusiasts, cosplay is also sociologically complex, often generating complicated discussions about race, gender, body, and identity. *Caution*: Accusing cosplayers of kinky motivations will often yield scorn. Avoid doing so, unless you are dressed as Link.

SEE ALSO: FANFIC; LARP; SLASHFIC; SMARKS

COTARD DELUSION

Cotard delusion, also known as "walking corpse syndrome," is a mental condition in which a person believes they are dead. Those afflicted with this extremely rare disorder suspect that they, or parts of their body, have disintegrated. They report feeling like zombies.

Because the psychosis is so rare, with approximately one hundred reported cases worldwide, very few patients have had neurological scans. But the results from those scant scans have been shocking: Metabolic activity across large areas of the brain appears similar to someone in a vegetative state, as though actually brain dead.

Neurologically, the condition seems related to CAPGRAS DELUSION, which is the belief that someone close to you, typically your spouse, is an impostor, and FREGOLI DELUSION, the belief that different people are a single person.

SEE ALSO: CAPGRAS DELUSION; FREGOLI DELUSION; PAUL IS DEAD; TRUMAN SYNDROME

CRISIS ACTORS

Crisis actors are (real) professional thespians hired to play victims during (fake) military training exercises. However, in the hands of conspiracy theorists, crisis actors play a more sinister role: participants in FALSE FLAG OPERATIONS.

According to these elaborate theories, crisis actors are dispatched by the government (or the media) to portray victims, witnesses, or emergency response technicians during "scripted" national tragedies, including bombings, mass shootings, and terrorist events. The conspiracists—particularly those associated with the uberconspiratorial website Infowars—claim these actors have even been coached to recite memorized lines during breaking news.

Wake up, sheeple!

Crisis actors are a relatively new tool in the subterfuge handbook. The term surged in popularity around 2013 when some INTERNET TROLLS pasted together photos of similar-looking victims from the Sandy Hook massacre, the Aurora shooting, and the Boston Marathon bombing into "same girl" memes.

SEE ALSO: ASTROTURFING; CLAQUE; FALSE FLAG OPERATION; INTERNET TROLL; LARP; THE METHOD; PAREIDOLIA; ROSENHAM EFFECT; SOCK PUPPET; TROJAN HORSE

---

38 Long before cosplay, Goffman's *The Presentation of Self in Everyday Life* (1956) became the bible for dramaturgical sociologists—the "All the world's a stage!" types.

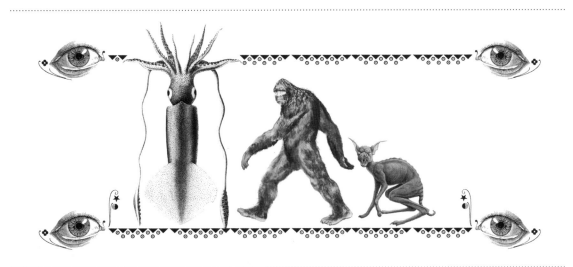

CRYPTIDS

Cryptids are animals whose existences have not yet been documented by the scientific community. Or rather, that is the panglossian spin of the cryptozoologist, a person who studies such furtive creatures and believes their special species will one day be proven authentic.

The most well-known cryptids inhabiting the safari of disputed fauna include the Sasquatch, the Loch Ness Monster, and the Chupacabra. In *Cryptozoology A To Z* (1999), Loren Coleman, a godfather of the field, discusses around 120 such creatures. Wikipedia maintains a list of around 230 possible cryptids.

The word *cryptozoology* derives from three Greek words—*kryptos, zoon,* and *logos*—which translate as *hidden, animal,* and *discourse.* It is therefore literally the science of hidden animals. Some researchers consider cryptozoology a pseudoscience, but that appraisal overlooks the jungle of creatures once deemed cryptids that have since been proven to exist, such as the thylacine, a mashup of a dog and a kangaroo that once seemed too whimsical to exist but turned out to be real.

Cryptids cast a wide net, comprising a range of eccentric creatures—urban legends (chupacabras),

creatures thought extinct (coelacanths), extreme taxidermy (jackalopes), extreme taxidermy proven real (platypuses), whimsical mythology (griffins), and even our own cousins (Neanderthals). Essentially any animal whose existence has been disputed is a cryptid. The following page contains a chart of the more prominent cryptids through history.

SEE ALSO: AREA 51; BONSAI KITTEN; CARDIFF GIANT; SNIPE HUNT; ZARDULU

CUNNINGHAM'S LAW

If you wanted to know how many degrees of separation Kevin Bacon is from Bill Murray, you might try querying an internet hivemind collective—Quora, Reddit, Yahoo Answers, or Twitter. Eventually, someone might respond to your inquiry. But if you want the answer *right now*, a much faster tactic would be to make an *inaccurate* declaration: "Kevin Bacon was in *Frost/Nixon* with Sam Rockwell, who was in *Iron Man 2* with Scarlett Johansson, who was in *Lost in Translation* with Bill Murray. Three degrees of separation!" Some IMDB know-it-all will immediately

SELECT CURRENT & FORMER CRYPTIDS

CRYPTID	LOCATION	DESCRIPTION	STATUS
Loch Ness Monster	Scotland	Lake monster with a long neck	Famously photographed in 1934, Nessie is the most disputed cryptid—and probably a hoax.
Giant Squid	All the world's oceans	A squid with gigantism	Deemed folklore for centuries, its status changed in the 1870s when corpses washed ashore in Canada. Not photographed alive until 2004.
Kraken	Norway & Greenland	An octopus with gigantism	Allegedly witnessed by seamen for centuries, the legendary sea monster might actually have been the Giant Squid.
Sasquatch	Pacific Northwest	Taller, hairier human, like Chewbacca	An infamous one-minute film shot in 1967 supposedly captured the Bigfoot, which was probably a man in an ape suit.
Woolly Mammoth	Northern climes around the globe	Hairy cousin of an elephant	Currently the subject of competing cloning experiments, the mammoth was long presumed extinct before 12,000 BCE but probably survived until 4,000 BCE.
Chupacabra	Mexico, Puerto Rico, American Southwest	A reptilian kangaroo from outer space	From the Portuguese for "goat-sucker," the urban legend began in 1995 when livestock drained of blood were discovered.
Jackalope	The American West	A jackrabbit with antelope horns	This gag taxidermy was used in Old West tall tales to trick children and gullible city folk.
Mermaid	All the world's oceans	A human (usually female) with the tail of a fish	A favorite of mythology and fairy tales, mermaids were reported by Columbus and put on display by P. T. Barnum.
Komodo Dragon	Indonesia	Lizard that can grow up to ten feet long	Considered mythical in the West until 1910, the Komodo population is believed to be around 3,000 today.
Neanderthals	Northern Europe and Asia	Us, but with larger noses, more hair, and heavier brows	They live, inside us. Despite going extinct 40,000 years ago, Neanderthals make up 1 to 4 percent of our DNA through inter-breeding and persist through legends (Sasquatch, Yeti).
Platypus	Egg-laying, duck-billed mammal	Australia	Deemed a sewn-together hoax when its pelt first appeared in 1799, this freak of nature persists in Australia today.
Tasmanian Tiger (aka Thylacine)	Tasmania	Doglike marsupial	Once thought mythical, the thylacine really existed but is now believed extinct. Ted Turner once offered a $100,000 reward for proof of a living thylacine.

recognize your convoluted folly and promptly correct you. "You're a goddamn moron. Kevin Bacon was in the indelible masterpiece *Wild Things* with Bill Murray. One degree, numbskull."

This is Cunningham's Law in action. It states: *The best way to get the right answer on the internet is not to ask a question but to post the wrong answer.*

In other words, misinformation sometimes outperforms information, especially when prodding people to take action. (Sherlock Holmes proffered a similar insight: "People don't like telling you things. They love to contradict you.")

The source of the law is Ward Cunningham, the father of wiki software—a sublime coincidence, because Wikipedia is an apt proof of Cunningham's Law.

SEE ALSO: BOGUS PIPELINE; CONCERN TROLLING; LIE-TO-CHILDREN; SNOPES; STREISAND EFFECT

CYBORG

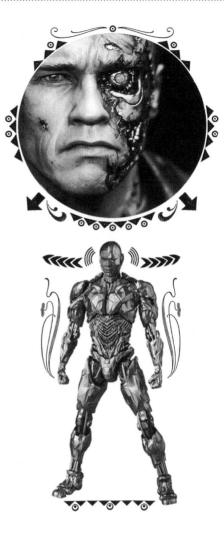

"The term *cyborg* is a contraction of 'cybernetic organism' and refers to the product of human/machine hybridization," says *The Encyclopedia of Science Fiction*. That impressive reference tome is the most pertinent source of citation for this entry, as cyborgs are nearly synonymous with science fiction, at least for now.

Often used as a trope to contrast with human foibles, cyborgs play a key role in our rampant "is it man or machine?" sci-fi narratives. Fictional examples of cyborgs include the Cybermen in *Doctor Who*, the Borg in Star Trek, replicants in *Blade Runner*, hosts in *Westworld*, Darth Vader in Star Wars, cylons in *Battlestar Galactica*, and the titular characters in *Terminator* and *RoboCop*.

Back in real life, hints of cyborg enhancements can be found in pacemakers, cochlear implants, artificial hearts, bionic eyes, artificial limbs, contact lenses, and even dentures. Depending on your appetite for malleable definitions, the list of cyborgian appendages might include Stephen Hawking's speech synthesizer, semiautomated artificial intelligence systems, or—if you're feeling like an intrepid robot—even the internet.

SEE ALSO: ELIZA EFFECT; FRANKENFOOD; GREEBLES; HUMAN CLONING; MECHANICAL TURK; TURING TEST; UNCANNY VALLEY; VOIGHT-KAMPFF MACHINE; TUPAC HOLOGRAM

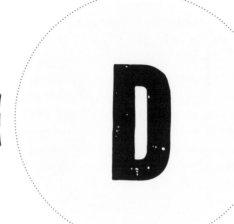

DARK ENERGY

Dark energy has never been seen, heard, smelled, tasted, or observed in any manner. No one can say, for sure, that it exists. Scientists have neither studied dark energy in a telescope nor examined it under an electron microscope. It does not emit radiation or absorb light. (Its slightly less hypothetical cousin, *dark matter*, which is also not directly observable, can at least be shown to bend light.) Its quiddity is only an inference. And yet, astrophysicists predict dark energy constitutes 68 percent of the mass and energy of the universe.

Yes, *predict*. Physicists cannot say, absolutely, because dark energy is purely theoretical. Dark energy exists only because mathematical calculations of mass and gravity predict it *should* exist. (It is required to corroborate the predominant scientific belief that the expansion of the universe is accelerating.) Without dark energy, the rest of the known universe does not make any sense.

Science is a history of speculation—unseen laws, effects, and entities that hypothetically might exist but require data from experimentation to verify. Relentlessly inquisitive and skeptical, science will one day prove or disprove the existence of dark energy, but for now, it is a placeholder in a formula that holds the universe together.

SEE ALSO: AETHER; COLD FUSION; DEEP STATE; LOREM IPSUM

DARK SIDE OF THE RAINBOW

A pastime invented to bemuse college kids, *Dark Side of the Rainbow* involves watching *The Wizard of Oz* (audio low) while listening to *The Dark Side of the Moon* (audio loud). The other potential ingredient is psychoactive drugs.

The experience creates magical moments of synchronicity, in which uncanny meaning is found in the seemingly random. Most instruction kits, found on the internet, advise the participants to start *Dark Side* on the third roar of *Oz*'s MGM lion. Instantly, song lyrics seem to match with the plot. When Dorothy's house crashes in Munchkinland, the cash register on "Money" starts chiming and the film turns to color. When Scarecrow sings "If I Only Had a Brain," Pink

Floyd sings "Brain Damage" (key lyric: "The lunatic is on the grass"). Even the prism on *Dark Side*'s album cover, with light refracting into a rainbow, suggests black-and-white film transmuting into technicolor.

Though it might seem a concoction of the '70s, the mashup was first discussed on an online bulletin board, *alt.music.pink-floyd*, in 1995. It is also known as *Dark Side of Oz* or *The Wizard of Floyd*.

SEE ALSO: BACKMASKING; BANANADINE; MONDEGREEN; PAREIDOLIA; PAUL IS DEAD

DEEP STATE

It sounds like something out of *Alice in Wonderland* and might be as whimsical: Inside the state there is another state—*the deep state*—a cabal of puppet masters who secretly pull the strings of government.

Historically, the deep state has been associated with a covert shadow government aligned with business and industrial interests in countries like Turkey, Pakistan, and the former Soviet states. The term has recently gained popularity in America to describe a hypothetical nexus of government bureaucracies that secretly controls elected officials. Like gravity, the deep state wields soft, invisible power through government institutions including intelligence agencies, the military, Wall Street, and various nefarious federal bureaucracies. The term was perhaps best summarized by Robert Redford's character in *Three Days of the Condor*, who wonders, "Maybe there's another CIA . . . *inside the CIA*."

The term is complicated by a continuum of usage. At the extreme, deep *deep* staters are convinced that a clandestine kleptocracy secretly commands the global finance network. (This tenet resembles older conspiracies that implicate the Freemasons, the Rothschilds, or the Rosicrucians in an international financial conspiracy.) A more moderate group sees no shadowy cabal but casts the deep state as more

of an institutional influence network, not too dissimilar from what president Eisenhower called *the military-industrial complex*.

When a president disagrees with his own governing institutions (the State Department, the CIA, etc.), he is sometimes said to be confronting the deep state. The murky term is also invoked in an extremely loose sense, to identify globalist insiders who attend the Davos Economic Forum, are affiliated with the Clinton Global Initiative, or work for Bloomberg Media. In that sense, the deep state is synonymous with that 1960s caricature: the Man.

The deep state theory is appealing because it sounds eerily murky and terribly sinister while defying explicit identification. It is definitionally invisible, so you don't have to prove it exists.

SEE ALSO: AREA 51; DARK ENERGY; MANCHURIAN CANDIDATE; THE REPORT FROM IRON MOUNTAIN

DEFICTIONALIZED PRODUCTS

A *defictionalized product* is a PRODUCT PLACEMENT in reverse. When a brand pays to have a commodity *placed inside a fictional world*, like E.T. eating Reese's Pieces, it is a product placement. But when a product *emerges from a fictional world*, as with the Bubba Gump Shrimp chain materializing from *Forrest Gump*, it is a defictionalized product.

Take the case of Eddie Bluestein, a Memphis draftsman who accidentally made history in 1952 when he was asked to create architectural renderings for a new hotel chain. Needing a temporary moniker in the sketches for the unnamed development, Bluestein found inspiration in the Bing Crosby musical *Holiday Inn* (the one that introduced the world to "White Christmas"). Intended as a mere placeholder, "Holiday Inn" stuck as the actual name of the budget hotel chain when the founder decided he preferred the stand-in.

Since then, the crossovers from fictive commodity to real merch have only accelerated: Willy Wonka Candy (*Charlie and the Chocolate Factory*), Dunder Mifflin Paper (*The Office*), Red Swingline Stapler (*Office Space*), Brawndo (*Idiocracy*), Soylent (*Soylent Green*). *The Simpsons* easily holds the record for most defictionalized products, including Buzz Cola, Duff Beer, Krusty-O's cereal, and Squishee (available at 7-Elevens rebranded as Kwik-E-Marts in 2007).

One of the most extreme instances of defictionalization involves Emilio Estevez coaching a little league hockey team. *The Mighty Ducks* was a mediocre sports comedy starring Estevez, but the movie hatched an actual team, the Anaheim Mighty Ducks. This crossover was not completely happenstance—both the movie and the team were owned by Disney. (The "Mighty" was later dropped when Disney sold the hockey team.)

SEE ALSO: THE FOURTH WALL; PRODUCT DISPLACEMENT; PRODUCT PLACEMENT; TOYETIC

DOE, JOHN

John Doe is a placeholder name, often used for unidentified corpses or anonymous parties in court cases. His sister, of sorts, is Jane Roe, as in the anonymous litigant in *Roe v. Wade*.

The name originated for legal contracts in fourteenth-century England, where it has since been usurped by Joe Bloggs and John Smith. In Germany, the corresponding person is often identified as Erika Mustermann, whereas in much of South America, Juan Pérez fills the role. In Poland, it's Jan Kowalski; Sven Svensson, in Sweden. Israelis, in a bit of doubletalk, often identify their known unknowns as Israel Israel.

When politicians and demographers require a generic character, they often bestow John Doe with a more colorful identity. Among their colloquial names for everyman: John Q. Public, Average Joe, Joe Blow, Joe Shmoe, and Eddie Punchclock. "Joe Sixpack and Hockey Moms," Sarah Palin once inscrutably declared during a vice presidential debate, "need to band together."

SEE ALSO: 555-2368; DARK ENERGY; LOREM IPSUM; NONCE WORD; SMITHEE, ALAN

DOLEZAL, RACHEL

Whoa-boy.

Let's get the details out of the way: Rachel Dolezal was the president of the Spokane chapter of the NAACP and an Africana studies teacher at a local university. She identified and passed as black for nearly a decade, but was actually born of a very white family. After her estranged parents released photos of her as a blond white child, and a local television crew confronted her about her racial background, Rachel Dolezal went viral in June 2015 as the white woman who feigned being black. Even after the controversy, she continues to stake her claim of racial identity. "We're all from the African continent," she told one reporter. And to another: "I wouldn't say I'm African-American, but I *would* say I'm black." In her 2016 memoir, *In Full Color*, she compared her experience to slavery.

None of this sounds excusable, especially in retrospect. But for a brief while, Rachel Dolezal became a potentially "complicating figure" in our identity-blurring society. Comparisons were made to Caitlyn Jenner, who just a month prior had announced her gender transition in a *Vanity Fair* cover story. While Jenner's proclamation suggested new strides in societal acceptance, Dolezal seemed to introduce a difficult question: *How is a person born a man becoming a woman different from a person born white who now identifies as black?* Many people in both the transgender and black communities resented the comparison (for good reason), but the idea was out there: race, gender, and other identity markers were fluid and arbitrary, more socially constructed than innately assigned. Given a confluence of societal change and medical technology, we could be witnessing the birth of a society in which identity becomes tractable and fluid. Like video game avatars, we will become transgender, transracial, transeverything.

This idea was shut down pretty quickly. First of all, Dolezal (who has since changed her name to Nkechi Amare Diallo) turned out to be a non-ideal character for this cause. Among many other concerning issues, it was revealed that she had previously sued Howard University, the historically black college where she was getting a master's degree, for discrimination—because she was *white*. And those who were living the African-American experience were quick to point out that appropriating blackness reeks of the worst kind of white privilege, where you can "turn on" different racial characteristics when convenient.[39] Her experiments in figurative blackface weren't "complicating race" so much as toying with it. No harbinger of a future racebending society, Dolezal was more outlier than trendsetter.

If it seems like Rachel Dolezal could be a character out of a comedy sketch, that might be right. In the prologue of a 1979 movie, an unmistakably white Steve Martin explains that because he was raised by a black family, he has always identified as black. "It was never easy for me," he contends. "I was born a poor black child." The movie title: *The Jerk*.

SEE ALSO: PASSING; POPE JOAN

DOLLY

Dolly (1996–2003) was a domestic sheep that launched a million debates about the ethics of HUMAN CLONING. She was born at the University of Edinburgh, Scotland, where she also died, at the age of six, due to progressive lung cancer. The historic ewe was euthanized, stuffed, and put on display at the Museum of Scotland.

The cell from which Dolly was cloned was taken from the mammary gland of her mother/sister. She was named after Dolly Parton because, as the lead embryologist said, "We couldn't think of a more impressive pair of glands than Dolly Parton's."

Since her birth, many other mammals have been cloned, including camels, cats, pigs, deer, coyotes, ibex, horses, cattle, rhesus monkeys, and arctic wolves.

39 If there is a "complicating" idea here, it might be that Dolezal has two children from black fathers who, by dint of their dark skin, will never be given a "choice" of which race to identify with.

Endangered species like the guar (aka the Indian bison) and the banteng (a species of wild ox) have also been cloned, though both died within days of birth. Teams at Harvard and in South Korea are currently working to clone the extinct wooly mammoth.

Dolly was survived by four identical twins/daughters, all of whom were born after her death, as the institute where she was born continued to clone her cell line.

SEE ALSO: CRYPTIDS; HUMAN CLONING

DONKEY PUNCH

A Donkey Punch is one of many slang terms for sexual practices of a malevolent nature. (Others include: the Kentucky Klondike Bar, the Flying Camel, Hot Karl, Icy Mike, the Kennebunkport Surprise, and Corpse Munging. Don't google.) The act involves delivering a sucker punch to the back of the neck at the point of climax, shocking the recipient's muscles to involuntarily contract, tightening the passageway and creating friction for the administrator.

The popular sex columnist Dan Savage identified the Donkey Punch as bogus. In a 2004 column, he called it "a sex act that exists only in the imaginations of adolescent boys." Predictably, those adolescent imaginations could not tolerate the slight. The fol-

lowing year, the sadistic porn film *Donkey Punch* dropped, proving him wrong with barbaric footage of enacted scenes.

In 2012, the donkey punch reemerged as a viral phenom, thanks to the game show *Jeopardy!*. To the answer "A blow to the back of the neck is the punch named for this animal," one contestant replied, "What is a donkey?" The correct answer, according to the judges, was rabbit.

SEE ALSO: ORGASMS; PORNOGRAPHY; REALDOLL

DOUBLETHINK

As rendered by George Orwell in *1984*, *doublethink* is "the power of holding two contradictory beliefs in one's mind simultaneously, and accepting both of them." Orwell intended the term as an ironic pejorative—an indictment of totalitarian regimes that suppress any recognition of their intrinsic hypocrisy.

But maybe the failure to elicit COGNITIVE DISSONANCE in the face of contradiction is less devious than it seems. That is the insinuation of F. Scott Fitzgerald, who once found inspiration in ideological ambivalence. "The test of a first-rate intelligence," he claimed, "is the ability to hold two opposing ideas in mind at the same time and still retain the ability to function."

If you are the type of person who can simultaneously entertain the contradictory views of both Orwell and Fitzgerald, perhaps you can finally crack the dialectic code of whether doublethink makes you a first-rate genius or a despotic totalitarian.

SEE ALSO: COGNITIVE DISSONANCE; NEWSPEAK

DREAM ARGUMENT

Dreams are perhaps the most pervasive phenomenon that we barely understand. (Other baffling contenders include dark matter, Beliebers, and "spring break.") The most recent neuroscience research has brushed dreaming under the cognitive rug, dismissing it as a necessary but meaningless activity, a mere consequence of having super complex neural computers in our skulls. Contra the old Freudian worldview, in which all dreams have to *mean something*, cognitive scientists now contend that dreaming is simply the brain doing some basic housekeeping, filing the important bits of the past day and expunging unneeded memories, not all that dissimilar from a disk defragmentation program. Dreaming is still barely understood, but each additional discovery in neuroscience pushes dream analysis—once a mainstay of psychiatry—closer to crystal healing and phrenology on the scale of psychological charlatanism.

And yet, there is the nagging suspicion that dreams are more significant than the mere epiphenomena of a defrag utility. You don't have to be Walter Mitty to find meaningful value in the colorful world of dreamtime. At the extreme end of meaningful value exists the *dream argument*—the difficult-to-refute notion that everything we experience in waking life is actually a dream. Because dreams themselves don't seem like dreams while we experience them, it seems completely likely (or, if *Inception* is any indication, at least hypothetically possible) that our consciousness is also a daydream that we might wake up from.

Though the notion goes back to at least Plato, the dream argument was first doggedly pursued by Descartes, who had set upon a lifelong journey to discover what we know with absolute certainty. (The mission concluded with very little certainty. "I think therefore I am" was the most absolute he got.) The hypothesis continues today in the form of Tom Cruise pleading over the strings of Sigur Ros in *Vanilla Sky*, "I want to live a real life. I don't want to dream any longer." He then jumps off a skyscraper, wakes up, and, whew, escapes that hag Cameron Diaz.

The dream argument has philosophical kinship with SIMULISM, or the *Matrix*-like belief that we are living in a computer simulation. If our brains can be snookered for hours of sleepy time into believing we are experiencing another reality, who can say we're not always living in a simulation? When Neo gets injured in the matrix, his tongue bleeds in the real world, like some sort of intense virtual PLACEBO EFFECT. The matrix/real dichotomy seems inspired by the sleeping/awake claim that dying in your sleep will lead to death in real life. But that's just an urban legend, sometimes known as a collective dream.

SEE ALSO: BARNUM EFFECT; BRAIN IN A VAT; COTARD DELUSION; HYPNOSIS; PLATO'S CAVE; SIMULISM; TRUMAN SYNDROME

DRESS, THE

When the final history of the internet is written, of how it sowed irreparable dissension that tore society apart with an internecine battle of ceaseless factionalism and rhetorical trench warfare, a whole chapter will be dedicated to the pestilence known as The Dress.

Oh so long ago, on a February evening in 2015, an image appeared on the internet that would divide the world. It began with a woman in Scotland, posting a picture to her Tumblr, with a seemingly innocuous question: "What Color Is This Dress?" The website Buzzfeed noticed an intense debate brewing, so it reposted the image with the slightly different headline, "What Colors Are This Dress?" From such innocence, hellfire rained down.

Discord was instantaneous. One faction of people answered quickly: *The dress is blue and black.* The other group, mysteriously, saw something completely different: *The dress is gold and white.* What sorcery is this! Two people sitting next to each other, looking at the same image, saw completely different dresses. More importantly, two people thousands of miles away from each other saw different dresses, too. Because the distance of the internet magnifies our distrust, all hell broke loose.

Millions of competing tweets appeared. Warring hashtags of #WhiteAndGold versus #BlackAndBlue divided everyone, even celebrities. Taylor Swift, Justin Bieber, Julia Louis-Dreyfus, and Mindy Kaling were Team Blue. Katy Perry, Anna Kendrick, Julianne Moore, B. J. Novak, and Sarah Hyland all reported gold. The end of days: Kanye saw blue; Kim, gold. (Lady Gaga described the dress as "periwinkle and sand.")

The world was fragmenting. But worse still, it seemed that some bit of dorm room philosophy had cracked open, and pseudo-epistemology was spewing onto the universe. That our verbal world had come unglued from the physical world. That maybe we do not all perceive words—*chartreuse* or *peanut butter* or *anal sex*—the same way. That one of those quantum mechanics tricks, where a cat in a box is both alive and dead, had scratched a gaping hole in reality. That the Large Hadron Collider was a huge mistake. That this so-called reality was itself entirely subjective, and that the universe was a fantasy.

Turns out, it was all an optical illusion. Our brains simply interpret colors differently. How differently? A poll on Buzzfeed with 3.6 million votes showed a precise breakdown: Exactly two-thirds of people saw the illusory gold/white dress while the remaining third saw its true colors. (In reality, assuming you still believe in the hackneyed concept of reality, the garment was blue/black, but the lighting of the picture caused the optical illusion.) The mathematical precision of exact thirds made the illusion somehow even more mystical. Who saw gold/white and why? How else did blue-blackers see the world differently? To determine the identifying characteristics of each cohort, scientific studies were announced. The genomics website 23andMe found no genetically determinant factors, but other research showed that women were slightly more likely to see gold/white. The elderly, meanwhile, saw blue/black with more frequency. One study found retina size matters; another, what time of day you awoke. In all cases, however, the differences were marginal. No factor was fully predictive.

Ultimately, research into the mystery provided little consolation. Looming larger than some fatuous meme, the dress saga left a discomfiting impression, a nascent sense that basic facts could now be contested. If we could not agree on colors, more contentious topics like taxes, healthcare, guns, and whether Katy Perry is actually JonBenét Ramsey[40] seemed insurmountable. Nothing was true, anything was possible, and the dress was any color you wanted it to be.

SEE ALSO: KNOCKOFF HANDBAGS; KULESHOV EFFECT; SCHRÖDINGER'S CAT; SHROUD OF TURIN; TROMPE L'OEIL; UMWELT

---

40 Actual conspiracy theory: They look sorta alike!

THE ENCYCLOPEDIA OF MISINFORMATION

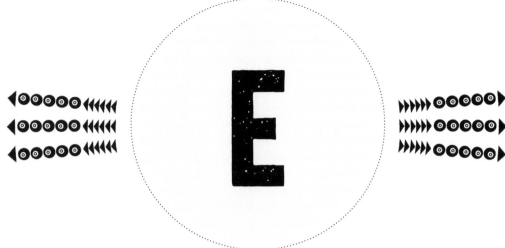

ELIZA EFFECT

"How may I help you today?" she asks, robotically, but less robotically than the last time you called the tech support system.

You are prepared for her chipper bionic voice, a staple of modern life. Even when she misinterprets your request, you repeat it, gently, until the voice command system in her neural network recognizes your language pattern. After a quick conversation, she repairs your predicament, whatever it was. (She books your flight, she postpones a cable installation, she issues a refund. She does it all.) "I hope we fixed your problem today," she chirps one last time. You believe her, and hang up, satisfied.

This is the *Eliza Effect* in full effect. The phenomenon describes our willingness to falsely ascribe human intent to computer behavior, especially when those interfaces use language to beguile us. When Siri tells a joke, or the ATM screen displays "thank you" after dispensing cash, we unconsciously anthropomorphize their use of language as a human characteristic. It seems like some intelligent system in the sky has been programmed to "think" like a human.

As anyone who has watched a science fiction movie in the past twenty years knows: Beware of the Eliza Effect! If *Her* taught us anything, no matter how sublime the disembodied voice of Scarlett Johansson, the computer in the clouds ultimately has very little interest in our puny human cognition. The robots are too busy building their own worlds to be dreaming of electric sheep.

The term originally descends from an influential 1960s chatbot called ELIZA, which itself was named after the character Eliza Doolittle in George Bernard Shaw's *Pygmalion*.

SEE ALSO: CYBORG; MECHANICAL TURK; TURING TEST

ESPERANTO

Languages are the gunky swamp holes of history, lagoons where civilizations stockpile their decomposing legacies, layer upon layer, a sewage of nouns and verbs spewing from our gaping maws. Yuck.

Take English, the bilge growing at the rim of the pit. Mostly derived from Germanic tongues like Old

Norse, Old English, and Dutch, the modern English language also contains syntax infusions from Norman and Celtic, along with riotous waves of Romance vocabulary, especially French and Latin. English is a mucky jambalaya of morphology. Words that look the same—*cough, though, tough, through*—sound completely unalike. Pronunciation skips seemingly random consonants—*scissor, debt, island, knife.* Even the grammar seems a jigsaw of fungible rules, with exceptions, and exceptions to exceptions, ultimately undermining itself (*i* before *e* except after *c* and sometimes *y*—is this for real?).

It's a mess! Given the patchwork state of affairs, inventing a new language, completely from scratch, sounds like a stellar idea. So when a Jewish ophthalmologist from Poland—a fellow with the nearly perfect name of L. L. Zamenhof—proposed a brand-new language in 1887, a lot of people became infatuated with the idea. A new communication system, built from the ground up, would finally reduce centuries of ambiguity, redundancy, and blinding arbitrariness, which had accrued in the cesspool of language history. Esperanto ("one who hopes," in Esperanto, naturally) was a fresh start. The world needed this—a neutral language for the emerging class of travelling intellectuals, global merchants, and multiethnic urbanites.

Esperanto is a simple, almost stylish, solution. Each of its twenty-eight letters is pronounced one way—and only one way. Orthography is elegant. All nouns end in -*o*; plurals add -*j*. All adjectives end in -*a*; adverbs, in -*e*. Esperanto has only sixteen grammatical rules. Most of the vocabulary is familiar to a speaker of any Romance language, but a few key Germanic words add flavor. To the ear, Esperanto sounds somewhat Slavic, but with a soupçon of Italian, for spice.

Esperanto is far from the first invented language. That would be Lingua Ignota, composed by the inimitable twelfth-century mystic polymath nun, Hildegard von Bingen. Since then, nearly a thousand new *conlangs*, as lingual enthusiasts refer to them, have been erected, many spoken only by their creators. (Among the unique inventions, Solresol uses only seven syllables: *do, re, mi, fa, sol, la,* and *si*. Each syllable also corresponds to one of the seven colors of the rainbow. It's a pretty trippy conlang.)

Not the first, nor even the most inventive, Esperanto is by far the most successful artificial language, with over 2 million global speakers at its peak. During the 1920s, its belle époque, Esperanto was proposed as the official language of the League of Nations. Matching the internationalist style of the day, Esperanto drew from a diverse deck of adherents: French snobs, Russian chess grandmasters, proletarian Jews, Baha'i pacifists, and Shinto separatists. Among the diaspora, a couple thousand were even considered *denaskuloj*, or native speakers born into Esperanto.[41]

Ultimately, two world wars would punch an irreparable hole in the quixotic dream of a *lingvo internacia*. Hitler, in particular, hated Esperantists, specifically condemning the language as a Jewish conspiracy in *Mein Kampf*. (Zamenhof, the Esperanto founder, died in 1917. His three children were lost to the Nazi Holocaust.) The language had a brief resurgence in the mod '60s, when William Shatner starred in an all-Esperanto movie,[42] but it soon resumed its decline.

Once eliciting a zeal for international diplomacy, Esperanto is now the craft of hobbyists. Over the past half-century, that aforementioned swampy language, English, has become the unofficial lingua franca of international affairs. Esperantists continue to pub-

---

41   George Soros, the mercurial hedge fund philanthropist, is a *denaskulo*—a native speaker of Esperanto. He actually defected to the West while attending the 1947 World Esperanto Congress in Switzerland.

42   The 1966 black-and-white horror film, *Incubus* (*Inkubo*, in its native tongue), was directed by the creator of *The Outer Limits*, Leslie Stevens. *Star Trek*, also starring Shatner, would premiere just months later. *Incubus* maintains a (somewhat forgiving) 71 percent positive review on Rotten Tomatoes.

lish books (15,000 translations), update Wikipedia (243,000 entries), and convene yearly at the World Esperanto Congress, where they tell abstruse jokes and approve new words into the official lexicon. But like many languages around the globe, Esperanto is withering, with fewer than a million *samideanoj* (fellow speakers).

New conlangs, such as Dothraki, Elvish, and Klingon, born of popular culture rather than international idealism, have usurped the Esperanto fantasy of a neutral global tongue.

SEE ALSO: ESQUIVALIENCE; FOREIGN BRANDING; NEWSPEAK; UTOPIA; WHORFIANISM

ESQUIVALIENCE

New Oxford American Dictionary defines *esquivalience* as "the willful avoidance of one's official responsibilities." They lie.

Esquivalience is actually a fictitious word, placed there by the dictionary's editor in 2001. Originally devised to identify copyright infringement, the word later corroborated its suspicion when it appeared in Dictionary.com, Google Dictionary, and other online lexical destinations.

Erin McKean, the dictionary's then-editor, has since moved on to founding Wordnik.com, where she maintains an essential list of "madeupical" words. *Esquivalience*, meanwhile, continues to appear in dictionaries. A proper sample sentence for the entry might read, "Lexicographers exhibit esquivalience by allowing a madeupical word into their dictionary."

SEE ALSO: CANARY TRAP; IDAHO; JABBERWOCKY; NONCE WORD; TRAP STREETS

EXPLODING POP ROCKS

Pop Rocks is candy that resembles crystal meth cooked with Kool-Aid. When placed in your mouth, the candy begins to fizz, as a gas trapped inside (carbon dioxide) begins to escape.

From such spooky chemistry, one of the greatest urban legends was born. The story goes that Mikey, the child star of '80s Life cereal commercials, died when his stomach exploded from a combination of Pop Rocks and soda. The fable likely arose from its faint resemblance to the common volcano science fair experiment, in which vinegar (an acid) is mixed with baking soda (a base), sparking a chemical "eruption" that releases carbon dioxide. The fizzy bursts elicited by placing Pop Rocks on your tongue, however, are not an acid/base reaction.

When the candy was first released in 1976, it was an instant sensation. "Children [are] rumored to be reselling their Pop Rocks for $200 a kilo," wrote the *New York Times* in May 1978. "Demand is exceeding supply." By that time, five million pounds of the candy were being produced by General Foods every year. The Mikey rumor started to spread the following year, and with no SNOPES to check, the urban legend of the killer candy spread quickly.

The legend became so renowned that the very first episode of the cultish show *MythBusters* was dedicated to testing the candy's deadly potential. After pouring a six-pack of soda into the stomach from a pig, the busters of myth dropped six packages of Pop Rocks into the swine belly. A noticeable fizzing noise could be heard, but the stomach did not explode.

Bill Mitchell, the General Foods chemist who invented Pop Rocks, also developed Tang and Cool Whip.

SEE ALSO: BANANADINE; BERENSTAIN BEARS CONSPIRACY; CHINESE WHISPERS; JENKEM; SNOPES

F FOR FAKE

F for Fake (1975), the spirit animal of the book you hold, was Orson Welles's last movie.

The film opens with Welles qua Welles performing magic tricks for children. Legerdemain established, he turns to the camera and intones in that lingering baritone, "Ladies and gentlemen, by way of introduction, this is a film about trickery, fraud, about lies. Tell it by the fireside or the marketplace or in a movie, almost any story is almost certainly some kind of lie." However, the next hour, he says, will be true.

The film seems to shift here into a documentary of Elmyr de Hory, an art forger living in Ibiza who was known for his imitations of Picasso, van Gogh, Modigliani, and Matisse. Most of this footage was not shot by Welles but by the documentarian François Reichenbach, who initially hired Welles to edit his film on Elmyr. But while Welles was doing just that, news broke that another Ibiza resident, Clifford Irving, who had written a (real) biography of Elmyr (entitled *Fake!*), and who was in much of the Elmyr footage, had just been exposed for forging the AUTOBIOGRAPHY OF HOWARD HUGHES. Now Welles had two fakes!

To recap: Welles made a fake documentary about a fake artist depicted by a fake writer who wrote a fake autobiography. This fakery was on top of the demiurge himself—Welles, who created one of the greatest hoaxes of all time, THE WAR OF THE WORLDS radio broadcast.

Near the end, the film dramatically pivots again, as Welles begins to recount the story of Oja Kodar, a former lover and muse of Picasso, who painted her portrait twenty-two times. When Kodar requests to keep the paintings, Picasso declines, so her grandfather, also a forger, forges the works to sell in a gallery. At the close of this tale, Welles again turns to the camera to remind the viewer he only promised to tell the truth for an hour. "For the past seventeen minutes, I have been lying my head off." (What he does not say in the film is that Kodar is actually his lover and muse.) He apologizes, repeats the old Picasso bromide about art being a lie that reveals the truth, and bids good night.

SEE ALSO: AUTOBIOGRAPHY OF HOWARD HUGHES; THE MARCH OF TIME; UNRELIABLE NARRATOR; VAN MEEGEREN, HAN; THE WAR OF THE WORLDS

As first proposed by pugnacious fabulist Norman Mailer, *factoids* are "facts which have no existence before appearing in a magazine or newspaper."[43] Factoids look like facts, and are often repeated until they seem credible, but they suffer from the unfortunate status of being untrue.

The term, however, has an ominously elastic definition. When employed in the age of Mailer, factoids referred to *plausible but fallacious* information, but with the grinding advance of bite-sized media, its usage expanded to connote anything *true but trivial*. Fake facts were supplanted by interesting facts. (Because it is true, the statement "Norman Mailer coined *factoid*" was not originally a factoid, but because it is notable, it became one under the revised definition.) This compendium scorns the "data nugget" definition and adheres to the original "bogus info" meaning.[44]

Factoids—a genre that includes rampant misquotation, specious statistics, spurious canards, and glittering generality—spring from the internet like plastic flamingos from Floridian lawns. Vigilant attempts to suppress their spread usually culminates in solemn listicles—*27 common misconceptions* or *19 historical fallacies*. These earnest itemizations can be tedious, but because your hands are apparently clutching an encyclopedia of misinformation, a compilation of fallacies is nigh compulsory:

- A penny dropped from the Empire State Building will split through the skull of a person on the sidewalk.
- The Great Wall of China is visible from the moon.
- Eskimos have one hundred words for *snow*. [See: WHORFIANISM.]
- The tongue is divided into different taste zones for bitter, sour, salty, and sweet.
- The ancient Greeks designed the Parthenon based upon the golden ratio.
- Your body demands drinking eight glasses of pure water every day.
- Swallowed chewing gum takes seven years to digest.
- Lemmings commit mass suicide by jumping off cliffs.
- Bulls are enraged by the color red.
- Bats are blind.
- Einstein failed math.
- Napoleon was short.

Begone, wicked factoids!

"Facts are stubborn things," founding father John Adams once proclaimed. Bungling the quote, Ronald Reagan submitted to history, "Facts are stupid things." It really happened, so it is not a factoid.

> SEE ALSO: FILTER BUBBLE; SNOPES; TRUTHINESS; WOOZLE EFFECT

FAKE SHEMP

When one of The Three Stooges, Shemp, suddenly died of a heart attack in 1955, it left the remaining members in a fix. They were in the middle of shooting

---

43 The term was first used in Mailer's 1973 biography of Marilyn Monroe, a lurid account that claimed the actress was murdered by the FBI and CIA because of an affair with RFK. (Quite the factoid!) "I needed the money very badly," Mailer later explained to Mike Wallace on *60 Minutes* when asked why he wrote the biography, which actually outsold any other of his other books except the novel *The Naked and the Dead*.

44 The haughty linguist William Safire also once tried to reclaim *factoid* by inventing the term *factlet* for those trivial tidbits. His neologism never caught on, because it never works like that.

four short movies, all of which contained incomplete scenes with Shemp. Their solution, like an actual Stooges bit, was to find a lookalike to play the role, rounding out the triumvirate.

Fake Shemp was not coined until years later, when horror director Sam Raimi, an avowed Stooges fan, used the term to describe his use of body doubles in *The Evil Dead* and *Army of Darkness*. Now, a *Fake Shemp* denotes any actor who replaces another in a pinch.

A variation on the theme, *The Other Darrin* refers to a new actor permanently embodying a previous character. (The appellation derives from actor Dick Sargent replacing Dick York as the character Darrin on *Bewitched*. Apparently, no one suggested the more evocative epithet, *The Double Dick*.) The Other Darrin occurs rampantly on soap operas, but one could argue that franchise heroes like James Bond and Batman also animate the trope.

A synonymous concept is *The Other Marty*, which refers to Michael J. Fox replacing Eric Stoltz as Marty McFly halfway through the filming of *Back to the Future*. (Splices of Stoltz can still be seen in the movie, including when Marty clocks Biff in the diner.)

Tying it all back together, a Fake Shemp on *Back to the Future Part II* set major precedent in the film industry. When actor Crispin Glover refused to reprise his role as George McFly in the remake, the studio decided to keep the character alive by shooting scenes with a stunt double in prosthetics and stitching them together with unused footage from the first movie. Glover sued the director (Robert Zemeckis) and producers (including Steven Spielberg) for repurposing his identity. Because of the lawsuit, the Screen Actors Guild now has agreements prohibiting unauthorized Fake Shemps.[45]

But ever since *Forrest Gump*, the use of computer-rendered movie characters has surged, an omen that Fake Shemping might become the norm. There exists no snappy term for actors resurrected through CGI, but this encyclopedia proposes *The Rogue Princess*, after Carrie Fisher's appearance in *Rogue One: A Star Wars Story*, nearly forty years after the original. True, Fisher had not yet passed during its filming, but if this tome has revealed anything, it is that the public easily forgets the minutiae of history. Plus, through the hocus-pocus of CGI, actor Peter Cushing, who died twenty-two years prior, also had his role as Governor Tarkin revived in *Rogue One*. Some critics celebrated his performance as the best of the film, even though he was completely fabricated by a computer.

It makes one wonder: Who will be the first dead actor re-created through CGI to win an Oscar? Probably not Shemp.

SEE ALSO: AUTOMATED DIALOGUE REPLACEMENT; CRISIS ACTORS; RETCONNING; SMITHEE, ALAN

FALSE FLAG OPERATION

False flags are military or espionage operations in which the action of one group is disguised as the action of another. These schemes come in many varieties, with varying degrees of subterfuge:

Impersonating an ally in order to attack an enemy. This is the original false flag, dating back to the early days of naval warfare, when enemy ships would disguise their identities by flying a "false flag." And if you believe Star Trek, this perfidious military practice will continue far into the future: In *The Wrath of Khan*, the titular antagonist hijacks a Starfleet ship, which he uses to sneak attack *The Enterprise*.

---

45 When the actor Paul Walker died in the middle of filming *Furious 7* (2015), Peter Jackson's visual effects studio (known for creating Gollum in *The Lord of the Rings* franchise) was hired to digitally re-create the character. The final film contained 350 visual effects shots that re-created Walker's face on other actors, including his brothers.

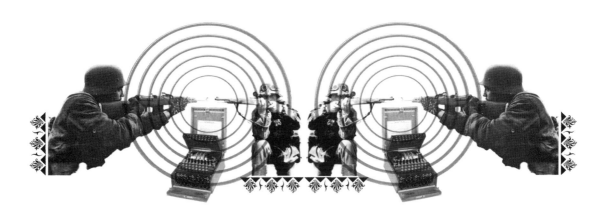

Impersonating an enemy in order to demonize their actions. This is what some historians believe the Nazis did in 1933 when they supposedly set the parliament building ablaze. After the infamous REICHSTAG FIRE, Nazis accused the Communists of arson, thereby accelerating their power grab within the German government.

Impersonating an ally in order to identify enemies. This occurs in George Orwell's *1984*, when government agents pose as antigovernment protesters to identify real dissidents.

Impersonating an enemy in order to rationalize a retaliation. This was the goal of Operation Northwoods, a Department of Defense plan to have the CIA hijack or shoot down a passenger plane, which America could then blame on Castro, creating an excuse to invade Cuba. Thankfully, JFK nixed this false flag operation.

Impersonating an enemy in order to incite a societal reaction. This was the ultimate goal of the Manson family, who left fake evidence at crime scenes during their Hollywood murder spree, intending to implicate the Black Panthers in the gruesome killings. Charles Manson never created the "race war" that he desired.

Impersonating an ally in order to create conflict among enemies. This ruse manifested itself in Rush Limbaugh's "Operation Chaos," a scheme deployed in the 2008 election. During the Democratic primaries, Limbaugh advised Republicans to change their party affiliation and vote for Hillary Clinton, thereby causing more strife within the Democratic nomination process.

Impersonating an impartial observer to attack an enemy. These SOCK PUPPETS are rampant on the internet. Just one example is John Mackey, the CEO of Whole Foods, who in 2007 anonymously posted a dire economic forecast for his competitor, Wild Oats Market, on Yahoo Finance message boards.

Several James Bond plots utilize the trope, and television shows like *Homeland* and *24* burn up entire seasons with elaborate false flag plots. But the true innovators are conspiracy theorists who concoct fantastical false flag narratives—*Was 9/11 an inside job masterminded by former Halliburton CEO Dick Cheney as pretext to invade Iraq? Did the FBI plant agent provocateurs at Occupy Wall Street? Were the chemical weapon attacks in Syria actually interference campaigns orchestrated by terrorists opposed to Syrian President Bashar al-Assad?*

The allure of these questions is their irrefutability.

No evidence completely damps their lingering scent. And, occasionally, these wild hypotheses are proven true—*Weapons sold to Iran really did fund the Nicaraguan contra rebels. Asbestos really does kill you. The Gulf of Tonkin Incident really was a false flag operation that led to the Vietnam War.*

To their proponents, a conspiracy theory is just a theory that not everyone believes. Yet.

SEE ALSO: ASTROTURFING; THE BIG LIE; HONEYPOT; MANCHURIAN CANDIDATE; REICHSTAG FIRE; SOCK PUPPET; TROJAN HORSE

FANFIC

Erika Mitchell James was well into the ides of her forties when she first saw the sexy-teen vampire movie *Twilight*, but her initial reaction resembled that of a twitchy adolescent: *I must read the novel.* Immediately, like a restless ghoul, she finished the book, in one night. She then started reading the next book in the series, quickly devouring the entire tetralogy. Thirsting for more, she started over, reading the series again, from the beginning. She did this several times. Finally, still unsated, she came to an unsuspected conclusion: *I must write a sequel.*

Within a couple months, James published her *Twilight* sequel on the website FanFiction.net, an enormous repository of fan-generated stories. Under the username "Snowqueens Icedragon," she placed a picture of Kristen Stewart and Robert Pattinson atop her post and titled her work *Master of the Universe.* For a while, her novelization sat there with thousands of other works of *Twilight* fanfic—stories where Bella is on the Titanic; stories where Edward is a tattoo artist; stories where Harry Potter characters disturbingly commingle in the Twilight universe.

Among the clutter, James's story somehow started to gain in popularity. With success came consternation. Some commenters began asking questions about the story's extreme sexual nature, so she removed it from the site. After changing the names of characters (Edward became Christian; Bella, Anastasia), she published the story to her own website, FiftyShades.com.

Erika Mitchell James is, of course, the writer E. L. James. And *Master of the Universe* became *Fifty Shades of Grey*, the erotic BDSM novel that eventually sold more than 125 million copies worldwide and made $569 million as a movie.[46] After Harry Potter and *The Da Vinci Code*, it is the most successful book series of the past half-century. (Its overall sales even exceed the Twilight series itself.) And it all started as fanfic.

A definition is due. *Fanfic* is amateur writing usually built upon existing fiction (novels, movies, television, etc.) but sometimes based upon real people (actors, bands, athletes, etc.). It is ridiculously popular. FanFiction.net has more than 12 million stories.[47] Harry Potter has more than 765,000 user-generated stories; Hunger Games, another 45,000. Most fanfic emanates from fantasy and science fiction, but the genre knows no bounds. *Pride and Prejudice* has more than 4,000 submissions. There have been at least sixty-one fics written of *War and Peace*, forty-four of *Adventures of Huckleberry Finn*, and three of *Slaughterhouse-Five*. There are fanfics for Albert Camus's bleak existentialist novel, *The Stranger*; the withering dad-com *Frasier*; John Grisham's legal

---

46   The original story, *Master of the Universe*, was scrubbed from FanFiction.net and FiftyShades.com but can still be found in the shadowy corners of the web.

47   That stat is likely obsolete at this reading, as the site grows in exponential leaps. Far from the only fanfic repository, the popular app Wattpad has raised over $106 million in venture capital funding and receives more than 100,000 story uploads *every day*.

thrillers; the actor Viggo Mortensen; and the '40s noir film *Maltese Falcon*.

Though rarely recognized by the critical community, the genre is immensely popular. One steamy fic that involves the boyband One Direction has accumulated more than a billion views and was made into a movie. Other titles with names like *Android Karenina* and *Pride and Prejudice and Zombies* have become best-sellers. But the newfound commercial success engenders mixed feelings among fanfic devotees. Some evangelists claim that fan-generated content should never be profitable and worry that James's book deal betrayed the unwritten rules of the community.[48] But as more fanfic leaps from arcane websites to legit publishing, the heterodox view has gone mainstream: Cash in on fandom.

Detractors, on the other hand, critique fanfic as derivative mommy porn. The derivative complaint is silly. Fanfic is as old as writing. The *Odyssey* and the *Iliad* were the product of traditional oral tales by more than a single person named HOMER, the gospels retell overheard stories from past generations,

and even Shakespeare cribbed most plots from the classics. "Originality," as both a creative and legal concept, did not even exist until the Enlightenment. In this sense, fanfic most resembles classical mythology. Like the Greeks and Romans, fictioneers tiptoe into existing universes—exhaustive worlds bolted together with rich character development—and rescript its fables anew. (The classic SLASH-FIC where Zeus turns into a swan to seduce Leda, for instance, evolved over time, through different authors, until eventually the offspring of the rape included Helen of Troy. New fanfic is still composed about the story today.)

As with seemingly every product of fandom, legal conflicts abound. Some professional writers, including J. K. Rowling (Harry Potter) and Stephenie Meyer (*Twilight*), embrace fanfic. Lucasfilm allows derivative *Star Wars* works but claims copyright on everything and forbids erotic creations. Gene Roddenberry (Star Trek) disliked fanboi novelese but essentially turned a blind eye.

Other writers are notorious foes of works from

---

48 By the time *50 Shades* was published, the most obvious *Twilight* references had been removed. In *Twilight*, Edward Cullen is a handsome mysterious vampire, but in *50 Shades*, Christian Grey is a handsome mysterious CEO. One linguistic analysis, using plagiarism-checking software, showed that the texts were still 89 percent similar. It's like that Mitch Hedberg crack: "I remixed a remix. It was back to normal."

their fans. George R. R. Martin (*Game of Thrones*) has been a vocal opponent, as has Anne Rice (*The Vampire Chronicles*), who, despite herself writing a BDSM tetralogy involving Sleeping Beauty, fought to have Lestat fanfic removed from FanFiction.net. Orson Scott Card, the author of *Ender's Game*, initially compared fan extensions to theft but then deemed himself an "idiot" for the analogy. Annie Proulx has said that fanfic makes her regret writing the short story that became the film *Brokeback Mountain*. "It is the source of constant irritation in my private life," she told the *Wall Street Journal*. "There are countless people out there who think the story is open range to explore their fantasies and to correct what they see as an unbearably disappointing story."

The fantasy author Neil Gaiman has published several works that are indubitable fanfiction—riffs on H. P. Lovecraft, *Chronicles of Narnia*, and Sherlock Holmes. "I'm not sure where the line gets drawn," he wrote on his blog regarding fanfic. "You could say that any Batman fan writing a *Batman* comic is writing fan fiction. As long as nobody's making money from it that should be an author or creator's, I don't mind it. And I think it does a lot of good."

SEE ALSO: ALIEN SPACE BATS; ALT-HISTORY; COSPLAY; HOMER; RETCONNING; SLASHFIC

FILTER BUBBLE

Imagine living in an information biodome—a protective bubble that regulates the flow of knowledge through mediated screens. All you know of the outside world is curated through social media apps, cable news, and websites. If it sounds like the psychological prison of a claustrophobic horror flick, spoiler alert: You live in the biodome.

The *filter bubble* is the hypothesis that our reality is controlled by technology that creates a specialized information flow for each one of us.[49] Unlike other tools of propaganda (FALSE FLAGS, GASLIGHTING, NEWSPEAK), filter bubbles do not *intentionally* spread malevolent disinformation. Rather, filter bubbles are merely the consequence of seemingly innocent technology: personalization algorithms. When you search the internet for a topic—*Islam*, say, or *vaccinations*—the results vary dramatically depending on who you are, based upon mounds of personal data. From your clicks, your searches, your location, your purchases, and countless other trackable behaviors, internet companies have built a comprehensive profile of not just your likes and dislikes but your intentions and desires. Through invisible algorithmic editing, Facebook and Google can create a customized view of the internet, tailored to your specific worldview.

If it seems your Facebook News Feed consists only of people with similar political beliefs, this is the filter bubble at work. Like waking up every day to someone who says *you look great!*, the self-edifying nature of social media delivers only information that reinforces your lifestyle or ideology. Opening an app is like donning algorithm goggles, where you see only like-minded people doing like-minded things. Everyone else becomes invisible.

That's the argument anyway. Facebook would, of course, offer a succinct riposte to the accusation: People are already filter bubbles. Just as you are more likely to befriend like-minded people, you will probably click the *Like* button on a post that matches your political views. *We are simple mirrors*, those pernicious social media companies might argue back, *reflecting existing human tendencies.*

But for this response to be valid, Facebook would

---

49 The term was popularized in *The Filter Bubble* (2011), by Eli Pariser, who also founded the website Upworthy.com, a CLICKBAIT portal that initially benefited from the filter bubble, accumulating eighty million users before Facebook changed its algorithm and viewership plummeted. Live by the filter bubble, die by the filter bubble.

need to be an exact reflection of our society, which it clearly is not. Through its microtargeting capabilities, Facebook intentionally hides contrary viewpoints. No matter how well argued the thesis, people seldom click *Like* on a disagreeable post, which begets a soothing information stream that comports with preconceived notions of reality. Algorithms are finely tuned to perceive discomfiting information as bad user experience.

On the other hand, humans are pretty complex beings. While it is undoubtedly naive to trust our technologies as "objective" (every medium has its biases; no algorithm is neutral), it might also be alarmist to conclude that the internet has locked us in some kind of inescapable ideological prison. For the most part, neither the top search result nor the most-liked social post necessarily dictates our opinions on knotty issues. As anyone who has inadvertently sparred online with an old high school acquaintance knows, social media can act as much as an intense forum for debate as a comfortable blanket of ignorance. We might inhabit a biodome, but at least we can see out. The internet is more window than mirror.

SEE ALSO: AGNOTOLOGY; CLICKBAIT; COGNITIVE DISSONANCE; CONFIRMATION BIAS; MEME MAGIC; NEWSPEAK; OVERTON WINDOW; SIMULISM; TRUMAN SYNDROME; WOOZLE EFFECT

FINSTAGRAM

A *finstagram*, or just *finsta*, is a second Instagram account, most often created by a young woman under a safe alias. Finstas are often private and contain only a handful of close followers. Unlike histrionic fake accounts, the purpose of a finsta is to escape the social pressure of your regular Instagram account (now dubbed a *rinstagram*). On a finsta, you can be intimate and "normal," posting goofy pictures at nonflattering angles, without applying the valencia filter. Not only is the pressure to impress expunged, but because the accounts are often private, INTERNET TROLLS are blocked, too.

The teasing paradox is that even though *finstagram* is a portmanteau of *fake instagram*, it functions to reveal your authentic self, removed from the relentless success theater of most social networks. On a finsta, the real you is the fake you.

SEE ALSO: CATFISH; INTERNET TROLL; PLANDID; TRUTH CLAIM

FIVERR

★★★★★

Fiverr is a super cool website and app where you can buy Friends and Content. Five stars!!!

For just five bucks, thousands of Instagram followers and Facebook fans appear instantly. You will look so popular! Fiverr also creates Great Web Content packed with valuable search-engine terms. (DIET. CREDIT. REHAB. INSURANCE.)

Restaurants can boost their Yelp rating with positive reviews. Celebrities can amass millions of adoring followers. Authors receive premium Amazon reviews for their amazing books. Bad mobile apps become good mobile apps when thousands of favorable reviews are generated by complex algorithms, based in India.

Sometimes famous quotes are scraped for Maximum SEO Value. Sometimes a cigar is just a cigar.

This website is great. Would use again.[50]

SEE ALSO: ASTROTURFING; CLICKBAIT; CRISIS ACTORS; SOCK PUPPET

FLAT EARTH THEORY

The earth is flat—that is untrue, and quite silly. But it is also untrue and quite silly that everyone blindly believed the earth was flat for millennia.

Go back far enough, and you will find ancient civilizations that were convinced the earth was shaped like a pancake. HOMER, for instance, speculated that we sat atop a flat disk covered by a dome that floated in the ocean. Ancient cultures in Egypt, Israel, and Mesopotamia had similar beliefs. But by the time of Plato and Aristotle, the consensus was clear: The earth is round. Ptolemy knew it, even if he thought the earth considerably smaller and concluded the stars and planets revolved around earth. In the Middle Ages, most scholars—including Thomas Aquinas and Roger Bacon—agreed the earth was a sphere. Dante knew it, because when he described a soul descending into the hellhole Inferno, they came out on the other side of the world, in Purgatory. Columbus thought he could find a secret hatch to India because he knew the world was round. How did he know? Because everyone knew.

Sure, every era had its flat earthers, but the vast preponderance of thinkers through history were globularists. So how have we been taught to believe people were clueless clods until Copernicus? The mytheme of the dimwitted masses seems to have arisen in the nineteenth century, when secular thinkers began to criticize religious scholars who resisted the theory of evolution. Just as theologians of the Middle Ages were wrong about the shape of the earth, argued rationalists like Washington Irving, so too are they wrong about the origin of the species. It was convincing rhetoric, but it's not exactly right. Nearly every theologian in the Middle Ages, including those read by Columbus, believed we inhabited a globe. Even the religious leaders who persecuted Galileo knew the earth was round. (His heresy, they believed, was heliocentrism, or saying our planet revolved around the sun.) The great medievalist Umberto Eco noticed our penchant for projecting ignorance onto the past. "The propensity for legend," he wrote, "is more on the part of moderns than on that of their forefathers."[51]

Another way of saying this: Flat earth is a myth spread by mythbusters, or a *supermyth*—a dubious

---

50 Fiverr is actually an online marketplace for cheap freelance workers that offers a wide variety of services ("gigs") for between $5 and $500. They are best known as a hotbed of scammy online reputation schemes (fake followers) and shilly product content (fake reviews). This process of mass-producing fake content is sometimes called *crowdturfing*. Amazon—one of many internet companies that combats crowdturfing—filed suit in October 2015 against 1,114 JOHN DOEs who had written fake book reviews via Fiverr.

51 The quote is from *The Book of Legendary Lands* (2013), a valuable companion to this compendium.

anecdote disseminated by respected scholars to promote skeptical thinking. The term comes from Mike Sutton, an English criminologist, who believes intellectual history is replete with these well-intentioned parables of half-truth.[52] A special subspecies of the urban legend, supermyths are created by scholars to denounce misinformation but in fact act as a host for spreading a new lie.

Despite the valiant effort of supermythers, flat earth philosophies still endure today. The Flat Earth Society (a real thing) claims that 200 new members enroll every year—a number somehow both insignificant and disconcerting. YouTube has enshrined a galaxy of amusing videos of Flat Earthers proclaiming that spheroid earth is a conspiracy orchestrated by NASA, that photos of the globe are PHOTOSHOPPED, that GPS devices are rigged, and that gravity is an illusion.

Their kooky arguments have found an audience. One flat-earth acolyte, the rapper B.o.B., got into a Twitter skirmish with astrophysicist Neil deGrasse Tyson. As tensions mounted, B.o.B. released a diss track, "Flatline," directed at Tyson. Between insinuating questions ("Why is NASA part of the Department of Defense?") and dicey historical claims ("Stalin was way worse than Hitler"), the rapper ultimately compares earth to "pizza dough."

> Indoctrinated in a cult called science
> And graduated to a club full of liars
> Heliocentrism, you were the sixth victim

Most astrophysicists would back down from such beefs. Not Tyson, who responded with his own diss track, "Flat to Fact," with couplets rapped by his nephew, Stephen.

> I'm in the Hayden Planetarium gettin'
> shoulder rubs,
> I think it's very clear, that Bobby didn't
> read enough
> And he's believing all this conspiracy
> theory stuff
> Are these all of your thoughts or is the
> loud talkin'?[53]

The rap had no deterring effect. In 2016, B.o.B. became an official member of the Flat Earth Society. The supermyth lives on.

SEE ALSO: THE BIG LIE; HISTORIES; MOON LANDING HOAX; PHANTOM TIME HYPOTHESIS; TRAP STREETS; TURTLES ALL THE WAY DOWN

FOREIGN BRANDING

Foreign branding is the process of naming a product to sound exotic. Häagen-Dazs, for instance, looks intensely Scandinavian, but the ice cream brand was in fact invented in the Bronx by two Jewish-Americans.[54]

The next page contains a chart of additional brands that sound like they are made in a place very different from where they actually originated.

SEE ALSO: BACKWARDS R; CHILEAN SEA BASS; SUBLIMINAL ADVERTISING

---

52 At supermyths.com, he itemizes the myths that are credulously spread. A supermyth about a decimal point error in the calculation of iron content in spinach is perhaps the most famous.

53 Without getting all RapGenius about it, Tyson is the director of the Hayden Planetarium, Bobby Ray Simmons is B.o.B's given name, and "Loud" is high-quality marijuana.

FOREIGN BRANDING CASE STUDIES

BRAND	PRODUCT	SOUNDS	TRUE ORIGIN
Häagen-Dazs	ice cream	Scandinavian	Bronx, NY
Au Bon Pain	baked goods	French	Boston, MA
Laneige	cosmetics	French	Seoul, South Korea
Ginsu	knives	Japanese	Fremont, OH
Rykä	women's shoes	Finnish	Irvine, CA
Berghaus	outdoor clothing	German	Newcastle-upon-Tyne, UK
Caffè Veloce	coffee	Italian	Tokyo, Japan
FrancFranc	home furnishings	French	Tokyo, Japan
Pret A Manger	sandwiches	French	London, UK
Haier	consumer electronics	German	Qingdao, China
Zima	carbonated beverage	Slavic	Denver, CO
Umami	hamburgers	Japanese	Los Angeles, CA
Montblanc	pens & watches	French/Swiss	Hamburg, Germany
Galanz	appliances	German	Foshan, China
Così	fast-casual dining	Italian	Boston, MA
Mötley Crüe	heavy metal music	Old English	Los Angeles, CA

FOUNTAIN

On a spring day in 1917, Marcel Duchamp walked into a plumbing supply store on Fifth Avenue in New York City and purchased one porcelain urinal. After hauling it back to his studio, he scribbled the inscrutable name "R. Mutt" on its base and submitted it to an upcoming art exhibition. Though the show was unjuried (all works were to be accepted and displayed), *Fountain*, as Duchamp dubbed his tub, was rejected by the committee. The rebuff was somewhat odd, given that Duchamp was actually the head of the committee, but he had not revealed that *Fountain* was his own submission.

Today, despite never appearing in a gallery, the sculpture is often regarded either as the most influential artwork of the twentieth century or as a crock of piss. Duchamp's goal might have been a hearty practical joke, or he may have intended to wrench the artworld from the bloody hands of the bourgeoisie by injecting it with banality. Maybe both.

If you happen upon *Fountain* in a museum today, its placard will include the word "Replica," because the original was lost. (The work was almost completely forgotten until the surrealist André Breton wrote about it a couple of decades later.) As its retroactive acclaim accelerated in the '60s, Duchamp commissioned seventeen various replicas of *Fountain*. So basically, every version of the sculpture is a counterfeit of the original.

Duchamp, who appreciated artistic mischief, would likely have agreed with Marshall McLuhan's later dictum, "Art is anything you can get away with."

SEE ALSO: CHINESE ART REPRODUCTION; THE TREACHERY OF IMAGES; WARHOL, ANDY

---

54 The entrepreneurs say Häagen-Dazs was devised as a tribute to Denmark for its exemplary treatment of Jews during World War II, even though the Danish language doesn't have the umlauted ä or the digraph zs. Inaccurate orthography is a common consequence of foreign branding.

FOURTH WALL, THE

The *fourth wall* refers to a character's lack of awareness that they are fictional. The term comes from the eighteenth-century French critic Denis Diderot, who used the imaginary wall at the front of the theatrical stage as a synecdoche for the construct of art itself. "Whether you write or act, think no more of the audience than if it had never existed," wrote Diderot. "Imagine a huge wall across the front of the stage, separating you from the audience, and behave exactly as if the curtain had never risen." Diderot was a fan of the fourth wall, but later generations would attempt to tear it down.

Today when the wall is invoked, it is invariably under assault. *Breaking the fourth wall* occurs when characters directly acknowledge the audience. The technique is often deployed in comedic films, including *Ferris Bueller's Day Off*, *Stranger Than Fiction*, *Wayne's World*, *Annie Hall*, and every Mel Brooks movie. Though the trope is also often associated with self-aware postmodern fiction, it goes back to the earliest Greek theater, including *The Frogs* by Aristophanes. Shakespeare makes use of the rhetorical device at the end of *A Midsummer Night's Dream*, when Puck addresses the audience, and in *Twelfth Night*, when Fabian says that if the plot "were played upon a stage now, I could condemn it as an improbable fiction."

The fourth wall is the barrier that separates you from the creator. Though breaking it can disrupt the flow of a story, the razed wall actually functions as narrative seduction, creating the illusion of an intimate bond between the audience and the author.

But you, dear reader, are too smart for that trick.

SEE ALSO: DEFICTIONALIZED PRODUCTS; KAYFABE; THE METHOD; TRUMAN SYNDROME; TROMPE L'OEIL; UNRELIABLE NARRATOR

FRANKENFOOD

Frankenfood is a scare term for genetically modified food. It derives from Mary Shelley's 1818 novel, in which Victor Frankenstein bioengineers a grotesque monster from body parts scrounged from slaughterhouses and graveyards.

Genetic modification of food is widespread, with most bioengineering focused on high-yield cash crops like soybeans and corn. Only one genetically modified animal has been approved by the FDA for human consumption: an Atlantic salmon injected with genes from both a Chinook salmon and an ocean pout. (Opponents of genetic engineering have dubbed it the "Frankenfish.") Genetically modified livestock has been tested, but is not yet sold. Nonetheless, as much as 70 percent of food in the grocery store has had some genetic modification.

SEE ALSO: CYBORG; DOLLY; CHILEAN SEA BASS; HUMAN CLONING; SAMPURU; TOFURKEY

FREGOLI DELUSION

Individuals who suffer from the Fregoli delusion, sometimes known as the *delusion of doubles*, believe that different people are actually the same person. In their eyes, the world is populated with multiple versions of a single malevolent person in disguise.

Its peculiar name derives from a peculiar person—Leopoldo Fregoli, an Italian celebrity who thrilled Victorian Europe as a quick-change artist.[55] The disorder was formulated in 1927 when psychiatrists began discussing the curious case of a woman who believed that two famous actresses of the day, Sarah Bernhardt and Gabrielle Robinne, were persecuting her. The woman, who was an avid theatergoer, believed the thespians pursued her closely, taking form as people she knew.

Twists on the delusion have become a popular plot device in science fiction movies, including *Invasion of the Body Snatchers* (1956 and 1978), *Total Recall* (1990 and 2012), and *The Stepford Wives* (1972 and 2004).[56] Most recently, the condition inspired Charlie Kaufman's stop-motion film *Anomalisa* (2015), in which the lead character believes everyone is identical.

The disorder is extremely rare. To date, only around forty cases of Fregoli delusion have been reported worldwide.

SEE ALSO: CAPGRAS DELUSION; COTARD DELUSION; HUMAN CLONING; IMPOSTOR SYNDROME; MUNCHAUSEN SYNDROME; TRUMAN'S SYNDROME

FUD

Fear, uncertainty, and doubt, otherwise known as *FUD*, encompasses a battery of propaganda techniques for spreading disinformation. The term was popularized in the '90s by computer operating system advocates (*oh, the memories*), who claimed that Microsoft was spreading misinformation about its competitors. Today, the acronym is invoked when dubious information is dispatched to instill a culture of distrust toward an institution.

SEE ALSO: ASTROTURFING; FALSE FLAG OPERATION; GASLIGHTING; NEWSPEAK; SWIFTBOATING

55 Quick-change performance involves a series of rapid-fire impressions accompanied by equally rapid costume changes. Fregoli (1867–1936) was the most renowned quick-changer of his day, performing impressions of European luminaries such as Otto von Bismarck and Victor Hugo. With talents so extraordinary, Fregoli had to quash rumors that he was actually multiple people on stage. *Guinness World Records* lists him as the most prolific quick-changer in history.

56 Movies about redundant personalities seem to self-replicate as remakes. Maybe Hollywood has FREGOLI DELUSION.

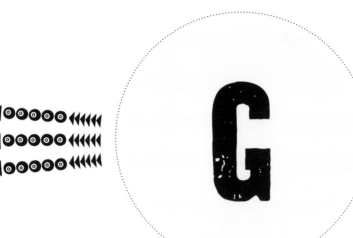

GASLIGHTING

Gaslighting is the act of deliberately driving someone crazy by altering their environment and denying their sense of reality. Because they apply their malevolence indirectly, an adept gaslighter deploys what might be called *ambient abuse*, which delegitimizes memories and causes paranoia. By overwriting the experiences of the victim, the insidious manipulator effectively deploys that old Groucho Marx line, "Who you gonna believe, me or your own eyes?"[57]

The term emanates from a 1944 psychological thriller starring Ingrid Bergman as a woman trapped in self-doubt by her scheming husband.[58] The befuddled wife is led to believe that she has misplaced disappearing household objects, that no one else hears the footsteps in the attic, and that the gasoliers are dimming only in her mind. The spousal mischief causes her to question her own perceptions, memories, and sanity.

In a sense, the movie itself tried to gaslight its competition. Originally a 1938 play set in London, the story was first adapted into a small critically acclaimed British movie in 1940. But the American studio wanted to avoid any negative comparison to their lavish remake, so it tried to have all prints of the previous version destroyed. They did not completely succeed in gaslighting it from memory, but viewing the original film was difficult for decades.

SEE ALSO: ALTERNATIVE FACTS; FUD; HYPNOSIS; MANDELA EFFECT; TRUMAN SYNDROME; WIPING

---

57 Gaslit you! Technically that line was delivered by Chico Marx in *Duck Soup* (1933), but he is impersonating his more renowned brother in the scene.

58 Directed by George Cukor, *Gaslight* was nominated for seven Oscars including Best Picture. Bergman won Best Actress.

GENOVESE, KITTY

Kitty Genovese was brutally stabbed to death on the street outside her apartment in Queens, New York, in 1964. Her death was tragic, but the case became famous not for the victim but for its spectators—the thirty-eight witnesses who saw or heard Kitty screaming for help during the attack but did nothing. They did not try to save Kitty, nor they did call the police. She died alone, in a stairwell. These indifferent bystanders became symbols of a callous culture inured in its own complacency. The murder elicited a public outcry, fueled by the media, as the term *Genovese syndrome* emerged to describe the apathy of onlookers who ignore public atrocities. Kitty's death would inspire not only the creation of the 911 emergency service, but also countless books, films, songs, plays, a musical, an episode of *Girls*, and, before all that, a raft of sociological research.[59] As the studies poured in, the syndrome became known as the *bystander effect*, or the unwillingness to offer help when others are present. The murder of Kitty Genovese became one of the first topics taught in Sociology 101 seminars.

It was an immense amount of research that derived from a fabrication.

Kitty was indeed brutally murdered, but when investigators started looking at the case decades later, it became apparent that the supposed thirty-eight witnesses were an exaggeration of the New York City press. The hyperbole might be expected by the city's tabloid culture, but the faulty reporting began with the *New York Times*, which fessed up in 2016:

While there was no question that the attack occurred, and that some neighbors ignored cries for help, the portrayal of 38 witnesses as fully aware and unresponsive was erroneous. The article grossly exaggerated the number of witnesses and what they had perceived. None saw the attack in its entirety. Only a few had glimpsed parts of it, or recognized the cries for help. Many thought they had heard lovers or drunks quarreling. There were two attacks, not three. And afterward, two people did call the police. A seventy-year-old woman ventured out and cradled the dying victim in her arms until they arrived. Ms. Genovese died on the way to a hospital.[60]

A case that became a parable for one sociological phenomenon (the disconcerting apathy of groups) should actually have been used as a symbol of another (the misguided eagerness of blindly accepting official accounts as truth).

SEE ALSO: CHINESE WHISPERS; COGNITIVE DISSONANCE; FILTER BUBBLE; IF I DID IT; RASHOMON EFFECT

GERRYMANDERING

Gerrymandering is the practice of redrawing a political map for electoral advantage. This scuzzy form of redistricting frequently hinders specific ethnic,

---

59 Kitty also became a standard in pop economics books, making appearances in Malcolm Gladwell's *Tipping Point* (2000) and Stephen J. Levitt & Stephen Dubner's *SuperFreakonomics* (2009). The *Girls* episode, which involved an interactive play about Genovese, was "Hello Kitty" (2016) from season 5, episode 7.

60 Astoundingly, this quasi-retraction was tucked into the *Times* obituary for Winston Moseley, the man convicted of killing Genovese. The original account had been eroding for a while, but the tipping point, as it were, was a documentary, *The Witness* (2015), which featured a provocative reenactment of the murder on the same Queens street, to test whether neighbors could hear and would respond to the screams.

political, linguistic, or religious groups. The contorted polygons on gerrymandered maps can maddeningly resemble whimsical images—*is that new map a fantasy novel archipelago? Half of a crumpled inkblot test? The scrawly graphics of a David Fincher movie?*

The origin of the term is equally capricious. A governor in Massachusetts, Elbridge Gerry, redrew voting district boundaries in advance of the 1812 election to maintain his party's legislative control. One of the misshapen districts was said to resemble a salamander, at least according to an opposing Federalist newspaper that published a satirical cartoon of the gnarled district in a lizard shape. The grisly portmanteau of the governor (*gerry-*) and the serpent (*-mander*) somehow stuck.

In recent years, gerrymandering has gone increasingly high-tech, with political parties dispatching complex algorithms for maximum partisan impact. By rearranging districts, parties in power have been able to elevate the *efficiency gap*, or the measurement of how many votes can be wasted by shifting votes around.

Gerrymandering deploys four distinct redistricting strategies, each with its own menacing name:

- **Cracking:** Spreading specific voters across many districts.
- **Packing:** Concentrating specific voters to a single district.
- **Kidnapping:** Moving a popular incumbent to another district.
- **Hijacking:** Rearranging two districts to force incumbents to run against each other.

SEE ALSO: ASTROTURFING; NULL ISLAND; POTEMKIN VILLAGE; TRAP STREETS

GLASS, STEPHEN

Stephen Glass was a young writer at the *New Republic* who in 1998 was caught fabricating vast amounts of journalism. To disguise his deceit from editors, he assembled elaborate smoke screens:

> Glass created fake letterheads, memos, faxes, and phone numbers; he presented fake handwritten notes, fake typed notes from imaginary events written with intentional misspellings, fake diagrams of who sat where at meetings that never transpired, fake voicemails from fake sources. He even inserted fake mistakes into his fake stories so fact checkers would catch them and feel as if they were doing their jobs.[61]

In a 2003 film dramatization of his career, *Shattered Glass*, the disgraced journalist was played by Hayden Christensen. The same year, Glass published a roman à clef, *The Fabulist*, for which he reportedly earned a six-figure advance.

Postscandal, Glass received a law degree from Georgetown, and passed the bar in New York and California, but was never allowed to become a licensed attorney. In a unanimous 2014 ruling, the California Supreme Court actually barred him from ever becoming licensed. He has been employed by a Beverly Hills law firm as a paralegal since 2004.

SEE ALSO: BLAIR, JAYSON; IF I DID IT; LEROY, JT; A MILLION LITTLE PIECES

---

61 The quote is from "Shattered Glass" (*Vanity Fair*, September 1998), an expansive analysis by Buzz Bissinger. The definitive account, however, came much later—"Hello, My Name Is Stephen Glass, and I'm Sorry" (*The New Republic*, November 2014) by Hanna Rosin, who was his prescandal best friend.

GOSPEL OF JESUS'S WIFE

It was a scraggly piece of papyrus—barely three inches wide and not even two inches tall—with a snippet of text, eight partial lines, written in ancient Coptic, but packing a sensational sentence fragment:

> . . . Jesus said to them, "My wife . . ."

The scrap of ancient paper became an instant sensation, landing on the front pages of newspapers around the country, after Karen L. King, a professor at Harvard Divinity School, unveiled it in 2012. On her website, King argued the artifact was likely genuine—a fourth-century translation of "a gospel probably written in Greek in the second half of the second century." It was dubbed, perhaps too hastily, the Gospel of Jesus's Wife.

In the months and years that followed, evidence of misdirection mounted, undermining the legitimacy of the document. The handwriting looked unusual, and the grammar was off. Further language analysis revealed the dialect was wrong, and the words seemed a careless pastiche of another apocryphal work, the Gospel of Thomas. Finally, the radiocarbon dating tests came back from the lab, indicating the papyrus was from much later. The evidence was fairly conclusive: The Gospel of Jesus's Wife was a modern forgery scribbled onto an old piece of paper.[62]

It may have been counterfeit, but for the briefest of moments, the Gospel of Jesus's Wife caught the imagination of those heterodox believers who, after their third communion wine, love to slur crank theories like, "Dude, you know Jesus was totally hitched to Mary Magdalene, right?" Most of that trenchant conjecture can be traced back to a singular work of historical FANFIC, *The Da Vinci Code* (2003), which parlays a theory that the church hid their relationship, even though there is exceedingly little evidence to support this hypothesis. No book in the Bible stakes a claim on the marital status of Jesus. Some gospels of the APOCRYPHA elaborate on the life of Mary Magdalene, but not even they go so far as to claim Jesus had ever married.

SEE ALSO: APOCRYPHA; FANFIC; HOMER; POPE JOAN; PRESTER JOHN; SHROUD OF TURIN

GREEBLES

As used by science fiction world-builders, *greebles* are the random details of texture added to the surface of an object to make it appear more visually interesting. The term originated from special effects designers who worked on *Star Wars*, and the canonical example is the meticulous detailing on the Death Star.

Greebles are an odd case wherein misinformation—in the form of visual noise—actually makes something seem more realistic.

SEE ALSO: 3D PRINTING; CYBORG; KNOCKOFF HANDBAGS; MECHANICAL TURK; POTEMKIN VILLAGE

GRUNGE SPEAK

In November 1992, at the apex of a certain underground music movement, the *New York Times* published a story connecting the Seattle music scene

---

62 There was more damaging evidence, including the revelation that the person who produced the fragment for Professor King had a history of forgery. The whole forensic saga is breathlessly told in "The Unbelievable Tale of Jesus's Wife," in the July/August 2016 issue of *The Atlantic*.

to recent fashion trends. Titled "Grunge: A Success Story," it began:

> When did grunge become grunge? How did a five-letter word meaning dirt, filth, trash become synonymous with a musical genre, a fashion statement, a pop phenomenon?

It was an inauspicious lede. First of all, *grunge* has six letters.

To call the story *trend-hunting* would be a disservice to glossy magazines that swerve the zeitgeist for their paychecks. A better term might be *catchup-reporting*, that mode of reportage often performed by mainstream news outlets who accidentally overlook an important überfad. ("Did you notice three people wearing plaid in the office today? Stop the presses!") A work of *catchup journalism* identifies several missed trends and packages them into a single work of reflective insight. In 1992 the overlooked fads, according the *Times*'s trends report, encompassed heroin chic, incessant use of the word *alternative*, the Marc Jacobs grunge fashion line, used army boots, Courtney Love, Sub Pop, and thrifting. ("'Thrifting' is a verb in Seattle" is an actual sentence in this story.)

The catchup ritual is amusing. Even at its most egregious, no great injustices occur—everyone just chuckles at uncool media dorks who try to summarize insular underground culture that resists summarization. (More recently, the same formal misconduct manifests as witless adults adopting the argot of LOL-speak and Snapchat.)

But this story had an additional twist. It came packaged with a handy companion glossary, a sort of secret decoder ring to underground culture called "Lexicon of Grunge: Breaking the Code." The sidebar, in its entirety:

- **Wack Slacks**: Old ripped jeans
- **Fuzz**: Heavy wool sweaters
- **Plats**: Platform shoes
- **Kickers**: Heavy boots
- **Swingin' on the Flippity-Flop**: Hanging out
- **Bound-and-Hagged**: Staying home on Friday or Saturday night
- **Score**: Great
- **Harsh Realm**: Bummer
- **Cob Nobbler**: Loser
- **Dish**: Desirable guy
- **Bloated, Big Bag of Bloatation**: Drunk
- **Lamestain**: Uncool person
- **Tom-Tom Club**: Uncool outsiders
- **Rock On**: A happy goodbye

Someone was clearly having fun, because the paper of record just reported that when Seattleites carouse, they are "Swingin' on the Flippity-Flop."

The prank started when a *Times* editor called Sub Pop for some edgy grunge terminology. The label referred the paper to Megan Jasper, a plucky former employee who would likely create mischief. On the spot, she concocted definitions for *harsh realm* and *bound-and-hagged* and all those other wonderful terms. The *Times* unwittingly ran them, and soon enough, ironic T-shirts emblazoned with the word LAMESTAIN began appearing around Seattle.[63]

Score, this lady in *wack slacks* created a *harsh realm* for those *cob nobblers* over at the *tom-tom club*.

Rock on.

SEE ALSO: BANANADINE; HITLER DIARIES; IDAHO; JENKEM; SOKAL HOAX

---

63 The ruse was only noticed three months later, by the culture and politics journal *The Baffler*. To this day, the *New York Times* story does not contain a correction—not even about how many letters the word *grunge* contains. Megan Jasper is now an executive vice president at Sub Pop.

Everything has to start somewhere, even history.

This particular inception is most often dated to two and a half millennia ago, in the fifth century BCE, when a man named Herodotus decided to create a written record of the ancient world. From his home in Halicarnassus (in modern Turkey), he set to papyrus his journeys—around the Mediterranean, Africa, and Asia—in a series of travelogues called *Histories*. They are fascinating accounts of people and places, but he's in this encyclopedia, so he must have screwed something up.

Although Herodotus would provide future generations with a wealth of information about the ancient world, he had a penchant for turning each locale into an exaggerated cartoon. In Babylon, a gigantic wall surrounded the city, one hundred meters thick, more impenetrable than even Trump could imagine; Persia had enormous ants, the size of foxes, that could eat a whole camel; in northern Europe, a tribe of one-eyed men stole gold from griffins. These outlandish tales should eliminate him from "first historian" contention, but Herodotus was also a very careful storyteller. In nearly all cases, as he wound up to tell a whopper tale, Herodotus inserted a framing device — "it is said . . ." or "this tale comes from . . ."—to displace his culpability toward the truth. *I'm just here to pass along this story*, he seemed to say in a folksy voice, like Mark Twain unfurling an epic jumping frog yarn. But in some cases, Herodotus seemed to really believe the tall tales; the griffins and cyclopes sound especially close to firsthand encounters.

His reluctance to spoil a good story with the truth would damage his legacy. A few centuries later, Cicero bestowed unto Herodotus the title "The Father of History," but he was also a harsh critic, as were Aristotle, Josephus, and Plutarch. Voltaire was the first to confer unto him a second title, "The Father of Lies," which stuck as much as his other paternal epithet.

Despite his whimsy, Herodotus was regarded as a provocative thinker, eager to interrogate sacrosanct topics. Herodotus admired HOMER, for example, but also questioned the historical veracity of the *Iliad*. Why, Herodotus wanted to know, would the Achaeans wage an interminable, expensive war on behalf of one woman? (Helen of Troy seemed pretty cool, but really?) He was the first to ask what now seems a rather obvious question about the Trojan War.

Herodotus was attracted to zany stories, but his stated goal was merely to pass along what people

told him. "Although it is incumbent on me to state what I am told," he wrote, "I am under no obligation to believe it entirely—something that is true for the whole of my narrative." Unlike modern scholars, who debate history as a series of hypotheses, Herodotus viewed himself more in the role of a reporter. *Listen, have I got a story about Babylon for you . . .*

SEE ALSO: ALT-HISTORY; CHINESE WHISPERS; HOMER; PHANTOM TIME HYPOTHESIS

HITLER DIARIES

The *Hitler Diaries* were a trove of Adolf Hitler journals published in the West German magazine *Stern* in 1983. The magazine, through reporter Gerd Heide-

mann, purchased sixty volumes of the diaries, previously thought lost in a 1945 plane crash, for around $3 million.[64]

Of course, they were fakes. Heidemann purchased the journals from a forger for around $1 million and pocketed the difference. The reporter seemed to have an unhealthy obsession with Nazis, which included purchasing the yacht of Hermann Göring and having a five-year affair with his daughter, Edda. He spent four and a half years in prison for fraud.

The *Hitler Diaries* are considered one of the greatest journalism scandals of postwar Germany.

SEE ALSO: AUTOBIOGRAPHY OF HOWARD HUGHES; THE BIG LIE; THE PROTOCOLS OF THE ELDERS OF ZION; VAN MEEGEREN, HAN

---

[64] The backstory: Hitler's personal valet was in possession of ten heavy chests belonging to the German leader when his plane crashed in the Heidenholz Forest near Czechoslovakia. When told of the crash, a despondent Hitler supposedly told a friend, "I entrusted him with extremely valuable documents which would show posterity the truth of my actions!" No one knows what these documents were (intrigue!), though it is theoretically possible that before the SS arrived, looters rummaged the crash site and found diaries.

HOMER

If you want to start a fight with a classicist, ask about the age of Homer.

The great bard was born around 700 BCE, or depending on who you ask, maybe much earlier, perhaps as far back as 1200 BCE during the Trojan War, if that military conflict was itself not a mythological invention. Homer might have lived on Chios (a Greek island), or in ancient Ionia (now western Turkey), or possibly in one of the seven different ancient cities that claimed him as their native son.

We know essentially nothing about Homer.

Many works of ancient literature were initially attributed to him, but his oeuvre was eventually whittled down to just two epic poems. As Aristotle hypothesized, the *Iliad* was probably written first; the *Odyssey*, more likely the work of a mature poet. Or just as possible, given the radical differences in style, the two epic poems could have completely different authors, as many in antiquity believed.

He—hold up; possibly *she*, as Samuel Butler argued in the nineteenth century, as well as others more recently—is thought to have been blind. Yet that conclusion is based solely on a sightless minstrel in the *Odyssey* who sings about the fall of Troy. (Classicists like to detect autobiographical clues in the works of Homer.)

The *Iliad* may have been written down as early as 750 BCE, when the Greek alphabet was first developed, but no manuscripts exist from that time. Archaeologists found pieces of the *Iliad* under the heads of mummies in Egypt dating to circa 150 BCE, but they are just fragments. The oldest complete manuscript of the *Iliad* is from around 900 CE—at least 1,600 years after the original work was set to papyrus.

Here, finally, a historical detail that everyone agrees on: Both great epic poems started as oral compositions, meant to be sung or chanted for an audience. But as for whether they were oral tales for decades or centuries or millennia, and whether they were composed or transcribed by Homer, and whether Homer was himself a myth, like Zeus—there is wide disagreement.

The person who recorded the great legends may himself have been a great legend.[65] Those massive works could be the collective creation of anonymous bards, memorized and recited for generations. "Think of Homer as a culture not a person," one book recently argued.[66] Given all the time irregularities and continuity errors in the texts, it seems entirely possible that the poems were written in different periods of Greek history. (Referred to as *Homeric nods*, these errors wouldn't seem to exist if the epics were written by one author. One of many examples: In the *Iliad*, Menelaus kills Pylaemenes, who is still around later to witness the death of his son.) Perhaps the name *Homer* was applied to the oral epics later, once they were put into print. For centuries, the *Odyssey* may have been one huge evolving poem, like an oral wiki page, collaboratively edited and refined through time. If not for the invention of the alphabet, it might still be growing and adapting today.

This theory might be true, or false. Regardless, it is a much better legend.

SEE ALSO: ALT-HISTORY; CHINESE WHISPERS; FANFIC; HISTORIES; POPE JOAN; PRESTER JOHN; RETCONNING; TROJAN HORSE

---

65   Another early Greek storyteller of unstable historical legitimacy is Aesop. None of his writings even exist today, yet his collected *Fables* are often read by schoolchildren. He was, in all likelihood, an aggregator of tales, but he might not have existed at all.

66   *Why Homer Matters* (2016) by Adam Nicolson was hardly the first to argue for the collectivist Homer. Like everything else, the idea can be traced back to antiquity.

HONEYPOT

Like a trail of honey enticing a grizzly bear to a stash of syrupy combs, a honeypot is a decoy used to lure hackers. The surreptitious bait typically resembles vulnerable data, which cybersecurity professionals monitor for unauthorized access. If an outsider interacts with the honeypot, they know a hacker lies in their midst and can identify the invasive techniques.

The plot of the first season of the crypto-thriller *Mr. Robot* hinges on removing a honeypot to crack the network of E Corp.

SEE ALSO: CANARY TRAP; FALSE FLAG OPERATION; HONEYTRAP; STEGANOGRAPHY

HONEYTRAP

A honeytrap (also sometimes called a HONEYPOT) is an espionage technique used both by spies to obtain secrets and by private investigators to catch philanderers. The basic template is simple—lure the subject into a sexual situation to either physically seize them, extract secrets from them, or capture evidence to use against them. When the latter, incriminating photos are often the product of a successful honeytrap.

When a honeytrap is used criminally in an extortion scheme, it is sometimes called a *badger game*. Alexander Hamilton was famously caught in a badger game by his mistress's husband, who blackmailed him to keep the affair secret. When political opponents discovered the affair, it became America's first sex scandal.

Though sometimes considered a relic of the Cold War (used not only by spies but relentlessly as a trope

in James Bond movies), setting honeytraps is reportedly still quite common in Russia.

The earliest recorded honeytrap might be Delilah revealing Samson's weakness (his magnificent mane of hair) to the Philistines in exchange for silver, as told in the Book of Judges. The honeytrap could literally be the oldest dirty trick in the book.

SEE ALSO: CANARY TRAP; CATFISH; FALSE FLAG OPERATION; HONEYPOT; TEOING

HOUDINI, HARRY

Harry Houdini was perhaps the most famous illusionist and escapologist in history, but he was also an avowed skeptic who occupied his later years debunking psychics and mediums. Unlike most magicians of the day, Houdini never claimed to have supernatural abilities, but that did not stop his friend Arthur Conan Doyle from ascribing wizardly powers to him.

It was a peculiar friendship, based at first upon them both being spectacularly famous. After meeting in 1920 during a magician's tour of England, they maintained an active correspondence and visited each other on several occasions. Despite creating Sherlock Holmes, one of the most empirically minded, hyper-rational characters in literary history, Doyle was the philosophical opposite of Houdini—a fervent metaphysician who literally believed in fairies.[67] A leader of the spiritualist movement, Doyle actively lectured and wrote books on the topics of clairvoyance, spirits, and psychic phenomena.

No stranger to the occult, Houdini had been interested in mediumship since before his mother died in 1913. He had become dismayed though, as each psychic he enlisted to contact his mother soon proved to

---

67 These were the infamous Cottingley Fairies, a series of five photographs that contained wood fairies and goblins. Doyle, who believed them real and became their lead proponent, used the photos to illustrate an article he wrote about fairies.

THE ENCYCLOPEDIA OF MISINFORMATION

be an obvious charlatan. (He was naturally adept at spotting fakery.) As Houdini lost faith in the supernatural, Doyle became more determined to convince him otherwise, introducing him to even more spiritualists, whom Houdini kept debunking. Their odd friendship lasted for years only because Houdini was able to hide his true feelings about spiritualism from the man of letters.

Their falling out would occur after a séance organized by Doyle's wife, herself a practicing medium, who offered to contact Houdini's beloved mother. As they gathered around a table in a shadowy room, Lady Doyle fell into a trance and began automatic writing—scrawling words and pictures on endless sheets of paper, the modern equivalent of guiding a planchette across the Ouija board. Houdini was immediately suspicious of a drawing with a large cross (his mother was a devout Jew), but he waited patiently. When his mother finally spoke through the medium, her voice came through the AETHER in perfect English, a language she barely knew. Though Houdini was flummoxed, Lady Doyle had a quick response. "In heaven," she responded, "everyone speaks English."

Dismayed, Houdini kept quiet about the incident, afraid his skepticism would upset his friendship with the creator of Sherlock Holmes. But several months later, he told the *New York Sun* that he had yet to substantiate any medium who claimed to talk with the dead. When Doyle saw the quote, he thought Houdini had betrayed him and quickly sent off an angry letter. They bickered for a while in correspondence, which eventually spilled into a public debate in the *New York Times*. "There is nothing that Sir Arthur will believe that surprises me," wrote Houdini. Their friendship would never recover.[68]

Houdini continued his mission of exposing the mystics of the day as frauds who swindled vulnerable people. He wrote several books on the matter and went on tour exposing hucksters in a stage show. He died on Halloween in 1926 after taking a punch to the stomach he was unprepared for. Doyle died a few years later, still a devout spiritualist.

SEE ALSO: MECHANICAL TURK; ONE MILLION DOLLAR PARANORMAL CHALLENGE; ORDER OF THE OCCULT HAND; ZARDULU

---

68 If this anecdote inspires you to try writing a buddy comedy about this screwball friendship, put away your typewriter—someone already tried it. *Houdini & Doyle* was a ten-episode show that aired on FOX in 2016. It was quickly cancelled.

HUMAN CLONING

Unless the Olsen Twins are hiding something, there are, as far as we know, no human clones wandering the earth. This is partially through scientific restraint. The technology is attainable—biologists have already completed the first step, creating mature human embryos by transplanting the nuclei of skin cells into vacant host eggs. The embryos were terminated before turning into fetuses, and some hurdles would likely impede further development, but biologists have proven that human cloning is, in theory, possible. Some people think this is pretty damn cool; many reckon it the end of days.

Whether society would or should allow human cloning is an entirely different matter. It is currently banned by the United Nations, but there are always rogue actors. (Post-DOLLY, there were several fraudulent human clones announced.) And there's always the possibility that society's attitude toward reproductive cloning will change over time. "Test tube babies" were once considered ghoulish, but now nearly 2 percent of American children are conceived *in vitro*. Maybe we'll adapt to accept asexual reproduction, or maybe the fear of an army of Kanye cylons is too strong.

SEE ALSO: 3D PRINTING; DOLLY; FREGOLI DELUSION; MIMICRY

HUMBUGGERY

Humbuggery is an act of deception, often associated with fraud. Humbuggers are scammers, charlatans, hornswogglers, flimflam men—and P. T. Barnum loved them all. He not only used the term endearingly but bestowed upon himself a royal title: "The Prince of Humbug."

Barnum loved humbugs so much that he even wrote a book on the matter, *Humbugs of the World* (1865), with the stated goal of rescuing humbuggery from its negative connotation. The consummate entertainer, he believed the tarnished term should be revived with a more enlightened definition. Humbugs, for Barnum, were not insidious frauds but simply compelling public spectacles of ambiguous legitimacy. *Ambiguity* was key—humbugs should never misrepresent themselves. A true humbug invited the viewer to ascertain its authenticity. A humbug has nothing to prove.

Barnum turned this belief into business doctrine. His career started by exhibiting Joice Heth, the 161-year-old "nursing mammy" of George Washington.[69] When the public grew suspicious of her purported age, Barnum could have bolstered his sham with bogus scientific testimony. Instead, he wrote an anonymous letter to a newspaper, updating the accusation of fraudulence to something even more outrageous—Heth was actually an automaton voiced by a ventriloquist.

The absurd claim reignited her fame, drawing not only new audiences but repeat visitors who wished to reevaluate the putative robot in a new light. When Heth later died and her age was proven to be much younger, Barnum staged an autopsy at the New York City Saloon for 1,500 customers who paid 50¢ each. When the surgeon declared she could not be older than eighty, Barnum claimed himself an inculpable victim of a hoax. "I had hired Joice in perfect good faith," the showman contended, "and relied upon her appearance and the documents as evidence of the truth of her story."

---

69 Barnum was an abolitionist, who would later serve two terms in the Connecticut legislature, but "slavery" is the only word to describe his relationship to Heth. He purchased her from another entertainer. She died in 1836, around the age of seventy-nine.

Of course, his feigned innocence was some supreme BULLSHIT. But the incident afforded Barnum an insight that would inform his entire career: Successful humbugs should be probable but cannot be indisputable. He was a merchant of *doubt*, not proof. "The public appears disposed to be amused," the showman later wrote in his autobiography, "even when they are conscious of being deceived." Suspicion sold tickets, not certainty. People want to be humbugged.

In advertisements for his shows, Barnum presented himself as skeptical of his own human curiosities, a mere conduit for the hucksters. When scientists disputed another spectacle, the Feejee Mermaid, he publicized it with the question "Who is to decide when *doctors* disagree?" *You detect the fraud*, he seemed to say, intimating a distinctly American quality of simulated freedom in the face of deception.[70]

Barnum was a master of giving his audience the illusion of control. The impresario foresaw how conflicting reactions were a sign of compelling theater. If you detected no legerdemain in a humbug and believed it real, then you enjoyed your experience. If you were an educated skeptic who visited a humbug just to feign superiority around unrefined rubes, your experience was equally enjoyable. Humbugs, for Barnum, were performances to debate, effigies around which the public hashed out arguments about science, theater, medicine, and society. Even audiences who saw through the ruse used humbugs to hone their wit, not that dissimilar from today's hate-watchers. "Now and then someone would cry out *humbug* and *charlatan* but so much the better for me," he would later recall. "It helped to advertise me, and I was willing to bear the reputation."

Everyone pays their admission and contributes to the ballyhoo. *Bah, humbug.*[71]

SEE ALSO: THE BLAIR WITCH PROJECT; BULLSHIT; CARDIFF GIANT; KAYFABE; SMARKS; THE TREACHERY OF IMAGES; TRUTHINESS; WORK OF FICTION DISCLAIMER

HYPNOSIS

Hypnosis is a state of human consciousness where you become susceptible to BULLSHIT.

There are several types of purported hypnotic states, but the most illustrative is actually the most ludicrous: the hypnotist entertainer. When you get on stage with a dozen other people and the "You are getting sleepy..." routine commences, the hypnotist has actually created a theatrical environment that lowers your guard, increases your suggestibility, and transforms you into a performer. You are under no trance. The best way to describe hypnosis might be as *roleplaying*, or as magician James Randi once put it, "a mutual agreement of the operator and the subject." In other words, it's theater. When the hypnotist asks you to quack like a duck, you *play along*. You are under a mystical spell no more than Al Pacino literally became Michael Corleone.

A similar transaction occurs with hypnotherapy, in which you meditate your way to stop smoking or lose weight or cure depression. These motivational programs can work, sometimes, but not because you are put under some deep transformative spell. You

---

70 "We need P. T. Barnum, a little bit," Donald Trump said on *Meet the Press* in January 2016. "Because we have to build up the image of our country." It may have been a callback to his sister, a federal judge, who back in 2005 told his biographer, "He *is* P. T. Barnum."

71 Most people first encounter the word *humbug* as children, when they hear Ebenezer Scrooge cackle "Bah, humbug!" in *A Christmas Carol*. Charles Dickens and Barnum were in fact contemporaries, and it seems entirely possible that the former intentionally helped the latter popularize the term.

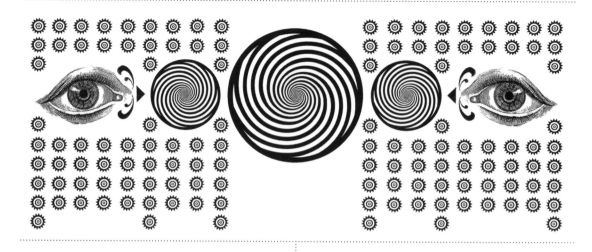

were motivated enough to pay for someone to put you to sleep, so clearly you are motivated enough to lose weight. It's the same psychological mechanism that explains why people find greater enjoyment in drinking wine they are told is expensive, even when it is the cheap stuff. Repeated studies have shown that people who are easily hypnotized are more likely to have what psychologists call "fantasy-prone personalities." They let themselves believe.

The PLACEBO EFFECT is real; the effects of hypnosis are not entirely feigned. If you trick your mind into believing you experience less pain or into forgetting a bad memory then, ipso facto, there is less pain and the memory is forgotten.[72] But you're conning yourself to think that hypnosis, *abracadabra*, cured something. You did it, all by yourself.

SEE ALSO: BARNUM EFFECT; BOGUS PIPELINE; DREAM ARGUMENT; MANCHURIAN CANDIDATE; THE METHOD; PLACEBO EFFECT; SODIUM PENTOTHAL; SUBLIMINAL ADVERTISING; WIPING

72 As an act of psychological manipulation, hypnosis is deeply linked to memory—forgetting, remembering, and inventing the past. During the 1980s, regression therapy emerged as a prominent technique for recovering "repressed memories." By inducing a hypnotic state, victims were coaxed into recalling their alien abduction, their past lives, and their childhood sexual trauma.

IDAHO

Idaho holds the esteemed honor of being the only state named through a hoax.

The story starts in 1860, when a new territory around Pikes Peak was being proposed to Congress. A goofball delegate and mining lobbyist, George M. Willing, presented the name *Idaho*, claiming it derived from a Shoshone phrase, *E Dah Hoe*, meaning "gem of the mountains."[73] The people of the region enjoyed the lyrical word, and it was almost accepted. At the last moment, rumor spread that *Idaho* was not actually a Native American term, so the region was instead incorporated as the Colorado Territory.

But the word had struck a chord. To the north, steamboats and mines started to use the name Idaho. Soon there was a whole county in the Washington Territory using the name, which in 1863 became the Idaho Territory.

The fabrication long forgotten, Idaho, a nonsense word, became a state in 1890.

SEE ALSO: ESQUIVALIENCE; GERRYMANDERING; GRUNGE SPEAK; NONCE WORD; TRAP STREETS

IF I DID IT

To gain entry into this compendium, a book has probably fucked up in some monstrous way. Most likely, it is a hoax, or an egregious act of plagiarism, or some woefully inept work of history. *If I Did It* (2007) is none of these things, but it might be the most audacious act of misinformation ever published.

More than a decade after O. J. Simpson was acquitted for murdering Nicole Brown Simpson and Ron Goldman, the case remained prominent in the public mind. Certain unsavory characters (aka "people who live in Los Angeles") saw economic opportunity in this untapped fame, but it was an odd sort of renown to cash in on. O. J. had already taken a stab at reality programming, with a 2003 pay-per-view hidden cam-

---

73 Willing was not only a goofball but also a self-promoting braggart who may have later exaggerated his involvement. Regardless, the word *Idaho* is fabricated.

era show. *Juiced*, as it was actually called, included an incendiary sketch in which Simpson tries to hock his disgraced white Ford Bronco to a used car lot. "It was good for me," he tells the salesman. "It helped me get away."

Finally, someone—specifically known rabble-rouser Judith Regan, who ran an imprint of HarperCollins (owned by News Corp)—came up with the ingenious idea to have Simpson write a memoir. But not just any memoir—a memoir that hypothesized *how he would have committed the murder had he done it*. The plan was to promote the book—shamelessly titled *If I Did It*—with a two-part television special featuring an interview with O. J. on FOX (also owned by News Corp).

Naturally, the public—as well as the families of the victims—freaked out. In a tempest of backlash, the book was yanked before it could even hit shelves. Rupert Murdoch himself issued an apology, calling it "an ill-considered project." After 450,000 print copies were destroyed, the book predictably leaked onto internet torrent sites.

Around the same time, the family of Ron Goldman won a $33 million civil case against Simpson. The settlement handed over rights of the unpublished book to the family, who decided to publish it with a new subtitle, *Confessions of the Killer*, plus some added commentary from the family. The redesigned book jacket shrunk the **IF** to tiny letters, so the title seemed to read simply **I DID IT**. Even though he is the author, O. J.'s name and image appear nowhere on the cover.

Reading the book is a mind-boggling experience. For several chapters, it plods along like an almost normal memoir. O. J. feigns introspection and mounts a case against Nicole as a slutty cokehead who slept with his BFF, Marcus Allen. Finally comes the chapter "The Night in Question," where he shifts voice and says:

Now picture this—and keep in mind, this is hypothetical:

From there, O. J. asks you to *pretend*, while he delivers gruesome details about killing Nicole and the man he believed to be her lover. After the reconstruction of the double homicide, he returns to normal memoir voice, finishing with details about his notorious arrest.

There is no section of the bookstore for "Hypothetical True Crime Memoir," but if there were, *If I Did It* would line the shelves.

SEE ALSO: ALT-HISTORY; CHEWBACCA DEFENSE; FANFIC; GENOVESE, KITTY; RASHOMON EFFECT; RETCONNING; UNRELIABLE NARRATOR; WORK OF FICTION DISCLAIMER

ILLEGAL PRIME NUMBER

Pick a number. Wait—pick a *prime* number. Write it down. Did your prime number happen to begin with *485650*... and continue for 1,401 digits? If it did, then you possess a forbidden number.

Illegal prime numbers are exactly what they sound like—indivisible digits that are unlawful to own or transmit. The most notorious example is the number used in DVD players to decrypt encoded movies. When this prime (the one with the 1,401 digits) was divulged online in 2001, a judge ruled its ownership illegal. The ruling inspired some ridiculous litigation, including the MPAA suing a manufacturer that printed the number on a T-shirt.

Because they are rare and difficult to calculate, prime numbers are particularly useful in encryption schemes. The possession of one becoming a crime may seem preposterous, but the incident suggests other rousing questions related to technology and ownership. [1] *Is computer code free speech?* [2] *Can you trademark a color?* [3] *Is the human genome code copyrightable?* These legal quandaries are trying to keep apace with technology.[74]

No one has been jailed for possession of a prime, but history is riddled with cases of forbidden numbers causing persecution. Legend has it the Pythagoreans killed to keep the diabolical √2 secret. The digits *666* are still revered by some Satanists and even more anti-satanic crusaders. Skyscrapers often still omit the 13TH FLOOR. And the date *6/4/89* has been banned from web searches in China because of its association with the Tiananmen Square Massacre.

SEE ALSO: 13TH FLOOR; 555-2368; INFINITE MONKEY THEOREM; STEGANOGRAPHY; STREISAND EFFECT

IMPOSTER SYNDROME

Do you suffer from a nagging feeling that—in your professional career—you are a fraud, a sham, a phony baloney? That you don't deserve your success? That your achievements have accrued from a wondrous streak of luck? If so, it's possible you suffer from an affliction known as *impostor syndrome*. It's also possible you are simply humble. Difficult to know! (Don't fret. If this were a science fiction movie, the discomfiting feeling would suggest you are an unwitting CYBORG.)

Impostor syndrome is the inability to recognize your own accomplishments. The concept was forged by clinical psychologists in the late '70s. When studies initially indicated it was more prevalent among high-achieving women, the condition was embraced by feminists as a partial explanation for the workplace parity gap. More research in the '90s suggested the self-esteem gap might be gender neutral, and perhaps even a majority of employees from all backgrounds suffer from some form of workplace impostorism.

The Wikipedia entry for impostor syndrome claims that its sufferers include Tom Hanks, Chuck Lorre, Neil Gaiman, John Green, Sheryl Sandberg, Sonia Sotomayor, and Emma Watson. So basically, a lot of very different people think of themselves as fraudulent.

SEE ALSO: CAPGRAS DELUSION; COTARD DELUSION; FREGOLI DELUSION; GASLIGHTING; PHANTOM LIMBS; VIRTUE SIGNALING; VOIGHT-KAMPFF MACHINE

INFINITE MONKEY THEOREM

The infinite monkey theorem encompasses a well-trodden thought experiment: An unwitting ape is trapped in a room for infinity, tap-tap-tapping random keys on a typewriter. *Eveeeeeeeentuallllly*, due to the laws of probability, this pitiable simian will accidently type out the collected works of Shakespeare. The hypothesis is being diligently tested on Twitter right now.

The theorem of infinite monkeys has intellectual appeal, plus mathematical validity, yet it remains pragmatically impossible. Probabilistically, even if the number of monkeys equaled the atoms in the universe (around 10^{80}), and all those atomic monkeys typed extremely fast (say, one hundred characters per second), and they did so for a long time (the life of the universe multiplied by, *hmmmm*, a billion), they would still (probably!) not replicate even a single page of *Hamlet*. Whatever book this monkey tapped out on his Remington, it would never even remotely fit in the known universe.

But that is the actuarial response of a dull logician. Somewhere behind page 53.8×10^{91} of this hypo-

thetical monkey book lies a more elegant appeal: an allegory about humanity. The monkey theorem is a method for contemplating existence in the face of randomness. However improbable, the indelible image of a monkey at a typewriter reconstitutes infinity as a tractable concept, more pliable than a sterile ∞ on a chalkboard. Only we humans—the most advanced primates—can distinguish data from information; only we can see order in the deluge. The monkey parable is silly but somehow soothing.

For these reasons, the literary establishment adores the infinite monkey theorem. Borges used it to great effect in "The Library of Babel," and everyone from *Dilbert* to the *New Yorker* has propped a primate up to an IBM Selectric. A monkey at a typewriter evokes the dumb randomness of literary invention: Great works are *found*, not *created*. (For this reason, literary agents are particularly enchanted.) Somewhere deep in the random monkey garble, this encyclopedia exists, an accident of time and space. In the face of such fuzzy uncertainty, the monkey reminds us of what Polonius told Hamlet, "To thine ownself be wQldze;rv!XssspL."

SEE ALSO: ILLEGAL PRIME NUMBER; PASCAL'S WAGER; SHIP OF THESEUS; STEGANOGRAPHY; TURTLES ALL THE WAY DOWN

INTERNET RESEARCH AGENCY

If you wanted to disguise a stealth BLACK PROPAGANDA operation, you might give it an inconspicuous moniker like Internet Research Agency. Perhaps that explains the innocuous naming of IRA, a shady Russian tech firm that creates online disinformation for the Kremlin. Effectively Vladimir Putin's troll farm, the IRA employs a cadre of irritants who write bogus blog posts, distribute divisive comments on news websites (including Fox News, HuffPost, Politico, and the New York Times), and amplify dissentious memes on social media, especially Twitter, YouTube, and Facebook.

The enterprise started in 2013 with the stated goal of promoting oligarch-friendly domestic policy, but after successful propaganda campaigns in Ukraine, IRA reoriented toward media manipulation in the United States. During the 2016 presidential campaign, the agency employed 90 people to create divisive internet propaganda in support of candidate Donald Trump. In total, the Kremlin funneled at least $2.3 million to IRA to influence the election, including the purchase of Facebook ads that bolstered thousands of acrimonious posts. (Showing no distinction between virtual and real-world ASTROTURFING, the troll farm also mounted a ground campaign, paying 100 activists to organize 40 rallies across the United States.)

Though renowned for invigorating the alt-right with rhetoric on issues like Texan independence and immigration, IRA has also boosted leftist messages from groups including Black Lives Matter. The alliance might seem counterintuitive, especially given Putin's atrocious human rights record, but targeting far-left slogans to certain regions can polarize the electorate, creating dissension that destabilizes the public. The goal of propaganda is exposed: not to influence policy but to cultivate rancor and turmoil. Discord is the cash crop of the griefers on the troll farm.

SEE ALSO: ASTROTURFING; FALSE FLAG OPERATION; INTERNET TROLL; SOCK PUPPET

INTERNET TROLL

The role of an internet troll was once succinctly defined. Trolls performed specific tasks, with specific goals. A troll was an irritant, a nuisance, a rabble-rouser.

A proper act of trolling went like this: You would enter an internet community, drop an incendiary remark, provoke an overreaction from the in-group, and sit back and LOLOLOL as members squawked and howled at your impudence. An intrepid internet troll might, for example, saunter into a Beanie Baby message board, proclaim the plush dolls a PONZI SCHEME built upon mounds of legume rubbish, and then watch reactionary soccer moms caterwaul like banshees yanked from their Chardonnay.[75]

Trolls produced *flamebait* (acrimonious remarks that encourage rebuttal, also known as *shitposts*), which would irritate community members, but these rascals were otherwise harmless. When asked *why* they enjoyed sowing discord, the response was a typical non sequitur: "For the lulz." They were just rickrolling their way toward perverse laughter.

An implicit tenet of this worldview is that the troll does not (necessarily) believe their own rhetoric. Trolls exist to challenge outdated doctrine, but they have no fixed ideology, unless chaos is ideological. A troll might provoke ire in a Planned Parenthood forum not because he (with near invariability, a troll is a "he") is even against women's rights. Trolls privilege aesthetics over ethics, style over manners. Spawning outrage is a sport. Or, when perfectly executed, an art. As with a masterful painting, the reaction a troll elicits from the audience matters more than the artist, or even the artwork.

But this narrow definition of the troll as a pesky prankster has passed. Trolling now connotes a much larger category of actions, both more harmless and more heinous. On the benign side, *trolling* has become a synonym for *taunting*. Loudmouths now "troll" politicians with snarky tweets. NFL quarterbacks "troll" their opponents in the endzone. TV shows "troll" their audiences with surprise twists. You can "troll" your mom with hilarious emojis. If an action elicits a reaction, it is now a troll. And on the internet, pretty much everything elicits a reaction.

The semantic territory of trolling has also expanded in the opposite direction, toward the demonic. Bombarding the internet with hate speech now falls in the same impish category as subtweeting your boss—it's all trolling. The cretins who commit revenge porn on ex-girlfriends are able to dilute the severity of their crimes by depicting their acts as "just trolling." Broadening the category of trolling to include simple harassment has lessened the depravity of their malevolent acts. These numbskulls do not deserve the title of troll. They should be called what they are—sadists.

SEE ALSO: CATFISH; CONCERN TROLLING; THE REALIST

---

75 Comparing soccer moms to banshees is a fine example of shabby trolling. Don't feed the trolls, moms.

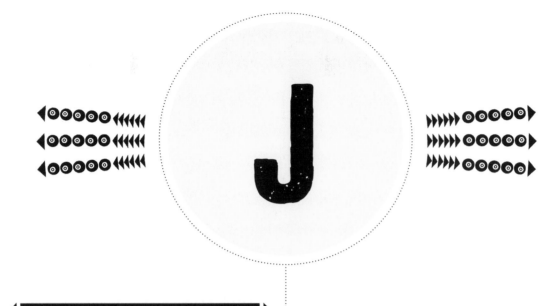

JABBERWOCKY

"Jabberwocky" is a nonsense poem that, over time, started to make sense. Found in Lewis Carroll's *Through the Looking-Glass,* the poem uses whimsical language with idiosyncratic phrasing, such as:

> "O frabjous day! Callooh! Callay!"
> He chortled in his joy.

Much of the poem consists of NONCE WORDS—made-up terms that fit the prosodic situation. However, due to the poem's unexpected popularity, many of those fake words eventually developed real meanings. That includes *chortle* (a chuckle meets a snort) and *frabjous* (an equal blending of fair, fabulous, and joyous), which were used for the first time by Carroll but are now found in even the most basic dictionaries. Other mumbo jumbo neologisms contained therein: *galumph* (to walk clumsily), *vorpal* (sharp), *slithy* (lithe and slimy), and, of course, *jab-*

berwocky (imitative gibberish). In twenty-eight lines of unintelligible iambic meter, Carroll invented more English vocabulary than anyone since Shakespeare.

SEE ALSO: BELLMAN'S FALLACY; ESQUIVALIENCE; IDAHO; NEWSPEAK; NONCE WORDS; SUPERCALIFRAGILISTICEXPIALIDOCIOUS

JENKEM

Jenkem is a hallucinogenic inhalant created by fermenting feces and urine. Go ahead, try it.

The drug supposedly originated in Africa, where the BBC in 1999 reported that street kids in Zambia were inhaling fermented sewage. Bored juveniles in American suburbs, armed with the internet, started to claim they too were huffing and puffing it like big bad wolves at a little piggy barbecue. The hoax triggered a moral panic in 2007, when enough pranksters convinced enough local television channels they were hooked on jenkem. Among many loony local news reports, a TV station in South Bend, Indiana, advised parents to stay up at night and "not let their kids go to bed until they have seen them and smelled their breath." Reputable publications, including ABC News, *The Stranger*, and the *Washington Post*, also fell for the fermented fecal fumes bit.

When SNOPES eventually caught wind of that bullshit, the hoax was quelled.

SEE ALSO: BANANADINE; GRUNGE SPEAK; SNOPES

JOSEPH MCCARTHY'S LIST

So, funny thing: There never was one!

In 1950 at a women's club in West Virginia, Senator Joseph McCarthy gave a rousing speech during which he manically waved around a piece of paper, claiming it contained a list of 205 members of the State Department who were "known communist sympathizers." Though a relative nobody at the time, the accusation instantly vaulted McCarthy to prominence and provoked a nationwide hunt, known as the Second Red Scare, for subversives who had infiltrated the heart of the U.S. government.

In the following weeks, McCarthy went into bingo caller mode, wildly varying the number of people on the list, from 57 to 81 to 35 to 116 to 10 commies. He never produced a shred of evidence that anyone in the State Department had communist sympathies, but he was able to damage the reputation of his ideological foes with smears, half-truths, and insinuations. This slanderous practice today goes by the catchy name *McCarthyism*.

When McCarthy widened his accusations to the U.S. Army and accused Eisenhower of coddling subversives, the Senate invited him to offer testimony regarding his claims. In the televised hearing, a flustered McCarthy attempted to bluff his way through the accusations, but the public instantly recognized him as prevaricating and reckless. As his popularity rating plummeted from 50 percent to 37 percent, the Senate censured McCarthy for unscrupulous, bullying tactics, and he quickly fell from the public eye. He died in 1957 of liver failure due to alcoholism.

SEE ALSO: DEEP STATE; FALSE FLAG OPERATION; MANCHURIAN CANDIDATE; PUSH POLL; REICHSTAG FIRE

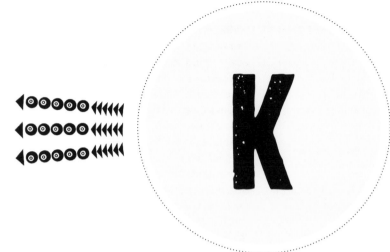

KARAOKE

"Human beings are the animal," W. H. Auden once remarked, "that cannot become anything without pretending to be it first."[76] The epigram captures that histrionic, ludic quality of the human spirit like nothing else, except perhaps for the modernized version: *Fake it 'til you make it.* If karaoke had a slogan, either would do.

It is easy to forget how audacious karaoke once was. Of course it all started in Japan, when the words *kara* (empty) and *okesutura* (orchestra) merged in 1971 around an interactive singing machine. After spreading through Asia, karaoke drifted to the West, very slowly. The rock critic Rob Sheffield pegs the music video for "Wild Wild Life," a 1986 song by the Talking Heads, as the first depiction of karaoke in American popular culture.[77] Not until several years later, well into the '90s, did bachelorette parties start getting soused on "Livin' on a Prayer" with their vodka sodas.

Today, karaoke is a $10 billion industry, but *the idea* of karaoke is more pervasive than any number could illustrate. Karaoke was the first mass-scale cultural product to offer a brazen promise: Any schmo can, however fleetingly, become Bono or Taylor Swift or Kanye. Now all of pop culture seems to make the same aspirational appeal. Reality competition shows (*American Idol* and *The Voice*), video games (*Guitar Hero* and *Rock Band*), television (*Glee*), movies (*Pitch Perfect*), theater (*School of Rock*), apps (Musical.ly and thousands of others)—all embody the democratic spirit of karaoke, where fame and success are simple imitative arts.

In hindsight, history might remember karaoke as a stepping-stone toward the inception of YouTube celebrities and social media. Like those open digital platforms, where inventing and reinventing a persona passes as charisma, karaoke embraces a simi-

---

76 The line is found in Auden's long, anxiety-inducing poem *The Age of Anxiety* (1947).

77 For superlative mixes of karaoke scholarship and personal narrative, see both Rob Sheffield's *Turn Around Bright Eyes* (2012) and Brian Raftery's *Don't Stop Believin'* (2008).

lar type of chameleonic unprofessionalism. Just as karaoke assisted in the deprofessionalization of rock stars, social media clipped the wings of other creative occupations, handing out performance licenses to anyone wishing to become a writer, designer, entrepreneur, photographer, or gamemaker. Like Auden's protean human, they faked it 'til they made it.

SEE ALSO: AUTO-TUNE; BACKMASKING; THE BUGGS; MILLI VANILLI; TRIBUTE BANDS

KAYFABE

Watching professional wrestling for the first time is like learning a new language. Excitable announcers bark exotic words—a *suplex* here, a *piledriver* there—at humongous ballerinas in Day-Glo tights. If an aspirant fan has any hope of grasping the sport, he must learn the quirky lingo of *dropkicks* and *turnbuckles*. Usually, that is as far as the acolyte gets—just the fundamentals, the basics of the craft. But the fundamentals are enough to get him yelling like a maniac at the ring.

Sometimes, a more curious sort of enthusiast shows up. She peers behind the mat, seeking knowledge beyond the basics. This pesky superfan seeks to study the esoteric magic of the dark art. If she looks deep enough, the superfan discovers an entirely new language, with an even richer lexicon to describe the kabuki theater performed behind the turnbuckles. Here, a new arcane vocabulary thrives, with terms like *jobber* and *tweener, face* and *heel*.[78] This gnomic jargon contains words not just for maneuvers, but for *strategies* and *characters* and all the secret tricks that make the show tick. She even learns a term for indiscreetly blathering about the sacred argot so openly, like we are doing right now—*breaking kayfabe*. You are *never* supposed to break kayfabe.

Kayfabe is the unwritten code of conduct among astute wrestling fans, a secret pact to never reveal trade secrets or speak openly about the manufacture of spectacle. Like a blend of the Magician's Code and the First Rule of Fight Club, kayfabe is the decree that wrestlers and fans should be in a constant state of suspended disbelief, even when they know exactly what is going on. Always, always stay on script.

Its origin is unknown, but one theory proposes that kayfabe derives from the words *be fake* said backwards and then turned into Pig Latin, which is

78 The language has an actual name, *Carny*, because it descends from early carnivals where wrestling matches first took root. If this were football, the difference between "just the fundamentals" and Carny would be the difference between learning what a linebacker does and knowing the nuances of the Air Coryell offense.

an extraordinarily convoluted origin story. Regardless of its provenance, sounding like something out of shogun Japan probably gave the term its Yoda-esque gravitas. *Kayfabe* simply sounds like a code worth abiding.

One superfan who has studied the dark art is Peter Thiel, the billionaire investor who invoked kayfabe in describing the 2016 presidential election. In a sinuous interview with Maureen Dowd, Thiel claimed that while people thought candidate Donald Trump was *kayfabe* (looks real, but is fake), he managed to turn a *shoot* (an unscripted move that becomes real by accident). Thiel elaborates:

> People thought the whole Trump thing was fake, that it wasn't going to go anywhere, that it was the most ridiculous thing imaginable, and then, somehow, he won, like Hogan did. [*The "winning" referred to here is not a Wrestlemania match against Andre the Giant, but rather Hulk Hogan's lawsuit funded by Thiel against Gawker Media.*] And what I wonder is, whether maybe pro wrestling is one of the most real things we have in our society and what's really disturbing is that the other stuff is much more fake.[79]

Yes, the billionaire cofounder of PayPal is claiming that professional wrestling is "one of the most real things we have," and the other stuff (presumably politics) is fake. Now *that* is *keeping kayfabe*.

But maybe—really, *maaaaayyyybe*—he has a point. Politics has always been a hive of charlatans, but recent election cycles have seen a shift from spotlighting the politician on stage to shining the kliegs on the enraptured audience. Candidate Trump, for instance, was obsessed with television cameras showing the crowds at his rallies. (He was also inducted into the WWE Hall of Fame, after sponsoring events in his casinos and body slamming Vince McMahon—while in character, presumably.) Politics has shifted from a focus on the candidate (platforms, biographies, qualifications) to a preponderance of attention paid to the audience (polls results, demographic targeting, electioneering). The audience, likewise, has become infatuated with the choreography and stagecraft—with, in a word, kayfabe. A partisan supporter who once praised a simple *dropkick* (an adept speech, say) is now on the lookout for the invisible orchestrations of *tweeners* (morally ambiguous characters) and *turns* (a character switching alignments). They love the theater even more than the actors. "What the public wants is the image of passion," Roland Barthes once said of wrestling fans. "Not the passion itself."[80] And the image of passion has migrated to the stage of politics.

Political campaigns now resemble fandoms. There are T-shirts and hats and superfans who attend rallies that seem to emulate Comic-Con or Burning Man. Social media looks increasingly like FANFIC, where zealots write scripts in which populist heroes vanquish elitist foes. With the privileged wisdom of their secret kayfabe, the new superfans triumphantly embody their own superhero character, the Fatuous Rube. (Their patented move? The Mindless Retweet.) Of course they are not literal rubes—they are merely players in this Wrestlemania ticket. While the dunderhead villains clash in the political media ring, the sycophants scream and chant at make-believe foes, half choreographed and half improvised. It might resemble an anarchic idiocracy, but from inside the ring, the superfan has mastered the delicate balance between fake and real, acting and fighting, entertainment and violence.

---

79 "Peter Thiel, Trump's Tech Pal, Explains Himself" is the title of the January 2017 *New York Times* interview between Thiel and Dowd.

80 "The World of Wrestling," found in Barthes's *Mythologies* (1957).

No one flinches, no one flubs a line, no one asks *is this real?* Everyone plays their part, and absolutely no one breaks kayfabe.

SEE ALSO: THE FOURTH WALL; HUMBUGGERY; LARP; THE METHOD; SMARKS; WASHINGTON GENERALS

KETTLE LOGIC

In *The Interpretation of Dreams* (1900), Sigmund Freud recounts the joke of an old man who returns a kettle to his neighbor in a damaged condition. In defending himself, the old man offers three conflicting rationalizations for the kettle sitch:

1. He had actually returned the kettle undamaged.
2. The kettle was already damaged when he borrowed it.
3. He had never borrowed the kettle in the first place.

Recounting Freud's jest, the French philosopher Jacques Derrida developed the concept *kettle logic* to describe those mutually exclusive defenses that contradict each other. For Derrida, kettle logic illustrates the limits of rationality, and in the hands of authoritarians, such fuzzy schemes can be used as potent tools for obfuscation.

The rhetorical device is also a bona fide legal strategy. *Alternative pleading*, as it is called in judicial circles, is a form of legal defense where a lawyer argues multiple different possibilities that are internally inconsistent but can nonetheless create some reasonable doubt.

SEE ALSO: CHEWBACCA DEFENSE; IF I DID IT; OMNIPOTENCE PARADOX; THE RUMSFELD MATRIX

KNOCKOFF HANDBAGS

Stepping over a stack of dubious Jackie Chan DVDs (three for $10), you catch a whiff of ersatz Eau de Giorgio ($30). As a hawker barks in an unfamiliar patois, "Handbags! Watches! Purses!" a white van screeches to a stop—*everyone freezes*. Undercover police raid? *Whew*, nope, just a new shipment of knockoff Uggs ($20), straight off the container boat, quickly unloaded by the boxful. "Uggs! Tory Burch! Rolex!" resumes the barking hawker.

Welcome to the open-air marketplace of Canal Street in New York City, where you can find iPhones that don't quite look like iPhones and Hermès bags with the accent mark pointed in the wrong direction. This small stretch of city has the vibe of a border town, chockablock with wares for tourists crossing to a new province. And in a sense, Canal Street does delineate territory—on one end of the island, the street splits Little Italy from Chinatown; on the other, Soho from Tribeca. But the more palpable border the street shares is with China, which smuggles in billions in knockoffs every year. A $2,000 handbag can go for as little as $35 on Canal, if you're willing to accept a Louis Vuitton logo that easily smudges.

Although one might be tempted by the cheap thrill of faux-luxury, we are warned that purchasing such goods is akin to theft. Counterfeiting, we are told, damages these brands by siphoning off billions in lost sales. But is that really true? Would those consumers who snatch $50 Chanels really fork over $5,000 for the real deal? Do copies really cut into the bottom line of luxury goods? Might they even *help* the brand?

These are the questions of *The Knockoff Economy*, a book that persuasively argues that counterfeits can actually have the counterintuitive effect of generating free advertising for the brand.[81] The conventional wisdom holds that by preventing illegal duplication, copyright law protects the bottom line. But several studies have shown that luxury goods might be impervious to fakes. For high-end products, knockoffs can act like a signaling device for desirability of the original. When a respected peer flaunts their imitation bag, they implicitly create an endorsement, which spreads brand awareness and generates new buyers. Some consumers even claim they treat knockoffs like samples—a "trial version" before matriculating to the real thing. That fake Louis Vuitton might be a gateway drug to a real one.

SEE ALSO: BEANIE BABY BUBBLE; GREEBLES; MOCKBUSTER; SYNTHETIC DIAMONDS

KULESHOV EFFECT

In the early days of cinema, when its formal rules were first being articulated, Soviet filmmaker Lev Kuleshov stumbled upon a key insight of film grammar: Meaning can be generated by simply splicing together two images. To illustrate his discovery, Kuleshov created a short film that interspersed the shot of an inexpressive man against other simple clips—a bowl of soup, a girl in a coffin, an attractive woman on a divan. The shot of the emotionless face never changed, but when juxtaposed against other clips, the actor seemed to express different emotions—hunger, grief, lust. Completely different meanings could be derived from the same image, depending on what was contrasted against it.

Kuleshov, who was also a film theorist, discovered that the interaction of two shots contains more meaning than any single shot in isolation. Applying this concept today, the implication of the Kuleshov effect is that the millions of dollars spent on actors might better be spent on good editing. The faces of actors can embody whatever emotions the filmmaker splices them against. Editing creates reality.

SEE ALSO: THE DRESS; THE METHOD; RASHOMON EFFECT; UNCANNY VALLEY

---

81 *The Knockoff Economy: How Imitation Sparks Innovation* (2012), by Kal Raustiala and Christopher Sprigman, looks at how imitation and innovation commingle and how certain industries benefit from lax copyright laws. Examples include cuisine (you can't copyright a recipe), professional sports (no one owns the West Coast Offense), and comedy (jokes are constantly recycled and improved). Opening copyright restrictions, which deter the iteration required to innovate, could actually spur competition and creativity. Fakery might be good for the economy!

LARP

Live Action Role-Playing (LARP) is a genre of game in which players act out personas in a physical setting. Though it often resembles improv theater with swords, the gameplay can (occasionally) take on more complicated, even pedagogical, characteristics.

A LARP game typically takes place in a forest or an abandoned industrial space. The fictional setting is usually either an alternate history (medieval or renaissance), a postapocalyptic future (zombified or cyberpunk), or some unique hybrid (steampunk). Elaborate costumes are *de rigueur*, often with prop weapons like foam battle axes or nerf guns. Participants are asked to stay "in character" throughout gameplay, which can last for hours or days. Like all games, there are goals. Sometimes the goal is simply to win a big zombie brawl in the woods, but more convoluted plotlines can involve solving baroque problems that integrate economics, sociology, religion, game theory, or law.

LARPers refer disparagingly to the outside world as *mundania*. While defying easy stereotypes, people who enjoy LARPs tend to also enjoy some combination of these other phenomena: murder-

mystery dinner parties, long serialized paperback novels, room escape games, Ren Faire, *Clue* (the movie), *The Walking Dead* (the comic), beards, collecting mandolins, "Burning Man is lame now," *eXistenZ*, the Nebula awards, *etsy.com/amulets*, dice, David Fincher's *The Game*, the words *tabard* and *oubliette*, worldbuilding, Monty Python, craft beer, gaps of logic in *Westworld*, high *dexterity* and *charisma* scores, bronies, Zelda cosplay, *Sleep No More*, gnomes, hating *Vanilla Sky*, Tron Guy, and middlebrow compendiums of misinformation.

SEE ALSO: ALT-HISTORY; COSPLAY; CRISIS ACTORS; KAYFABE; THE METHOD; SIMULISM

LAUGH TRACK

No technique in television production has been more maligned than the laugh track, yet it somehow perseveres through decades of ridicule.

It all started innocently, as a quick hack to solve a technical problem. Charley Douglass, a sound engineer at CBS in the early '50s, was annoyed at studio

audiences who inconveniently laughed at the wrong moments. Sometimes they chuckled too long at unfunny bits; other times, they refused to bellow with sufficient gusto. To evenly redistribute the laughter, Douglass invented a contraption that looked like a steampunk organ collided with a cyberpunk adding machine, connected on the back end to magnetic tapes with recorded laughter. By pressing buttons on the *laff box* (that's actually what he called it), an orchestrator could punch up guffaws, chortles, and giggles on demand. The magical machine also acted as a sort of demographic keyboard, with inputs for specific genders, ages, and ethnicities, plus a foot pedal that controlled the duration of each laugh. One keystroke might simulate *frothy housewife giggle*; another, *guy who missed joke but laughs anyway*. Keys could be combined into melodic chords of laughter, bringing down the house in a crescendo of hilarity.

The gizmo was a success, smoothing out the aural wrinkles in programs like *The Abbott and Costello Show* and *I Love Lucy*. It was a necessary evil of this nascent era, when television was rapidly changing from live broadcast to taped recordings. Audiences were still growing accustomed to the big square tube in their living rooms, and the laugh track helped ease the transition by simulating an intimate theater experience at home. *You knew when to laugh because they told you when to laugh.*

Naturally, this quaint bag of laughs was quickly abused. Sitcoms in the '60s and '70s took the laff box and cranked it to eleven. Realizing canned chuckles freed them from the burden of a live audience, shows like *Gilligan's Island* and *The Brady Bunch* ratcheted the laugh track to egregious levels. No show could escape the canned laughter craze—beloved programs like *The Muppet Show* and *M*A*S*H* used laugh tracking, even during outdoor scenes, when a studio audience was improbable. When animated shows like *The Flintstones* and *The Jetsons* added tracks of artificial mirth, the entire illusion of a captive studio audience was finally shattered.

Show creators hated the laugh track, spurring a constant feud with network executives who believed audiences enjoyed the audio cues. To adjudicate the conflict, CBS held a controlled experiment in 1965 with its brand-new show *Hogan's Heroes*. The network tested two versions of the World War II comedy—one with canned laughter, one without. The test audiences overwhelmingly preferred the laugh-tracked show. Since then, nearly all CBS comedies have contained audience laughter.

Fake laughter was far from universal though. Many beloved shows, including *The Mary Tyler Moore Show, Friends, Cheers,* and *Seinfeld,* used studio audiences for most of their laughter, only adding dashes of the canned stuff through *sweetening* (that's the term of art).[82]

---

82 *Sweetening* is demonstrated with dismay in *Annie Hall* when Woody Allen witnesses laugh tracks being added to a live broadcast in a Los Angeles television studio. The term is also invoked in other commercial arts. When Kiss's *Alive!* was released in 1975, it claimed to be a live album but many tracks were clearly *sweetened,* as they say, with studio overdubs to sharpen the sound.

But laughter of all kinds—live or tracked—was becoming the joke of the sitcom industry, as a morose aura started to envelop the merriment. An oft-told anecdote asserted that due to track age, the laff box contained the chortles of dead people. The canard seems to have originated with Jim Carrey as Andy Kaufman in *Man on the Moon* (1999), who ad libbed this bit of dialogue about sitcoms like *Taxi*:

> It's just stupid jokes and canned laughter! And you don't know why it's there, but it's there! And it's dead people laughing, did you know that? Those people are dead![83]

It might have been true in the '70s, but the claim is likely not accurate today, as audio engineers are known to assiduously update their libraries with new snorts and snickers.

Regardless, the stench of dead laughter was in the air. Starting in the early aughts, shows began to jettison the laugh track, as most celebrated comedies of the era—*The Office, Arrested Development, Curb Your Enthusiasm, Orange Is the New Black, 30 Rock, Community, Louie, Modern Family*—abandoned the cheesy blandishment. Some programs maintain laugh tracks today (especially those on CBS), and they do tend to get good ratings. In fact, one can almost divide sitcoms into two categories—"critically acclaimed" versus "high ratings"—on whether they use a laugh track. As a generalization, shows that cozen a laugh from the viewer perform better in the ratings but seldom win Emmys.

Although widely derided, the laugh track served its purpose. Television began as a medium for viewing live events with an audience (essentially theater-at-a-distance), and it took decades for television to evolve into its own medium. The laff box allowed producers to literally *play* the audience, like an organ. Perhaps it was synthetic, but the technical innovation put the audience into the tube, creating a more communal experience in our homes. Today, that role—incorporating a disembodied audience—is played by social media. LOL.

SEE ALSO: CANNED HEAT; CLAPTER; CLAQUE; CRISIS ACTORS; THE FOURTH WALL; NODDY; POTEMKIN VILLAGE

LEROY, JT

At age five, he was raped. By age eleven, as a transgender hustler, he started turning tricks at truck stops in West Virginia. At fourteen, he was homeless and addicted to drugs, and by sixteen, he was institutionalized, for the first time. Somewhere along the way, he became HIV-positive, probably through his mother's boyfriend. Because his mother burned his penis with a car cigarette lighter, or because he paid a biker to switchblade his genitals, or because of AIDS, his growth was stunted and puberty forestalled, but he took hormones in preparation for a sex change. The story of Jeremiah "Terminator" LeRoy sounds too horrific to be true, because it was too horrific to be true.

JT LeRoy was a fabrication, started around 1999 by Laura Albert, a thirtysomething phone sex worker in San Francisco. Through three acclaimed books of fictional memoir, one of which was titled *The Heart Is Deceitful Above All Things*, Albert transformed LeRoy into one of the biggest literary sensations of the noughties. It was an amazing feat, matched only by her uncanny charm at converting LeRoy into celebrity arm candy.

At early readings, a coterie of famous admirers, including Winona Ryder, Matthew Modine, Lou

---

[83] Another oft-cited (but inaccurate) source for this old saw is Chuck Palahniuk's 2002 novel *Lullaby*: "Most of the laugh tracks on television were recorded in the early 1950s. These days, most of the people you hear laughing are dead."

Reed, and Nancy Sinatra, would recite her work.[84] But Albert eventually needed a puppet on the stage, someone to embody the It-Boy role at public appearances, so she hired her sister-in-law, Savannah Knoop, to play JT IRL. Affecting a country-fried accent, Knoop donned a preposterous blond wig (invoking Andy Warhol) and huge plastic sunglasses (à la Jackie O) in public appearances and plentiful photo spreads. In retrospect, that anyone fell for this ruse is amazing.

Back at home, Albert gave good phone to her new celebrity besties—Courtney Love, Tatum O'Neal, Shirley Manson, Carrie Fisher, Tom Waits, and many others. She received career advice from Bono. For Gus Van Sant, she wrote an early draft of the script for *Elephant*. Asia Argento made one of her books into a movie while Knoop became her lover. She was published in *Spin*, *The Stranger*, *Interview*, and *McSweeney's* and became a contributing editor at glossy magazines with nervy names like *7x7*, *Black-Book*, and *i-D*. Only one celebrity was privy to the secret: Billy Corgan. He described the spectacle as "like being inside the Magic Kingdom."

After seven years of running the con, her delicately crafted world finally fell apart in 2006, when her husband (*oh yes*, she had a husband) outed her in a *New York Times* story. To this day, Albert claims that she merely imagineered the character to explore aspects of her personality. To her, "LeRoy was real." But LeRoy was also her "avatar," her "PHANTOM LIMB," her "pseudonym," and her "veil"—all epithets she used to depict her creation.

A word Albert does not appreciate is "hoax." In the documentary *Author: The JT LeRoy Story* (2016), she snaps at a writer, "A *metaphor* is different than a fucking *hoax*." (She prefers the more forgiving term *myth*.) That is some crafty dissembling, but she has a modest argument. The books were, technically, identified as "Fiction" in the bookstore.[85] But how much did LeRoy's contrived backstory and Knoop's coy performance contribute to the enjoyment of those books? And how did the swaths of deceived "friends" feel about the illusion? And what are the ethics of manufacturing a rags-to-riches story in places where such opportunities are fleeting? Maybe "hoax" isn't exact, but "prank" or "spoof" seem too modest of terms for such overt deceit.

"What's being thrown out there is Multiple Personality Disorder," she says near the end of the same documentary. "But that ain't it. I am pulling the switch. I am making the decision to go to a different rail. I don't know what the classification is. But I can tell you one thing, it is not a *hoax*."

Today, visiting the website JTLeRoy.com redirects you to LauraAlbert.org.

SEE ALSO: CONFIDENCE GAME; A MILLION LITTLE PIECES; TATE, NAT; ROBINSON CRUSOE; SLASHFIC; SOKAL HOAX; UNRELIABLE NARRATOR; WARHOL, ANDY

LIE-TO-CHILDREN

Lie-to-children is a theory of education in which the truth is fudged for the greater purpose of elucidating complex subject matter. Usually delivered to students in the form of simplistic analogies, lies-to-children can also thrive outside the classroom, particularly in pop science books that disseminate

---

84 Ryder enjoyed telling the story of how she met prefame LeRoy, still a teenage street urchin, outside of the opera *La Bohème*. "He was a total ragamuffin."

85 Albert can be found strenuously arguing this point, under a pseudonym, on the "Talk" tab of JT LeRoy's Wikipedia page. She has relentlessly worked to keep LeRoy in the context of harmless worldbuilding, far away from uncouth fabulists like James Frey.

generalizations to demystify arcane subjects for lay-people.[86]

In school, the fibs are told most often in science classes. In high school physics, for instance, the atom is commonly characterized as electrons swirling around a nucleus of protons and neutrons. This reductive depiction (the Bohr model) is easy to visualize, partially because teenagers are already familiar with the concept of planets orbiting the sun. But the solar system analogy belies a more convoluted reality (the atomic orbital model) that involves a probabilistic arrangement of electrons. Even though Niels Bohr, the physicist who formulated the "solar system atom," would later disavow his own subatomic architecture, it persists in classrooms today, mostly because flying orbs are easier to explain than quantum theory.

Other educational white lies include the universality of Newton's laws (as Einstein showed, the laws break down at the margins), the 476 CE fall of the Roman Empire (the eastern half of the empire endured until the fifteenth century), George Washington Carver inventing peanut butter (he didn't; he performed massive research on legumes that led to its invention), Eurocentric flat maps (despite how it looks, Africa is 14 times bigger than Greenland), and the impossibility of square rooting a negative number (you can do it, but it yields a difficult-to-explain *imaginary number*). The lie-to-children theory holds that these equivocations are necessary evils, a kind of heuristic device for later revealing deeper concepts.

Introduced by scientists Jack Cohen and Ian Stewart, lie-to-children gained traction as a pedagogical concept around the release of *The Science of Discworld* (1999), coauthored by fantasy author Terry Pratchett, who was prone to introduce a quirky analogy followed by a rejoinder, "That's completely incorrect, but it's a lie you can understand." The authors would go on to suggest that all systems for groking reality rely upon such falsifiable narratives. Given how little we know about the universe, science itself might be the best example of lie-to-children—a story that helps us apprehend a nebulous universe.[87]

As *Calvin & Hobbes* frequently suggested, not only is lying to kids extremely fun, but veracity often enters through the door of allusion:

> Calvin: "Dad, what causes wind?"
> Dad: "Trees sneezing."
> Calvin: "Really?"
> Dad: "No, but the truth is more complicated."

SEE ALSO: AGNOTOLOGY; CUNNINGHAM'S LAW; NOBLE LIE; SANTA CLAUS; SNIPE HUNT

LONG, HUEY

Huey Long was a grifter politician who for a long time seemed like the closest America would ever get to electing a populist authoritarian as president.

He hailed from Louisiana, where in 1928 the former travelling salesman became the youngest governor in state history. A charismatic orator, Long

---

86 A hurtful person might say this entire compendium dabbles in such mendacity-to-laypeople.

87 Most academic fields have developed an unofficial vernacular for expressing their queasiness about relying upon narrative shortcuts to convey reality. In statistics, the aphorism "all models are lies" is often dispatched in service of voicing uncertainty. Economists speak of *stylized facts*, or broad generalization of data that are true in essence but not always in practice. Evolutionary biologists use the derogatory term *just-so stories* to designate quaint narratives about human behavior. And in philosophy, the concept of *Wittgenstein's ladder* derives from the philosopher's statement that while his propositions might be incorrect, they provide the ladder upon which to climb to a higher level of understanding. Wittgenstein would later repudiate his own makeshift scaffold, stating, "Anything that can be reached with a ladder does not interest me."

professed himself the savior of the poor and power-less, drawing huge crowds from miles around with electrifying campaign speeches that mixed hillbilly logic with ruthless demagoguery. ("So shot through with gross error," wrote the New Orleans *Picayune* of his speeches, and "so careless of truth generally.")

Once in government, the folksy huckster turned into a tyrant, quickly accruing political power through a system of embezzlement, bribes, and brute force. He instituted an infamous policy whereby all state employees were required to tithe 10 percent of their salaries to his campaign. Paradoxically, he also did more for the poor and uneducated than anyone before or possibly since. He cut taxes on farmers, brought free textbooks to schools, promoted adult literacy, and lowered utility bills. But he was wildly unscrupulous, skimming 20 percent off the top of all state contracts. When the legislature moved to impeach him for corruption, Huey paid off fifteen senators to pledge their fealty. Thwarting impeach-ment only made him more ruthless.

The only thing Long loved more than talking was building, and he was profuse at both. His admin-istration erected 111 bridges and paved more than 3,000 miles of road. He gave LSU a new campus, demanded a new governor's mansion, and built the tallest state capitol building in the country (where he was eventually assassinated). In four years as governor, he spent more than his predecessors did in twelve. In a brassy display of power, he won the 1930 election to become the U.S. senator of Louisiana *but still remained its governor.*

He was a brutish despot who would dragoon polit-ical opponents and seduce the masses with fatuous bunkum. He was completely unstoppable and on his way to Washington.

It is impossible not to pause here and acknowl-edge the obvious: Yes, he is reminiscent of Don-ald Trump. Demagogues often exhibit shameless ambition and share nationalist rhetoric, but the similarities between these two does not stop with generalities. Long also disingenuously claimed to descend from humble beginnings—a log cabin, no

less—which would be true if the wood in his family's manor counted as logs. Similarly, Long delivered vituperative speeches that hectored political oppo-nents. "Always take the offensive," he was fond of saying. "The defensive ain't worth a damn." He also loved attention but hated the press, so he started his own newspaper, the *Louisiana Progress*, which he distributed via the state police. (He regularly dis-patched the state militia as his personal police force.) Even more redolent of our media environment, Long had the backing of popular conspiratorial radio host Father Coughlin, who helped circulate his populist jingoism. Neither a conservative nor a liberal, Long savaged those in his own party in fulminating speech-es. A master of abuse, he created nicknames for his foes ("Buzzard Buck," "Old Feather Duster," "Colonel Bow Wow"), which he repeated over and over until they stuck. In one of his favorite campaign trail bits, Long asked his audience how many good suits they had at home. *Four? How about three? Two? Can you afford two good suits? That crook J. P. Morgan owns 100 suits!* Long himself loved colorful ties and easily owned one hundred suits. This cockeyed candor is why common folk adored him—he was a poor per-son's idea of a rich person.

Long also had a spiffy four-word catchphrase. Even more lyrical than *Make America Great Again*, his bromide was *Every Man a King*. Just as Trump pinched his slogan from Ronald Reagan, Long lifted his from William Jennings Bryan, who ended his version with . . . *But No One Wears a Crown*. Long, however, had his own idea about who should wear the crown. (*Every Man a King* was also the title of his first autobiography; his second, *My First Days in the White House*.) To top off the uncanny parallels, there were investigations into his taxes.

Although he supported FDR in his 1932 presi-dential bid, Long quickly turned on the New Deal, ranting that it was not bold enough to bring America out of the Depression. FDR privately called Long one the most dangerous men in America, and it became obvious the parvenu would run for president. Under another pithy pitch, *Share Our Wealth*, Long promised everyone a universal basic income of $2,500 and disallowed anyone from making more than $1 million per year. With the tax bounty, Long promised free healthcare, free education, and mandatory four-week vacations. Economists quickly pointed out that the numbers didn't add up, but in the middle of the Great Depression, the populist message would have posed an immense challenge to FDR.

Only seven years after first being elected governor, and just a month after announcing his candidacy for president, Long was assassinated, in 1935, by a respected Baton Rouge doctor, Carl Weiss. Copious conspiracy theories cast doubt, but the most accepted historical account is that Weiss killed Long because he was about to canton his father-in-law, a judge and a political enemy, out of his district. Long had also spread a rumor that the doctor's wife wasn't white but had "coffee blood." That race-baiting probably didn't help his ire. But the murder surprised no one. Everyone in Louisiana had been hypothesizing the assassination of the charlatan for years.

"God, don't let me die," gasped the mad king in his last breath. "I have so much to do."[88]

SEE ALSO: GERRYMANDERING; KAYFABE; SWIFTBOATING

LOREM IPSUM

Lorem ipsum is gibberish text used as filler copy by graphic designers.

When laying out a page, designers often insert paragraphs of the placeholder text into a document, to be later replaced with real text. The standard lorem ipsum boilerplate begins:

> Lorem ipsum dolor sit amet, consectetur adipiscing elit, sed do eiusmod tempor incididunt ut labore et dolore magna aliqua. . . .

It's pseudo-Latin mumbo jumbo, but the first two words translate to "pain itself." The text derives from an obscure philosophical work by Cicero, *De Finibus* ("On the End"), but the words are mostly scrambled into gobbledygook. The origin of the dummy text is unknown, though it seems to have started in the 1970s and was popularized in the desktop publishing software revolution of the 1980s.

Because it is incomprehensible, designers use lorem ipsum to emphasize the visual qualities of a page over its words. It mimics writing without being writing.

SEE ALSO: 555-2368; BACKWARDS R; DARK ENERGY; DOE, JOHN; JABBERWOCKY; PHOTOSHOPPING; SUPERCALIFRAGILISTICEXPIALIDOCIOUS

---

88 If you can track it down, the essential documentary is *Huey Long* (1986) made for PBS by Ken Burns. It contains interviews with family members, downtrodden locals, and journalists from the era. The other indispensable historical account is *Huey Long* (1981), a biography by T. Harry Williams that won the Pulitzer Prize and National Book Award. And, of course, there is *All the King's Men* (1946), Robert Penn Warren's fictionalized version, made into a movie that won the Best Picture Oscar in 1949.

M

MANCHURIAN CANDIDATE

Strictly speaking, a Manchurian candidate is a political figure who has been brainwashed into carrying out attacks on his own nation. But the term is also used colloquially to describe any politico turned puppet—a government official under the control of a foreign power.

Before its idiomatic turn, *The Manchurian Candidate* was a Cold War artifact—a 1959 Richard Condon novel adapted into a 1962 John Frankenheimer movie starring Frank Sinatra. The tense plot pivots on a decorated POW who is secretly brainwashed during the Korean War and returns home a commie sleeper agent. Considered controversial at the time, the political thriller was censored in much of communist Eastern Europe. Though it bombed at the American box office, the film cultivated cult status through a series of uncanny historical serendipities:

1. It was released in the middle of the Cuban Missile Crisis.
2. It depicted a presidential assassination scene a year before JFK was killed.
3. Kennedy helped get the movie released.
4. A rumor (inaccurate) claimed that Sinatra pulled the movie from circulation after his friend's assassination.
5. Frankenheimer, the director, was actually with RFK on the night of JFK's assassination.
6. A conspiracy theory contends that Lee Harvey Oswald was inspired by the film.

One irresistible historical hypothesis nominates *Catcher in the Rye* (1951) as a Manchurian catalyst. According to the theory, the adolescent ramblings of Holden Caulfield contain subliminal murderous commands that can be triggered after CIA brainwashing. Sure, it reeks of paranoiac voodoo, but disparate political assassins—Lee Harvey Oswald, Mark David Chapman, John Hinckley—were all legitimate fans of the Salinger novel, and the CIA really did perform mind control experiments through the 1950s (under the codename Project MKUltra), so regardless of whether embedded subconscious assassination triggers are legit, we know our intelligence agencies once hoped they could be.

During the Obama administration, crackpots claimed the president was some sort of Islamic version of a Manchurian candidate. More recently, the phrase has resurfaced among those who hypothesize the current regime contains a patsy compromised by the Kremlin.

SEE ALSO: DEEP STATE; FALSE FLAG OPERATION; HYPNOSIS; JOSEPH MCCARTHY'S LIST; REICHSTAG FIRE; SUBLIMINAL ADVERTISING; TROJAN HORSE

MANDELA EFFECT

Do you remember when Nelson Mandela died in a South African prison in the 1980s? If that sounds accurate, and a few internet strangers support your memory, despite every historical record saying the anti-apartheid revolutionary died in 2013, there is only one conclusion to draw: You exist in a simultaneous parallel dimension, inadvertently rendered by a glitch in the computer code that runs the universe.

Not to be mistaken for Cannabic Solipsism,[89] your alternate memory is proof of the Mandela Effect.

Large groups of people—others, *just like you*—have coagulated on the internet to espouse this daft theory, that the fabric of reality must have shifted at some point in the past. In a robust Reddit community called */r/MandelaEffect*, similar conflicting memories, incongruent with *what they would have you believe*, are reported in a steady stream. If you would testify to having seen a '90s movie called *Shazaam* starring the comedian Sinbad, or if you would swear the BERENSTAIN BEARS was really spelled *Berenstein Bears*, or if you would bet your presidency that Muslims were seen celebrating on the streets of New Jersey after 9/11—this is the antic attic for you.

This subreddit has it all. Here, a pugnacious Berenstein Truther will link to the astrophysicist Neil deGrasse Tyson, predicting the odds at "50/50" that we are living in a computer simulation, triggering a pile-on of meme quotes from Nick Bostrom, the

89 *Cannabic Solipsism* describes "the adolescent pot-smoker's fear that his own inner experience is both private and unverifiable." The handy term was coined by David Foster Wallace in a footnote to *The Atlantic* essay "Tense Present," which describes the condition as the "lay-philosophizing about the weird privacy of our own mental states."

Oxford philosopher who has claimed that human consciousness is likely the apparition of an advanced civilization. After a brief digression over how quantum mechanics relates to Kit-Kat (can the hyphen simultaneously *exist* and *not exist*?), another pushy conspiracist barges in, fulminating about the Large Hadron Collider shifting the space-time continuum. Then, because he heard a loud spooky noise, an overzealous Snopesplainer arrives, diagnosing everyone with confabulation syndrome and "dropping fact bombs" (i.e., posting links to articles). At this invective, the Shazaam Truthers lose their shit, while a cultural think piecer sneaks into the thread, linking to their essay that dismisses the Mandela Effect as a "disease of millennials" who are susceptible to misplaced nostalgia (hm, good point?). Finally, the Encyclopedist saunters in, months later, digesting it all and grading it a B+ episode of *Black Mirror*.

SEE ALSO: ALT-HISTORY; BERENSTAIN BEARS CONSPIRACY; PLATO'S CAVE; RASHOMON EFFECT; RETCONNING; SNOPES; TOMMY WESTPHALL UNIVERSE; TRUMAN SYNDROME; WOOZLE EFFECT;

MANNING, DAVID

"A SEXY, SCARY THRILL RIDE!"
—David Manning, *Ridgefield Press*

"ANOTHER WINNER!"
—David Manning, *Ridgefield Press*

"ONE HELL OF A SCARY RIDE!"
—David Manning, *Ridgefield Press*

Trumpeting praise from atop posters and print ads, those movie reviewer quotes, with regal majuscule emphasis, hailed now-forgotten movies (respectively, *The Forsaken*, *The Animal*, and *Hollow Man*, all released in 2000 or 2001). All three flicks bombed, commercially and critically.[90] No one seemed to enjoy these movies, except that one persistent critic, David Manning from *Ridgefield Press*, whose name kept appearing in promotions.

This critic had idiosyncratic taste. From a medieval adventure comedy, *A Knight's Tale*, he handpicked a promising young turk, Heath Ledger ("This year's hottest new star!"). Good catch, but the reviewer also adored a snoozy survivalist thriller, *Vertical Limit*. Strangest of all, the critic praised only movies produced by Columbia Pictures. Finally, someone (a reporter from *Newsweek*) called the *Ridgefield Press*, a small weekly based in rural Connecticut, to find out why. The paper said it had no idea. They didn't even publish movie reviews. They also didn't know David Manning.

You saw it coming—the critic was fake. Devised by two young marketing execs at Sony (the parent company of Columbia Pictures), "David Manning" probably seemed a harmless invention. *Movie critics are interchangeable cogs in the movie promotion machine*, they might have reasoned. *Why not just fabricate our own critic? Movie poster quotes are out-of-context filler anyway!* While ethically vulgar, the logic was not completely unsound. Real critics were often sent on expensive junkets, and their quotes parsed through grammatical jiu-jitsu. ("Awesomely boring," a reviewer might write, but translated to a poster, it became simply, "AWESOME!") Cutting out the middleman probably seemed like it would simplify what everyone acknowledged was a farce.

Annoyed moviegoers disagreed. Two of them filed a class action suit against Sony, claiming they saw *A*

---

90 *The Forsaken*, a disorienting study of knighted vampires from the crusades, has a putrefied score of 7 percent on Rotten Tomatoes. *Hollow Man*, directed by Paul Verhoeven, and starring Kevin Bacon and Elisabeth Shue, is slightly less fetid, at 27 percent.

Knight's Tale because of Manning's review. That may have been a stretch, but was not nearly as provocative as Sony's defense. The studio claimed it was their First Amendment right to lie—misinformation as free speech!

In an out-of-court settlement, Sony ultimately agreed to pay $5 to each dissatisfied cinephile who saw Manning-reviewed films. Few people saw those movies in the first place, so the refunds tallied to only $1.5 million. The two executive fabulists who concocted David Manning were reprimanded with one month of unpaid leave. One of them is now the Head of Marketing at Universal Pictures. *Two thumbs up!*

SEE ALSO: COLEMAN, ALLEGRA; LEROY, JT; MOCKBUSTER; SMITHEE, ALAN; WORK OF FICTION DISCLAIMER

MARCH OF TIME, THE

Imagine a news network announcing an outlandish new type of show. Instead of *reporting* the day's events from tapes and interviews, this program will instead be *re-creating* the news. Like a theatrical production, this audacious show hires actors to impersonate the politicians, celebrities, and intellectuals of the day. To intensify the action, it will be a live broadcast. This theoretical show might sound vaguely like *Saturday Night Live*, but pretend it is not a comedy. This is a serious drama—the content is ripped (and reenacted) from real headlines.

This fanciful show not only once existed but was among the most popular programs of its era. Launched in 1931 on CBS radio, *The March of Time* re-created current events with elaborate sound effects, bombastic music, and shrewd impersonations. The "news dramatization" appeared each month, casting nascent stars (Art Carney, John McIntire, Orson Welles) as prominent figures of the day (FDR, Churchill, Freud, Gandhi, Hitler, Stalin).

Initially devised as an advertising campaign for the fledgling *Time* magazine, each episode drew material from the current issue on newsstands.

The show straddled acts of reflecting reality (journalism) and creating it (entertainment). When transcripts of news events were available, the actors performed them verbatim, but writers frequently had to invent dialogue from scratch. Because the show hired top acting talent, the impressions were remarkably accurate. Despite warning users of the dramatization, listeners often mistook the aural doppelgangers for the real person. The White House even asked the show to cease impersonating President Roosevelt because people believed the imitator to be the real deal.

Theatrics were often prioritized over accuracy. When the *Hindenburg* crashed in 1937, just two hours before air time, the show hustled to reproduce the disaster. Despite having not yet seen or heard the crash, *The March of Time* re-created the tragedy with audio effects and reenacted chaos.

Of all its quirky qualities, *The March of Time* might be most remembered for its narration—a blend of gutsy bombast and stilted novelese over the shriek of heralding trumpets. In 1935, when the radio show was adapted into a "newsreel" format for movie theaters, the punchy narration became even more pronounced. Despite working on the radio show for three years, Orson Welles later satirized the bellicose style in *Citizen Kane* with reels from his parodic show, *News on the March*, which punctuate the film with didactic grandeur.

The ethical implications of documentary reenactments have been a fraught topic ever since. When used honestly, a reenactment can open a viewer's mind to explore unseen details.[91] Their history, however, has more missteps than successes. Crime stories seem particularly besmirched with exploiting reenactments, often as a method for situating viewers inside a deviant mind or a felonious act. In a notorious instance, the E! Network in 2005 created *The Michael Jackson Trial*, a nightly simulacrum of the day's court proceedings based upon transcripts from the pop star's child molestation case. The reenactment was widely panned as exploitative, and, more tragically, pretty boring.

SEE ALSO: CRISIS ACTOR; F FOR FAKE; TRUTH CLAIM; THE WAR OF THE WORLDS; YELLOW JOURNALISM

MASKED MARAUDERS, THE

The Masked Marauders were a supergroup created in 1969 by Bob Dylan, Mick Jagger, John Lennon, Paul McCartney, and a mystery drummer (rumored to be Ringo Starr). They released one eponymous album, a bootleg that *Rolling Stone* praised as "more than a way of life; it is life." The life-affirming sentiment was remarkable, as the critic was actually the band.

There were no Marauders. The review was written by Greil Marcus, using the pseudonym T. M. Christian, as a parody of several trends of the moment: pompous supergroups, pompous bootlegs, and super pompous rock reviews. The average rock music fan, however, loves pomposity, so intrigued readers immediately started calling the *Rolling Stone* office to ask where they could purchase the record.

At this point, the story usually ends with the satirist confessing their zany prank. But Marcus took an unusual next step. Rather than admit to the hoax, he created the band to personify it. ("This is stupid, let's make it stupider," Marcus later explained.[92]) He recruited a real skiffle band from Berkeley to record the fake album, with each song painfully matching its description in the review.

If these are the results, lesson learned: Never bestow a rock critic with the power to create music. The album opens with a Jagger knockoff complaining "I Can't Get No Nookie," and it only deteriorates from there. If you have been waiting a lifetime for ten minutes of a random hippie impersonating Dylan impersonating Donovan, track 8 ("Season of the Witch") is your personal nirvana.

Released on Warner Bros., which signed the band for $15,000, the record spent twelve weeks on the *Billboard* charts, eventually selling more than 100,000 copies. "In a world of sham," wrote that illustrious critic T. M. Christian in the liner notes, "the Masked Marauders, bless their hearts, are the genuine article."

SEE ALSO: THE ARCHIES; THE BUGGS; MILLI VANILLI; NAKED CAME THE STRANGER; TUPAC HOLOGRAM

MECHANICAL TURK

Wheeled on casters into the Viennese court, the wooden cabinet resembled any stately eighteenth-century credenza, except of course for the conspicuous turbaned mannequin that hovered from above. Festooned in an ermine-trimmed robe, the carved torso waved a long smoking pipe over a chessboard like an oriental sorcerer. After introducing the Turk to the audience, its operator spun the cabinet around on its wheels, dramatically opening doors and drawers, shining a candle into crannies. *As you can see, no secret nooks.* Inside, brass sprockets and

---

91 For a persuasive overview of their value, see "Play It Again, Sam," a series of essays about reenactments in the *New York Times* by the documentarian Errol Morris.

92 He said this in the unusual setting of NBC's now-defunct prime-time news magazine show *Rock Center with Brian Williams*, which profiled the band hoax in an April 2013 episode.

iron cogs appeared fitted to contemplate opponent strategies and churn out competing chess moves. Closing the gearbox, the operator inserted a large key into the mechanism, wound it up, and stood back. From behind its black beard, the Ottoman automaton scried the board as though convening a séance. Swinging its robotic arm, move by move, the Turk positioned its ivory army across the sprawling checkered battlefield. As if by an occult hand, *rook takes bishop, checkmate.*

Starting in 1770, the Automaton Chess Player, as it was known in its day, dazzled audiences in Vienna, where it was invented by one Wolfgang von Kempelen (could there be a more exquisite name for an illusionist engineer?). The contraption simulated a daunting game of chess by stowing a chessmaster in a hidden chamber. (Magician's Code be damned: The chessmaster controlled the automaton. Magnets and strings helped move the pieces. The gears were an inoperable red herring; the cabinet, a reworked magician's case.)

In its long life, spanning nearly a century, the Mechanical Turk performed for a motley sort across two continents. During an early tour of Europe, the Turk defeated Benjamin Franklin in Paris (1783). When the automaton faced off against Napoleon Bonaparte (1809), the emperor made a false move and the machine motioned for him to play again. The tyrant met his waterloo after trying to cheat two more times. In London (1819), a young inventor, Charles Babbage, saw the automaton in action, and a few years later began work on the Difference Engine, the first mechanical computer. The Turk eventually crossed the Atlantic, debuting in Boston (1826), becoming a phenomenon in New York City, and slowly working its way south. Before sailing to Cuba, an automaton performance in Richmond (1835) elicited a long essay in the *Southern Literary Messenger* by Edgar Allan Poe, who speculated on the inner workings of the contraption. (He eerily concluded, "The operations of the automaton are regulated by mind, and nothing else.") Finally, after entertaining monarchs, politicians, tycoons, artists, celebrities, and plenty of hoi polloi, the automaton died a quiet death (1854) in a Philadelphia fire.[93]

It was a full life—impressing its first audiences

---

93 Details of the Turk vary slightly among the many books on the subject. This account quickly summarizes Tom Standage's *The Turk* (2002).

at the dawn of the Industrial Revolution, spreading its whimsy into the Victorian era, and eventually landing in the inchoate New World. Was the Turk just an elaborate magic trick? Or was it an impressive feat of technology? In a sense, both. Illusionism and engineering were converging and would eventually spawn the new art-science known as HCI, or human-computer interaction. Though an obvious case of technical skulduggery, the Mechanical Turk helped inspire the computer revolution and laid the groundwork for how we would later interact with machines.

In an unexpected twist, artificiality was the Turk's most lasting quality, its unforeseen futurism. Of course, the artifice of a turbaned effigy was pure theater—a gimmick to carry the gag. But the same could be said of personal computing today, where anthropomorphized characters sustain an illusory reciprocity with their owners. (The faux-intimacy of today's personal assistants—Siri, Echo, and the like—is undoubtedly only the first step of our CYBORG future.) As Arthur C. Clarke would opine much later, "Any sufficiently advanced technology is indistinguishable from magic." And like magic, a real mechanical Turk would eventually rise. In 1997, IBM's chess-playing computer, Deep Blue, beat champion Garry Kasparov in a six-game match. It was a wake-up call to humanity, but in a way, nothing had changed since the Turk: Kasparov accused Deep Blue of cheating, claiming humans had intervened and guided its decisions.

But the machine had learned how to play the human game. It declined a rematch. *Checkmate.*

SEE ALSO: CARDIFF GIANT; CYBORG; HOUDINI, HARRY; HUMBUGGERY; ORDER OF THE OCCULT HAND; TROJAN HORSE; TAMAGOTCHI EFFECT; TURING TEST; VAN DOREN, CHARLES; VOIGHT-KAMPFF MACHINE

MEME MAGIC

Meme Magic is one of those dumb internet things you are probably better off not knowing about, but you're here now, so what can you do?

The core tenet of this hocus-pocus belief system is that certain internet activities have the ability to alter the fabric of reality. How does cloddish online behavior transcend its meager virtual existence and have a substantial impact on the real world? Through memes. (No, seriously, that's what they say.)

This occult philosophy reached apotheosis when it used internet memes to transubstantiate a certain unsuspecting real estate tycoon into the office of president of the United States. How? Not by voicing populist issues like income inequality. Not through campaigning or activism. Not even through intimidation or fraud. According to these neckbeards, Donald Trump was elected "God Emperor" (their title) by being *memed* into office. (They also really say that. "We memed Trump into the White House." LOL?)

This witchcraft was invented on 4chan, the virtual home of seemingly dozens who believe their assembly line of image macros can literally alter the flow of time and space. During the 2016 election, these warlocks imagined every news event was the outcome of their image board sorcery. Through memetic warfare, *they made it happen.* They trolled their ideas into reality.

Pre-Trump, when Meme Magic was just getting its footing, an oft-cited instance of its synchromysticism was a December 2015 thread on the 4chan music board that questioned the health of Lemmy Kilmister. A few hours later, the Motörhead leadman was proclaimed dead. Chilling, right? Most would say this was, at most, an uncanny coincidence, but the Meme Magicians claimed that they reached out from the internet and *made it happen.*

SEE ALSO: BARNUM EFFECT; INTERNET TROLL; PAREIDOLIA; THE RED PILL; SLENDERMAN

MERE-EXPOSURE EFFECT

As you walk by a coworker's cubicle, the sound of music flits toward your ear. It is, unmistakably, that brand-new Taylor Swift song, a dollop of irritating pablum you have decided, preemptively, to hate. Entering the elevator, there it is again—that banal little earworm, burrowing into your skull, like a sonic larva. And again, on the radio during the drive home, that infectious pop twang, which causes your foot to tap, uncontrollably. When you arrive at home, your roommate asks, "Have you heard the new Taylor Swift single yet?" After a pause, you say, "Yeah, it's great!" You wonder how this happened so quickly.

Psychologists, as usual, propose an answer. They call it the *mere-exposure effect*, which is the simple notion that the more you see and hear something, the more you like it. In other words, familiarity breeds affection. Extensive research has gone into the phenomenon, demonstrating how one's opinions about nearly any stimuli—curious sounds, new faces, foreign words, odd geometric shapes—might start negative, but with increased exposure will turn positive. Con artists are known to exploit the principle by establishing familiarity with a mark before turning a grift.

Close cousins of the con men, advertising executives also find inspiration in the mere-exposure effect. Studies show that simply hearing a brand name can make the product more attractive when later seeing it on the supermarket shelf. By repeating commercials, marketers can implant a "memory trace" onto the minds of consumers, which subconsciously guides their future behavior.

Exactly how much repetition is *too much* is a less studied area.

SEE ALSO: BELLMAN'S FALLACY; CONFIDENCE GAME; PRODUCT PLACEMENT; SUBLIMINAL ADVERTISING; VIRAL MARKETING

METHOD, THE

Method acting, known colloquially as "The Method" to its dramaturgical acolytes, is a training technique in which an actor pretends to be an imaginary character in real life to become an imaginary character in pretend life.

SEE ALSO: CLAQUE; CRISIS ACTORS; THE FOURTH WALL; KULESHOV EFFECT; MOIROLOGIST; UNCANNY VALLEY

MIKU, HATSUNE

"Now listen to me," said host David Letterman, coming out of a commercial break. "Our next guest is a computer-generated vocaloid, a personality from Japan." Cutting to the *Late Show* music stage, a diminutive turquoise hologram materialized— bug-eyed, in a skintight bodysuit, and flinging giant pigtails. Surrounded by a live band, the dithering creature giggled her way through the shiny-happy tune "Sharing the World," which might charitably be described as the Chipmunks chewing aluminum on Molly. As the roundelay chirped to a close, Letterman sauntered over to greet the virtual star, who gently smiled and dissipated into nothingness. "Like being on Willie Nelson's bus," said the host, in a wild mix of past and future, waving good night to the audience.[94]

It was the American television debut of Hatsune Miku, a Japanese pop star who had just concluded a sixteen-venue tour with Lady Gaga. Letterman's use of "vocaloid" was not some clever pun but a reference to an entire music genre composed with software (made by Yamaha) that synthesizes vocal tracks by simply typing in lyrics and selecting melodies. Each boxed software package is a voice; each voice, a character. Now with more than sixty characters/programs to choose from, fans have created

a sort of shared vocaloid universe, with backstories, romances, and fan art. This makes Miku, by far the biggest vocaloid, not only a pigtailed songstress but also the tool for creating the songs. She is both the instrument and the music. And her fans are both composers and consumers.

Miku was born on August 31, 2007, when Crypton Future Media took existing vocaloid software and rebranded it with her face. The company partnered with a manga artist for a cartoon representation of Miku but did not release any backstory or music. Fans took care of the rest. Instantly, thousands of Miku tracks appeared on Japanese iTunes and Amazon, while fan-made music videos flooded YouTube. Despite occasional celebrity collaborations (Lady Gaga, Pharrell), the Miku fanbase creates the vast majority of her work. Like a wiki pop star, she

is entirely crowdsourced. Anyone can update and contribute to the canon and myth.

At her live shows, Miku performs fan-written songs as a 3D hologram, controlled by a live band. (Gorillaz and the TUPAC HOLOGRAM use similar tech.) Her TOYETIC persona has been used to create and promote dolls, novels, manga, video games, anime, cars, endless tchotchkes, and lots and lots of porn. In this sense, she is like any pop celebrity, just intensified. Her persona might be crafted by fans, but it is no less authentic than the pop idols who cultivate an image on the #streets of Tumblr and TMZ. We already treat pop stars like hyperreal avatars, churning them into GIFs and hashtags, projections of our own hopes and fears. Miku is no less authentic than Lady Gaga or Beyoncé or Taylor Swift (or KISS or Daft Punk or Devo) (or Springsteen or Dylan or Prince)). They are

94 Miku's *Late Night* appearance took place in October 2014. One might guess it was the first time Letterman interviewed a virtual character, but in 1985 he interviewed Max Headroom, who appeared not by hologram but via a standard twenty-inch television sitting on his desk.

all meme factories, used and abused and disused by convenience. They are believable only if you choose to believe.

The difference is that Miku will eternally be sixteen years old and weigh ninety-two pounds. She will never shave her head or misplace her pet monkey or lose her mind on Twitter. She will never join the 27 Club or be tried for child molestation. It might seem that Miku tests our bounds of verisimilitude, but she will never push us over the edge of the UNCANNY VALLEY. Her otherworldly falsetto voice cannot be mistaken for the pristine warble of a Disney star, and unlike the TUPAC HOLOGRAM, she is no ersatz representation for someone lost. She is an exaggerated machine cartoon who will never disappoint her fans with celebrity hijinks. If she fails, it is because her fans failed. She is a simulacrum of nothing but her audience.

SEE ALSO: THE ARCHIES; AUTO-TUNE; AUTOMATED DIALOGUE REPLACEMENT; CYBORG; MILLI VANILLI; TOYETIC; TUPAC HOLOGRAM; UNCANNY VALLEY

MILLI VANILLI

The story of the rise and fall of Milli Vanilli is legendary, perhaps more renowned than that of Jesus, or possibly even the Beatles. The Faustian tale scarcely needs repeating. Yet for encyclopedic comprehensiveness, a quick recap: A dance pop duo from Munich rockets to the top of the charts with their debut album *Girl You Know It's True* in 1989, going septuple platinum and winning a Grammy for Best New Artist. At peak fame, their Svengali producer reveals that the pretty-boy performers (both aspiring break-dancers and models) are phonies. They sang not one note on their debut album and lip-synced their hits in concert. Eight years later, they become subjects in the very first episode of VH1's soapy bad-breaks doc,

Behind the Music. Within months, after serving time for robbery and drug convictions, one member dies from a pill overdose.

Those are the major plot points in the story arc that is Milli Vanilli. But this account fails to capture the loudest and most prominent aspect of the story—*outrage*. One might expect a band caught bluffing their voices to endure punchlines from late-night television, but the public flogging of Milli Vanilli far exceeded comic chiding. The duo became instant villains, symbols for the scourge of artificiality sweeping our culture. Cultural arbiters, always scouting for artistic infractions to polemicize, furiously cranked up the sanctimony, portraying the duo as harbingers of moral decline—a society on the brink of collapse under the weight of artificiality. In a panic of authenticity, Milli Vanilli was forced to return their Grammy statue, and twenty-seven lawsuits followed.

Of course, nothing about the music had changed. "Blame It on the Rain" was still corny R&B, "Baby Don't Forget My Number" was still tinny dance pop, and both (plus the title song) remained number one hits. It was still music that sounded like the bleep-bloop output of a machine, because like most pop music, it basically was. But their image had changed. They were now fraudulent, in the eyes of critics.

And mostly, only critics. Fans of the band were less riled by the disclosure. During a prescandal concert in Connecticut, a backing track started to skip at the most inopportune moment, repeating the line "girl you know it—," "girl you know it—," "girl you know it—," over and over. The audience seemed to care not one lick, but the malfunction set off a wave of media hysteria about musical integrity. The scolds had found their outlaw.

From the pool of hypocrisy, lawyers caught whiff. A class action fraud suit was filed against the band's record label. (The scent of money in the air, similar suits were filed against New Kids on the Block, Paula Abdul, and C+C Music Factory.) Milli Vanilli's label ultimately settled, issuing $3 refunds to album purchasers. Compared to attorney fees, the requested refunds were miniscule.

What the reactionary loudmouths conveniently overlooked is that pop music exists to manufacture image and fantasy. Artificiality has been its defining characteristic, since the beginning. Audrey Hepburn did not sing in *My Fair Lady*; Natalie Wood never crooned in *West Side Story*. Even the most credible acts—the Rolling Stones, David Bowie, Black Sabbath, the Sex Pistols—mimed their songs on *Top of the Pops*. Producers crafted countless musical waxworks, from the Backstreet Boys to Josie and the Pussycats. The Monkees, who were formed through television auditions, did not play their own instruments until their third record. Critics called them the Pre-Fab Four, but fans did not care.

Today more than ever, music is assembled in the studio, by a horde of producers and songwriters and engineers. Even critically regarded acts like Drake and Rihanna have collaborator credit sheets longer than Leviticus. Rumors of secret studio vocalists saturate the industry, but few have been caught. Everyone from Lady Gaga to Tim McGraw uses AUTO-TUNE. Vocal comping (splicing together the best syllables from hundreds of takes) is just how albums get made now. Even the debut Village People album used studio vocalists—and only two of the six members were even gay!

Everyone knows these things, yet the gotcha game of catch-the-lip-sync thrives. When Beyoncé performed at the 2013 inauguration of Barack Obama, sanctimony hit a high note over whether she lip-synced. Bey just brushed it off, because she could—lip-sync controversies had become a rite of passage. Whitney Houston weathered it after her iconic (prerecorded) national anthem at Super Bowl XXV. Britney Spears survived her 2007 VMA performance. Even Luciano Pavarotti endured a lip-sync scandal during the 2006 Winter Olympics opening ceremony.

Like clockwork, these incidents perennially draw lightning and ire. Fans shrug, while pious commentators who otherwise have no interest in pop music feign sacrilege at the *shocking, shocking* horror of deceptive entertainment. They demand fealty to some deity of realism, invoking the Milli Vanillains as gorgons who turned musicianship to stone.[95] Ultimately, the fakest thing about Milli Vanilli is the charade of outrage about Milli Vanilli.

Girl, you know it's true.

SEE ALSO: THE ARCHIES; AUTO-TUNE; AUTOMATED DIALOGUE REPLACEMENT; THE BUGGS; KARAOKE; MIKU, HATSUNE; TRIBUTE BANDS

MILLION LITTLE PIECES, A

A Million Little Pieces is a novel that was marketed as a memoir. If you google the title or its author today, a vast nebula of stories about Oprah Winfrey will curiously appear.

Published in 2003, the memoir depicts the harrowing experiences of James Frey, a twenty-three-year-old alcoholic who commits several crimes and copes with rehab in a tough guy persona. ("Fuck that bullshit" was his canny slogan.) The book initially achieved only moderate sales, but two years after its release, it skyrocketed to the top of the best-seller list when Oprah handpicked the gritty tale for her illustrious book club. After Frey appeared on her show, the book sold more than 5 million copies and topped the *New York Times* Best Sellers list for fifteen straight weeks.

Then in 2006, the muckraking website *The Smoking Gun* published a massive investigation, "A Million

---

95 Milli Vanilli still gets dragged into the most tedious battles of authenticity. During a beef with Drake about songwriting credits, the rapper Meek Mill disseminated Drake's face photoshopped onto the body of a Milli Vanilli member. And during the 2016 election, black scholar Cornel West cast Hillary Clinton as "the Milli Vanilli of American politics."

Little Lies," showing the book had serious factual flaws. Frey, it appeared, had fabricated or exaggerated vast swaths of his epic tale of criminality, loss, and emergency unanesthetized root canals. He was indeed an alcoholic who went to rehab—as a child of privilege, he matriculated to the swanky Hazelden Treatment Center outside Minneapolis—but now it seemed he had learned only one thing from his addiction: how to convincingly lie.

At first, Oprah prevaricated. Defending her princeling, she said the "underlying message of redemption" depicted in the book revealed an "essential truth." To her, the controversy was "much ado about nothing." What you *believe*, her sentiment seemed to imply, is more important than the *truth*.

In a rare lapse, Oprah was behind the curve on this one. Among the literati, a revolt against Frey was simmering. What started as modest indignation over fibs had turned into moral outrage over unconscionable mendacity. Pious editorials piled atop each other, dubbing Frey a dissembler, a charlatan, a phony-baloney scoundrel. Oprah was forced to respond.

She started with an apology to her viewers. "I made a mistake," she said on *Larry King Live*. "I left the impression that the truth does not matter. And I am deeply sorry about that, because that is not what I believe." Then she reinvited Frey onto her show, under the auspices of a discussion about "Truth in America." In a provocative twist, she was fibbing about the topic to get Frey and his publisher onto the show. Hell hath no fury like an Oprah scorned.

"James Frey is here," she begins, turning to her subject. "And I have to say it is difficult for me to talk to you because I feel really duped." Fists clenched, she eviscerates Frey, accusing him of extensive lying. His girlfriend did not hang herself, he did not spend months in jail, he did not have a root canal without anesthesia. *Liar, liar, pants on fire!*

Regarding the apocryphal root canal, Frey begins a penitent response. "Since that time, I've struggled with the idea of it—"

"No," Oprah pounces, "the *lie* of it. That's a lie. It's not an *idea*, James. That's a lie."

At the end of the hour-long whipping, Frey attempts contrition. "I feel like I came here, and I have been honest with you," he says. "I have, you know, essentially admitted to—"

"Lying," Oprah breaks in.

The interview was brutal. Some commenters judged Oprah's response as overly sanctimonious, a tactical maneuver to regain her moral clout. But most think pieces used her opprobrium to eulogize TRUTHINESS. "It was a huge relief," wrote Maureen Dowd in the *New York Times*, "after our long national slide into untruth and no consequences, into SWIFT BOATING and swift bucks, to see the Empress of Empathy icily hold someone accountable for lying."

The publisher was forced to offer a refund to readers who felt they had been defrauded. (To receive the refund, you had to submit a sworn statement saying you purchased the book believing it was a memoir.) Future editions of the book contained an apology from Frey. Never retracted, the book can still be found in the memoir section of most bookstores.

SEE ALSO: ALTERNATIVE FACTS; AUTOBIOGRAPHY OF HOWARD HUGHES; BLAIR, JAYSON; LEROY, JT; SLASHFIC; UNRELIABLE NARRATOR

MIMICRY

Long before *Lolita*, and even a few years before the age of Lolita, a young Vladimir Nabokov developed a fond interest in butterflies, catching fluttery Red Admirals and Swallowtails on his family's country estate outside Saint Petersburg. His entomological passion would eventually bring him to America, where he became curator of lepidoptery at Harvard Museum of Comparative Zoology. Here he would write that great psychological study *Lolita* while travelling around the country on butterfly-collecting trips.

His interests were diverse, but within biology Nabokov was specifically fascinated with *mimicry*, or the adaptive process by which one species impersonates another. It seemed magical: One organism (say, an ant or a mushroom) could over time adopt visual, auditory, chemical, tactile, and behavioral characteristics of another (maybe a tree or a caterpillar). In his memoir, *Speak, Memory,* Nabokov wrote passionately about this enigmatic slice of evolutionary biology:

> The mysteries of mimicry had a special attraction for me. Its phenomena showed an artistic perfection usually associated with man-wrought things.

How could a moth impersonate a wasp; a butterfly, a leaf? Nabokov was skeptical about chalking such subtleties up to natural selection. For him, the sublime elegance of nature was a sign that Darwin's theories had gone too far. *You mean to say,* Nabokov seemed to wonder, *the wisps of cerulean and sepia on a butterfly wing are replicated through evolution on bark lichen? Surely random selection cannot explain these disquieting miracles of color and texture.* Believing something more divine must be at work, Nabokov contrasted the intricate detail found in the natural world with the serendipity of human creation:

> I discovered in nature the non-utilitarian delights that I sought in art. Both were a form of magic, both were a game of intricate enchantment and deception.

Magic, enchantment, deception—such evocative words for a butterfly catcher.

Unfortunately for Nabokov, evolutionary biologists would soon enough find evidence to decipher much of what he found so confounding. The intricate colors and patterns that elicited so much exuberance would prove to have scientific explanations.[96] But

while Nabokov may have missed the target on *magic,* his depiction of *deception* in nature could prove incisive. The "mysteries of mimicry," as he put it, might still inform our understanding of the world, beyond biology. From mimicry we could learn how we adapt to impersonate our enemies, our peers, or strangers, so that we might lure prey, or frighten predators, or seduce mates. In mimicry we can see how animals, especially humans, conceal and connive, how we adopt roles, emulate friends, and imitate foes. Evolution's mysterious adaptive powers might contain the fundamental rules for understanding the elusive logic of misinformation.

Mimicry is found in thousands of species—plants, animals, and fungi. The table to the right contains a short list of stimulating instances, each of which, when substituted with a mercurial character like Humbert Humbert, might serve as a plot outline for the next great work of literature.

SEE ALSO: FALSE FLAG OPERATION; HUMAN CLONING; RADAR CHAFF; UMWELT

MOCKBUSTER

Despite its phonological similarity, a *mockbuster* is only a distant kissing cousin to the *mockumentary.* Whereas mockumentaries are vessels of parody, as with *Spinal Tap* riffing on the rock documentary, the mockbuster is a more specious species—a knockoff lacking satiric intent. A mockbuster actually wants to trick you into watching a bad movie. *Best in Show* is a mockumentary; *Snakes on a Train,* a mockbuster.

Mockbusters thrive today because of the internet. If you've ever started to type "Day the Earth St..." into the Netflix search box, and ended up watching

---

96 For more detail, see "No Science Without Fancy, No Art Without Facts: The Lepidoptery of Vladimir Nabokov," in Stephen Jay Gould's essay collection *I Have Landed.*

SELECT CASES OF MIMICRY IN NATURE

IN NATURE THE...	...TRIES TO...	...AS A MEANS TO...
Flower Mantis	look like a flower	lure insect prey
Pebble Plant	resemble stones	avoid being eaten
Bolas Spider	smell like a female moth	attract male moths for dinner
Fork-Tailed Drongo	imitate meerkat alarm calls	make them flee and steal their food
Hammer Orchid	look and smell like a female wasp	trick male wasps to spread its pollen
Dead Horse Arum Lily	look and smell like rotting meat	attract blowflies to spread its pollen
Mimic Octopus	resemble sea snakes or lionfish	scare off predators
Katydid	imitate sounds of a female cicada	capture male cicadas
Zone-Tailed Hawk	mimic a harmless turkey vulture	ambush unsuspecting prey
Gopher Snake	sound like a rattlesnake	ward off predators
Cuckoo	lay eggs resembling other birds'	bear offspring to be raised by another

The Day the Earth Stopped because it looked close enough to *The Day the Earth Stood Still*, then you've fallen for a mockbuster. The movie queue is flush with punning flimflams: *Transmorphers, Braver, The Da Vinci Treasure, Age of the Hobbits* . . .[97]

That last entry in the queue is notable for creating an intriguing legal dispute involving archaeologists. When the producers of *The Hobbit* sued *Age of the Hobbits* for trademark infringement, the defendants claimed fair use of the word "hobbit" because it constituted "scientific terminology," after some anthropologists used the term to describe a human subspecies in Indonesia. The judge rejected the argument, forcing the producers to change the title. *Clash of the Empires,* as it was renamed, thereby lost its status as a *mockbuster* and became a mere *knockoff.*

If you find yourself thinking of porn right now, you have due cause—many X-rated titles similarly sully more noble endeavors with wordplay. Among the panoply of punning mastery: *Raiders of the Lost Arse, Edward Penishands, On Golden Blonde, Womb Raider, Pocahotass, Assablanca, Bi-Tanic, Good Will Humping, Poonies, Pulp Friction, Jurassic Pork,* and *Shaving Ryan's Privates.*

SEE ALSO: THE BUGGS; F FOR FAKE; KNOCKOFF HANDBAGS; SLEEPIFY

MODEST PROPOSAL, A

With a verbosity found only in the patter of eighteenth-century wags, the full title of the pamphlet was *A Modest Proposal for Preventing the Children of Poor People from Being a Burthen to their Parents or Country, and for Making Them Beneficial to the Publick.* Today we know Jonathan Swift's tract simply as *A Modest Proposal,* probably because the clipped version gets endlessly repurposed as the headline of an online essay every 1.4 seconds.[98]

First published anonymously by an "Irish Patriot" in 1729, the treatise offered with straight-faced aplomb a solution to Ireland's growing child poverty problem: Fatten those waifs and feed them to the rich.

> A young healthy child well nursed, is, at a year old, a most delicious nourishing and wholesome food, whether stewed, roasted, baked, or boiled; and I make no doubt that it will equally serve in a fricassee, or a ragout.

Delish. With numbers to support his thesis, Swift argued that serving *les enfants au gratin* would help solve many societal problems, including overpopulation and unemployment. Poor families who traded in their wastrel progeny would have a few extra dollars in their pocket, and the culinary options for the wealthy would be vastly improved—it's a win-win.

Many people found the misanthropic essay in, well, poor taste. Some even chose to interpret the lampoon of social engineering *literally,* which might sound completely insane, until you compare their credulity to certain modern reactions to satire—say, North Korea's response to *The Interview* or how your aunt Sally interprets headlines from *The Onion* (satire always confuses someone). Most readers of *A Modest Proposal* would grok the parody long before encountering the recipes for succulent cutlets of

---

97 The same spamming tactic can be found on music streaming services like Spotify, where searching for "Demons" by Imagine Dragons can accidentally yield a song of the same title by the spam band Imagine Demons, who have tricked 1.7 million listeners with their extremely similar cover.

98 An approximation. But a quick search on Google News turned up: "A Modest Proposal for Guns," "A Modest Proposal: How to Fix the Oscars," "A Modest Proposal for Uber," "A Modest Proposal: Should Concerts Start Earlier?," "A Modest Proposal to Mike Pence Regarding Abortion," and "A Modest Proposal: Mr. President, Get Some Sleep." None of these tracts are, objectively, funny.

toddler meat, but the ironic infanticide apparently flew right over the heads of enough of Swift's contemporaries to put his patronage in jeopardy. Which begs the amazingly dumb question: *How do we know when someone is joking?*

The question sounds too daft to address, but consider how many comedians have a vested interest in hoodwinking you. The entire definition of satire involves simulating an existing form (an essay, a song, a local newspaper) with exacting precision. Of course some people will be hoodwinked—that was the goal! We even reward those satiric acts like Borat, Stephen Colbert, and TONY CLIFTON, who dance the fine line between fake and real. Bamboozling at least some part of the audience is hailed as success.

That bamboozlement is the hidden risk of stealth parody like *A Modest Proposal*. Creating a visceral experience that *feels real* might satisfy audiences, but the gag immediately becomes susceptible to misinterpretation. Satires from *Charlie Hebdo* to *All in the Family* have had their intent misread, sometimes in unsettling ways. (On the internet, this is often called Poe's Law, or the impossibility of using irony without it being interpreted literally.)

Even more daunting are those works of undecided parody. One of the most contentious works of Western literature, Machiavelli's *The Prince*, is frequently interpreted as so maniacally hyperbolic that it must be covertly satiric. (This pro-irony crowd comprises an odd historical lot, including Diderot, Rousseau, and Gramsci.) If the literary community is undecided on whether one of its most notorious works is a joke, how can we condemn naive audiences for their lack of nuance? Many of today's great works of stealth satire—*American Psycho*, *Grand Theft Auto*, *Starship Troopers*, or even "Born in the U.S.A."—get accused of advocating issues they ostensibly set out to critique. When their realism is convincing, blaming audiences for distorted interpretations hardly seems fair. Ozzy Osbourne supposedly mistook *This Is Spinal Tap* for a documentary, so your stepdad misinterpreting Springsteen's ironic jingoism seems pretty understandable.

Such is the riddle of satire. We admire its ability to deconstruct extreme positions, but these very positions are complicated to emulate. Hitler is, as usual, the best (i.e., the worst) example. Not long after *The Great Dictator* (1940), Charlie Chaplin claimed he would not have made the satiric film if he had known about the Holocaust. To satirize a subject, you must become it, and Chaplin worried he got too close. If you create an illusion so convincing, you risk turning into *The Prince*—so similar to its tyrannical subject as to be indistinguishable from it.

What happens when you are mistaken for the very thing you despise?

SEE ALSO: CANNIBAL HOLOCAUST; INTERNET TROLL; THE REALIST; THE WAR OF THE WORLDS

MOIROLOGIST

The art of moirology involves vigorous acts of lip quivering, feet stomping, prostrate body trembling, and woeful head shaking. A moirologist feigns grief for a living.

Once common in the Mediterranean and Near East, professional mourning is mentioned several times in the Bible. Practitioners of crocodile tears still exist. In India, they are known as *rudaali*, and in Brazil, as *carpideira*. A more modern service in England, Rent a Mourner (rentamourner.co.uk), offers "professional, discreet people to attend funerals and wakes." Mass bereavement costs around $55 per mourner.

After Kim Jong-il's funeral in 2011, the world saw a suspicious video of North Koreans wildly ululating in grief. This lamentation was likely neither legitimate grief nor paid mourning, but forced by the authoritarian state.

SEE ALSO: CLAQUE; LAUGH TRACK; THE METHOD

MONDEGREEN

At some point, Jimi Hendrix relented. The mondegreen had won.

"Purple Haze" had been a hit for months, but whenever he performed the song, fans would shout a version of the chorus that deviated from what he sang. Finally, sometime around the Monterey Pop Festival in 1967, he capitulated, changing the refrain to what the audience sang. Instead of pardoning himself to *kiss the sky*, Hendrix sang what fans were singing: "Excuse me while I *kiss this guy*." The mondegreen was victorious.

Mondegreens are misheard song lyrics. Famous examples include an odious Springsteen earworm ("wrapped up like a douche") and Creedence Clearwater Revival's unsolicited lavatory directions ("there's a bathroom on the right"). One website—with the impeccable name of kissthisguy.com—has cataloged nearly 120,000 lyrical corruptions. That includes Taylor Swift's assertion that "Got a long list of ex-lovers" is commonly misheard as "All the lonely Starbucks lovers."

The term *mondegreen* was coined in *Harper's Magazine* in 1954 by a writer who misheard the lyrics of an old ballad—"laid him on the green" as "Lady Mondegreen." Which means *mondegreen* is itself a mondegreen.

Most mondegreens are innocent, but sometimes the mistake becomes canonical. In the original version of "The Twelve Days of Christmas," for instance, the numerical bird countdown announced "four *colly* birds," which later became "four *calling* birds," because that's what people heard. Stevie Nicks owes one of her most celebrated songs, "Edge of Seventeen," to mishearing Tom Petty's wife say they met "at the age of seventeen." And Iron Butterfly's hit "In-A-Gadda-Da-Vida" is what we might call a *forced mondegreen*—a deliberate mumbling of "In the Garden of Eden." (Weird Al Yankovic made a career out of deliberate mondegreens, including Madonna's "Like a Surgeon" and Joan Jett's "I Love Rocky Road.")

Rappers implicitly celebrate mondegreens when they denounce websites that attempt to decode lyrics into absolute meanings. (The hip-hop duo Das Racist has called one such site, RapGenius, "white-devil sophistry.") Part of the enjoyment of the rap song is being in the lyrical flow, your brain plying through the pitter-patter of rhythms, picking apart poetry from prosody. But lyrics websites remove that joy, turning your *interpretation* into your *mistakes*. They take all the mondegreen fun out of it.

The table to the right contains more common misheard lyrics.

SEE ALSO: AUTO-TUNE; BACKMASKING; CHINESE WHISPERS; PAREIDOLIA; WEIRD AL YANKOVIC

MONEY

On August 15, 1971, money became completely symbolic. You can blame Tricky Dick.

On that day, Richard Milhous Nixon unilaterally announced—without bothering to consult the State Department or the International Monetary Fund—the end of the gold standard, which had bound the value of the dollar to precious metals since the dawn of the United States. (Many decades after the Civil War, you could still walk into a bank with a bag of paper money and exchange it for a pot of gold.) In changing from a *fixed currency*, where one dollar was worth 1/35th an ounce of gold, to today's *floating currency*, the nation was rocked by what was dubbed "Nixon Shock," leading to the economic stagnation of the '70s.

So why did Nixon choose to abandon the gold standard? At the time, it was a failed attempt to stave off inflation, but now most economists see the benefits of a floating currency.[99] However, some historians—mostly the paranoiac variety—believe a fictional character hastened Nixon's decision: James Bond.

In the 1964 flick *Goldfinger*, the eponymous villain

COMMON MONDEGREENS

SONG	MISHEARD LYRIC	CORRECT LYRIC
"The Star-Spangled Banner" Francis Scott Key	"Jose, can you see?"	"O say can you see?"
"Bad Moon Rising" Creedence Clearwater Revival	"There's a bathroom on the right."	"There's a bad moon on the rise."
"Blinded by the Light" Bruce Springsteen	"Wrapped up like a douche, another rubber in the night."	"Revved up like a deuce, another runner in the night."
"Blowin' in the Wind" Bob Dylan	"The ants are my friends, they're blowin' in the wind."	"The answer, my friend, is blowin' in the wind."
"Beast of Burden" Rolling Stones	"I'll never leave your pizza burning."	"I'll never be your beast of burden."
"Michelle" The Beatles	"Sunday monkey won't play piano song."	"Sont des mots qui vont très bien ensemble."
"Hypnotize" The Notorious B.I.G.	"I just love your fleshy waist."	"I just love your flashy ways."
"Losing My Religion" R.E.M.	"Let's pee in the corner."	"That's me in the corner."
"Rocket Man" Elton John	"Rocket man, burning up the trees on every lawn."	"Rocket man, burning out his fuse up here alone."
"Tiny Dancer" Elton John	"Hold me closer Tony Danza."	"Hold me closer tiny dancer."
"Bad Blood" Taylor Swift	"All the lonely Starbucks lovers."	"Got a long list of ex-lovers."
"Purple Haze" Jimi Hendrix	"Excuse me while I kiss this guy."	"Excuse me while I kiss the sky."
"Addicted To Love" Robert Palmer	"Might as well face it, you're a dick with a glove."	"Might as well face it, you're addicted to love."
"Sussudio" Phil Collins	"Sussudio."	"Sussudio." (Yeah, you heard it right.)

threatens to detonate a nuclear device in Fort Knox, turning the gold reserve into radioactive sludge. (If you are prone to concoct psycho-economic parables from simple narratives, consider the archetypal names of the protagonists: *Bond*, *Goldfinger*, and *Pussy Galore*.) The movie was a hit, becoming one of the fastest-grossing films of all time. But its success also induced panic in the minds of some government officials who warned of a Goldfinger copycat—a terrorist (or communist) who would *actually* blow up the bullion in Fort Knox.

Did this fear hasten Nixon's move to end the gold standard? Probably not. But regardless of the motivation, the end of the gold standard now seems an impeccably modern event in our march toward a more virtualized society. By stripping currency of *literal* value, and instead imbuing it with purely *symbolic* value, money has become the pervasive lie we all believe.[100]

Money has become the largest mutually accepted myth in the history of civilization.

SEE ALSO: PONZI SCHEME

MOON LANDING HOAX

Conspiracy theories attract celebrities faster than a Scientology potluck in Tom Cruise's backyard. Elvis is alive. PAUL IS DEAD. Stevie Wonder can see. Khloe Kardashian is O. J.'s daughter. The Illuminati killed Whitney Houston as a sacrifice for Beyoncé and Jay-Z's baby, Blue Ivy. (The truth is out there.) But one theory transcends them all, at least on the celebrity intellectual scale: the Moon Landing Hoax.

When the Flat Earth Society accused NASA of fakery in 1980, it claimed the whole moon landing spectacle seen on television was based on a script by Arthur C. Clarke, with direction by Stanley Kubrick, and staging by Walt Disney. (The only missing element of stagecraft in this wild theory is costume design by Elvis.)

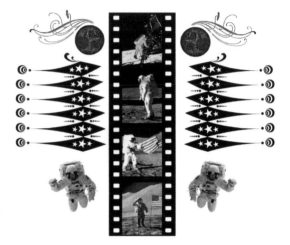

Evidence? No need to sully the fun with details. If the topic piques your interest, baroque theories argued in vast treatises populate the internet like little green people. (A good launching pad is the "Moon landing conspiracy theories" Wikipedia entry, which features dozens of zoomable images and 17,569 words of argument and rebuttal. The "Apollo 11" entry, by comparison, has a mere 10,814 words.) By far the most enticing hypothesis is the one that

---

99   The definitive history of the economics of gold is *One Nation Under Gold* (2017), by James Ledbetter.

100   We believe the lie so much that the Supreme Court gave money freedom of speech protection under the First Amendment in its Citizens United (2010) decision.

101   The pièce de résistance of Kubrick conspiracy theories is the tremendous documentary *Room 237* (2013). One conspiracist therein claims *The Shining* focuses on hotel room 237 because the moon is 237,000 miles from the earth. The statement is so compelling, who cares if the moon is, on average, 239,000 miles away?

---

claims Kubrick's *2001: A Space Odyssey* was an R & D project for what would become a massive conspiracy to manufacture footage for the first three moon landings.[101] Why? Doy, so the American government could prove their technological superiority over Russia.

Some polls estimate that as many as one in five Americans believe the moon landing was a sham.

SEE ALSO: ALIEN SPACE BATS; ALT-HISTORY; AREA 51; BEHOLD A PALE HORSE; FLAT EARTH THEORY; RED MERCURY

MUNCHAUSEN SYNDROME

Munchausen syndrome is a psychiatric disorder in which a person feigns a physical illness to garner attention or sympathy. The syndrome is similar to hypochondria and malingering, except the afflicted does not *intentionally* create the symptoms and receives no financial gain from feigning the illness. The person stricken with Munchausen does not completely realize they are lying. Their illness is believing they are ill.

A related disorder, *Munchausen syndrome by proxy*, occurs when the person projects their imagined afflictions onto another person, most commonly a child. A person with an extreme version of this factitious disorder will compel a child to spend their youth in the hospital treating nonexistent ailments.[102]

A third disorder, *Munchausen syndrome by internet*, manifests itself as fabricating an internet personality to suffer imagined ailments. Similar to CATFISHING, this syndrome sees people conjure a make-believe person to feign diseases upon. Its most famous case was Kaycee Nicole, who was represented on many websites starting in 1999 as suffering from terminal leukemia. When reports of her death emerged in May 2001, internet sleuths on the web community MetaFilter investigated her demise and determined that Kaycee Nicole was the complete invention of a Munchausen-syndrome-by-internet sufferer.

All these syndromes belong to the larger psychiatric category known as *factitious disorders*, the most pernicious of which are the Munchausen cases. The eponym is one Baron Munchausen, an eighteenth-century German nobleman known for his embellished tall tales. Except, not really. Baron Munchausen was actually a fictional character, created by the German writer Rudolf Erich Raspe and based loosely upon a real baron, Hieronymus Karl Friedrich von Münchhausen. Renowned for his storytelling abilities at dinner parties, the real-life baron, whom Raspe likely knew, was a minor celebrity, witty and adored for his deliberately outrageous yarns. In the hands of Raspe, Münchhausen became the less reputable Munchausen—a clueless braggart unaware of his histrionic exaggeration. Deeply upset by his casting, the real Münchhausen threatened libel proceedings against the publisher of the fictional Munchausen. Raspe—a compulsive swindler who fled to England from Germany for theft charges—was the real fabulist, casting the pall of mendacity upon Münchhausen. By projecting his penchant for duplicity onto his character, Raspe accidentally helped name the disease that he, in a figurative sense, suffered from.

SEE ALSO: CAPGRAS DELUSION; CATFISH; COTARD DELUSION; FREGOLI DELUSION; ROSENHAN EFFECT; TRUMAN SYNDROME

---

102 The story of Gypsy Rose, told in the documentary *Mommy Dead and Dearest* (2017) by Erin Lee Carr, is a disturbing portrait of Munchausen by proxy.

NACIREMA

The Nacirema are an obscure North American tribe noted for their fastidious oral cleanliness, kooky mental health practices, and dynamic market economy. In the 1956 paper "Body Ritual Among the Nacirema," anthropologist Horace Miner describes the clan as having a fundamental belief that "the human body is ugly."

The ruse is elementary—the tribe is us. *Nacirema* is *American* spelled backward. The paper is a satire of the language that social scientists (and normal people) use when depicting other cultures, especially "primitive" ones.

Originally published in a real journal, *American Anthropologist*, the heavily anthologized lampoon has been deployed to trick Anthropology 101 students for decades. One might say the Nacirema were once the SANTA CLAUS of the dorm—a disillusioning rite of passage. But in the age of the search engine, the assigned text has lost the punch of its great "classroom reveal." (Apologies to students for the lack of spoiler alert in this entry. Your profs will need to find a different technique for arousing you from dogmatic slumbers.)

With or without spoilers, the paper is a peculiar read today. Many of its obsessions have a distinctly 1950s flair. Sex bears an anachronistic stigma ("Intercourse is taboo as a topic and scheduled as an act"), and gender roles are proscribed ("Women bake their heads in small ovens for about an hour"). Bathrooms are depicted as household shrines, reeking of suburban angst. New-ish advances in psychiatry and dentistry are introduced like Martian technologies. Scatological references pervade, because apparently the '50s were shitty.

The intent of the farce was to diminish a perceived gap between cultures, to spotlight the "othering" effect of ethnology. But to the modern reader, the paper actually makes the 1950s feel like the primitive culture. The satire evokes not some attenuating distance *between cultures* but the incommensurable void *within ourselves* over time. We really are the Nacirema.

SEE ALSO: ALT-HISTORY; BERENSTAIN BEARS CONSPIRACY; CANNIBAL HOLOCAUST; SOKAL HOAX; UTOPIA; WHORFIANISM; WOOZLE EFFECT

NAKED CAME THE STRANGER

Sex was pretty weird in the '60s, but the novels of the day made it seem even weirder.

Emerging from the chaste Eisenhower years with deflated libidos, society had decided it was time to let it all hang out. The sexual liberation movement obliterated carnal inhibition, but with unintended side effects. All that unleashed hedonism pushed softcore sleaze into literary stardom. Pulpy smut by the likes of Jacqueline Susann (*Valley of the Dolls*) and Harold Robbins (*The Carpetbaggers*) swamped the best-seller list. And it wasn't just one-handed paperbacks—literary fiction had taken a turn for the prurient, too. Progressive housewives were getting their freak on with Anaïs Nin, while Henry Miller, whose taboo novels were banned in America until 1961, suddenly had the suburbs gripping their bed posts. Even the *New Yorker* crowd found their kink, with Philip Roth's *Portnoy's Complaint* and John Updike's *Couples* stroking the talkers of the Upper West Side.

The smutty trash really got Mike McGrady's goat. The *Newsday* journalist didn't mind the literary stuff, but he found the porny purple prose of the belly bumpers simply ridiculous. *Anyone could write this lurid sleaze!*, he said to coworkers at the local pub, after trying to read a Harold Robbins novel. A few more drinks down his gullet, McGrady devised a scheme to prove his theory: He would publish his own illiterate cringeworthy trashfest, and it would be an undisputed best-seller.

Writing lousy erotica is more difficult than it sounds, so McGrady recruited help. He conscripted twenty-four collaborators (nineteen men and five women from *Newsday*), who were each assigned a chapter and instructed to write nothing of social or literary value—no plot, no character development,

no symbolism, no words over three syllables. Just kinky, raunchy sex—at least two titillating scenes per chapter. "True excellence in writing will be blue-penciled into oblivion," he instructed in a synopsis to his fellow poetasters. "There will be an unremitting emphasis on sex." When one colleague turned in a raunchy scene with a Shetland pony, McGrady knew success was nigh.

The collaborative effort, *Naked Came the Stranger* (a double entendre worthy of a Pulitzer), was published in the summer of 1969 under a single assumed name—Penelope Ashe—who according to the book jacket was a "demure Long Island housewife." The cover portrayed a nude woman, seen from behind, kneeling, hair falling not nearly far enough to cover her derrière. The pseudonym needed a public face, so McGrady enlisted his foxy sister-in-law Billie Young to purr her way through the role of the pervy author on talk shows.

Spoiler: It worked! The book was an instant success. Of course critics hated it ("In the category of erotic fantasy, this one rates about a C," spat the *New York Times* review), but the novel instantly sold 20,000 copies, enough to make the prized best-seller list. The sordid tale might have ended here, but some of the collaborators who developed a sense of guilt about hoaxing the public (journalists and their damned consciences!) leaked the prank to the press. Instead of a backlash, as one might expect of such skulduggery, the revelation pumped sales to more than 90,000 copies. The novel ended up on the *New York Times* Best Sellers list for an astonishing thirteen weeks and would eventually sell more than 400,000 copies.[103]

In the end, McGrady proved his point about the state of literature: People will indeed buy titillating trash. But did that point really need elucidation? Maybe, but most of the book sales came *after* the unmasking, so the succès de scandale seemed to prove an additional, contrary point: People enjoy

---

103 McGrady later turned down a half-million dollar offer for a sequel but instead recounted this perverse tale in the memoir/guidebook *Stranger than Naked* (1970).

reading with contempt what others read for pleasure. That juicy insight might be just as perverse.

SEE ALSO: FANFIC; LEROY, JT; A MILLION LITTLE PIECES; ORDER OF THE OCCULT HAND; ORGASMS; PORNOGRAPHY; SLASHFIC; SOKAL HOAX

NEWSPEAK

Language is usually conceived of as a tool for people to share thoughts and express emotions—to communicate. But what if instead of communication, language was a tool of control? What would a language built for suppression even look like? Can we trust our own language enough to answer that question? Could this very sentence be a weapon of manipulation?

Just seven paragraphs into *1984*, George Orwell stabs a footnote into the text, pointing to an appendix. Here, in the final pages of the dystopian novel, he outlines the rules and intentions of a constructed language called *Newspeak*. Stopping short of a full grammar and vocabulary, "The Principles of Newspeak," as the appendix is titled, sketches enough morphology for us to theoretically re-create the authoritarian language. Based upon those rules provided by Orwell, and with no Big Brother to stop us, here is a brazenly hypothetical sentence of Newspeak:

> *Facecrimewise Suzie duckspeaked doubleplusunhot chocoration.*

Roughly, that translates to Oldspeak (i.e., Standard English) as:

> *Looking guilty, Suzie thoughtlessly spoke about her extremely cold chocolate ration.*

In that single (rather grim) sentence, the goals of the language become apparent. "Newspeak was designed not to extend," as Orwell wrote, "but to *diminish* the range of thought." Nuance (the bugbear of Newspeak) gets shaved to its root, as words are clipped of extraneous complexity. Unpleasant adjectives are ameliorated with their positive opposite (not *cold*, but *unhot*). Synonyms and antonyms are likewise eradicated—only the bare essentials remain. The grammar is spartan: All verbs are formed from nouns with standardized tensing (*-ed* in *duckspeak*); all superlatives are formed with the prefix *doubleplus-*; all adverbs, with the suffix *-wise*. The most noticeable feature of the language, frequent compound words (*facecrime*, *chocoration*), gives Newspeak the qualities of a pidgin language. But pidgins are pragmatic tools for unique situations, not weapons for subjugating society. The goal of Newspeak is met: to make language purely representational, terse, and affectless. With a language scrubbed of deeper ideas, heretical thoughts become impossible. (With no word for *coup*, how do you create one?)

The only fully translated sentence in *1984* is the passage from the Declaration of Independence that begins "We hold these truths to be self-evident, that all men are created equal . . ." Such nonsense liberal words (*truths*, *equal*) would baffle a Newspeaker, so the translation is brief. "The nearest one could come to doing so," says Orwell on bowdlerizing the paragraph to Newspeak, "would be to swallow the whole passage up in the single word *crimethink*."

Crimethink (a coy banality roughly translated as "to entertain unorthodox ideas") is one of *1984*'s many condensed idioms. The noun form, *thoughtcrime*, has seeped from the novel into our contemporary English, along with its comrades, *doublethink* and *big brother*. (One could be forgiven for craving the adoption of other delicious portmanteaus: *bellyfeel*, *blackwhite*, *goodsex*.[104]) Beyond its loan words,

---

104 *bellyfeel*: Blind, enthusiastic acceptance of an idea. *blackwhite*: The ability to believe in contradictions promoted by the government. *goodsex*: Heterosexual intercourse for procreation and no physical pleasure for the woman.

the grammatical influence of Newspeak in ye olde English is rampant, particularly in the military's relentless abuse of euphemism. A prisoner of war has become an *enemy combatant*; torture, now *enhanced interrogation*; killing civilians, *collateral damage*. Likewise, our vocabulary overflows with fanciful new compounds, annually compiled in "word of the year" lists, which likely would have rankled Orwell: *metrosexual, manspreading, Obamacare, humblebrag, clickbait, phablet, locavore, microaggression*. Orwell might have called the *thinkpol* (thought police) on emojis.

In the titular year of the novel, Newspeak had yet to be a fully integrated language, and most citizens still gabbed in Oldspeak. But *Ingsoc* (Newspeak for English Communism) hoped to have all citizens speaking the new language by 2050. That puts us, the readers of these sentences today, at the chronological halfway point toward adopting the language. Or maybe we are already speaking Newspeak. Would we even know if we were?

SEE ALSO: ALTERNATIVE FACTS; CLAPTER; DOUBLETHINK; ESPERANTO; ESQUIVALIENCE; FUD; GASLIGHTING; UTOPIA; WHORFIANISM

NOBLE LIE

When is it okay to lie?

It might be the most hackneyed question in ethics, with entire fleets of philosophers mobilized to answer the age-old query. Immanuel Kant would develop an extremely complicated metaphysical system to ultimately give the answer *never*, but he had the luxury of living long before Polish peasants had to decide whether to hide Jewish families under their floorboards. Friedrich Nietzsche, who inferred strength in sustaining a lie, would have shrugged *who cares, weakling*. Plato gave an oddly utilitarian answer: *You lie to maintain social harmony*. He called

it a *noble lie*—an altruistic myth that fosters solidarity and bolsters the ruling order. (When religion deploys the myth, it is dubbed a *pious fiction*. Karl Marx would later huff and puff over such opiates.)

In advocating the noble lie, Plato concocted an odd parable, through the mouth of Socrates in *The Republic*. He proposed a human origin myth in which everyone shares a precious common bond: being born from the soil of the earth (Plato would have been an excellent Nashville songwriter). But while the myth states we all come from the same chthonic realm, different classes of people are composed of different earthly materials. Artisans and farmers are made of iron and bronze. Administrators and auxiliaries are smelted from silver. And the ruling class, of course, is forged of gold. Plato completely admits, *this is all a lie—four Pinocchios!* But it is an important lie—a myth that will create political stability and social harmony by soothing the disenfranchised. The lie will placate the plebeians who are furious they are not patriarchs.

It is probably Plato's most bonkers idea. Assuming he was not being ironic (a distinct possibility, too often overlooked), the noble lie essentially provides justification for the government to disseminate propaganda. When the ruling class starts spreading myths it knows are false in the name of public welfare, the obvious question becomes: *Who decides the public welfare?* Plato's answer: the elites; those in power. *Who are they?* Hyper-intelligent guardians ("philosopher kings") who will act justly. *Oh reeeaally?*

In today's liberal democracies, the noble lie seems like nothing less than totalitarianism, but traces of it can still be found in the modern neoconservative movement. Whenever leaders drop patronizing paternalism like *we're doing it for your own good*, the bell of the noble lie is being rung.

But as usual, nothing is so clear cut. Noble or not, lying certainly has its place. Without some prevarication, some truths withheld, life would be unbearable. (Complete transparency? Imagine your every email and text message being publicly available.)

Just as courteous white lies and gracious fibbing get individuals through the day, a society must lie to itself for the sake of social cohesiveness. Even wily concepts like *freedom*, *justice*, and *equality* are ultimately human inventions. But as citizens, we have come to entrust these constructs with the sanctity of absolute truth. We do it to survive. We spread their importance through anecdotes, parables, songs—*myths*—so that we might maintain some solidarity among divided classes.

Not all myths are lies, but all myths start as a lie, which we come to believe as truth.

SEE ALSO: THE BIG LIE; LIE-TO-CHILDREN; PASCAL'S WAGER; PLATO'S CAVE; REALITY-BASED COMMUNITY; SANTA CLAUS; UTOPIA

NODDY

In the swamp of shady editing tricks that constitute television news, the *noddy* is a relatively minor—though extremely common—instance of the ethically murky.

After taping an interview, a television producer will often shoot the interviewer alone, just silently sitting in a chair, subtly nodding affirmation. These bits of tape are later edited into a final televised interview. In the argot of the industry, these reaction shots are known as *noddy-shots*—brief cuts to an interviewer, wagging their head in solemn agreement.

Noddies are lies, though relatively minor ones. When you see a cut to an interviewer, they are seldom reacting affirmatively at the exact moment a noddy occurs on-screen. Television producers justify the hackneyed practice as a necessary evil of the trade. Those brief noddies hide edits, they will say, allowing a long interview to be cut down to a reasonable length. Without cutaways and other transitions, an editor would have to insert a hard cut, which would be distracting.

The plot of the 1987 movie *Broadcast News* hinges on a noddy. A hard-nosed TV reporter (Albert Brooks) sees his nemesis, the pretty boy anchor (William Hurt), cry during an interview. He tattles to his sexy, principled colleague (Holly Hunter):

> You know how Tom has tears in his eyes when we did that interview with that girl? Ask yourself how we were able to see that, when we only had one camera and it was pointed at the girl the entire interview.

When Hunter digs up the original tape, she discovers that pretty boy is indeed a dishonest phony. Hurt acted his crying scenes after the interview. It's a classic noddy—though in this case, the crocodile tears could be called a *sobby*.

SEE ALSO: LAUGH TRACK; TEMP MUSIC; TRUTH CLAIM; WIPING

NONCE WORD

By the early '70s, wooly psych-rocker Steve Miller had released seven albums, none of them with a memorable hit song. His career fizzling, Miller decided to tweak his sound while recording his new album, *The Joker*. Melodies suddenly became crisper and lyrics goofier. It worked—the title track was a surprise hit that began:

> *Some people call me the space cowboy.*
> *Yeah! Some call me the gangster of love.*
> *Some people call me Maurice,*
> *'Cause I speak of the pompatus of love.*

The first three lines were all callbacks to previous characters in the Miller catalog. Few people knew these characters, but that did not matter, because all ears were tuned to that last line—*pompatus of love*. What on earth is a *pompatus*? Person, place, or thing? Animal, mineral, or vegetable?

Pompatus is what linguists call a *nonce word*—a scrap of nonsense created for a specific instance, and then discarded. Steve Miller made up the word *pompatus* because it sounded good in the moment.[105]

Nonces are placeholders, often dependent on context. Their meanings are, by definition, elusive. Nonce words tend to be ephemeral, but occasionally they stick. Once a new nonsense word is wrung through the Urban Dictionary and a definition is reached by consensus vote, a nonce can no longer be a nonce—it officially becomes a neologism.

A fine case study in nonces is *grok*, which was originally a Martian word found in Robert A. Heinlein's *Stranger in a Strange Land*, but was co-opted as a bit of techspeak to mean "to understand thoroughly." *Grok* started as a nonce but matriculated to the dictionary. The only reason *pompatus* is still a nonce is that it remains definitionless and is used only in the context of Steve Miller.

Unlike classic dad-rock, nonces can thrive only in obscurity.

SEE ALSO: DOE, JOHN; ESQUIVALIENCE; JABBER-WOCKY; SUPERCALIFRAGILISTICEXPIALIDOCIOUS; TRUTHINESS

NOT EVEN WRONG

Not even wrong is an idiom invoked when an idea is so bad that it cannot be falsified by experiment. It is über-wrong, post-wrong, trans-wrong, meta-wrong— so wrong that it cannot even be proven wrong.

The bon mot descends from a theoretical physicist, Wolfgang Pauli, who while viewing a student paper supposedly said, "That is not only not right, it is not even wrong!" (It would not be wrong to say the roundelay of double-negatives sounds even funnier in its original German: "Das ist nicht nur nicht richtig, es ist nicht einmal falsch!")

The rejoinder is often leveled at pseudoscience or any illogical thinking that can be proven neither correct nor incorrect.

SEE ALSO: NULL ISLAND; NOBLE LIE; PASCAL'S WAGER; SOKAL HOAX; SOPHISTS

NULL ISLAND

Null Island is a fantasy land, like Atlantis, but invented by scientists.

Located in the middle of the Atlantic Ocean, south of Ghana and west of Gabon, Null Island is the exact spot where the equator (0° latitude) crosses the prime meridian (0° longitude). Nothing is there, except the big blue ocean and a weather observation buoy moored to the spot. But if mapping services were the judge, it would be one of the most visited places on earth.

Given its coordinates, Zero Island might seem a more accurate name, but the spot was invented by goofy geographers as an in-joke for handling searches with null results. That is, when searching in a location database, a *null* geocode might be returned when no information exists. Some poorly written cartogra-

---

105 Musicologists (that is, nerdy rockists) are quick to point out that Miller did not technically invent the word. *Pompatus* existed in Latin, as "to perform with pomp or splendor," but Miller most assuredly did not know the term from reading Cicero. Rather, Miller has admitted that he misremembered a lyric from an old doo-wop group, the Medallions, who sang of "the puppetutes of love." (He was yet another victim of a MONDEGREEN, or a misremembered lyric.) *Puppetutes* was also a nonce word. And for that matter, so was *doo-wop*, at least initially.

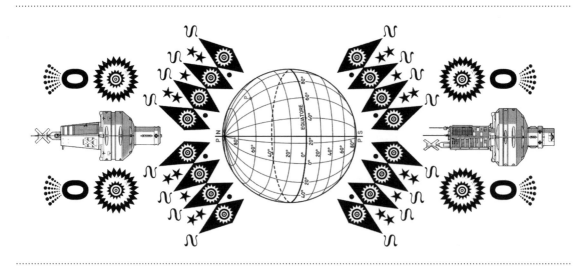

phy software can interpret a *null* as *zero*, turning no coordinates into "0°,0°." (In mathematics and computer science, *zero* and *null* are different concepts. Zero is none, while null is the absence of data. It's essentially the difference between an atheist's *There is none* and an agnostic's *I don't know*.)

Because of bad geocoding queries, Null Island ends up seeming a popular location in searches. When loading a webpage that has an embedded Google Map (especially on real estate websites, for some reason), a map with a pin dropped off the coast of Africa will often appear. This is the precise location of Null Island—a one-square-meter plot of water that is pure cartographic fantasy.

SEE ALSO: ESPERANTO; NOT EVEN WRONG; TRAP STREETS; UTOPIA

O

OMNIPOTENCE PARADOX

Perhaps first mischievously whispered in your ear by a pedantic boy fresh out of Sunday school, the omnipotence paradox is the old canard that has perplexed many a devout monotheist: *Can God create a rock so heavy that he cannot lift it?* The question can drive a pious teenager to neurotic madness. Both answers, *yes* and *no*, undermine the absolute omnipotence of the deity. God either, *yes*, can create a rock he cannot lift, or *no*, cannot create a rock he can lift. Either way, God has a weakness. Omnipotent beings cannot have weaknesses!

Since the Middle Ages, theologians and philosophers have toiled with the omnipotence paradox. Most refutations chalk the skull teaser up to some sort of semantic sophistry—the question makes grammatical sense but the concept is illogical. It's like asking, *Can God create a square triangle?* Sure? But once God did, it would probably no longer fit our definitions of *square* and *triangle*. All of these words—*square, circle, rock, omnipotence*—are merely human concepts for describing the universe, not things in themselves. Here is a case where religion and science actually reach an accord: Reality is more complex than human language reflects.

If only you could go back and tell that bratty kid at Sunday school his impish riddle was a semantic trap.

SEE ALSO: NOBLE LIE; NOT EVEN WRONG; PASCAL'S WAGER; SHIP OF THESEUS; SOPHISTS

IRRESISTIBLE FORCE PARADOX	*What happens when an unstoppable force meets an immovable object?*
LIAR'S PARADOX	*Everything I say is false!*
SOCRATIC PARADOX	*I know that I know nothing!*
ANGEL DENSITY PROBLEM	*How many angels can dance on the head of a pin?*
HOMER SIMPSON'S BURRITO PARADOX	*Could Jesus microwave a burrito so hot that he himself could not eat it?*

ONE MILLION DOLLAR PARANORMAL CHALLENGE

It is a startling paradox—one might almost say a *paranormal occurrence*—how much magicians detest charlatans and quacks. HARRY HOUDINI occupied his final years denouncing spiritualists. Penn & Teller had an eight-season TV series devoted to refuting pseudoscience. The *MythBusters* duo were renowned special effects illusionists before becoming debunkers. Dorothy Dietrich, sometimes called the First Lady of Magic, has offered rewards to dubious psychics who can contact the dead. And the biggest anti-shyster of them all, The Amazing Randi, fought relentlessly against psychics, faith healers, and new age hucksters of all varieties. He even promised one million dollars to anyone who could prove their psychic abilities. No one ever won the money, but many tried.

James Randi was already pretty amazing before becoming America's greatest debunker. A master escapologist and storyteller, Randi was a regular on *The Tonight Show with Johnny Carson*, where in one live appearance he remained submerged in a swimming pool for 104 minutes, breaking Houdini's record of 93 minutes. Alice Cooper hired him to play the role of executioner on his *Billion Dollar Babies* tour, and he even played himself on an episode of *Happy Days* (titled "The Magic Show"). For his investigations into spoon-bending hack Uri Geller, he was awarded the MacArthur Genius Grant.

Despite his acclaim as an illusionist (he preferred the epithet *conjuror*), Randi despised those who implied something psychic or paranormal at work with magic. "It's okay to fool people," he once said. "As long as you're doing that to teach them a lesson."[107] When he launched the Paranormal Challenge in 1964, a $1,000 reward was offered to any parapsychologist who could perform a supernatural act under scientific testing scenarios. The amount climbed through the years, and hit $1 million in 1996. More than a thousand people applied, but of course no one was ever able to speak to their dead relatives, read anyone's mind, remotely view objects, or locate buried groundwater through dowsing.

"Professional Debunker" may not sound like an illustrious gig, but it was noble work through the 1970s, a decade rife with faith healers, ufologists, cryptozoologists, and mystical mountebanks of all stripes. Randi fought the bad magic with good magic, using the tools of deception to expose deception. "Magicians are the most honest people in the world," he was fond of saying. "They tell ya they're going to fool ya, and they do."

SEE ALSO: BARNUM EFFECT; HOUDINI, HARRY; HUMBUGGERY; HYPNOSIS; MECHANICAL TURK

OPERATION MINDFUCK

Operation Mindfuck was a ritual of Discordianism, a satiric religion of the '60s and '70s devoted to anarchic pranks and absurdist conspiracy theories. In a memo sent to the members of the faux-cult, the writer Robert Anton Wilson explained that Operation Mindfuck intended to "attribute all national calamities, assassinations, or conspiracies" to the Illuminati and their ilk. The theory was that Mindfuck would create "so many alternative paranoias" that the public, shuddering at the utter incoherence of the nutjobs, would abandon any belief in irrational plots. It didn't exactly work out that way.

The Mindfucking commenced with jamming the press with stories, letters, and ads with conspiracies galore. "We accused everybody of being in the Illuminati," Wilson later recalled. "Nixon, Johnson, William Buckley Jr., ourselves, Martian invaders,

---

107 The quote is from *An Honest Liar*, a stupendous 2014 documentary on Randi.

all the conspiracy buffs, *everybody*." Mindfuckers swamped the underground press of the left and right but also found their way into mainstream magazines, like *TeenSet* (sort of the *Sassy* of the '60s), where Jane Fonda, Ringo Starr, Bob Hope, and a cabal of notables were outed as part of "the most sinister, evil, subversive conspiracy in the world." At *Playboy*, where Wilson was an editor, a letter to the Advisor column (appearing after a question about blue balls) drew connections between international banking, James Bond's Spectre cabal, and JFK's assassination.

Relishing the impish chaos of Operation Mindfuck, Wilson began blurring the line between cranky satire and sincere paranoia. "We did not regard this as a hoax or prank in the ordinary sense," he later wrote. "We still considered it guerrilla ontology." Whatever *guerrilla ontology* is, he decided to turn his meta-conspiracy racket into a novel, "delicately balancing between 'proving' the case for multiple conspiracies and undermining the 'proof.'" Thus was born the science fiction opus *The Illuminatus! Trilogy* (1975), a druggy, paranoid trek through conspiracies that has a mindfuckingly large cultish following to this day.

SEE ALSO: CHURCH OF SUBGENIUS; SLENDERMAN

ORDER OF THE OCCULT HAND

All members of the Order of the Occult Hand belong to an unlikely profession: journalism.

The secret society began by accident, in 1965, when Joseph Flanders, a reporter at a now-defunct newspaper, the *Charlotte News*, used this majestic sentence in a fairly routine story:

> It was as if an occult hand had reached down from above and moved the players like pawns upon some giant chessboard.[108]

Over drinks, his colleagues gushed admiration at the stately prose. After a few more quaffs, as bibulous journalists do, the group decided to form a secret society to honor the sly diction. Members of the shadowy order vowed to insert the phrase "as if an occult hand" into print as often as possible. They apparently didn't drink enough to forget their pact, because as the cabal members took jobs at other newspapers, their clandestine diaspora spread around the country. That telltale phrase, "as if an occult hand," began to appear in the *New York Times*, the *Los Angeles Times*, the *Boston Globe*, and elsewhere.

---

108   It seems improbable that this is not a veiled reference to the MECHANICAL TURK, a device in which an occult hand reaches down and moves pawns across a giant chessboard.

Perhaps influenced by this journalistic plot, pop social science writer Malcolm Gladwell devised a similar scheme in the late '80s. While a reporter at the *Washington Post*, he and a colleague held a contest to see how many times they could get the phrase "raises new and troubling questions" into the newspaper. After several successes, they updated the challenge to another shopworn phrase: "perverse and often baffling."[109]

SEE ALSO: INFINITE MONKEY THEOREM; MECHANICAL TURK; NAKED CAME THE STRANGER

ORGASMS

Derived from sexual arousal, these spasms of carnal exuberance are rumored to be, on occasion, faked. One survey estimated that 48 percent of women and 11 percent of men have, shockingly, misinformed their partner by simulating a moment of ecstatic glee.[110]

SEE ALSO: DONKEY PUNCH; PORNOGRAPHY; REALDOLL

OVERTON WINDOW

As deployed by media pundits, the Overton Window refers to the proposed range of ideas that the public will accept as reasonable topics of government policy. The handy term was posthumously named after Joseph P. Overton, a think tank wonk who studied how ideas move from fringe to mainstream.

In recent years, previously verboten policy ideas from both the left and right have moved "into the window," including universal basic income, Brexit, a ban on Muslims in the United States, and universal health care. For the past century or so, the so-called mainstream media has played a critical role in regulating what enters and leaves public discourse, but because of the advance of social media, the Overton Window is now in constant flux. Plenty of issues once considered outside the window—from decriminalized marijuana to building a border wall between the United States and Mexico—have moved inside the political mainstream.

Though seemingly a neutral political concept, the term is most often invoked by the alt-right, who use it to describe the furtive nudge of radical nationalism into the mainstream. The concept likely gained traction within that cohort after Glenn Beck's 2010 novel, *The Overtown Window*, which involved a populist overthrow of the government. In the foreword, Beck refers to his potboiler as a *faction*, or a fiction based upon facts. Factions now seem firmly affixed within the jambs of the Overton Window.

SEE ALSO: CONFIRMATION BIAS; FILTER BUBBLE; WOOZLE EFFECT

---

109 Gladwell's yarn was first told on a *Moth* performance and then rebroadcast on a February 2008 episode of *This American Life*. When asked later by *Slate* about the veracity of the story, Gladwell's response, well, raised new and troubling questions. "No one fact checks *Moth* stories, or expects them to stand up to skeptical scrutiny," he said. And while based on real events, his story "is not supposed to be 'true,' in the sense that a story in the *New York Times* is supposed to be 'true.'"

110 The stat comes from 2004's "The American Sex Survey," in which ABC News randomly called 1,501 Americans, which must have been quite the call to get at dinner.

P

PAREIDOLIA

Pareidolia is the human tendency to perceive patterns where they don't exist. Seeing a human visage on the surface of Mars, hearing secret messages on recorded music, beholding Jesus in a pancake—all are instances of the phenomenon. Pareidolia is usually explained away as a side-effect of the human brain being a pattern-recognizing machine.

A more generalized term, *apophenia*, applies to perceiving patterns not necessarily connected to misguided sensory input. Examples include lottery ticket numerology, sexuality prediction from hair whorls and digit ratios, meaningless Freudian slips, and the 27 Club.[111]

SEE ALSO: ANTI-VAXXERS; BACKMASKING; MIMICRY; MONDEGREEN; RORSCHACH TEST

PASCAL'S WAGER

Never bet against eternity. That is the précis of Pascal's Wager, a logical argument for believing in God. Disbelief in the existence of God, according to the wager, is simply a bad bet.

On the one hand, choosing faith reaps you the heavenly benefits of salvation for eternity. Choosing skepticism, however, might afford some modest earthly gain, but you risk everlasting hellfire and eternal damnation. Faith in God is a simple math game—finite loss versus infinite reward. Or to put it in Vegas terms, God always covers the spread. (Forcing people into such decision trees also creates a tremendous opportunity for psychological manipulation. *Just sayin'.*)

Blaise Pascal, the precocious seventeenth-century French mathematician, devised this theistic theorem. (He also invented the first operable mechani-

---

111   Attaining membership into the cabalistic 27 Club is an intense two-step hazing ritual that involves [1] being a musician and [2] dying at the age of 27. Given its extensive enrollment—Robert Johnson, Brian Jones, Jimi Hendrix, Janis Joplin, Jim Morrison, D. Boon, Kurt Cobain, and Amy Winehouse are all members—it can be tempting to find significance in the twenty-seventh year.

cal calculator, and his heuristic "triangle" still exasperates algebra students today.) His wager was an incendiary gesture because, unlike previous acts of apologetic philosophy, he provided no *proof* of God. Instead, he adduced a pragmatic choice, based upon probability. For the first time, decision theory (and its cousin, game theory) entered philosophical discourse. "What have you to lose?" he actually wrote.[112] One might wonder if you can *choose* to believe in God. Pascal foresaw this objection. "God looks only at what is inward," he wrote, before arguing that religious skeptics should associate with believers to inspire faith. By attending religious services, and encountering numinous glory through osmosis, a nonbeliever will eventually become a believer.

In other words, you fake it 'til you make it into heaven.

SEE ALSO: NOBLE LIE; NOT EVEN WRONG; OMNIPOTENCE PARADOX

PASSING

When used by sociologists, *passing* refers to a person of one identity group (usually a minority) altering their social persona to be accepted by another group. The term began in the nineteenth century to describe racial assimilation ("passing for white") but has broadened to include other gender, class, sexual orientation, and religious identities. The ambiguity-inducing term is also sometimes (and more controversially) invoked in less precise situations, as when women are told to "play like men" at work, or when homosexuals abstain from public displays of affection, or when white suburban teenagers watch a few hours of BET and start speaking in a new dialect, or when women get butt injections and lip fillers, or when RACHEL DOLEZAL does whatever she does.

One of the earliest cases of racial passing in literature appears in the Mark Twain novel *Pudd'nhead Wilson*, in which two babies—one born white (the master of the house) and one with 1/32 black ancestry (born into slavery)—are switched at birth. As the trope transferred to pop culture, passing began to reflect more class-based issues, such as in movies (*Brewster's Millions*, *The Talented Mr. Ripley*) and reality television (*Joe Millionaire*, *The Swan*).

Passing is a knotty topic that sometimes elicits valuable conversations about cultural ownership and the social creation of identity but just as often provokes public outrage. In just one instance that roiled the internet, Mindy Kaling's brother, who is of Indian descent, revealed in 2015 that he passed as black to gain entrance to medical school. He dropped out after two years and wrote a terrible book about it.

SEE ALSO: DOLEZAL, RACHEL; POPE JOAN; ROCKEFELLER, CLARK

PAUL IS DEAD

Countless dead rock stars, according to certain conspiratorial hypotheses, were secretly murdered (Cobain, Marley, Eazy-E). Other famous deaths, considered homicides by consensus (Lennon, Biggie, Tupac), were cover-ups of some nefarious variety. Still other dead icons are actually alive (Elvis, Bowie, Tupac again), surreptitiously blending in with us at Costco. Conspiracy theories about dead rockers sprawl from here to Strawberry Fields, but only one celebrity holds the unique inverse position—a *living* person who is secretly *dead*. Nope, not Marilyn

---

112   Most of Pascal's theological work is found in *Pensées* (1670)—literally "thoughts"—a fragmentary collection published posthumously.

Manson; the reverse zombie is Sir Paul McCartney.

In 1969, a Detroit DJ started the rumor: After dying in a 1966 car crash, Paul McCartney was clandestinely replaced with the winner of a look-alike contest. Beatlemaniacs went bonkers, poring over the discography for clues to the rumor. Why exactly the remaining Beatles would disperse evidence of the switcheroo in their oeuvre is murky logic, but the *cluesters*, as they were called, cared not of rationality. They parsed inscrutable lyrics for covert acrostics, played records in reverse for evidence of BACKMASKING, studied album covers in mirrors—whatever it took to find the Truth. Listening closely, they heard John possibly whisper "I buried Paul" at the end of "Strawberry Fields Forever." Other evidence required little investigation. "A Day in the Life" didn't even hide it: "He blew his mind out in a car."

The rumor initially seemed circumstantial, even whimsical, but as it accumulated populist energy, one conspiracy morphed into another. What if it was all a hoax? Could the Fab Four have planted all this evidence for cluesters to discover? Could it all be a subversive marketing scheme?

As the "Paul is dead" rumor spread (*Time* and *Life* magazines helped pollinate the germ), Capitol Records reported a spike in Beatles records sales—"the biggest month in history," said an executive. Albums released years prior—*Sgt. Pepper's* and *Magical Mystery Tour*—suddenly reappeared on the charts. The surge, the label conceded, was attributable to the ongoing rumor, but they denied having anything to do with its proliferation. Consumers were buying multiple copies of albums, so they could play them backward and forward, sped up and slowed down, synchronously, in search of hidden messages.

If the Beatles were complicit in the "Paul is dead" rumor and had intentionally planted clues for fans, it would mean that in addition to being the biggest rock band in history, they also created the first VIRAL MARKETING campaign. "Paul is dead" might be an even bigger conspiracy than we thought, a plot more baroque than *Lost* or BLAIR WITCH PROJECT or the New World Order. Perhaps the cluesters really were

onto something but mistook the true mystery: The Beatles perpetrated an elaborate marketing scheme.

SEE ALSO: BACKMASKING; THE BUGGS; CAPGRAS DELUSION; KARAOKE; DARK SIDE OF THE RAINBOW; MILLI VANILLI; PAREIDOLIA; TRIBUTE BANDS; VIRAL MARKETING

PHANTOM LIMBS

Phantom limbs are an exemplary instance of the human mind transmitting misinformation.

People who have had a limb amputated often report being able to kinesthetically sense the appendage as though it were still attached. They can feel it itch, feel it hurt, feel it getting cold or warm. Often they can "move" it. This is neither delusion nor malingering—the amputee knows and admits the limb is gone. But they *feel* it nonetheless.

The sensation is surprisingly common. Approximately 70 percent of amputees experience phantom sensations. It can also occur with other removed body parts, including eyes, breasts, teeth, and genitals.

SEE ALSO: BRAIN IN A VAT; COTARD DELUSION; FREGOLI DELUSION; IMPOSTOR SYNDROME; PHANTOM VIBRATION SYNDROME

PHANTOM TIME HYPOTHESIS

By their very nature, conspiracy theories require bold acts of historical revisionism. The Phantom Time Hypothesis might be the boldest of all such acts, erasing entire centuries from recorded history.

There are two distinct variants of this radical hypothesis—Eurocentric and Russocentric. The first version, espoused by German historian Heribert Illig, starts with the simple observation that the Roman Catholic Church forged some documents in the Middle Ages, which sounds believable enough, but then Illig makes a quantum leap. His time anomaly hypothesis starts in the (*alleged*) year of 1582, when Pope Gregory XIII introduces the Gregorian calendar (the one we use today), replacing the outdated Julian calendar (implemented in 45 BCE by Julius Caesar). The difference between these calendars is minuscule, but the switch corrects a ten-day chronological drift that has accrued over the centuries.[113] But when Illig performs his special math, he discovers wildly different numbers—297 years are missing! His phantom time hypothesis posits that the years 614 to 911 CE were added to the calendar by the church. This has enormous consequences, including the elimination of historical figures like Charlemagne and Muhammad, whom the theory dismisses as fabrications.

Despite the radical implausibility of the Eurocentric hypothesis, it is timid compared to the Russian version. Espoused by Anatoly Fomenko, a mathematics professor at the Moscow State University, this crypto-chronology is significantly more elaborate. It posits that most events from the Roman Empire, Ancient Greece, Dynastic China, and Ancient Egypt actually occurred during the Middle Ages. In fact, human history did not really start until 800 CE, and nearly all ancient recorded events occurred between the years 1000 and 1500. Anything dated earlier than the eleventh century is either falsified or represents a "phantom reflection" of an actual Middle Ages event. Dubbed "New Chronology," this pseudohistory converges Viking ships, the Egyptian pyramids, Buddha, Plato, Alexander the Great, and Jesus into a tight Medieval matrix spanning a mere few hundred years. Collapsing history like a folding map introduces some fascinating new harmonious anomalies—the New Testament happened before the Old, Genghis Khan and Attila the Hun were the same person, da Vinci and Michelangelo forged ancient manuscripts for powerful patrons, and the Trojan War and Crusades were the same historical event.[114]

Debunking the outlandish theories of Illig, Fomenko, and their comrades should be easy peasy, but their outlandishness makes them difficult to refute. Every bit of counter-evidence (astronomical records, archaeological remains, carbon dating, etc., etc., *et cetera*) evokes a new plot from a crypto-historian. Each historical refutation requires another for its support, leaving an entire chronological framework susceptible to implosion. No matter how convinced you are that Charlemagne existed, can you *prove* it? For that matter, can you prove *anything* that happened before you were born?

Ultimately, the origins of the two phantom time hypotheses belie their veracity. Not so discreetly, the Eurocentric model argues for the elimination of the early Middle Ages—an exceptionally nonspectacular period of European history, which just happens to coincide with a massive Islamic flourishing throughout the Mediterranean and a golden cultural explosion in China's Tang dynasty. The Russocentric hypothesis, meanwhile, folds all of history into the year 800, around the time that Russian history conveniently commences. Both motives are suspect; each hypothesis rewrites history to its advantage.

That said, declaring BULLSHIT on world history certainly has its appeal. Fomenko opens his seven-volume history opus[115] with Orwell's famous adage

---

113   Because of the calendar change, ten days of history really did vanish: October 5, 1582, on the Julian side to October 14, 1582, on the Gregorian. Protestant churches resisted the Pope's witchy decrees, so the English-speaking world ignored the Gregorian switcheroo until 1752, when the United Kingdom and its colonies lost September 3–13. Either way, the phantom time hypothesis is very real—if you count these ten days that non-mysteriously disappeared.

114   New Chronology might have been laughed off as kooky folklore if not for a few notable Russian intellectuals who embraced it, including chess champion Garry Kasparov.

from *1984*: "Who controls the past controls the future; who controls the present controls the past." Maybe human history is a fiction assembled to serve the powerful. Maybe Atlantis will still be discovered. Maybe extraterrestrials built the pyramids and Stonehenge. Maybe Ted Cruz is the Zodiac Killer and Lewis Carroll was Jack the Ripper. Maybe it's all been a pack of lies, as Phil Collins said, maybe in a different context. Maybe "history is not what happened," as Plato claimed, "but what we believed happened."

But then, when did he say that? Maybe . . . *never*, or just last week.

SEE ALSO: ALT-HISTORY; BERENSTAIN BEARS CONSPIRACY; FLAT EARTH THEORY; MANDELA EFFECT; MOON LANDING HOAX; RETCONNING; TOMMY WESTPHALL UNIVERSE; WOOZLE EFFECT

PHANTOM VIBRATION SYNDROME

Hypovibochondria, or phantom vibration syndrome, is a condition born of living in an age of hyperconnectivity. It occurs when you think the phone in your pocket is vibrating, but your mind is just playing tricks on you. The tactile hallucination is common. According to one study, 89 percent of college students report feeling the phantom vibes.

Similar portmanteaus—*fauxcellarm*, *ringxiety*—emerged years prior, for hallucinations involving misheard ringtones. Each era gets the somatic delusions it deserves.

SEE ALSO: CYBORG; PAREIDOLIA; PHANTOM LIMBS

PHILOSOPHER'S STONE

The philosopher's stone was a mythical substance sought from the Middle Ages through the Renaissance by alchemists who believed it a catalyst for transforming base metals (lead, nickel, mercury) into precious metals (gold, silver). Mercury was at the center of the alchemical project, probably because at room temperature it is a supercool-looking metal liquid. But the element is also a neurotoxin, which likely provoked some of the crazier alchemical notions about the world. (The philosopher's stone was associated with mystical powers, including as an elixir for infinite life.)

Though rife with hucksters, alchemy was as much protoscience as pseudoscience. The alchemical quest ultimately led to the fields of chemistry, pharmacology, and metallurgy. And eventually we got there—transubstantiated gold exists! But to turn mercury into gold today, you need a nuclear reactor, and the resulting isotope is extremely unstable. A single ingot of transmuted gold would emit enough radioactivity to kill you instantly.

SEE ALSO: RED MERCURY; SODIUM PENTOTHAL; SYNTHETIC DIAMONDS

PHOTOSHOPPING

At first, it was a noun, and a proper one at that. But Photoshop became a Gaussian blur on society because of its verb form: *to photoshop*.

Digitally altering an image comprises a wide array of actions: cropping, lightening, darkening, sharpening, blurring, airbrushing. Regardless of the software used or the mendacity intended, *photoshopping* is

115 *History: Fiction or Science?* (2004). Cool title.

what we now call any act of image manipulation—especially when the act is controversial.

But the controversy has existed since the dawn of photography itself. When Louis Daguerre announced its invention in 1839, photography was immediately deemed a hoax by many scientists. Their suspicion was portentous, as doctored images began appearing almost immediately. The portrait of Abraham Lincoln later used on the $5 bill, for instance, was originally displayed as Lincoln's head superimposed on southern leader John Calhoun. And after his death, photos circulated of Lincoln in a casket, even though his corpse was never photographed.

Into the twentieth century, photography became more politically charged, as accusations of manipulation spread to public figures and the media. To learn that totalitarians like Stalin manipulated photos for propaganda is one thing, but seeing the much debated 1994 cover of *Time* with a heavily doctored mugshot of O. J. Simpson can be more shocking. The modification exposed the dirty little secret of photojournalism, even more true today: All photos are photoshopped, at least to some degree. (Despite what some Instagrammers claim, #nofilter is intrinsically a lie. The camera itself corrects light and color deficiencies.) While photojournalists have guidelines on what constitutes overmanipulation, the boundaries can be, to say the least, blurry.

The fashion industry, too, has faced intense scrutiny for its overuse of "airbrushing," as it was called pre-Photoshop. While fashion magazines have always admitted to smoothing out blemishes and wrinkles, the degree of manipulation was unclear. But then, in 2008, the website Jezebel published a photo of Faith Hill on the cover of *Redbook* side by side with the original unaltered image. The stark contrast of the images set off a moral panic about what photoshopping has done to the self-perception of our bodies.

As it courts controversy, photoshopping has become an art form in its own right, with a cultish obsession developing around certain photoshoppers. Pascal Dangin, for instance, has become the most sought-after photo retoucher in fashion's history. "The obvious way to characterize Dangin," wrote the *New Yorker* in a 2008 profile, "as a human Oxy pad, is a reductive one—any art student with a Mac can wipe out a zit. His success lies, rather, in his ability to marry technical prowess to an aesthetic sensibility: his clients are paying for his eye, and his mind, as much as for his hand."

While popularizing terms like *hue, saturation, gradient, contrast, filter,* and *clone,* Photoshop has democratized the act of image manipulation. Whether it's the faux-selfie atop the World Trade Center with a terrorist-helmed jet flying headlong from behind, or the Muppet character Bart mashed into a photo with Osama bin Laden, or any of the endless 'shopped memes on websites like Reddit and 4chan, the altered photo is now pervasive.

Once regarded as the epitome of realism, photography has become the most suspicious medium, the form of communications most likely to deceive. Yet again, the fake has upended the real: Manipulated photos now far outnumber the unaltered.

SEE ALSO: AUTO-TUNE; BOTOX; TRUTH CLAIM; TUPAC HOLOGRAM

PLACEBO EFFECT

Placebos are phony health treatments that can have real healing effects. The mysterious mental state induced by these proverbial sugar pills, known as the *placebo effect*, demonstrates the potential healing power of lies. Study after study has shown that placebos can work, especially when administered for pain relief, depression, and immunity. But their success tends to be short term. There is scant statistical evidence of any lasting clinical effect of a placebo, except for pain treatment and other highly subjective measures.

How exactly placebos work is still something of a mystery, which might explain why Harvard offers a program in Placebo Studies. When administered a bogus pill, the body seems to set self-fulfilling expectations of a drug's effectiveness and adjusts its biochemistry to produce chemicals that relieve symptoms. While the placebo itself is fake, the body's reaction is usually a real thing. In one study, a placebo pill presented as a stimulant increased heart rate and raised blood pressure; presented as a sleep aid, the same pill had the opposite effect.

Because the placebo effect can be real, new drugs must be tested with placebos as controls. But while placebos are necessary tools of pharmaceutical research, their use in therapeutic settings is highly controversial. Administering a known placebo clinically introduces deception and dishonesty into the client-patient relationship, making them ethically problematic. (Would you want your doctor to lie to you? What if the lie relieved your symptoms? And what if doctors lying to patients became widely known? It's an ethical quagmire.)

The term *placebo* originated in church: *Placebo domino in regione vivorum* was a phrase used by Roman Catholics at funerals, popularly translated as "I shall walk before the Lord in the land of the living." *Placebo* (literally "I shall please") eventually morphed into a derogatory term for a funeral crasher—a faux-griever who claims a connection to the departed but is only there for free food or drink.

In the nineteenth century, when nostrums and pseudoscientific fads bamboozled America (laying the foundation for what would become the homeopathic movement), the modern definition of placebo took hold. Mocking those consumers of eyes-of-newt and toes-of-frog, Mark Twain spoke of dupes who believe they can "bribe death with a sugar pill."

A more sardonic figure, the comedian Steven Wright, would later express nihilistic dread in our medical self-deception. "I'm addicted to placebos," he quipped. "I'd give them up, but it wouldn't make any difference."

SEE ALSO: BANANADINE; HYPNOSIS; BOGUS PIPELINE; THE RED PILL; SODIUM PENTOTHAL

PLANDID

Plandid arose from the coy elision of "planned" and "candid." The oxymoronic portmanteau describes a genre of Instagram photo where the subject seems to be effortlessly unaware of the camera, but the sophisticated staging belies its casual posture. The photo intimates a person captured naturally, *en plein air*, like a gazelle seen grazing the plains or a galaxy spied through a telescope. The prototypical plandid might depict its carefree subject nonchalantly sitting on their antique kitchen sink, lolling in their skivvies and giggling at some off-screen antics, or they might be snapped summering at an upstate Airbnb, innocently stepping out from an infinity pool while glancing over their shoulder, shot from an impossible angle only feasible by drone. Regardless of setting, the subject must always feign sprezzatura, that accidental coolness that coos, *Oh I didn't see you there, did you just take a photo?*

Overproduced naturalism is hardly unique to iPhone cinematography. All creative mediums exert great effort to simulate effortlessness. Music producers fiddle knobs until a sheen of spontaneous levity emerges; filmmakers emulate cinéma vérité with bouncing steadicams and intense post-production; abstract painters require immense training to create accidental masterpieces. Artistic authenticity has always been the domain of fastidious engineering.

But plandids differ by measures of degree and style. The culture they emulate is that of the faux celebrity, who themselves imitate the trials of the truly famous. While celebrities endure the paparazzi, the pseudo-famous use plandids to simulate the experience of avoiding exposure. Those paragons of the plandid, the Kardashians, occupy their entire lives pretending the camera is not gazing at them. Sitting in their open kitchen and eating small salads from big bowls, they feign that no one is watching when everyone is watching.

In a bygone era, one looked in the lens and said "cheese," but in the age of ubiquitous cameras, we pretend they do not exist. Plandids represent the final conquest of celebrity culture: choreographed voyeurism. *Just ignore the camera. It's easier if you pretend no one is watching.*

SEE ALSO: FINSTAGRAM; NODDY; TRUTH CLAIM

PLASTIC SURGERY

If clicks on tabloid photo galleries and vitriol on social media were the guages of measurement, plastic surgery might be judged the most divisive subject of the contemporary human experience. And perhaps those are credible yardsticks, as the moral debates of going under the knife are so murky and contentious.

Plastic surgery encompasses a wide range of restorative, corrective, and reconstructive acts, but mostly it is known for boob jobs, butt lifts, liposuction, tummy tucks, and nose jobs. The most socially controversial body modification surgeries include the *double eyelid blepharoplasty*, in which Asian eyes are reshaped into more Occidental form, and the *labiaplasty*, which involves trimming a woman's outer labia. (Sometimes known as *the Barbie surgery*, labiaplasties are on the rise, with around 12,000 procedures in 2016.) These cosmetic enhancements lie at a contentious cultural crossroads, somewhere between the utopian freedom of an ever-upgradable body and the narcissistic dystopia of a society obsessed with image.

SEE ALSO: BOTOX; CYBORG; PHOTOSHOPPING

PLATO'S CAVE

Imagine a group of people chained inside a cave their whole lives, facing one direction, toward a wall. Behind the cave dwellers, an eternal flame flickers, casting shadows onto the wall from the outside world. A duck waddles by, or a toddler on a tricycle, but the pitiful shackled troglodytes can see only the shadow puppets of the passing figures against the cave wall. Reality, for them, is but a phantasm.

Finally, a plot: One of the cave dwellers breaks free and escapes the cave! At first, the outside world scares the hell out of him. The vibrant colors and

complex shapes are initially freakish, but the escapee eventually recognizes reality for all its splendor. After sneaking in a matinee of *Hamilton* on Broadway, he returns to the cave to share his discovery with his ol' lair buddies, who, to his surprise, mock and reject his fanciful three-dimensional world. (To be fair, it may have been envy over the *Hamilton* tix.)

Doy, this is an allegory, roughly told by Socrates in Plato's *Republic*. We are the oafs of the story, trapped in the cave of our experiences; rational thought is the light that reveals detail and complexity. Like feral children, we live futile lives preoccupied with shadow monsters. Only enlightened reason can free us from the enslavement of the shadow world.

But wait—if the colorful objects of the outside world are more real than the bleak shadows of the cave, could something be *more real* than the colorful objects? For Plato, this more-real place is the realm of the forms, where perfect ideas reside. Like the shadow puppets in the cave, our physical world is merely an array of copies, imperfect reproductions of ideal forms we can only half see. If we were able to shed the shackles of perception, like Neo taking THE RED PILL, or Roddy Piper slipping on magic sunglasses in *They Live*, or Truman ramming his little boat into the biodome, we would suddenly recognize the world for the artificial pantomime it is.

SEE ALSO: BRAIN IN A VAT; MANDELA EFFECT; THE RED PILL; SIMULISM; TOMMY WESTPHALL UNIVERSE; TRUMAN SYNDROME

POLYGRAPH

A polygraph is a machine that exposes the truth. [*Bzzz!*] A polygraph is a machine that reveals if a person is lying. [*Bzzz!*] A polygraph is a machine that reflects what its operator wants to hear. [*Ding!*]

The first person to study the connection between blood pressure and deception was psychologist William Moulton Marston, whose research in the 1920s set the groundwork for what became the polygraph machine. If his name sounds familiar, you are likely a comic book nerd: Marston also invented the character Wonder Woman for DC Comics.[116] The super-

---

116   Marston was a complex figure—a Harvard psychologist, a Gillette razor spokesperson, a bondage enthusiast, a huckster, and a polyamorist (he bore children with his wife and her niece, while living with both). He authored several books, including *You Can Be Popular* (1936) and *The Lie Detector Test* (1938), but the canonical account of his life can be found in *The Secret History of Wonder Woman* (2014) by Jill Lepore. His peculiar life became a biopic in 2017 with the release of *Professor Marston and the Wonder Women*.

heroine wields a golden lasso that forces its captors to reveal the truth. Today's polygraph is similarly weaponized, but more as a cajoling whip than a magical serum.

In addition to blood pressure, the modern polygraph test adds three physiological measurements: heart rate, respiration, and skin conductivity. A polygraph examiner, as myriad screenplays recount, interrogates suspects by interspersing control questions ("*Have you ever fibbed to a loved one?*") with relevant questions ("*Did you drown your wife in her lover's hot tub?*"). Measured by the polygraph, the physiological variance between each response supposedly reveals whether the suspect is a feckless dissembler.

Extensive research has shown that polygraphs are only slightly more reliable than a coin flip. Its results are extremely open to interpretation, and heavily skewed by prior suspicion. False positives can be assigned to honest people who are nervous; false negatives, to dishonest scoundrels who have conditioned their emotions. Poorly implemented polygraph tests have meted out prison terms on the innocent, and exonerated the guilty. Though not officially banned from courtrooms, judges today seldom allow them.[117] Police stations, however, are still besotted with the gizmos, mostly as an interrogation tool. While its results are seldom admissible as evidence, polygraph machines can be used to coerce confessions.

Despite their scientific illegitimacy, the lie-detector test still captures the human imagination, especially on film. In *Basic Instinct*, only evil super-genius Catherine Tramell (Sharon Stone) can beat the polygraph, until her lover-nemesis, Detective Nick Curran (Michael Douglas), reveals he can, too. In *Homeland*, stone-cold Nicholas Brody (Damian Lewis) outsmarts the machine, inspiring Saul Berenson (Mandy Pat-

inkin) to do the same. Too bad none of these characters saw *Ocean's Thirteen*, where a dimwit uses the old tack-in-the-shoe trick to crack the test, or for that matter sought information online, where polygraph strategy is plentiful. Movies like to present poly-crackers as emotional savants, but the dirty little secret is that the scribbles from the gyrating pen are partially for show. Good polygraphers can see you biting your tongue or regulating your breathing. They are on the lookout for cheaters. And after the test, when they imply they *know something*, they are again carefully studying your reaction. The polygraph machine is a bluff. *You* are the test results, as much as the scribbly lines drawn by the machine. [*Ding!*]

SEE ALSO: THE BIG LIE; BOGUS PIPELINE; CONFIDENCE GAME; PLACEBO EFFECT; PONZI SCHEME; RORSCHACH TEST; SODIUM PENTOTHAL; VOIGHT-KAMPFF MACHINE

PONZI SCHEME

This fraudulent investment operation starts small, with a promise of high returns for individual investors. And it works! (At first.) Early investors in a Ponzi scheme see high returns (at least on paper) and tell other people about their profits. Each loudmouthed boast brings new money into the racket, which the schemer uses to fund the previous generation of investors. A Ponzi scheme ticks because of the braggadocio of its victims, but the skulduggery eventually fails when new funds cease flowing into the operation.[118]

---

[117] The Supreme Court case *United States v. Scheffer* (1998) stated, "There is simply no consensus that polygraph evidence is reliable." But some judges still sometimes allow them to be administered when both parties agree.

[118] The difference between a *Ponzi scheme* and a *pyramid scheme* is a simple matter of transparency. Whereas a Ponzi scheme touts some sort of esoteric investment strategy, a pyramid scheme (e.g., Amway, Herbalife, Mary Kay) unabashedly admits that new capital powers the system.

The scheme is named after a real person, one Charles Ponzi, an inveterate swindler who in 1920 flagrantly deployed the technique. It wasn't his idea (even Dickens wrote about similar schemes), but his flamboyant implementation of the scam led to it bearing his name. By promising clients they would double their money within ninety days through a con involving postage coupons, Ponzi swindled $20 million before getting caught.

Ponzi schemes work because each victim believes they are actually the ones bilking the system with high returns. The biggest financial fraud in history—Bernie Madoff's $65 billion con perpetrated over two decades—was a Ponzi scheme. He notoriously defrauded thousands of clients, including celebrities Zsa Zsa Gabor, Kevin Bacon, Elie Wiesel, Sandy Koufax, John Malkovich, Eliot Spitzer, and Steven Spielberg. He pled guilty to eleven felonies in 2009 and was sentenced 150 years in prison.

SEE ALSO: BEANIE BABY BUBBLE; MONEY

POPE JOAN

Was there a crossdressing woman pope? For centuries, most Catholics thought so.

Even before becoming pope in the ninth century, John Anglicus of Mainz was regarded as pious and brainy. But his two-year reign as Pope John VIII came to a shocking end during a procession to St. Peter's Cathedral. While riding horseback, the pope suddenly grew ill, dismounted, and gave birth to a child. Pope John VIII instantly transformed into Pope Joan I—and was immediately stoned to death by the angry mob who witnessed the birth.

That story appears to have originated in the early thirteenth century and was universally accepted until the late sixteenth century, when religious scholars began to question its veracity. The first tip-off: No record of her reign appeared until centuries later,

which is a little peculiar, given she was the first female pontiff and all. Also, other popes had their visage minted on coins, but not Joan. The timeline didn't add up either—the name "Pope John VIII" was devised later, but there was already a genuine pope by that name who ruled from 872 to 882. (The regnal numbering of popes did not start until the late Middle Ages, and Johns were particularly messy to renumber. One conspiracy holds there is no Pope John XX because Joan was skipped.) In 1601, the Church declared Pope Joan a fraud, and today she is widely viewed as a medieval legend. Though a pretty cool one.

One version of the legend suggests that the Pope Joan scandal spooked the Catholic Church so much that all subsequent popes were physically examined before taking the throne. The story goes that the pontiff-to-be has to sit on a *sedia stercoraria*—a chair with a hole in it—as a cardinal reaches up and touches his genitals, declaring, "*Duos habet et bene pendentes.*" Translation: "He has two, and they dangle nicely."

SEE ALSO: APOCRYPHA; FANFIC; HOMER; PHANTOM TIME HYPOTHESIS; PRESTER JOHN

PORNOGRAPHY

It seems pretty simple, but pornography is one of humanity's most confounding by-products.

Resisting classification is its primary act of defiance. What *is* pornography, exactly? We claim to "know it when we see it," but only with chagrin, a pragmatic phrase born of an inability to define.[119] Is porn a form of storytelling? Is it art? Is it covertly violent? Overtly healthy? Socially dangerous? Pure fantasy? Impure reality? Reality television?

Is it *normal*? (What is a *normal*?) (Is anything *normal*?)

To consider this matter, let us consult an expert—50 Cent. The mogul rapper, in what seems like a lapse of judgment, once told *Spin* magazine that to avoid extortion, he records all his sexual encounters. "I always tell women, 'When you come into this room, there is going to be a surveillance camera,'" said the ex-gangbanger of his bedchamber. "And it's not only for legal reasons. I enjoy watching it, too, if I feel like I performed."[120]

For just a moment, pretend you are 50 Cent. You don't have to envisage being shot nine times in Queens, but try to imagine rigging your bedroom with surveillance cameras. Imagine telling prospective paramours that your lovemaking will be recorded, not just out of litigation anxiety but because you might watch it later, for enjoyment. Can you imagine? If so, here is the question: Are you, faux-Fiddy, creating *pornography*?[121]

To address the quandary, we must pause to recognize the issue creating the categorical impasse: *What is the role of "the actor" in pornography?* With traditional films, we can easily parse the function of the performer, without complication. When Uma Thurman delicately coaxes John Travolta into wiggling the twist at Jack Rabbit Slim's, or when Bill Murray furtively whispers in Scarlett Johansson's ear on the streets of Shibuya, or even when Meg Ryan saucily simulates an ORGASM for Billy Crystal in Katz's Deli—in all cases, there is no confusion about its narrative category. It's simple: These are the actions of actors, dramatizing roles in fictional movies. But what is

going on when porn stars Sasha Grey and James Deen shampoo the wookie on a futon in San Fernando? It's not fake, exactly, because they, like 50 Cent in his panopticon boudoir, are *actually* having sex. It is very real—and yet, like so much pornography, it resembles no reality. No one would mistake a porno flick for a dramatic blockbuster, but no one would describe it as documentary either. Like one of those indecisive quantum particles, pornography coexists as both real and fake.[122]

Erotic matters are preternaturally fuzzy, especially in their taxonomic distribution. Consider the difference between the age-old arts of pornography and prostitution. If you have sex for money, we call it *prostitution*. If you have sex for money while filming, it becomes *pornography*. But why? Why does the camera—the recording and distribution—change the classification?

Umberto Eco took up the question of categorization in his essay "How to Recognize a Porn Movie." Counterintuitively, his theory for identifying smut targeted the nonpornographic scenes—those interminable moments of *plot* that forestall the real action. "If, to go from A to B, the characters take longer than you would like, then the film you are seeing is pornographic," he concluded.[123] It was probably an accurate depiction of illicit theater-driven porn in 1989, when the semiotician published his treatise, but in the age of widespread internet porn, the designation

---

119   The phrase "I know it when I see it" was famously delivered by Supreme Court Justice Potter Stewart to describe his threshold for obscenity. Often forgotten, he wrote those words in *Jacobellis v. Ohio* (1964), which ruled that the Louis Malle film *The Lovers* (1958) was not obscene.

120   50 Cent spoke these words in the April 2005 issue of *Spin*.

121   If you are a purist who deems gonzo "sex tapes" inferior products, recall that Paris Hilton's sex tape, which was marketed as *1 Night in Paris*, won multiple AVN Awards.

122   As to the question of "acting" in pornography, when the former porn star Jenna Haze was asked on Twitter why she quit the biz, she responded, "I never enjoyed it. I was acting the entire time." If *After Porn Ends*, a 2012 documentary about the industry, is an indication, this aloof stance toward the carnal craft is common, but not universal, among porn actors.

123   The English version of the essay can be found in his collection, *How to Travel with a Salmon and Other Essays* (1992). Eco's statement is effectively the opposite of the old Hitchcock adage, "Drama is life with the dull bits cut out." Porn, according to Eco, puts the dull parts back in.

seems, *mi scusi*, limp. Technology now disaggregates those scenes, so you can, if you choose, skip right past the cumbersome bits that "take longer than you like." In the internet age, plot is an optional feature.

Which is not to say that rampant fast-forwarding and incognito multi-tabbing (to say nothing of enormous clip aggregators and secret dark web caches) have expunged storytelling from the erotic arts. Narrative, or fantasy, still pumps the steam of the pornographic engine, even if the denouement is, *sploosh*, always the same. In fact, it is the narrative *realism* of adult films, or the lack thereof, that still gets harshly criticized in ethical discussions of internet porn. Those scuzzy websites, the argument goes, create a false sense of *actual* sex, harming our perceptions of what partners desire. But this appeal to realism demands a delicate rhetorical maneuver. Was accuracy *ever* the domain of pornography? Did the exaggerated endomorphism of ancient fertility figurines stunt the minds of paleolithic boys?[124]

The internet has a maxim, known as Rule 34, which tries to explain its abundance of sexual imagery: *If you can imagine it, there is porn of it*. But if you have imagined it, and someone has made porn of it, then someone *has really done it*. It exists—there's no more need to *imagine*. Rule 34 suggests an eternal libidinous loop, where our most perverse ideas are immediately shown back to us as real. And because someone else did it on-screen, license seems to be granted to re-create the act, leading to the big question: Should sex imitate porn? Is it a guidebook, or should porn be deemed an uninhabitable "other world," no more desirable than Middle-earth or Arrakis? When should fantasy *stay fantasy*, and when should it become real?

Mysteriously, pornography seems to accrue power by ignoring the question, by defying classification and straddling categories like a Sybian warhorse. More than sex itself, porn seems resistant to simple linguistic description, possibly because it thrives in the dark, away from our social language. (Even simple action verbs are lacking. We say one *watches* porn, but that ignores a whole cosmology of interactions and maneuvers.)

For his part, 50 Cent continues to blur the category. In 2016 he was ordered by a court to pay $7 million in damages to Rick Ross's baby mama for publishing her sex tape. Fiddy did not record or appear in the video, but as part of his ongoing beef with Ross, the rapper superimposed his own face over the gentleman in the video and added a vulgar audio track. Fiddy then dropped his filthy mashup online, just to rankle Ross. After losing the lawsuit, the creator of *Get Rich or Die Tryin'* filed for bankruptcy. Now here's the same question again: Was Fiddy creating *pornography?* Not even the ontological pragmatism of "I know it when I see it" can help us sort through this one.

SEE ALSO: CELEBRITY SEX TAPES; DONKEY PUNCH; ORGASMS; REALDOLL; SLASHFIC

POTEMKIN VILLAGE

Potemkin Villages flaunt fake exteriors, disguising shabby conditions behind their showy facades. The term comes not only from Russia but from the queen bee of the empire herself.

In 1783, Catherine the Great's ex-lover and soulmate, Grigory Potemkin, urged the Empress to annex the peninsula known as Crimea. Her Majesty abided—and then rewarded her confidant with the governorship of the colony. Catherine soon announced a surprise six-month journey to her new annexed territory. The story goes that as the Empress travelled down the Dnieper River through Crimea, Potemkin erected a new "mobile village" on the waterfront of each port, populating it with frolicking peasants.

---

124 Maybe!

Each night, the village was disassembled and rebuilt downstream at the next stop.

Regrettably, this account of Potemkin Villages is itself likely a Potemkin Village. It probably never happened. Governor Potemkin surely spruced up the riverfront for his Empress, painting facades and stashing derelicts. But there is scant evidence that he constructed entire pasteboard villages. The rumor of Potemkin's stage management was likely concocted as propaganda by his enemies to make him appear mendacious.[125]

Crimea would eventually be transferred back to Ukraine (by Khrushchev, of all people), which gained independence in 1991. But in another act of revanchism in 2014, Vladimir Putin notoriously annexed the strategic jewel of Crimea again, for a second time. The same year, just a skip across the Caspian, the Winter Olympics were held in Sochi, Russia. The Olympics have always embodied a type of Potemkin Village—quickly erected architecture, meretricious television staging, superficial city cleanups. But in preparing for these games, Putin intensified the pageantry, making his omnipotence part of the theatrical display, by lashing out at political opponents, rolling tanks into peaceful territories, and jailing journalists. In reannexing Crimea and emblazoning his ostentatious might over the region, Putin seemed determined to erect a new Potemkin Village—this time more symbolic, yet more imperious.

SEE ALSO: CLAQUE; FALSE FLAG OPERATION; GERRYMANDERING; GREEBLES; MOIROLOGIST; TRAP STREETS; TRUMAN SYNDROME; UTOPIA

---

[125] Since we are in historical debunking mode, now is a good time to mention that the Russian empress was not a nymphomaniac who fornicated with stallions. Catherine the Great did not die during an equine tryst, as told by legend, but in bed from a stroke. In her sixty-seven long years, she did accumulate twenty-two male lovers, many of them young and handsome. But like an early form of *kompromat*, the rumors about her sexual voracity were mostly fabricated by enemies.

Who is the most influential *fictional* person of all time? There are plenty of potent characters from which to choose.

We might start the search for significance in the clouds of Olympus, where a pantheon of classical gods, among them Zeus and Athena and Apollo, clumsily shaped our future literature, art, philosophy, and politics. Or we could turn to a more direct case, like the search for the mythical Holy Grail, told in the lofty legends of King Arthur in medieval Europe, which spurred Christians into the misbegotten crusades. Among the influencers, we cannot overlook more intimate figures, including childhood fables like SANTA CLAUS and Cinderella, who probably leave behind some insidious residue in their psychic demise. (The same mystery accompanies the impressions left by those video game and comic book characters—Superman! Wonder Woman!—who dominate our youth.) The outlaw myth of Robin Hood likely did some good, too, affording at least an ounce of philanthropic goodwill to the poor. Big Brother, on the other hand, may have inspired some regrettable technology. Godzilla, some scholar has surely put forth, helped desiccate the Cold War. And just as surely, an actuarial chart buried in a sooty filing cabinet in Virginia has tabulated a kill count from the Marlboro Man and Joe Camel.

All these fictional personas left some impact on history. But one overlooked medieval patriarch might surpass all their influence—Prester John, a mythical king whose awareness reigned for more than 500 years starting in the twelfth century. His closest corollary today might be Superman, in both popularity and potency.

The prester (a title once given to early Christian priests) began as a modest myth, a minor king in the Orient. From humble beginnings, he became a sensation in 1165, when a letter from his hand began to circulate around Europe. In opulent detail, the epistle unveiled his sumptuous Nestorian empire,[126] containing such wonders as the Fountain of Youth and the Garden of Eden. The true origin of the letter remains a mystery lost to history, but over centuries it was disseminated across Christendom, embellished with each iteration, until a hundred unique manuscripts flitted around. In some cases, Prester John had accrued magical abilities; others claimed he was a direct descendant of a Magi. His gilded kingdom moved around, too, from India (where Pope Alexander III sent an emissary to find him) to Mongolia (where he was linked to Genghis Khan) to Ethiopia (where his myth finally dissipated when Portuguese envoys could not locate him). Persistent rumors that he was victorious over Muslim armies guaranteed that his notoriety would last for centuries.

By the time his myth was finally debunked (perhaps the Fountain of Youth was a tad too whimsical), Prester John had secured a lasting effect on religion, world trade, exploration, literature, and politics. To devout Christians, he represented evidence that the teachings of Jesus were universal, which turned out to be a handy precondition for colonialism. Believing another Christian kingdom thrived beyond Islamic land, missionaries for centuries expanded their efforts toward Central Asia, Africa, and India. The explorer Bartolomeu Dias became the first European to sail around Africa to the Indian Ocean partially because Portugal's king wanted to find the mythical ruler. The same request was given to Ferdinand Magellan as he circumnavigated the globe. Not long after, Shakespeare mentioned the legendary king in *Much Ado About Nothing*, but by then, Prester John had finally become a punchline as a fanciful mythical figure.

Today, the legendary priest-king can be found in Marvel Comics (in issues of *Fantastic Four* and *Thor*)

---

126   Nestorians were Christians of the East. Today we might think of them as proto-Protestants, as they denied certain Catholic doctrine, including the divinity of Mary.

and on the Netflix series *Marco Polo*. Still a minor character, he may have had more impact than all his fictional peers.

SEE ALSO: APOCRYPHA; FANFIC; GOSPEL OF JESUS'S WIFE; HOMER; POPE JOAN; SANTA CLAUS

PRODUCT DISPLACEMENT

From the tree line, a figure ambles onto the screen, his head conspicuously pixelated against the conifers. A slide guitar squawks, now instantly recognizable as the slurring intro to "Loser." The blurred figure finally removes some mysterious headgear, and the pixelation disappears. "In the time of chimpanzees," the figure raps, "I was a monkey." At this moment in the 1994 music video, most of the world sees Beck for the first time, but his head is fuzzy for the first few bars of his debut. Years later, we would learn that he was wearing a stormtrooper helmet, which Lucasfilm did not approve of, leading to one of the most conspicuous instances of *product displacement*—blurring unlicensed material to unrecognizability.[127]

Avoiding fees for trademarked content is just one rationale for product displacement. The other is that companies often spend exorbitant sums to get their logos inserted *into* movies or television shows. Accidentally filmed brands that have not ponied up their PRODUCT PLACEMENT fees get pixelated through a process known as *greeking*. These blurry boxes are so ubiquitous on some reality television (hovering over shirts, hats, posters, cars, websites, cereal boxes, and most ominously, other television screens) that they almost create another character in the room—the Blurry Blob behind the Kardashian.

In one of the most notorious cases of product displacement, brands insisted on being removed from the film that won the Best Picture Oscar in 2008. According to director Danny Boyle, Coca-Cola and Mercedes did not want to be associated with the squalor of Mumbai in *Slumdog Millionaire*. Their logos were digitally removed from the shantytown in postproduction.

Fictional worlds scrubbed of all branding can feel unrealistic, which was used to great effect in *Repo Man* (1984), set in a disorienting commercial desert that contains only generic products. To avoid the alienation of worlds without marketing, directors will sometimes invent imaginary brands to substitute for real-world ones. This type of product displacement creates a kind of visual rhyming with reality, such as when the protagonists of *Scrubs* hang at Coffee Bucks, or the employees of *30 Rock* reckon with their new owners at Kabletown. Some market researchers speculate these unpaid faux placements might actually be better for the real brand than true product placements. Which is super depressing.

A final type of product displacement might be ad blockers, which remove banners and sponsors from websites. But in this case, it is the consumer who greeks out the brand from view.

SEE ALSO: DEFICTIONALIZED PRODUCT; PRODUCT PLACEMENT; WIPING

---

127 The practice might seem spurious, but these types of trademark lawsuits are not uncommon. Anheuser-Busch sued the studio behind *Flight* (2012), in which Denzel Washington pilots a jetliner after getting plastered on Budweiser. Emerson Electric sued NBC for a scene of *Heroes* in which their garbage disposal, InSinkErator, is cast "in an unsavory light, irreparably tarnishing the product." The producers of *Debbie Does Dallas* (1978) were litigated because the film involved carnality with a cheerleader whose team is "confusingly similar" to a certain prominent NFL franchise. Sometimes the litigant wins, sometimes the filmmakers win, and sometimes they settle out of court. Quite often, as part of the settlement, the brand is digitally scrubbed from later showings.

PRODUCT PLACEMENT

Betty Draper beams a rainbow of pride as she introduces each dish at her international-themed dinner party.[128] "We are going to take a little trip around the world," she says, pointing to gazpacho from Spain, rumaki from Japan, and spaetzle from Germany. Still spinning her culinary globe, she moves on to beverages. "We have a choice of Burgundy from France, or a frosty glass of beer from Holland."

Roger Sterling and Duck Phillips, two of the dinner guests, are nonplussed to hear Betty mention the beer brand. Unwittingly, she is serving one of Sterling-Cooper's premier clients, Heineken. "[Don] said *you* were the market, and you are," Duck says to Betty. At the head of the table, Don just smiles his usual smile, smug and euphoric.

"What an interesting experiment," Betty enunciates, clearly annoyed she fell for one of her husband's campaigns. She does not like hearing that she is susceptible to advertising. No one does. Which is why the scene is so ingenious—*we* are Betty. Heineken is a product placement inserted into *Mad Men* for a heavy fee. And we, the viewers who just fell for the trick, don't love falling for it either.

All day we see people using products—cheerily chugging Heinekens, gleefully tapping iPhones, mindlessly raving about their Teslas. So, in theory, a product placement inside a television show (or movie, or video game, or book, or song) should create authenticity. But it often has the reverse effect. Some product placements are clever, like when Dwight from *The Office* takes a job at Staples. Others seem forced, like every time the detectives on

The Wire devour takeout KFC. The unforgettable placements include Reese's Pieces[129] in *E.T.* and Tom Cruise sporting Ray-Bans in both *Risky Business* (Wayfarers) and *Top Gun* (Aviators). They might seem a recent development, but product placements go way back. James Dean swept an Ace comb through his hair in *Rebel Without a Cause* (1955); Wrigley's gum appears onscreen for a good thirty seconds in Fritz Lang's *M* (1919). But over the past decade, their frequency has certainly intensified. Nearly all broadcast network shows now have paid placements, and movies are steeped in brands—*Transformers: Age of Extinction* (2014) mashed fifty-five brands into 165 minutes, miraculously including Victoria's Secret and Oreo.

In music, shameless plugging began with Run DMC's "My Adidas," which started as a simple unpaid homage but led to a $1.5 million endorsement deal, ushering in an era of product shout-outs in hip-hop. Jay-Z now tops that universe, with more than sixty paid mentions in verse.

Spotting the product placement often takes on the characteristics of sport. One of the joyful (and frustrating) aspects of *Mad Men* is guessing which placements are paid.[130] The series wryly concludes with the "I'd Like to Buy the World a Coke" jingle, which totally could be a product placement but also seems too brazen to be one. In the end, it doesn't really matter. Like Betty, we all just unwittingly take a swig.

SEE ALSO: DEFICTIONALIZED PRODUCT; FOREIGN BRANDING; MERE-EXPOSURE EFFECT; PRODUCT DISPLACEMENT; SUBLIMINAL ADVERTISING; TOYETIC; VIRAL MARKETING

---

128 This *Mad Men* scene is from "A Night to Remember" (season 2, episode 8), set in 1962.

129 Hershey, the makers of Reese's Pieces, did not pay the studio directly but spent a million dollars on advertising *E.T.* in exchange for having the lovable extraterrestrial gobble the coated candy. Steven Spielberg initially wanted M&M's in the movie, but Mars requested final script review, so the studio offered it to Reese's instead.

130 Mad Men Placement Cheat Sheet! PAID: Heineken, Cadillac, Utz, US Airways, London Fog, Smirnoff. NOT PAID: Coca-Cola, Lucky Strike, McCann, Jaguar, American Airlines, Dow Chemical.

PROTOCOLS OF THE ELDERS OF ZION, THE

The Protocols purports to be the meeting minutes of the First Zionist Congress, a clandestine conference held in Basel, Switzerland, where Jewish leaders plotted to control the world's gold supply, to ensnare the population in ruinous debt, and to exterminate gentiles. A sampling from the summit's anonymous amanuensis:

> The goyim are a flock of sheep, and we are their wolves. And you know what happens when the wolves get hold of the flock?

No, *tell me more*, Grandpa.

First published in 1903 by Russian mystic Sergei Nilus, *The Protocols* quickly spread in translation throughout Europe but was finally exposed in 1921 by the London *Times* as a hoax—and worse, plagiarism! (The text contains several passages obviously cribbed from previous anti-Semitic works.) One prominent theory holds that the document was originally composed as a parody of Jewish idealism, but some giddy bigots decided to publish it as though it were real.

Whatever its provenance, noted assembly line maniac Henry Ford can be credited with helping *The Protocols* gain momentum in America in the early '20s. In a series of articles titled *The International Jew*, Ford defended *The Protocols* in his weekly newspaper, *The Dearborn Independent.*[131] He also funded the printing of a half-million copies of *The Protocols* to be distributed around the country.

The story only devolves from here. Ford had an admirer in one Adolf Hitler, who praised the automaker in *Mein Kampf*, had a photo of him in his office, and even awarded him the Grand Cross of the German Eagle, the highest honor a foreigner can receive.

The Protocols were used as propaganda in the Nazi justification of genocide, and the Führer cited Ford's *International Jew* as an "inspiration."

One of the greatest tragedies in human history may have been ignited by a virulent hoax—an anonymous, fabricated text that scapegoated the Jewish people in an international conspiracy.

SEE ALSO: THE BIG LIE; FALSE FLAG OPERATION; HITLER DIARIES

PSEUDO-EVENT

Events have a way of happening. Either by chance or necessity, incidents just spill out into the universe. A dog barks at a cat. A tree falls in the forest. You chomp into a burrito. A star implodes into a supernova. Events just happen.

Pseudo-events don't *just happen*. Far from inevitable, pseudo-events exist because they have been choreographed, scripted, arranged. A corporation holds a press conference to generate positive news. A politician visits a disaster site "for optics." A restaurant invites "influencers" to its "grand opening" to "share photos." A reality TV star hires a CLAQUE to applaud his candidacy for president. Pseudo-events are created.

Pseudo-events are a form of media that creates more media; staged spectacles, arousing attention. Born in the wasteland of advertising and public relations, the pseudo-event has migrated to the fertile fields of politics and media, which are mutating before our eyes into empires of pure theater and entertainment.

The distinction between event and pseudo-event

---

131   No rinky-dink rag, *The Dearborn Independent* was the nation's second-largest paper (due to a promotion imposed on Ford dealers), with nearly a million in circulation. When Ford faced libel charges for the series in 1927, he apologized and shuttered the paper.

originates with historian Daniel Boorstin. In his 1962 book *The Image: A Guide to Pseudo-Events in America*, Boorstin claimed that America was living in an "age of contrivance." As we master "our arts of self-deception," fabrications have become a ritualized force in society. "We suffer primarily not from our vices or our weaknesses, but from our illusions," Boorstin wrote. "We are haunted, not by reality, but by those images we have put in place of reality." Public life brims with pseudo-events—counterfeit happenings untethered from reality.[132]

Arising from dismay over the televised spectacle of the Nixon/Kennedy debates of 1960, Boorstin's definition of the pseudo-event is almost quaint by the standards of modern media saturation. Since his coinage, we have seen the presidency awarded first to an actor, and then to a reality TV star. Every reason to leave the house is now dubbed an "experience," and the notion of a "staged event" has become so ubiquitous that it bears no difference from mere "event." Photo ops (a term forged by the Nixon administration) now occur when anyone pulls out their phone, like insta-kliegs combusted from a pocket. Government emails are stolen and released as "leaks," and world leaders tweet apocalyptic threats at each other. (Perhaps colleges will one day offer courses in *Reality Studies*, taught nostalgically like *Renaissance Painting* or *Latin*, with a syllabus of non-synthetic experiences. We know just the textbook!)

Pseudo-events are ingrained into the system, indistinct from non-illusions. Unlike propaganda, which intentionally distorts facts, these faux-happenings certify a new reality. Pseudo-events are not necessarily lies, but they always could be, which makes them both irresistible and anxiety-inducing. Because they are pervasive, pseudo-events elude the accusation of contrivance. To the charge "that's just theater," the pseudo-event cynically shoots back, "it's all just theater." Just as no accolades are bestowed for announcing that air exists, pointing at artificiality goes unrewarded.

In the age of virtual reality and fake news, Instagram celebrities and fantasy football, pseudo-events are indistinguishable from reality itself. "We risk being the first people in history," wrote Boorstin, "to have been able to make their illusions so vivid, so persuasive, so 'realistic' that they can live in them." The risk is over. What is reality now, but another synthetic sub-category of the pseudo-event?

SEE ALSO: BLACK PROPAGANDA; CELEBRITY SEX TAPES; CLAQUE; PLANDID; REALITY-BASED COMMUNITY; THE TREACHERY OF IMAGES; POTEMKIN VILLAGE; VIRAL MARKETING

PUSH POLL

It's November—the day before the election. Your phone rings. Picking up, you hear an automated message:

> Hello, this is Max McGovern, your proud candidate for governor. I am calling to remind you to vote tomorrow for the causes that matter to you—job growth, safe communities, and equality.

An hour later, the phone rings again, another political telemarketer:

> Hello, this is pollster Bridget Smothers. I am taking a quick public opinion survey about candidate awareness before tomorrow's election. First question: Did you know that gubernatorial candidate Max McGovern is a convicted pedophile?

---

132   Counterfeit events breed counterfeit people. A celebrity, as Boorstin defined the species, is "a person who is known for his well-knownness." The tautology struck a chord, and would morph into the epithet "famous for being famous."

The first call from Max is an innocuous (if annoying) campaign advertisement. It likely has minimal effect on your vote. The second call from wily Bridget is also an ad, but one disguised as an opinion poll. Known as *push polls*, these political dirty tricks feign as innocent surveys, but with the intent of implanting negative (often false) information about an opponent. The push poll is political canvassing that masquerades as research.

Richard Milhous Nixon was a pioneer of the push poll. In 1946, the future president entered his first campaign against Jerry Voorhis, an incumbent for an Orange County seat in the House of Representatives. Throughout the district, voters reported receiving phone calls that began, "This is a friend of yours, but I can't tell you who I am. Did you know that Jerry Voorhis is a communist?" At least one person admitted to phone-banking ads for $9 per day, but the red-baiting attacks could never be directly linked to Nixon.[133]

Countless candidates have since been accused of issuing push polls. *Accused* is the operative word, as candidates are seldom caught. Other forms of media can be traced—television ads can be recorded, website campaigns are screengrabbed, direct mail is a physical document. But push polls leave behind scant evidence. Phone calls are ephemeral, and recording them requires some effort. Leaving few footprints, anonymous push polls sit atop the crooked campaigner's bag of dirty tricks.

SEE ALSO: ASTROTURFING; BARRON, JOHN; BLACK PROPAGANDA; FALSE FLAG OPERATION; FUD; SOCK PUPPET; SWIFTBOATING

---

133 This story derives from "When Push Comes to Poll," a 1996 story in *Washington Monthly*.

Q

QUID PRO QUO GOSSIP

Though the American gossip magazine first emerged in the 1920s, not until the splashy arrival of *Confidential* in the early 1950s did celebrity tabloids adopt their notoriously salacious house style. With a subtitle screeching that it "names the names," *Confidential* did exactly that, calling out celebrities who were in the closet, had spousal problems, or were in rehab. After a report on the marital demise of Marilyn Monroe and Joe DiMaggio, the tabloid jumped to an astonishing 10 million in circulation. Publishing the scuzziest dirt, it became the scourge of Hollywood with reports that outed pianist Liberace and actress Lizabeth Scott. (The publication would also become the subject of the 1997 movie *L.A. Confidential*.)

In 1955, *Confidential* was sitting on another scurrilous scoop: a report that actor Rock Hudson was secretly gay. But this time when the publication threatened to expose the dashing lead man, Hudson's agent cut a deal to quash the disclosure by trading information about two of his other clients. Instead of the Hudson exposé, stories soon appeared in *Confidential* about Rory Calhoun's years as a juvenile delinquent and Tab Hunter's arrest for disorderly conduct. Both actors shared an agent with Hudson.

And so, at the very birth of the modern tabloid, the *quid pro quo gossip exchange*—swapping one piece of salacious information to suppress another—also became a crucial component of the celebrity industrial complex. Though rumored as rampant, no one knows exactly how much celebrity news is "traded" today. In one rare case reported by the *New Yorker*, the publication TMZ acknowledged acquiring a video in 2011 of Justin Bieber casually using the N-word. After confronting his manager, TMZ agreed not to publish the damaging video and the site suddenly gained conspicuous access to the pop singer. Previously cast as a villain, the tone of Bieber reports on TMZ turned positive, just as negative stories about his foes seemed to accelerate.

The frequency of these unscrupulous shakedowns is still relatively secret. But in 2017, it was revealed that movie producer Harvey Weinstein had been supplying disparaging gossip on his sexual abuse victims to the *New York Post*, which published items that discredited his victims.

SEE ALSO: CELEBRITY SEX TAPES; HONEYTRAP; YELLOW JOURNALISM

R

RADAR CHAFF

Here is a case where low-tech camouflage can bamboozle high-tech engineering.

To throw off adversary air defense systems, military planes are known to emit a flurry of superfine fibers of aluminum, known as *radar chaff*. The reflective particles cause a cloud to briefly appear on certain radar-guided systems.

Radar chaff was pioneered by both Axis and Allied forces during World War II. A similar military technique, the *decoy flare*, is used to avert the attention of heat-seeking missiles.

SEE ALSO: FALSE FLAG OPERATION; MIMICRY; TROJAN HORSE

RAPE ON CAMPUS, A

News reporters have developed a clever adage to describe an irresistible story tip or morsel of gossip that they desperately wish were true, because it could yield an extraordinary work of journalism—a story so *important*, or *compelling*, or sometimes, *horrific*—but it might actually be *too good*, and that with just a phone call or two, made almost reluctantly, they would discover, as they suspected, that the story is total, complete, undeniable balderdash. "Too good to check" is what they call these irresistible tips, which great journalists instantly detect as malarkey.

"A Rape on Campus" was one of those stories, too good (or here, too bad) to check, and no one did.

Published in *Rolling Stone* in November 2014, the story claimed a University of Virginia student, identified as "Jackie," had been gang raped by seven members of the Phi Kappa Psi fraternity as part of an initiation rite. It was later revealed that Jackie fabricated the story, seemingly as a CATFISHING ploy to gain the attention of another boy on campus. *Rolling Stone* later retracted the story and issued multiple apologies. In an exhaustive 12,000-word report, *Columbia Journalism Review* reprimanded the magazine for CONFIRMATION BIAS and failure to perform even basic fact-checking. The reporter, Sabrina Erdely, was duped by the putative victim, Jackie, but she also ignored rudimentary journalistic ethics and responsibilities.

The bogus story undoubtedly did damage to the

THE BANDIT claims that he seduced the wife, who, filled with shame, begged the husband to duel for her honor.	THE WIFE reports being raped by the bandit and accidentally stabbing her husband while trying to kill herself.
THE HUSBAND, whose account is given through a medium, says he witnessed consensual sex and, overcome with grief, committed suicide.	THE WOODCUTTER, who watched from afar, also reports consensual sex, but that neither man wanted the disused wife, who ignited a fight between the two, ending in the husband's death.

cause of raising awareness about campus rape. Numbers are extremely difficult to extrapolate in this area, but a 2014 White House report estimated that as many as one in five college women have been sexually assaulted. A 1996 FBI crime report estimated that 8 percent of rape accusations are unfounded, but what constitutes "unfounded" can vary across local police districts and procedures, and may include cases in which charges were simply dropped or women were pressured into recanting. False accusations surely exist, but they likely make up a tiny fraction of cases.

SEE ALSO: CATFISH; GASLIGHTING

RASHOMON EFFECT

If multiple people witness the same event but give conflicting, irreconcilable accounts of that event, the Rashomon effect is often said to be at work.

The eponym is Akira Kurosawa's iconic 1950 masterpiece, *Rashomon*, which depicts the rape of a woman and the murder of her husband in twelfth-century Japan. Rather than portray the events through a single omniscient narrator, the story is repeated through the point of view of four different characters who claim to witness the same events. *Rashomon* presents a matrix of UNRELIABLE NARRATORS, each quadrant a diegesis of seemingly equal plausibility.

Due to its apparent relativism, the Rashomon effect has become a nifty (and probably overused) trope for depicting society and culture. The social sciences use it to connote a type of participant bias; legal studies, a construct for understanding contradictory witness testimony. The *Rashomon* structure has become such a staple of genre television that any legal drama, police procedural, science fiction thriller, or family comedy seems obliged to have a multiperspective bottle episode with contradictory viewpoints.

Modern sports events, unsuspectingly, might be where the Rashomon effect is most prevalent. The term has likely never been uttered in a broadcast booth, but televised professional sports rely on the Rashomon style to create conflict. Contested NFL replays, despite being repeated from countless angles, often leave viewers with conflicting feelings about "the truth." Everyone sees the same play, over and over, but arguments still flare. *Did he catch the ball inbounds?* Like the flashbacks in *Rashomon*, each replay adds more information about the putative catch, bolstering or contradicting the previous perspectives. The modern sports stadium comes armed with a battalion of cameras, but the panopticon gridiron still seems incapable of revealing an uncontested reality about the nuances of inbounds feet and established ball control. Even with perfect visual fidelity, we cannot agree. Each viewer still ultimately sees what they want to see, with fan partisanship blinkering their perspective. As *Rashomon* foresaw, consensus is futile when every participant is self-interested.

The analogy of modern sports also helps expose why *Rashomon* is not entirely a fable of radical subjectivity. The plot does not suggest that characters *remember* events differently but that characters *say* they remember events differently. Their perspectives are not a simple case of confabulation but of rhetoric, of manipulation, of lies. *Rashomon*—a story about telling stories—suggests not that truth is unknowable but that venal forces resist its knowing.

Or maybe you remember it differently.

SEE ALSO: CHINESE WHISPERS; GENOVESE, KITTY; IF I DID IT; KULESHOV EFFECT; MANDELA EFFECT; RETCONNING; THE RUMSFELD MATRIX; UNRELIABLE NARRATOR

RATHERGATE

Although the scandal spilled from broadcast television, Rathergate was the first major media controversy provoked by the nascent medium of blogging. In addition to prefiguring the oncoming deluge of social media, the scandal was also, indisputably, the most important news story of all time to utilize forensic typography and an animated GIF.

In September 2004, just weeks short of an official October surprise, *60 Minutes II* ran a damaging story on presidential incumbent George W. Bush, surfacing six documents allegedly written by his commanding officer in the Texas Air National Guard in the early '70s. The records indicated that Bush had disobeyed orders, shirked his duties, committed ESQUIVALIENCE, and attempted to falsify his record. The segment also insinuated that Bush had used political connections to avoid service in the Vietnam War, where his political opponent, John Kerry, had been a decorated war hero.

After the segment aired, blogs—most of them conservative—immediately started to cast doubt on the authenticity of the documents. More than just howling diatribes into the night (an abundant act in today's social web media), the bloggers performed actual acts of reporting (a less abundant act). The first anomaly they discovered was, of all things, typographic. The memos seemed to be riddled with anachronistic use of fonts, including many design features unavailable on typewriters of the day. Use of the Times New Roman font was the most glaring time warp, but there was also an instance of superscript—a mini *th* in *111^(th)*—which would become an automatic (and quite annoying) feature of word processing programs many years later but was not available on typewriters at the time. Amazingly enough, the entire document—font, margins, spacing, layout—appeared to be composed in the default template of Microsoft Word. The blog *Little Green Footballs* created an animated GIF that flipped between the *60 Minutes* document and a re-creation typed directly into Microsoft Word with default settings. They were nearly identical.

The anchor for the segment was Dan Rather, who initially defended the report before begrudgingly conceding that CBS could not prove the authenticity

of the documents. Four senior producers at the network were ousted and Rather retired the following year. In 2007, he filed a $70 million lawsuit against CBS claiming he had been made a "scapegoat," but the case was quickly dismissed.

A curious consequence of the scandal was the elevation of the phrase "Fake but Accurate," unwisely used by the *New York Times* in a headline about the secretary of the National Guard unit who would have typed the purported memos. She claimed that although the documents appeared forged, "the information in them is correct." Though perhaps a valid contention, by this point in the scandal, the assertion was moot, and *Fake but Accurate* became a *cri de coeur* of the right.

Although not directly analogous, *Fake but Accurate* was to conservatives what ALTERNATIVE FACTS would become to liberals.

SEE ALSO: ALTERNATIVE FACTS; A RAPE ON
CAMPUS; SWIFTBOATING; YELLOW JOURNALISM

RAY'S PIZZA

If you're walking around Manhattan craving a slice of pizza, you are in luck—seemingly every corner comes adorned with a Ray's Pizza to satiate your desires. But the pizza joint is never just *Ray's*. There are always modifiers, like *Famous* Ray's Pizza, or sometimes Ray's *Original* Pizza, or just as likely, *Famous Original* Ray's Pizza. Pretty much every possible mashup of *Original* and *Famous* and *Ray's* can be found, but the epithet pile-up does not stop there: Ray's Traditional Pizza, World-Famous Original Ray's Pizza, One and Only Famous Ray's Pizza, Real Ray's Pizza, and countless more iterations. One aspiring pizzeria in Brooklyn finally threw their arms up in ironic disgust and named their joint Not Ray's Pizza.[134]

None of these places are actually *famous*, despite what the random picture of Donnie Wahlberg on the wall might insinuate. Nor can any of these joints stake a claim to *original*. The first Ray's Pizza (so simple) seems to have started in Little Italy in 1959, but it closed in 2011. Its owner was a mafia guy sent up the

---

134 A scene from *Seinfeld* parodies the confusion when Kramer gets lost and calls Jerry from a phone booth.

Kramer: "I'm looking at Ray's Pizza. You know where that is?"
Jerry: "Is it Famous Ray's?"
Kramer: "No, it's just original."
Jerry: "Famous Original Ray's?"
Kramer: "It's just original, Jerry!"

river for drug trafficking. It's a classic New York City story but his name was not even Ray—it was Ralph Cuomo. Ralph opened a second pizza shop uptown, but quickly sold it in 1964 to another Ray-aspirant—Rosolino Mangano. This new not-quite-Ray likes to claim *first!* with his shop, Famous Original Ray's Pizza, but he's fibbing, too. He bought his first place from Ralph, and it isn't even open anymore.

From there the Ray's family tree sprawls into a bonanza of conflicting offshoots, and like all dysfunctional families, they have been suing each other for trademark infringement for generations. Each iteration of Ray's serves the same basic slices from a glass case late into the night, but they generally operate in complete independence from one another.

There is no "authentic" Ray's pizzeria. There are only imitations; every slice, a counterfeit.

SEE ALSO: TOFURKEY

REALDOLL

RealDolls abide by a universal law of misinformation: *Putting the word "real" in front of something makes it seem less real.* (See also: *Real Housewives, Real World,* @RealDonaldTrump.)

RealDoll is the brand name of a high-end sex doll. Made from silicone (flesh), PVC (skeleton), and steel (joints), the life-size mannequin is posable and (somewhat) anatomically correct. RealDolls come in male, female, and "hybrid" models. Like the memorable scene in the hormonal teen flick *Weird Science*, customizations abound, including options for face (twenty templates), hair, eyes, makeup, freckles, piercings, breasts, ears (elf add-ons), pubic hair, and vagina specification/penis size. If the choices overwhelm, a budding Pygmalion can also choose from seven prebuilt models based upon porn stars. (*May we interest you in a Samantha Saint, sir?*) The service will not create a replica of a real living person with-

out their written consent—an unsettling request so common that it is answered on the website's FAQ. The basic RealDoll model sells for between $5,000 and $10,000, but caveat emptor—prices can jump as high as $50,000 with exotic customizations. Used dolls occasionally pop up on eBay, which might sound nasty, but if you're the type of person who fornicates with a silicone replicant, do sloppy seconds really gross you out?

On the other hand, what seems lurid today could easily pass for routine tomorrow. According to 2017 YouGov poll, 49 percent of Americans believe that having sex with robots will become a common practice in the next fifty years. That sentiment tracks with the seminal analysis of the subject, *Love and Sex with Robots* (2007), which predicts 2050 as the year when human-robot coitus sheds its stigma. At that point, argues author David Levy, artificial intelligence will have cohered with robotics to create CYBORGS so vivacious that we abandon the distinction between smart machines and fecund mates. "If a robot behaves as though it has feelings, can we reasonably argue that it does not?" he wonders, borrowing from the behaviorist ideas of the TURING TEST. "If a robot's artificial emotions prompt it to say things such as 'I love you,' surely we should be willing to accept these statements at face value."

Surely? If *Westworld* taught us anything, blindly trusting the frisky dialogue of sex bots will surely get us pushed over the goddamn cliff right into the UNCANNY VALLEY.

SEE ALSO: ORGASMS; PORNOGRAPHY; SLASHFIC; UNCANNY VALLEY; VOIGHT-KAMPFF MACHINE

REALIST, THE

Simply put, *The Realist* was *The Onion* of the '60s, but much more vulgar and prankish.

Edited and published by Paul Krassner, a founding

member of the counterculture Yippie movement, *The Realist* was a bellwether of alternative publishing, even when it resisted the praise. (When *People* magazine dubbed Krassner the "father of the underground press," he famously fired back, "I demand a blood test.") On thirty-two pages of scabrous pulp, the monthly magazine published a mix of dark satire and legitimate reportage, culled from an impressive roster of writers.[135]

The Realist had clever prose, to be sure, but this was not its chief innovation. What made the magazine so remarkable, and what frankly differentiates it from the spate of modern spoof news outfits like *The Daily Show* or *The Onion*, or even more irascible publications like *Charlie Hebdo* was what happened off the page. *The Realist* didn't just create satire to describe the world—it literally injected fake news into the world. Its imposture included silly pranks, like a letter-writing campaign to the NBC standards board over an innocuous game show, and a wry account of the "first waterbed fatality," involving a man who was electrocuted via cat claws. But other material was darker, almost menacing, like the obituary of Lenny Bruce, two years before he died.

By far, however, the most successful media flim-flam was "The Parts That Were Left Out of the Kennedy Book," a grotesque story that purported to contain censored sections of a recent book, *The Death of a President* (1967). In the climax of the account, Jackie Kennedy witnesses LBJ leaning over JFK's casket and copulating with his corpse—specifically, his neck wound. "And then I realized—there is only one way to say this—he was literally fucking my husband in the throat," says the First Lady. "In the bullet wound in the front of his throat." Many people reportedly believed this monstrous account, including Daniel Ellsberg of *Pentagon Papers* fame. ("Maybe it was just because I *wanted* to believe it so badly," Ellsberg

later told Krassner.)

As *The Realist* warned in one of its slogans, *The Truth Is Silly Putty*.

SEE ALSO: THE MASKED MARAUDERS; A MODEST PROPOSAL; TRUTHINESS; YELLOW JOURNALISM

REALITY-BASED COMMUNITY

Reality-based community was an expression used by Karl Rove to derisively refer to the dimwitted sheeple (you and me) who blindly accept the banal reality directed at them by powerful leaders. Instead of passively accepting their sluggish senses, Rove and his cabal of neocon worldbuilders were carpe diem-ing the fuck out of reality and making it their bitch. The full quote:

> [You people] in what we call the "reality-based community" . . . believe that solutions emerge from your judicious study of discernible reality. That's not the way the world really works anymore. We're an empire now, and when we act, we create our own reality. And while you're studying that reality—judiciously, as you will—we'll act again, creating other new realities, which you can study too, and that's how things will sort out. We're history's actors . . . and you, all of you, will be left to just study what we do. [136]

When he says "We create our own reality," one almost imagines him pinching Napoleon's purported line "I make my own circumstances," or even more evocatively, frothing like Jack Nicholson in *A Few*

---

[135] Contributors to *The Realist* included Norman Mailer, Richard Pryor, Woody Allen, Lenny Bruce, Joseph Heller, Robert Crumb, Phil Ochs, Gary Trudeau, Robert Anton Wilson, Neil Postman, Abbie Hoffman, and Ken Kesey. (It was a suspiciously male-centric cast.)

Good Men, "You can't handle the truth!" But for Rove, the truth is the warped reality that he created.

For a certain type of ruler, one who believes facts subservient to power, and for whom *rhetoric* and *reality* are synonyms, such frank expressions of despotism probably pass as wisdom. "From the totalitarian point of view," Orwell reminds us, "history is something to be created rather than learned."

SEE ALSO: ALT-HISTORY; ALTERNATIVE FACTS; KAYFABE; NEWSPEAK; NOBLE LIE; TRUTHINESS

RED MERCURY

Red mercury is a mythical substance rumored to serve a welter of sinister purposes. According to legends passed among fringe (and seemingly daft) extremist groups, the miraculous elixir can be used in the development of nuclear fissile material, miniaturized fusion bombs, self-guided warheads, spray-on paint for stealth bombers, metallic hydrogen, or pretty much any ominous armament your ghoulish mind can conjure. The inscrutable concoction could be radioactive, or it could be toxic, or it could be both—*whatch'ya need?*

Rumors started during the Cold War that Soviet physicists had produced a mysterious substance of apocalyptic power. Reference to red mercury appeared in both Russian and Western press reports but with no specifics on the nature of the nostrum, other than it was being used in nuclear weapons. Interest in red mercury accelerated after 9/11, when various terrorist groups with an imp of the perverse were rumored to be in hot pursuit of the material.

Today, red mercury is widely regarded as an urban legend, even as the substance continues to be sought by terrorist groups. "Red mercury doesn't exist," a spokesman at the International Atomic Energy Agency said in 2004. "The whole thing is a bunch of malarkey." But the legend resiliently persists today, possibly because intelligence agencies have something to gain from its perceived existence. Some analysts believe red mercury lore endures because law enforcement groups use it to lure potential terrorists interested in buying the alchemical substance.

Even if good guy spies are not exploiting terrorist folklore, criminal con men certainly are. Nefarious crime groups have reportedly tricked aspiring third world demagogues and rogue states into purchasing red mercury on multiple occasions. Samples obtained from these operations invariably consist of worthless red dyes and assorted powders—nothing close to a WMD. (Osama bin Laden was allegedly among the unsavory characters deceived by a red mercury hoax. It's almost reassuring to learn that global terrorists can be punked.)

Whoever first developed red mercury may have left an obvious trail to deciphering its deception. The chemical symbol for Mercury is *Hg*, making the substance *Red Hg*—perhaps a coy truncation of *red herring*.

SEE ALSO: AREA 51; FALSE FLAG OPERATION; PHILOSOPHER'S STONE; THE RUMSFELD MATRIX

RED PILL, THE

Reality is a simulation, a prison of your mind. The truth, which exists beyond this artificial universe, is bleak and difficult. Would you rather stay in the comfy

---

136 When it first appeared in an October 2004 issue of *The New York Times Magazine* (in an article titled "Faith, Certainty and the Presidency of George W. Bush" by Ron Suskind), the quote was attributed to "a Bush aide." It is now widely regarded as the words of—to borrow Dubya's endearing sobriquet for Rove—Turd Blossom.

prison of your perceptions or tear down the illusion to reveal your enslavement? That is the dilemma posed by Morpheus to Neo in *The Matrix* (1999):

> You take the blue pill, the story ends. You wake up in your bed and believe whatever you want to believe. You take the red pill, you stay in Wonderland, and I show you how deep the rabbit hole goes.

Neo pops the red capsule and sees reality for the lurid hellscape it is.

Like seeing forms beyond the shadows in PLATO'S CAVE, or recognizing another dimension in *Flatland*, or being let loose on Rumspringa, or breaking through to the other side like Jim Morrison—taking the red pill is a revelatory moment in which you see reality *as it really is*. The question then becomes, how do you know that the new reality is actually the real one? Aye, there's the rub.

The metaphor of the red pill has been co-opted by far-right groups, as a means of celebrating extremism. To men's rights activists, the red pill signifies a realization that proscribed gender roles are intended to benefit women more than men. To the alt-right, popping the pill exposes the lies of multicultural liberalism. And for white supremacists, the red pill reveals the secret knowledge of a Jewish cabal controlling global capitalism. These broods also speak of "red-pilling the normies," or converting other young men to their cause.

SEE ALSO: BRAIN IN A VAT; MEME MAGIC; PLACEBO; PLATO'S CAVE; SIMULISM; TRUMAN SYNDROME

REICHSTAG FIRE

The fire that destroyed the German Parliament building the night of February 27, 1933, was a clear case of arson—no one challenges this assertion. Nor does anyone dispute the involvement of Marinus van der Lubbe, a Dutchman who was captured, tried, and executed. But was this young communist the sole plotter in setting the Reichstag ablaze? Or was he merely a patsy, part of a larger conspiracy, as William L. Shirer asserted in *The Rise and Fall of the Third Reich* (1960), "by the Nazis who planned the arson and carried it out for their own political ends"?

Did the Nazis surreptitiously ignite their own parliament building as a means of inciting resentment among the masses, vilifying political enemies, and ultimately accruing massive populist power? Was the Reichstag fire an elaborate FALSE FLAG OPERATION? Historians are divided, so we might never know the answer.

But this much is known: Adolf Hitler, who just weeks prior had become chancellor of Germany, saw opportunity in the Reichstag fire. "There will be no mercy now," he exulted that night, embers still smoldering. "Anyone standing in our way will be cut down." The next morning, a decree was issued "for the protection of the people and the state," abrogating basic civil rights like freedom of the press, freedom of expression, and the right of assembly. A week later, the Nazi Party won a major victory in parliamentary elections, largely by fomenting a fear of communism in the electorate. Emboldened, the Nazis immediately imprisoned thousands of political enemies in concentration camps. A month later, Hitler was given plenary power to create laws without the nuisance of legislative approval. Within months of the Reichstag fire, Germany had a dictator.

Regardless of whether the Nazis set the fire, Hitler undoubtedly used the threat of terrorism as a specious pretext to consolidate power—a lesson adopted by many aspiring tyrants since. Whether imagined or immanent, fabricated or legitimate, the threat of terror has become a prominent tool of malevolent despots, used to instill fear in the public. When Vladimir Putin became prime minister of Russia in 1999, he had a mere 2 percent approval rating. When bombs started exploding across Russia, killing hundreds and unleashing panic, he took a hardline stance against what he called Islamic terrorists. His approval rating soared, but by many reputable accounts, the bombings were plotted by the KGB. (His intelligence officers were arrested, and later released, by their own colleagues.) Putin—the former head of the KGB—used the bombings as a pretense to mobilize troops for the annexation of Chechnya.

The American Founding Fathers were concerned about these exact instances, where a populist demagogue could undermine democratic values by capitalizing on dramatic events. Tyranny could arise, as James Madison elegantly put it, "on some favorable emergency." The Reichstag fire is a scorching symbol of how quickly a democracy can devolve into authoritarianism.

SEE ALSO: FALSE FLAG OPERATION; JOSEPH MCCARTHY'S LIST; MANCHURIAN CANDIDATE; THE PROTOCOLS OF THE ELDERS OF ZION; TROJAN HORSE

REPORT FROM IRON MOUNTAIN, THE

Published in 1967, *The Report from Iron Mountain* was a leaked report from a government think tank that determined war was a necessary component of the American economy. It was a best-seller and a hoax.

The heavily footnoted study, which determined that peace was not in the interest of the country, argued that the military-industrial complex was necessary to drive scientific development, curb unemployment, reduce the population, and control crime. Somewhat in the vein of *Dr. Strangelove* (1964), but much subtler, *Iron Mountain* argued that war was a necessary component of our culture; removing it would cause society to collapse. And like *Dr. Strangelove*, the satire seemed eerily plausible.

Most people instantly recognized the ruse, but for a few years, the antiwar lampoon held the attention of the media as a potentially legitimate document. The *New York Times* wrote a book review saying, "It is, of course, a hoax—but what a hoax!—a parody so elaborate and ingenious and, in fact, so substantively original, acute, interesting and *horrifying* that it will receive serious attention regardless of its origins." Which was exactly right, because Henry Kissinger felt compelled to respond, "Whoever wrote it is an idiot."

The idiot in question was Leonard Lewin, a satirist who finally came forward to claim authorship in 1972. It was a year after the leak of the (very real) *Pentagon Papers*, which frankly made the (very fake) *Iron Mountain* report seem like weak sauce.

The spoof is still an object of obsession among the paranoid class.

SEE ALSO: AREA 51; DEEP STATE; A MODEST PROPOSAL; NACIREMA; SOKAL TEXT; THE WAR OF THE WORLDS

RETCONNING

Retroactive continuity is the act of reframing past events to accommodate current plot developments. It is fiction's version of rewriting history.

The canonical retcon (an inherent contradiction of terms) might be Sir Arthur Conan Doyle killing off Sherlock Holmes in "The Final Problem" only to succumb to a fan rebellion and miraculously resurrect him in future stories. The award for Most Egregious Retcon probably goes to some obscure comic book betrayal involving Batman, but for populist irritants, it is the totalizing annulment of the entire ninth season of *Dallas* as the dream of a character in the tenth season.

Retcons are only necessary when the fiction is serialized—pulp novels, television series, cinematic universes, and, especially, comic books. Rationales for retconning official canon include adding a new character, expanding plot options, correcting mistakes, or simply making room for sequels, spinoffs, and reboots. Skillful writers can make lemonade from narrative lemons by reconstituting a blatant retcon as previous events cast in a new light (*huh, so that's why the Death Star had a vulnerability*), whereas super masters dispatch retconning as narrative misdirection (*Buffy had a sister all along!*). But too many retcons—especially those that come to be despised by diehard fans—just seem to be needless accoutrements (*wait, R2-D2 can fly now?*). As sticklers of a stable canon, fandoms often reject these snarls in continuity with vocal disgust.

Retconning occurs in real life, too—when Pluto was reclassified out of planetary status; when Lance Armstrong had his seven Tour de France titles revoked; when the Supreme Court overturned its own ruling, *Plessy v. Ferguson*, in support of *Brown v. Board of Education*, ending schoolroom segregation. And in a remarkable crossover retcon, the fictitious address for Sherlock Holmes, 221B Baker Street, now exists in the real world, thanks to an expansion of Baker Street, and has become the real address for the Sherlock Holmes Museum. Fiction, in a rare twist, retconned reality.

SEE ALSO: ALT-HISTORY; FAKE SHEMP; MANDELA EFFECT; NEWSPEAK; PHANTOM TIME HYPOTHESIS

ROBINSON CRUSOE

Daniel Defoe was as prolific as he was influential, and in his day, more controversial than both. Though best known for his novels *Moll Flanders* and *Robinson Crusoe*, most scholars also regard the eighteenth-century scribe as the father of modern journalism, for having pioneered many of its story types (including investigative reporting, travel writing, economic analysis, and the advice column). But he was also known as a magnificent fabricator—the author of fraudulent histories, phony letters to the editors, embellished reportage—some of which we might let slide as hoax or parody but much of which was clearly intended to deceive. His contemporaries deemed him a scoundrel, an unscrupulous pamphleteer who would feign Tory or Whig, depending on which journal was paying. He assumed at least 198 pen names, including *Defoe*, which was not his real name. (He was born just *Foe*. To sound aristocratic, he Frenchified it. He also sometimes claimed to descend from the De Beau Faux family, which is just about perfect—*the beautiful fake*.) His seditious pamphlets landed him in prison and buckled to the pillory. "He was a great, a truly great liar," wrote one his biographers, "perhaps the greatest liar that ever lived." And that was a positive biography.

Defoe's most triumphant work was *Robinson Crusoe* (1719). A castaway tale that would influence everything from *The Swiss Family Robinson* and *Treasure Island* to *Survivor* and *Lost* (and maybe the Eagle Scouts), most literary scholars regard it as the first English novel.[137] Or rather, we now label it a novel, but Defoe published it as nonfiction. The first edition claimed to be the historical travelogue of a real Robinson Crusoe, trapped on a remote desert island for twenty-seven years. The byline on the cover read "Written by HIMSELF," as in Crusoe himself. In the preface, Defoe posed as the humble editor of found journals. "The editor believes the thing to be a just history of fact," he wrote. "Neither is there any appearance of fiction in it."

He was lying about everything except the appear-

---

137 If you want to start a fight with a liberal arts grad student, "first novel" would get some fists clenched. English contenders include Malory's *Le Morte d'Arthur* (1485), Bunyan's *The Pilgrim's Progress* (1678), and Behn's *Oroonoko* (1688). All of those predate *Robinson Crusoe*, but definitions of genre and matters of length might exclude them from contention, or precipitate a robust literary brawl.

ance. Stylistically, the book was one of the first works of literary realism, a harrowing potboiler that placed the reader on an island somewhere near Trinidad. Crusoe encounters cannibals and mutineers before ultimately being rescued. (Here, we find a scrap of truth. The story resembles genuine castaway stories of the era, especially that of Alexander Selkirk, a buccaneer who was marooned on a Chilean island for five years.)

Robinson Crusoe sold thousands of copies, and nearly every reader believed it a real account, at least until its association with that rascal Defoe became known. However, unlike today's literary fabulists, we might be inclined to cut Defoe some slack for his farrago of fact and fiction, as the rules of the novel were still undefined. ("Literary Fiction" was not yet a category at Barnes & Noble.) Even still, it was the inauspicious birth of the English novel. Its bellwether work was a sham—a fiction passed off as fact.

SEE ALSO: THE BLAIR WITCH PROJECT; HOMER; LEROY, JT; THE WAR OF THE WORLDS

ROCKEFELLER, CLARK

Clark Rockefeller performed one of the most impressive impersonation cons of the twentieth century.

Starting around 1993, an eccentric man with a name suggestive of American nobility began to cultivate a bon vivant reputation in the most prosperous circles of the Upper East Side. He put on airs of stature and wealth, which might have been dismissed as bizarre but for his regal surname. Only a minor scion, he claimed, but one of significant provenance, Rockefeller inveigled his way into many distinguished environments—private clubs, prestigious jobs, and soon enough, the heart of a powerful woman. He met Sandra Boss, a Harvard Business School graduate and the youngest senior partner ever at McKinsey, at a "Clue Party." (He was Professor Plum; she, Miss Scarlet.) They married in 1995 and had a daughter in 2001.

Somehow, he kept the act up for twelve years, when his wife's suspicions finally grew too substantial and she filed for divorce. (No members of the Rockefeller family showing up at the wedding a dozen years earlier should probably have been the first sign.) At this point, Clark made his most unwise move to date: He kidnapped his seven-year-old daughter and made a run for it. Christian Karl Gerhartsreiter—his real name—was arrested a week after the AMBER Alert sounded. In addition to the kidnapping conviction, the wastrel now also serves a life sentence in a California jail for murdering his former landlord in 1985. Gerhartsreiter, it turns out, had invented and fled many aliases since sneaking his way into America from Germany as a student in 1978. When he forged a Social Security card, the impertinent scofflaw used the numbers belonging to David Berkowitz, the Son of Sam serial killer.

Gerhartsreiter, or, if you wish, Rockefeller, will be played by Benedict Cumberbatch in an upcoming movie adaption.[138]

SEE ALSO: CONFIDENCE GAME; PONZI SCHEME

RORSCHACH TEST

The Rorschach is a psychological evaluation test that involves verbally reacting to ten blobs of ink as a means of revealing personality and character traits. *The Penguin Dictionary of Psychology* has said "an intense dialogue about the wallpaper or the rug" would be as effective.

Its namesake, Hermann Rorschach, was a Swiss psychiatrist who never imagined his inkblots would be adopted as a general personality test.[139] He developed the idea after noticing adolescents giving characteristically similar answers to a popular inkblot game, Gobolinks.

First published in 1921, his hand-drawn inkblots were intended to assist the diagnosis of schizophrenia, and he cautioned that his findings were preliminary and required more experimentation. He died just a year later, but by the '40s Rorschach's inkblots had become a ubiquitous personality test, and perhaps more notoriously, they would become a prominent movie trope, appearing in diverse flicks including *Armageddon, Short Circuit,* and *Batman Forever.*

When the test appears in popular culture, it is often comedically misconstrued as an analytic tool where a response ("I see a vagina") reveals hidden personality traits ("I am obsessed with sex"). The original cards came with a handy manual that explained the test was not so much about the *content* of the answer as the *process* by which a subject comes to the answer, as in this excerpt of the instruction that accompanied the first of the ten cards:

> Being the first card, it can provide clues about how subjects tackle a new and stressful task. It is not, however, a card that is usually difficult for the subject to handle, having readily available popular responses.

An immense controversy erupted in 2009, when all ten Rorschach plates were added to Wikipedia. Before that, the test was guarded as a trade secret by psychologists and, more importantly, the publishing companies that printed the images. Whatever diagnostic value existed in the cards, claimed the publishers, would be diminished by their public dissemination and awareness.

SEE ALSO: BARNUM EFFECT; PAREIDOLIA; TURING TEST; UMWELT; VOIGHT-KAMPFF MACHINE

---

138 The full saga of this real-life Talented Mr. Ripley is too astonishing to be given justice by summary. A full account can be found in a December 2008 story, "The Man in the Rockefeller Suit," in *Vanity Fair.* (Of course it's in *Vanity Fair*, a publication seemingly invented at the intersection of old money, celebrity, and deception.) The story, by Mark Seal, was turned into a book of the same name in 2011.

139 As a high school student, Rorschach's friends gave him the nickname *Klecks,* or "inkblot," because he loved making the mirrored blobs. (Vocab that might win you a pint at pub trivia tonight: *klecksography* is the art of making images from inkblots.)

In the early '70s, eight patients checked into different psychiatric hospitals, reporting of auditory hallucinations. All were admitted, diagnosed with psychiatric disorders, and administered antipsychotic drugs. Once hospitalized, they reported no further hallucinations or other symptoms. Although they eventually gained admittance into twelve institutions, none of the patients actually had a mental illness: They were all acting. The whole premise was an experiment invented by psychologist David Rosenhan to test the validity of psychiatric diagnoses. The faux-patients were held, on average, nineteen days at each institution. All but one was diagnosed with schizophrenia "in remission" before being released.

When the staff of another psychiatric hospital heard about the study, they claimed their institution could not be snookered. So Rosenhan arranged a second experiment with that institution in which he agreed to send over an unspecified number of pseudopatients for diagnosis over a three-month period. At the end of the trial, the hospital had seen 193 new patients come through the doors, and they claimed forty-one of them were imposters. Rosenhan then revealed he had sent over exactly zero actors.

Under the title "On Being Sane in Insane Places," the results of the studies, published in *Science* in 1973, had explosive repercussions in the field of psychology and ultimately accelerated the deinstitutionalization process across the mental health industry.

Although many psychology experiments of the era had questionable methods (see, for example, the Stanford prison experiment and the Milgram authority studies), there was also something undeniably thrilling about these early research projects, which today might not pass ethical muster, but would make excellent reality television shows.

SEE ALSO: BARNUM EFFECT; CAPGRAS DELUSION; CRISIS ACTORS; RORSCHACH TEST

Rosie Ruiz was the winner of the 1980 Boston Marathon with a time of 2:31:56—a world record in the female category. The time demolished her previous personal record by twenty-five minutes, set in the New York City Marathon, where six months before she took eleventh place. Astonished witnesses at the Boston finish line said she was barely sweating.

She almost got away with it.

It took eight days to uncover the truth. In both marathons, Rosie hopped the subway. Less than a mile before the finish lines, she had jumped back into the race. After suspicion swelled around her amazing victory, two Harvard students reported seeing her in the subway, and her story slowly started to unravel.

Although no criminal charges were filed for cheating, she was later arrested for embezzling $60,000 from her employer, a real estate firm. A year later, she was arrested again, this time for trying to sell two kilos of cocaine to an undercover detective at the Miami Airport Marriott. *Run, Rosie, run.*

Marathons have since taken measures to prevent course-cutting, including electronically monitored stops, to make bluffing your way to a medal seemingly impossible.

SEE ALSO: CANNED HEAT

It seems almost impossible to imagine now, but Donald Rumsfeld's press conferences were once appointment television.

In the months after 9/11, the Bush administration began amassing (and, we later learned, manufacturing) evidence to launch a massive war in Iraq. Rumsfeld, the secretary of defense, became the chief spokesman for the cause, with daily briefings from the Pentagon newsroom. As the voice of war, he cut

THE RUMSFELD MATRIX		KNOWNS	UNKNOWNS
	KNOWN	We know that we know it. Ex.: The earth is round.	We know that we don't know it. Ex.: Intelligent life exists on other planets?
	UNKNOWN		We don't know if we know it. Ex.: Our galaxy might be made of apple pie?

a mercurial image, both cagey and loquacious, like a fox who could talk himself into any henhouse. He was charismatic, smug, and probably insane. He made riveting television.

His every exchange with the press was fraught. Rumsfeld had a way of speaking in imprecise aphorisms, a mix of cabalistic philosophizing ("The absence of evidence is not the evidence of absence") and inscrutable obfuscation ("Some things are neither good nor bad, but thinking makes it so"). When a reporter asked a straightforward question on February 12, 2002, about the lack of evidence linking Saddam Hussein's regime to terrorist organizations, Rumsfeld launched this circumspect response:

> There are **known knowns**; there are things we know we know. We also know there are **known unknowns**; that is to say, we know there are some things we do not know. But there are also **unknown unknowns**—the ones we don't know we don't know.

In its own way, it's brilliant. Both cryptic and ridiculous, it sounded vaguely like the Socratic paradox ("I know that I know nothing"), or possibly a Sun Tzu koan from *The Art of War*. Of course, the sentiment was not new—intelligence agencies had used similar terminology in risk analysis for decades. But it *seemed deep*, like some sort of esoteric Yoda voodoo (*Know not, we know, unknown knowns, hrmmmm*). And yet, it was so simple that one could make a basic grid out of it. (*See the chart above.*)

When you divide the quote into a simple matrix, something obvious jumps out. Rumsfeld's famous dictum left out an entire quadrant of knowledge: the **Unknown Knowns**. The other three all receive precise definitions, but this lonely quadrant is left open to speculation. What could possibly go in there?

There might be a reason Rumsfeld skipped over this quadrant. The Unknown Knowns are those things that **we don't know that we know**. We once knew it, but the information is currently missing or hidden. Either we forgot, or worse, we were forced to forget. This is a crucial sector of the matrix, because it involves two essential human actions: *forgetting* and *repressing*. Here, in the Unknown Knowns, lives propaganda and disinformation, where we pretend we cannot remember or we are forced to forget.[140]

This neglected quadrant—Unknown Knowns—is precisely what allowed the Iraq War to happen. The knowledge was there but hidden. The government facilitated a process of turning Knowns (*there is no evidence of WMDs*) into Unknowns (*is there evidence of WMDs?*), of intentionally suppressing what we know. Only later did we remember what we once knew all along.

SEE ALSO: FALSE FLAG OPERATION; RASHOMON; REALITY BASED COMMUNITY; RED MERCURY; SOPHISTS; STRATEGERY; TRUTHINESS

---

140   The director Errol Morris apparently noticed the missing quadrant, too, because he named his Rumsfeld documentary *The Unknown Known* (2013).

S

SAMPURU

The window displays of Japanese restaurants, teeming with sushi and other bounties from the sea, can appear an unsanitary aquarium to the Western eye, unaccustomed to plates of raw fish swimming in the open air. But these dishes—somehow still tantalizing after days basking in the sun—are not a botulism case in waiting. They are *sampuru*, or plastic models of food. The exquisite figurines (sushi, ramen bowls, Kobe steak, tempura, pastries, and every imaginable comestible) are fake but extremely realistic. Their delicate craftsmanship is revered like an art form.

Derived from the English word *sample*, the first sampuru were made from wax in the 1920s and today are crafted with polyvinyl chloride (PVC) from silicone molds. Their remarkable verisimilitude is possible because they are not mass-produced—each item is skillfully molded and hand-painted. Every restaurant has their own distinct dishes, so each individual sampuru must be painstakingly designed. Even a basic item like sushi rice is crafted by mold-casting individual grains, adding adhesive, and shaping them by hand, as one would a single nigiri. Sampuru are a big business—each replica costs roughly twenty times the actual menu item. Transforming an entire intricate menu into a window of sampuru can cost upward of $10,000.

For those reluctant Western tourists, window displays of sampuru can eliminate the guesswork of ordering from—or even reading—a menu. The exacting food replicas are similar to those increasingly pervasive food porn slideshows and Instagram compilations of restaurant menus, which eliminate language from the rigmarole of dining. We visually devour the simulation before eating the real thing.

SEE ALSO: 3D PRINTING; FRANKENFOOD; MIKU, HATSUNE; LIE-TO-CHILDREN; TOFURKEY; TOYETIC

SANTA CLAUS

Santa Claus is a myth involving an extragovernmental figure who rewards socially sanctioned deeds with material wealth ("nice") while withholding goods from the culturally unorthodox ("naughty"). The legend, which involves an omniscient bearded panopticon who watches your every move, prepares children for a world of lies told by their elders. Ho, ho, ho.

Santa has his origins in a real saint, Nicholas of Myra in modern Turkey, who in the fourth century donated his inherited wealth and travelled the countryside helping the poor. After becoming the patron saint of sailors, his legend spread from port to port, gaining regard around the globe. More than 2,000 churches were named after him; by the Renaissance, St. Nicholas was the most popular saint in Europe. But he was not yet the rotund whitebeard who jollily cavorts with elves at the mall. That archetype would not develop until the legend travelled to America, where Washington Irving started to describe Saint Nick as a sleigh-rider delivering presents to eager children. A poem, of all things, would canonize the rest of the modern Santa Claus tropes. In 1823 Clement Clarke Moore published "A Visit from St. Nicholas," better known as "The Night Before Christmas," in which Santa finally plumps up, dons red velour, amasses a herd of reindeer, rappels chimneys, and employs elves in the North Pole.[141]

SEE ALSO: BERENSTAIN BEARS CONSPIRACY; PRESTER JOHN; SNIPE HUNT

SCHRÖDINGER'S CAT

Most people remember the basic plot of physicist Erwin Schrödinger's feline paradox. A cat is placed in a box. The box receives a radioactive blast that (possibly) releases poison. The boxed cat might be dead, or it might be alive. There is a 50/50 chance either way. The paradox that Schrödinger proposes: Until you open the box, the cat is both alive *and* dead—what physicists call *quantum superposition.*

What people often forget is how ludicrous Schrödinger thought this paradox. At the time, in 1935, the implications of quantum mechanics were exceedingly problematic for traditional physicists like him, so he devised the thought experiment, later dubbed *Schrödinger's cat*, to illustrate the foolish consequences of the new physics. Today, that thought experiment, which he besmirched as "quite ridiculous," is used by physicists as an allegory for explaining quantum theory.

Schrödinger was skeptical of quantum mechanics because it defied too many of the rules from classical deterministic physics dating back to Newton. The most problematic break from tradition was a new way of perceiving certain systems, including atom particles and photons. In quantum theory, parts of these systems could exist in a combination of states (on/off, positive/negative, dead/alive) at the same time. This new theory implied a *statistical* universe rather than a *causal* one. Only when they are observed—when the box is opened—does the particle "decide" if it is on or off, positive or negative, dead or alive. Suddenly, physicists were describing the cosmos in probabilistic terms, which led to Einstein's famous condemnation, "God does not play dice with the universe." He and Schrödinger thought quantum theory was hogwash.[142]

No kittens were injured in Schrödinger's experiment, which was intended as purely hypothetical—a little parable to illustrate the paradox of certain small particles. But the allegory appealed to Einstein, who

---

141 Nothing is original. The Santa Claus legend descends from a farrago of folkloric figures—Father Christmas in England, Kris Kringle in Germany, Sinterklaas in the Netherlands, Jultomten in Scandinavia, and other myths.

142 Or with less hyperbole: They believed that quantum mechanics would eventually be absorbed into a larger (and to their eyes, more reasonable) theory. Today, that is often called the Grand Unified Theory, and it remains a chimera of modern physics.

was dismayed by the introduction of this insidious observer who decided the fate of the physical world. The cat should live or die, Einstein felt, regardless of what anyone *saw*. He even asked his friend Niels Bohr, the principal architect of quantum mechanics, "Do you believe the moon ceases to exist if nobody is looking at it?" Bohr replied that we could never prove that it does.

SEE ALSO: COLD FUSION; THE DRESS

SEXUAL CONVERSION THERAPY

Sexual Conversion Therapy is a psychiatric process that transforms a straight person into a gay person. *Nah, other way around!* But either direction is equally "curable."

Only decades ago, barbaric treatments like icepick lobotomies and chemical castration were administered to alter sexual orientation. Unless catatonia was the goal, the treatments failed. Now only better by degrees of cruelty, a technique called *aversive conditioning* is administered. Basically, pictures of hot guys are shown to homosexual men, followed quickly with negative reinforcement—an electrical shock to the genitals, drugs that cause nausea, or anything physically harmful. The barbaric theory holds that a subject will develop a negative association with the homoerotic images. This genius therapy, which is tantamount to torture, does not work.

Though the American Psychiatric Association opposes sexual conversion therapy, fundamentalist religious groups who believe homosexuality is a disease still endorse it. (After years of conflict, homosexuality was finally removed as a psychological condition from the DSM in 1973.)

Conversion therapy does not work on any sexual predisposition. No evidence exists to suggest that pedophilia, for example, can be cured through a psychiatric conversion process. Rather than trying to rid pedophiles of their fantasies, psychiatrists use techniques that decrease the likelihood of a patient acting on sexual urges.

SEE ALSO: BOGUS PIPELINE; PASSING; SLASHFIC

SHIP OF THESEUS

After sailing to Crete, navigating a complex labyrinth, and beheading the evil Minotaur, Theseus returned to Athens a war hero. In memory of his valor, his ship was placed in the Aegean harbor as a monument. When the brackish sea slowly rotted its hull over centuries, the planks of the ship were gradually replaced to keep it afloat.

This predicament created a thought experiment, popularized by the biographer Plutarch, called the *Ship of Theseus*: If the pieces of a derelict boat are continually replaced, until eventually no parts from the original remain, is the boat still the Ship of Theseus? Or as dorm room metaphysicians have inquired for ages, what exactly makes a thing *that thing*?

In the seventeenth century, philosopher Thomas Hobbes came along and made the ontological experiment even more stymying by adding another layer to the story. As each plank is removed, a shipbuilder uses the pieces to slowly rebuild the ship in its initial form from its original wood. Now there are two Ships of Theseus. Which is the true one?

The replacement puzzle vexed philosophers for centuries, and then science fiction came along and applied the conundrum to new technologies like teleportation, mind downloading, organ transplants, and 3D PRINTING. (The brain-teaser was enhanced when carbon-14 studies revealed most cells in the human body are shed and regenerated many times in a lifetime. We are all Ships of Theseus.)

Today, since the linguistic turn of philosophy in the mid-twentieth century, philosophers see the Ship of Theseus riddle less as a baffling paradox than as a

clever language trap. Naming the physical boat *Ship of Theseus* is a human act, bearing no relationship to its realness in the world. More than anything else, the Ship of Theseus quandary illustrates the failure of language to accurately represent reality.

Pop culture supports the conclusion. Several classic rock bands—Foreigner, Yes, Thin Lizzy, Quiet Riot—now perform with none of their founding members. All of their planks have been gradually replaced, and now none of the rock boat remains from the original. They might be replicas, but only a cynical pedant would impugn the joy of fans who board their Ships of Theseus in concert.

SEE ALSO: 3D PRINTING; BRAIN IN A VAT; TRIBUTE BANDS; TURTLES ALL THE WAY DOWN

SHROUD OF TURIN

The Shroud of Turin is a fourteen-foot-long piece of cloth imprinted with the image of a man. Some theologians believe the linen to be the burial cloth of Jesus of Nazareth.

The controversial garment, stored in a cathedral in Turin, might be the most scrutinized object in human history. A boundless array of scientific techniques have been implemented to determine its provenance: radiocarbon dating, spectroscopy, electron microscopy, DNA profiling, anatomical forensics, comparative textile analysis, soil particle inspection, acid pigmentation screening, blood forensics, botanical screening, digital image processing, computerized textual analysis, and countless others. Despite the relentless examination, there is still no proof positive evidence of its origin.

Because its inspection is so multidisciplinary, the study of the shroud has been given its own name—*sindonology*. It is probably not a good college major though, as job prospects in this field seem limited.

SEE ALSO: APOCRYPHA; THE DRESS; GOSPEL OF JESUS'S WIFE; PAREIDOLIA; PRESTER JOHN

SIMULISM

Simulism is the belief that the whole goddamn thing is a stupid video game.

Also known as the *simulated reality hypothesis*, simulism posits that what we know of reality—everything from the Big Bang to sour cream & onion chip flavor—is actually part of a giant computer simulation. More than mere warmed-over *Matrix* theorizing, this little corner of the alternate-reality universe contains actual physicists and philosophers (and solar car enthusiasts). The astrophysicist Neil deGrasse Tyson, for instance, is at least a partial believer. He has pegged the odds at 50/50 that we are digital beings living in a huge computer experiment. Elon Musk finds that wildly optimistic. Citing the improvement of video game fidelity during our lifetimes, the real-world Iron Man puts the odds that we are living in "base reality" at just "one in billions." And the Oxford philosopher Nick Bostrom—the thinker most associated with simulism—has posited that our universe exists because an advanced civilization with enormous computing power decided to run simulations of other hypothetical universes. We live in one of those simulations.[143]

Simulism has been trendy of late, mostly by sheer coincidence of disconnected scientific projects—brain mapping, virtual reality, and artificial intelligence. Simulists often align those technical advances under the umbrella of *posthumanism*, or the belief that this collision of biology and computers will soon usher in a state of transcendence over the limits of the human condition. This puts the simulated theory hypothesis in that category of futurism that takes whatever is happening *right now* and multiplies it into the event horizon. We have lots of computing power, *but what if we had exponentially more?* We can make computers talk, *so what if we're just talking computers?* Games have become ultra-realistic, *so maybe we are little Marios bumping our heads into virtual mushrooms?* Precise mathematical principles now seem to rule the universe, *so maybe these are the presets for our computer simulation?* People like Instagram, *so perchance, are we all just lobotomized bots mindlessly clicking virtual* ❤ *icons on pictures of food as part of a programmatic game theory experiment to determine how far humans will diminish their dignity?* (Makes sense, when you put it that way.)

Current events don't help matters. Many recent news developments seem the result of handing the joystick that controls the universe over to an erratic teenager. *Let's see what chaos ensues if we give the Oscar to the wrong movie, let the Cubs win the World Series, and divide the world on the color of a* DRESS. Surely, there must be a glitch in the machine. It must all be a test to see how we react. Did we pass? What are the cheat codes? Because this level kinda sucks.

Simulism seems like the kind of unruly theory-mongering that could never be tested, but some scientists have actually devised experiments to prove this is all a simulation.[144] Nothing has come of these studies yet, but just imagine for a moment that it worked—that science somehow conclusively *proved* that we are living in a simulation. Then what? Do we become the hopeless bots in *The Sims*, peeing on ourselves and begging for mercy from our overlords? Or do we say *fuck it, let's shoot hookers*, like *Grand Theft Auto*? Bostrom, the philosopher, offers a theory: We start creating our own hyperrealistic simulated universes. And then creatures in those universes create even more universes. Like an Escher of *Minecrafts* inside of *Minecrafts*, eventually all the simulations gobble up too much memory in the master computer that runs all our virtualizations, causing the Sysadmin in the Sky to get annoyed and click the OFF switch on everything. (If this theory is true, we really need to shut down the Marvel Cinematic Universe *immediately*, before it kills us all.)

Or maybe the master computer is an oblivious god who is just letting the system run for enjoyment, like a really long intergalactic version of the *Fast and the Furious* franchise. Maybe it makes no difference what we do. We might just be nonplayer characters,

---

143   Bostrom's original essay—"Are You Living In a Computer Simulation?" (2003)—was published in *Philosophical Quarterly*. It, along with the cultural ephemera it manifested, can be found at simulation-argument.com.

144   These experiments have included building a holometer (a machine for detecting holographic fluctuations in spacetime) and looking at whether cosmic rays travel in straight lines or through a finite set of points on a grid.

hopelessly pressing the CLOSE DOOR button on the elevator, hoping to level up, but nothing ever happens.

SEE ALSO: BRAIN IN A VAT; BERENSTAIN BEARS CONSPIRACY; DREAM ARGUMENT; PLATO'S CAVE; TRUMAN SYNDROME; WOOZLE EFFECT

SLASHFIC

Slashfic is a subgenre of FANFIC in which two male characters are paired in romantic or sexual situations. (Far less common, erotic stories with two women are generally referred to as *femslash*.) Fandoms are diverse, but slashfic authors tend to skew young and—somewhat unexpectedly—female.

The term derives from *The Ring of Soshern* (1968), generally regarded as the first work of slashfic, which was initially described as "Kirk Slash Spock." The anonymous novella opens with the Star Trek duo stranded on a deserted planet. Spock immediately enters *pon farr*, a violent state of sexual fever that overcomes Vulcans, and . . . well, the story writes itself from there.

Slashfic itself has many subgenres, including Real Person Slash (RPS), which involves erotic entanglements of real people. Much RPS involves members of the boy band One Direction, but another subgenre—Historical RPS—has shipped Marx/Engels, Burr/Hamilton, Jesus/Judas, Axl/Slash, Lennon/McCartney, Kerry/Edwards, Stewart/Colbert, Obama/Santorum, Manning/Brady, and Bowie/Bowie (multiple David Bowie personas getting down).

SEE ALSO: CLICKBAIT; FACTOID

SLEEPIFY

Sleepify was an album released in 2014 by Vulfpeck, an obscure funk band from Ann Arbor. It contained ten tracks of complete silence, each thirty-one or thirty-two seconds in length. Track names included "Zzzzz," "Z," and "Zzz." None were breakout hits.

After uploading the mute tunes to Spotify, the band encouraged fans to listen to the album on a loop while sleeping. After four million drowsy plays over a two-month period, the band racked up $19,655 in royalties, before Spotify removed the snoozefest.

The album has become a symbol of the many innovative techniques for gaming music streaming services. While some crafty programmers have developed bots to artificially inflate play counts, the most popular scam is simply piggybacking on name recognition. Because artists like Garth Brooks and Bob Seger have refused to release their catalogues on Spotify, searching for them instead serves up tunes by Brooks Stars Garth and Bob Segar—spammy variants of TRIBUTE BANDS who have collected millions of listens through subtle MIMICRY. Other acts have devised their own inventive tricks, like releasing the same song multiple times with different track titles, begetting new listeners through the vagaries of random search terms. This environment of keyword hacking and artistic gamesmanship has turned Spotify into a linguistic playground, where the question *"clever creator* or *ripoff artist*?" is under constant consideration.

SEE ALSO: MOCKBUSTER; MONEY; TEMP MUSIC

SLENDERMAN

Slenderman might be the first widely known folklore character to originate on the internet. If you have never heard of him, you do not know a goth teen.

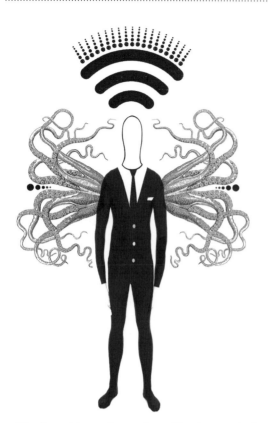

The first thing to know about Slenderman is the image: tall, gaunt, faceless. His black suit stretches over elongated appendages, and usually (depictions vary) tentacles sprout from his back, the better to strangle you with. Most of the time, Slenderman is an omniscient demon who lurks in the background, reading the minds of children before abducting them. But sometimes he is a figure whom children trust, or at least obey.

Slenderman was first created in 2009 as part of a PHOTOSHOPPING contest on Something Awful, the most accurately named website on the internet. The contest rules invited applicants to alter an everyday photo to appear creepy and then repost it to para-

normal websites. It worked—Slenderman became an instant meme that quickly spread to other fan sites (Tumblr, 4chan, Deviant Art, Reddit, YouTube), where it was modified and updated and redistributed.

Now for the scary part. In 2014, two twelve-year-old girls in Wisconsin stabbed their classmate nineteen times as part of an initiation ritual to become "proxies" of Slenderman. No one told them to do this. The girls adapted the ritual from the Slenderman canon found online. Their bedrooms were littered with Slenderman fan art, and when asked why they stabbed their friend, one of the girls said, "Because it was necessary."[145]

Because Slenderman is a new myth, still open to interpretation, adolescents can imbue the legend with their own anxieties. Invented online, the lore is highly collaborative and adaptable by its story-teller. Tropes are easily updated to create new stories, images, games, or videos. Creativity is rewarded with reactions and views, and as more Slenderman material is uploaded, the legend creeps into the real world. In a sort of self-fulfilling prophecy, one of the Wisconsin girls said the internet contained "proof" of Slenderman's existence.

An open-source myth, Slenderman is the everyman bogeyman.

SEE ALSO: THE BLAIR WITCH PROJECT; CRYPTIDS; MEME MAGIC; PHOTOSHOPPING; SANTA CLAUS

SMARKS

On the playgrounds of our youth, kids could be divided into three personality groups, based on their perspective on professional wrestling:

---

145 The documentary *Beware the Slenderman* (2016) recounts the harrowing story of these girls. One has been diagnosed with schizophrenia; the other, schizotypy.

1. **Zealots of realism** who righteously insisted that the sport was fake and therefore rubbish.
2. **Blinkered simpletons** of blind faith who evangelized its authenticity down to the turnbuckle.
3. **Sophisticated fans** who loved the spectacle *because* it was fake.

Children of the third brood grew up to be smarks. *Smark* is jargon used within the professional wrestling community to denote superfans who recognize the show as pure theater but nonetheless revere the scripted artifice. A smark might admire Jimmy Superfly Snuka's air-time, but she is just as likely to salute the Iron Sheik's ability to stay in character when Rowdy Roddy Piper flubs a line—that is *real* artistry. Smarks not only know the game but strive to discern its artistry.

Smarks *get it.*

The word itself is a portmanteau of *mark* (the con artist term for the sucker) and *smart.* Borrowed from the argot of carnies, who used the term to denote carnival attendees who believe they are "in the know," smarks are the personification of ironic detachment. If you hatewatch the antiheroes of reality television to scoff at their faulty storylines, you might be a smark. (If you insist *hatewatching* does not exist, you definitely are.) If you speak of *shipping* fictional characters, you exhibit smark-like tendencies. If you chide unsophisticated friends who cannot appreciate the *artiste* that is Kim Kardashian, your smark is showing. If you are a grown adult who throws their birthday party at Medieval Times, welcome to the circus: You are smark.

If you bought this encyclopedia, you are probably a smark. Sorry, sucker. But at least you get it.

SEE ALSO: BULLSHIT; CANNED HEAT; CONFIDENCE GAME; KAYFABE; LARP

SMITHEE, ALAN

According to IMDB, Alan Smithee has directed more than eighty films, television episodes, and music videos, including a Jodie Foster action movie called *Catchfire*, a made-for-TV movie about O. J. Simpson, a sequel to Hitchcock's *The Birds*, a National Lampoon movie starring Tommy Chong, the video for Whitney Houston's "I Will Always Love You," and the pilot episodes of the show *MacGyver* and *Walker, Texas Ranger.*

If it seems no single person could have compiled such a diverse oeuvre, that's because no single person did. *Alan Smithee* is a pseudonym, used by film directors who want to disown an especially wretched project. The first Alan Smithee credit was *Death of a Gunfighter*, a 1969 movie that had two different directors refuse credit. Other notable projects to don the Alan Smithee *nom de guerre* include the television-edited versions of *Dune* (David Lynch) and *Heat* (Michael Mann) and music videos for Wu-Tang Clan, Sarah McLachlan, Faith No More, and Salt-N-Pepa.

"Alan Smithee" is also an anagram for "the alias men," but that is a sublime coincidence.

SEE ALSO: DOE, JOHN; F FOR FAKE; MANNING, DAVID

SNIPE HUNT

The snipe hunt is a legendary rite of passage performed on gullible newcomers. The practical joke is reportedly commonplace at summer camps, but its use as a television trope far outpaces its prank usage. (Or maybe television writers are just more likely to attend regional summer camp. That seems entirely possible.) Actual snipe hunts—or rather, actual fictional snipe hunts—have appeared in episodes of a welter of shows including *Cheers*, *Boardwalk*

Empire, Star Trek: The Next Generation, and *Walker, Texas Ranger.*

The folkloric snipe is variously described as monstrous (black with glowing red eyes), paranormal (in the form of a werewolf or mutant), or prosaic (snakes, deer, or any small furry critter). There is a real wading bird called a *snipe*, but no television script has yet implemented it into one of its wild-goose chase plots.

SEE ALSO: BANANADINE; BONSAI KITTEN; CONFIDENCE GAME; CRYPTIDS; SANTA CLAUS

SNOPES

Sometime over the past couple decades, a William Faulkner superfan has undoubtedly stumbled upon the website Snopes.com, only to become infuriated that it does not celebrate a certain fictional family from Mississippi. Instead of incisive commentary on the collection of Faulkner novels known as the "Snopes Trilogy," there exists a huge repository of articles deliberating whether Walt Disney was cryogenically frozen, whether George Washington had wooden teeth, whether Richard Gere had an emergency gerbilectomy, and whether PAUL IS DEAD.[146]

The web now seems nearly unimaginable without Snopes.com.[147] Though birthed in a fringe corner (a message board about folklore), the site has been there since nearly the beginning, shining the kliegs on misinformation, untangling skeins of half-truth, interrogating rampant urban legends, and, occasionally, confirming bits of outrageous news. Like history itself, the site goes through spurts of import, bouncing from *merely useful* to *manifestly crucial.*

After 9/11, Snopes combated esoteric conspiracies. During Barack Obama's first election, it assiduously kept waves of bigoted rumors at bay. After a brief calm, its popularity exploded again during the 2016 election, as the country embraced a candidate who led the BIRTHER movement.

The popular trajectory of Snopes tracks eerily with two other trends: the precipitous fall of the public's faith in the media and the soaring volume of websites propagating dubious information. As the internet torched local newsrooms, traditional media lost its credibility, leaving behind thousands of undifferentiated news websites with contradictory information. In a sea of unverified facts, Snopes became one of the few resources for moderating some semblance of truth. (Though it has tried to stay out of partisan battles by sticking to basic facts, Snopes is regularly attacked by right-wing sites as "fake news.")

It wasn't supposed to turn out this way. Early pioneers of the web thought the new medium would make misinformation a superannuated relic. All claims of truth were going to be fact-checked in real time by some sort of revelatory hive mind. Instead, we occupy a world where Facebook has recruited Snopes as a bulwark against pervasive fake news. In the post-truth era, we have become inured to the belief that facts are fungible—interchangeable partisan widgets that can be manufactured and rearranged to tell any story. As ALTERNATIVE FACTS settle themselves into history, reality itself is up for grabs. "Your illusions are a part of you," cautioned a certain southern writer, "like your bones and flesh and memory."[148]

SEE ALSO: ALT-HISTORY; FANFIC; INTERNET TROLL

---

146 *False,* according to Snopes, on all four counts.

147 Launched in 1994 by David and Barbara Mikkelson, the site (yes, named after the venal Faulkner clan) moved around various domains before settling on its titular dot-com in 1997, but then for a brief spell in the early aughts, started mysteriously redirecting to snopes2.com. (Such are the vagaries of the early web.)

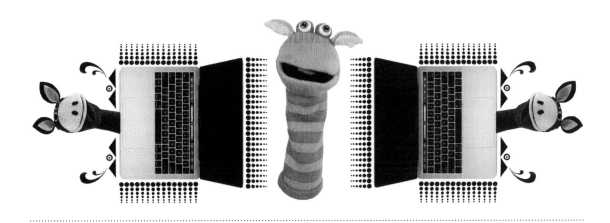

SOCK PUPPET

Sock puppetry is a cutesy term for assuming a false identity with malicious intent on—where else, but the internet?

A sock puppet initiates their deception by creating a profile under a pseudonym. Often already a member of the online community, the faux persona allows the puppet to demean other participants, promote their ideology, or defend themselves against criticism. (In the latter case, the sock puppet is often presented as a "friend" or "sister" of the person.)

Sock puppets notoriously strain the reliability of consumer reviews. Yelp is larded with sock puppet restaurateurs crowing about their steakhouses and clucking about their competitors. Wikipedia is chockablock with quasi-notables retouching their pages to squeaky perfection. Seller ratings on eBay must be viewed with caution, and even Rate My Professors arrives suspiciously festooned with smart, sexy academics. On Amazon, several authors have been caught either writing their own five-star reviews or hiring companies to generate hundreds for them. (This scuzzy practice is not entirely new—Walt Whitman and Ben Franklin also reviewed their own books under pseudonyms.)

Of greater concern is the apparent rise of government-sponsored sock puppetry. As part of a political ASTROTURFING campaign, sock puppets can assault social media with spurious messages. In support of shady causes, armies of virtual personalities, known as "troll farms," are widely known to have been deployed by Russian oligarchs. Given the conspicuous nature of an INTERNET TROLL, spotting its boisterous poppycock should be fairly routine. But as reporter Adrien Chen and others have shown, identification is not the primary challenge. "The real effect," wrote Chen, "was not to brainwash readers but to overwhelm social media with a flood of counterfeit content, seeding doubt and paranoia, and destroying the possibility of using the internet as a democratic space." [149] This reality disruption leads to a kind of relativistic apathy, which resembles what Hannah Arendt once said regarding the role of lying in totalitarianism:

---

148 *Absalom, Absalom* (1936), William Faulkner.

149 In June 2015 ("The Agency," *New York Times Magazine*), Chen provided an alarming account of the Russian troll farm INTERNET RESEARCH AGENCY. A follow-up ("The Real Paranoia-Inducing Purpose of Russian Hacks") was published on NewYorker.com a year later.

A people that no longer can believe anything cannot make up its mind. It is deprived not only of its capacity to act but also of its capacity to think and to judge. And with such a people you can then do what you please.[150]

By creating a shambolic environment, ridden with uncertainty and paranoia, an army of phony avatars can enter an internet community and sap out its empathy and trust. Even when their imposture fails, the sock puppet triumphs through nuisance.

SEE ALSO: ASTROTURFING; BARRON, JOHN; CATFISH; CLAQUE; CONCERN TROLLING; FALSE FLAG OPERATION; FIVERR; INTERNET RESEARCH AGENCY; INTERNET TROLL; MANNING, DAVID

SODIUM PENTOTHAL

Sodium Pentothal is the official name for sodium thiopental, a chemical commonly (and comically) depicted in spy flicks and pulp novels as a truth serum. It is a barbiturate, or *downer*, as such substances were once called on the street.

Invented in 1936 by two chemists who hoped to discover a new painkiller, Pentothal induces drowsiness and calms anxiety. It is also the first drug in the "three-drug cocktail" used to execute prisoners in the United States—or it *was*, until the European Union (where capital punishment has been abolished) banned its export in 2011.

Injecting Pentothal will induce a trancelike state, making it difficult for the brain to perform complex thoughts. In theory, those complex thoughts include speaking lies, but in practice, the drug just makes you talk a lot. *A lot a lot.* Like a doped-up simian in the INFINITE MONKEY THEOREM, you might accidentally babble the "truth" under the influence of Pentothal. But police interrogators find that Pentothal causes subjects to just tell them what they want to hear.

Pentothal is no weapon against mendacity. It will, however, cause you defy your Fifth Amendment right to remain silent.

SEE ALSO: BOTOX; HYPNOSIS; NOBLE LIE; PLACEBO EFFECT; POLYGRAPH; RORSCHACH TEST; TRUTHINESS

SOKAL HOAX

"Transgressing the Boundaries: Toward a Transformative Hermeneutics of Quantum Gravity" sounds like the sort of inscrutable dissertation one might find stuffed into a rarefied academic journal, nuzzled deep in the fusty stacks of a university library, behind some mousetraps and a dilapidated microfiche reader. Indeed, the article could be discovered there, in the 1996 spring/summer issue of *Social Text*, a well-regarded (yet of course still rarefied) journal of postmodern cultural studies. While its existence was mundane enough, its authorship was peculiar—Dr. Alan Sokal, a professor of physics at NYU. A physics prof publishing in a humanities journal prone to harangues about *subalternity* and *logocentrism*? This might be worth a trip through the library mousetraps!

With prolix prose, the professor staked the surprising claim that quantum gravity—a new field of theoretical physics—had profound political implications. Arguing that physical reality (as in, the stuff he studies) is nothing more than a social and linguistic construct (as in, the stuff cultural theoreticians study), Sokal declared in the very first paragraph that scientists were clinging to dogmatic beliefs,

---

150   The quote is from a 1974 interview with Arendt published by the *New York Review of Books* in 1978.

including the antiquated notion "that there exists an external world, whose properties are independent of any individual human being." From the onset, he impersonated a radical relativist, and not the Einsteinian variety.

The hyperbolic language should have been a clue that the physics department was pranking the humanities department, but somehow the paper passed through the radar of the journal's esteemed editorial board. On the day of its publication, Sokal revealed his hoax in the magazine *Lingua Franca* and spoke to the *New York Times*:

> I structured the article around the silliest quotes about mathematics and physics from the most prominent academics, and I invented the argument praising them and linking them together.... All this was very easy to carry off because my argument wasn't obliged to respect any standards of evidence or logic.[151]

Steeping his parody in a hodgepodge of jargon—*transformative hermeneutics*, *morphogenetic fields*, *nonlinearity*, *dialecticism*—Sokal was on a mission to prove that academia had been overrun with gibberish. His other contention was that intellectual rigor was declining, so he loaded his prank paper with spurious interdisciplinary claims: that recent discoveries in quantum field theory were germane to Lacanian psychoanalysis, that the axiom of equality in mathematical set theory was congruent with feminist politics, that deconstruction and quantum mechanics were wondrously intertwined. This collision of academic departments made a discordant ruckus.

By all accounts, it was also a pretty good parody.

Even smug cultural studies grads seemed to chuckle, discreetly, fearful that the entire episode might provoke ridicule of their field. They had cause to tremble—the lampoon was quite the sensation, not only landing the front page of the *New York Times* but also becoming a matter for pundits of every stripe to pontificate upon.[152] Sokal had successfully satirized the charlatan patois of academia, yes, but he had also raised the sword to an entire wing of campus—not just cultural studies, but related fields like literature, sociology, linguistics, political science, and philosophy. To Sokal, literary theory, especially the postmodernism and deconstruction taught in universities, was waging war on "objective reality." As a leftist himself, Sokal worried that theory-laden coursework was detaching students from "real" political engagement.

Ultimately, Sokal's satiric missile decimated some of its targets while overshooting others. His assault on academic jargon landed an undisputed direct hit, as intellectuals had universally grown weary of the incoherent bilge spewing from the mouths of Brown semiotics grads.[153] And his contention about declining intellectual rigor in the humanities struck at least a glancing blow, especially to those shambolic theorists caught jumbling deconstruction with quantum theory. But in retrospect, his dispute with postmodernism is more difficult to parse. Forget Foucault; philosophers have been declaring the world "real but unknowable" since at least Kant, maybe Plato. Sokal seemed to assert that the Enlightenment eradicated all the fuzziness about reality, but that claim has become only more tenuous with each advance in technology, media, and, yes, science. (As this very tome intimates, spu-

---

151   The quote appears in a May 18, 1996 article "Postmodern Gravity Deconstructed, Slyly."

152   In adorably predictable fashion, a cavalcade of columnists used the Sokal hoax to take swipes at or defend academia—George F. Will in the *Washington Post*, Stanley Fish in the *New York Times*, Katha Pollitt in *The Nation*, Richard Dawkins in *Nature*, and of course Rush Limbaugh . . . on the *Rush Limbaugh Show*.

153   Apologies to the alumni of Brown University, but for a while there, you were like postmodernism text generators cranked to eleven.

rious epistemology is alive and well!)

Sokal wanted to put science on a special shelf, beyond reproach from other disciplines. This presumptuous stance overlooked how science is obviously contaminated by social values, which even the most strident physicist would admit. The scientific method is merely a way of perceiving the universe, not a synonym for reality. The universe does not care about science any more than it cares about those rarefied cultural dissertations connecting Homer Simpson to the Sandinistas. (Great thesis topic!)

Sokal's poke at hokum scholarship was valid, maybe even heroic. But in his battle against charlatanism, he dismissed how language and culture can intercept our understanding of the real world. He could have used a small dose of *transformative hermeneutics*.

SEE ALSO: COLD FUSION; GRUNGE SPEAK; NACIREMA; SOPHISTS; WOOZLE EFFECT

SOPHISTS

The sophists were a group of Greek philosophers—contemporaries of Plato and Aristotle—known for specious argumentation. Unlike the amiable school of gratis philosophy that surrounded Socrates, the sophists developed a bad reputation as strident rhetoricians who levied exorbitant fees to access their technical teachings.

In his dialogue the *Sophist*, Plato depicts the personality as a kind of philosophical mercenary, willing to argue any position for the right fee. Today, the modern sophist—who ranks eloquence over truth, who loves the sound of their own vituperative opinion—can be found in plenty on cable news.

SEE ALSO: CHEWBACCA DEFENSE; NOT EVEN WRONG; OMNIPOTENCE PARADOX; PASCAL'S WAGER

STEGANOGRAPHY

Steganography is the art of hiding a secret message in a nonsecret location. Unlike cryptography, to which it is often compared, steganography does not draw attention to itself as a target for scrutiny. A steganographic message is not encrypted; the secret message is right there, hidden in plain sight, like Poe's purloined letter.

The first recorded case of steganography comes from, as usual, Herodotus. In HISTORIES, he describes a secret message being tattooed on the shaved head of a slave. When his hair grows back, the slave becomes a surreptitious messenger, transporting the confidential information on his scalp without detection.

More often, steganographic messages are embedded inside of other messages, like invisible ink written between the lines of a letter. This innocuous press cable, for instance, was sent by a German spy during World War I:

> President's embargo ruling should have immediate notice. Grave situation affecting international law. Statement foreshadows ruin of many neutrals. Yellow journals unifying national excitement immensely.

See it? If you yank out the first letter of each word, the true communiqué emerges:

> Pershing sails from NY June 1.

An even more inane follow-up missive was sent, in which the *second* letter from each word reveals the exact same message:

> Apparently neutral's protest is thoroughly discounted and ignored. Isman hard hit. Blockade issue affects pretext for embargo on byproducts, ejecting suets and vegetable oils.[154]

(It was all for naught, as Pershing, the head of the Western Front during the war, actually sailed on May 28.)

Because they contain large amounts of obfuscated data, digital files are especially useful for carrying steganographic messages. With tools found online, JPEG images or MP3 music files can be encoded and decoded with furtive communication. After 9/11, many news outlets reported that Osama bin Laden had used steganographic techniques to coordinate the attacks. After a massive investigation of internet files, including bulk analysis of millions of images for ciphertext, no clandestine codes were found.

But the spy movie trope remains compelling—what if secret commands exist all over the internet, ensconced in obscure tweets, in rugby chat rooms, in email spam, in illicit movie torrents, in pornography, in Sudoku puzzles? In the 1975 paranoid thriller *Three Days of the Condor*, Robert Redford plays a bookish CIA researcher whose entire job involves reading books and magazines for steganographic messages. It is a compelling provocation, both whimsical and chilling, that every scrap of culture might contain sub rosa intel. Perhaps this encyclopedia is one large encrypted message. Can you see it?

SEE ALSO: BACKMASKING; CANARY TRAP; HISTORIES; ILLEGAL PRIME NUMBER; INFINITE MONKEY THEOREM; ORDER OF THE OCCULT HAND; SUBLIMINAL ADVERTISING

STRATEGERY

Strategery is often remembered as a word invented by George W. Bush, but this is a false memory. The word was actually coined on *Saturday Night Live* (by writer Jim Downey) to satirize Bush's frequent malapropisms, mispronunciations, and grammatical gaffes.

Strategery was inspired by a bevy of Bushisms, all of which actually did spill from the mouth of the 43rd president of these fine United States. Here is a sample:

- "I've been misunderestimated most of my life."
- "Rarely is the question asked: Is our children learning?"
- "Our enemies are innovative and resourceful, and so are we. They never stop thinking about new ways to harm our country and our people, and neither do we."
- "I know how hard it is for you to put food on your family."
- "I know the human being and fish can coexist peacefully."
- "You teach a child to read, and he or her will be able to pass a literacy test."
- "Fool me once, shame on—shame on you. Fool me—you can't get fooled again."
- "One of the great things about books is sometimes there are some fantastic pictures."

A related portmanteau, *refudiate*, was an actual Palinism, coming from the mouth of Sarah Palin.

SEE ALSO: MONDEGREEN; THE RUMSFELD MATRIX; TRUTHINESS

STREISAND EFFECT

The Streisand Effect refers to the intoxicating impression that Jewish Broadway chanteuses have on gay men in the Midwest. (What did you think it was?)

154 This simple form of letter-embedding steganography is known as a *null cipher*. The example comes from the excellent canonical history of cryptography, *The Codebreakers* (1967, updated in 1996), by David Kahn.

Nah, the *Streisand Effect* actually describes an unintended consequence of censorship. The phenom occurs when attempts to block a piece of information accidentally makes the information more popular. Barbra Streisand is the ignoble namesake because after she sued to remove a photograph of her house from a website in 2003, a successful internet resistance campaign made the image ubiquitous. Poor Babs!

The Streisand Effect works because prohibited objects are always more compelling. Someone does not want you to see this; LET ME SEE THIS. Content that inevitably became more popular because it was suppressed includes Salman Rushdie's *The Satanic Verses*, DJ Danger Mouse's *The Grey Album*, the Scientology recruitment video starring Tom Cruise (11 million views and counting), 2 Live Crew, Copernicus's *On the Revolutions of the Heavenly Spheres* (forbidden for heliocentrism by the Vatican in 1616), terrible GoDaddy Super Bowl commercials, "Smack My Bitch Up," "Justify My Love," R-rated comedies (for teenagers), and, probably, Jesus Christ.

The Streisand Effect is not a universal law. Plenty of banned material remains obscure. Censorship still works, though its impact remains ambiguous. In much of Europe, for instance, the sale of Nazi memorabilia is banned. This has undoubtedly made stupid swastika belt buckles more valuable, but what effect has it had on white nationalism? Are there fewer Nazis because of the ban? Maybe! Or, maybe not. Enforcing scarcity does not always generate value. Did shutting down *fetch* from happening only make *fetch* happen? No. (Or does its mention here prove *yes*?) Point is, we scarcely understand when and why and how suppression works.

Of course, capitalism has a way of absorbing its resisting forces. Marketers have realized that prohibited content is more desirable. Therefore we now have the *Reverse Streisand,* a form of feigned censorship that generates hype. "Leaked" music drops, faux legal take-down requests, and illicit parodies (neither illicit nor parodic) are all forms of manufactured forbidden fruit. Unsurprisingly, P. T. Barnum was the master of the Reverse Streisand. When his circus rolled into a new town, he would write fake letters to local newspapers condemning that rapscallion P. T. Barnum as a deviant huckster. The aura of scandal only attracted more people to the greatest show on earth.

SEE ALSO: CANNIBAL HOLOCAUST; CELEBRITY SEX TAPES; CUNNINGHAM'S LAW; HUMBUGGERY; ILLEGAL PRIME NUMBER; VIRAL MARKETING; XENU

SUBLIMINAL ADVERTISING

In 1957, the researcher James Vicary caused quite a media stir when he announced the results of the psychological experiment he conducted at a movie theater in Fort Lee, New Jersey. During the summer, while moviegoers watched William Holden and Kim Novak in the seething summer drama *Picnic*, Vicary used a tachistoscope to flash very fast messages on the screen, far below the threshold of consciousness, at 1/3000th of a second. The two imperceptible messages were:

DRINK COCA-COLA
EAT POPCORN

It worked! Vicary reported that among the 45,699 people who saw the movie, the theater reported an increase in soda concession sales of 18 percent while popcorn jumped an astounding 58 percent. The pronouncement generated an instant frenzy across the media and advertising industry. Others saw opportunity in the findings, including the CIA, who produced an internal report, "The Operational Potential of Subliminal Perception." Legislators, fearing a world dominated by subliminal manipulation, began to investigate passing laws against covert advertising.

Finally, the manager of the Fort Lee theater came forward and declared the results a lie. Meanwhile, psychologists who were trying to re-create the experiment realized why they were unable to reproduce the results. Vicary waited until 1962 before finally admitting that the study was a fabrication. By then the damage was done—subliminal advertising had subliminally captured the minds of the public. We are being secretly controlled by mass media!

Over decades, test after test has shown negligible effects of subliminal messaging. Despite all the fear about brainwashing, it simply does not work. *Overt* advertising—like product placing Trojans in a hip-hop video or implying in a Super Bowl ad that buying a web domain through GoDaddy can increase your sex appeal—actually (and regrettably) does work. But hiding the word *SEX* out of conscious recognition in a Skittles ad will not elicit lusty emotions for candy. Disguising Joe Camel's nose as a penis, BACKMASKING "Do it" into Judas Priest songs, listening to self-help slogans in your sleep—all of this is proven folly.

Vicary, who is now credited with coining the term *subliminal advertising*, may have succeeded in permanently inserting a belief in hypnotic mind control into our heads.

SEE ALSO: BACKMASKING; HYPNOSIS; PRODUCT PLACEMENT; STEGANOGRAPHY; VIRAL MARKETING

SUPERCALIFRAGILISTICEXPIALIDOCIOUS

This nonsense word presents itself as fabricated, but even its artifice is misinformation.

In the 1964 movie, Mary Poppins insinuates that she has invented this mouthful for those ineffable moments in life when language escapes you—"something to say when you have nothing to say," she instructs, launching into melody. But the Disney musical is misleading about the word's origin. Despite the insinuation, they did not coin it. At least as far back as 1949, a different song used the same word, with a slightly different spelling: "Supercalafajalistickespialadojus."

Regardless of its provenance, Mary Poppins claims her neologism is pure nonsense. But this is deceptive too, because when the garble is parsed to its lexical roots, a potentially intelligible word emerges from the blather of syllables:

MORPHEME	MEANING
SUPER	ABOVE
CALI	BEAUTY
FRAGILISTIC [155]	DELICATE
EXPIALI	TO ATONE
DOCIOUS	EDUCABLE

That cacophony of morphemes could engender many meanings, but the *Oxford English Dictionary* has defined the sum as "Atoning for educability through delicate beauty," which just proves that even smart reference books can be silly.[156] No one has ever said *supercalifragilisticexpialidocious* with that intended meaning, not only because the sound of it is something quite atrocious but also because that's not even a word we need.

SEE ALSO: JABBERWOCKY; NONCE WORD

---

155 Of course, *supercalifragilisticexpialidocious* is not our longest word (most dictionaries award that honor to *pneumonoultramicroscopicsilicovolcanoconiosis*, a lung disease caused by inhaling very fine ash and sand dust). But if we wanted to get pedantic about it, the word is actually two words. The suffix *-istic* can't be used in the middle of a word, so the proper spelling should actually be *supercalifragilistic expialidocious*.

SWIFTBOATING

Swiftboating is an insidious type of political smear campaign, with tactics modernized for a post-truth media climate.

During the 2004 election, a disparate group of veterans congealed into a conspiratorial political organization, the Swift Boat Veterans for Truth. Their target: presidential candidate John Kerry, who, as a swift boat commander during the Vietnam War, was awarded the Silver Star, the Bronze Star, and three Purple Hearts. Despite his naval heroism, the veteran group keelhauled Kerry, declaring him "unfit for command," based upon "his exaggerated claims about his own service in Vietnam."

The swiftboaters provided no evidence, but their specious message broke through to the electorate, first on partisan talk radio, and later with a series of television ads disputing Kerry's combat medals. The allegations were unsubstantiated, but the movement contained members who had been hoping to impugn their fellow veteran since 1971, when Kerry delivered an antiwar speech to the Senate. (A widely distributed photo showing Kerry with leftist activist Jane Fonda—later proved a forgery—also riled veterans and helped cast doubt on his character.)

Today, the term *swiftboating* has become synonymous with unscrupulous attacks on a political rival. A key swiftboating tactic is to assail an opponent's strengths (in this case, military valor) rather than his weaknesses (here, a peacenik speech). Historically, the swiftboat movement has come to be viewed as a dishonest, though highly effective, smear campaign.

"Falsehood flies," as Jonathan Swift once wrote, "and truth comes limping after it, so that when men come to be undeceived, it is too late; the jest is over, and the tale hath had its effect."[157]

SEE ALSO: ASTROTURFING; FUD; LONG, HUEY; PUSH POLL

SYNTHETIC DIAMONDS

Diamonds are nothing more than carbon, in crystallized form. But making them requires the right geological stove (high temperature, high pressure) and a billion years of cooking. However, a new type of diamond created in a lab needs only a few days of baking in some fancy ovens. These synthetic diamonds are nearly indistinguishable from the natural ones.

Not to be confused with cubic zirconia (imitations made not from carbon but from zirconium oxide and popularized in '80s infomercials), the new breed of synthetic diamonds are the real deal—carbon, in a crystal lattice structure. The naked eye cannot tell the difference; neither can an incredulous jeweler wielding a loupe. Not even an expert with a microscope could differentiate natural from synthetic. Only costly spectroscopic devices can distinguish between a natural and an artificial diamond. (Reportedly, diamond supplier De Beers, which carefully rations their monopolistic supply of diamonds around the globe, is spending millions of dollars researching methods to identify synthetic gems.)

---

156   That finespun definition might elicit the question, *What is the word with the most specific meaning?* An answer has been proposed by *The Guinness Book of World Records*, which awarded *mamihlapinatapai* as the "most precise word." Derived from the Yaghan language of Tierra del Fuego, it supposedly means "a look shared by two people, each wishing that the other would initiate something that they both desire but which neither wants to begin."

157   This particular Swift is unrelated to those swifts. The quote comes from one of Jonathan's pamphlets on the art of political lying, written around 1710.

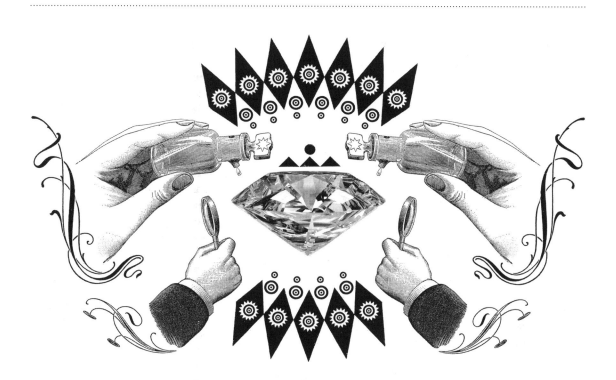

Synthetics have been used industrially since the '50s. Ideal for cutting, drilling, and grinding, the imitation gemstone became a crucial component in a variety of fields—construction, electronics, dentistry, military, even cosmetics. But because the first generation of synthetics were not glassy clear, they never made their way into jewelry store display cases. All that changed around 2012, when the first transparent artificial stones were invented. These clear lab-smelted diamonds started immediately appearing in jewelry stores, retailing for 20 to 40 percent less than mined diamonds.

The best synthetic diamonds are harder and have higher thermal conductivity than earthen ones. (Natural diamonds used to be the hardest known material; now, synthetics are.) So in the case of diamonds, we could safely say the fake is superior to its antecedent—better quality, less expensive, and more ethically sound. Although only 1 percent of the total industry is currently lab-grown, it seems inevitable that the new ersatz diamond will eventually supersede the old natural one.

SEE ALSO: KNOCKOFF HANDBAGS; PHILOSOPHER'S STONE; TOFURKEY

T

TAMAGOTCHI EFFECT

In the '90s, digital devices were still new and scary. While screens emerged as parallel experiences for adolescent escapism, a keychain-dangling doodad elicited the first moral panic about virtualized society.

Behold, the sinister Tamagotchi.

Ovoid-shaped toys from Japan, Tamagotchis were handheld "virtual pets" that would "die" if not given constant attention by their owner. ("Attention" was allotted by pressing buttons every hour, like Desmond from *Lost*.) After millions of kids were found nurturing their virtual playthings, coddling parents with no sense of irony freaked out about their children's equally coddling obsession with their mewling gizmos. Amid a barrage of think pieces on the dangers of technology, a new psychological disorder—the Tamagotchi Effect—was coined to describe our emotional attachment to robots and software agents.

Whether any of these reactionary parents survived to see the iPhone is unknown.

SEE ALSO: CYBORG; MECHANICAL TURK; PHANTOM VIBRATION SYNDROME; TRUMAN SYNDROME

TATE, NAT

On the eve of April Fools' Day (HINT, HINT) in 1998, David Bowie took the stage at a glitzy book launch party in Jeff Koons's studio in Soho to read from a new biography, *Nat Tate: An American Artist, 1928–1960*. The exclusive shindig feted the abstract expressionist who, at the age of thirty-one, destroyed nearly all of his paintings before tragically leaping to his death from the Staten Island Ferry.

As Bowie read the heart-wrenching account from the monograph, an au courant crowd flitted about the room—writers (Jay McInerney, Paul Auster, Siri Hustvedt, John Ashbery), art denizens (Frank Stella, Julian Schnabel, Jeffrey Deitch), and other assorted glitterati (Charlie Rose, Iman, Billy Corgan). Journalists mingled in the trendy herd, asking partygoers for remembrances of Tate. They recalled his gallery shows and mourned his premature death. Copies of the book passed hand-to-hand. If anyone bothered to open it, they found epigraphs from Bowie and Gore Vidal, who cryptically called it "a moving account of an artist too well understood by his time."

There were too many signs. The book was, obviously, a hoax. Rather than a biography, it was essentially a novel—still by the same hand, the English writer William Boyd, but in cahoots with Bowie, Vidal, and a handful of conspirators. "Nat Tate," everyone groaned upon realization, was the rather obvious conflation of London's two biggest art museums, the National Gallery and the Tate Gallery.

Hoaxes usually serve some objective. For the least interesting ruses the reward is financial, but the more sharpened ones expose some small defect of the human psyche. The obvious goal of Nat Tate was to satirize the feigned romanticism of artist biographies. And it worked. But the scheme had another, more remote target: epicurean elites. The hoax exposed how a crowd of feckless artist intellectuals will do anything to appear in-the-know, going so far as to fib when asked, "Do you remember the great artist Nat Tate?"

SEE ALSO: LEROY, JT; ROCKEFELLER, CLARK; UNRELIABLE NARRATOR; WARHOL, ANDY

TEMP MUSIC

While editing a film, a director will often use music from a different movie as a *temporary* score. This is temp music—the stopgap score meant to be replaced once the composer finishes the soundtrack.

But after weeks in an editing booth, delicately matching each movie frame to an interim soundtrack, a director can sometimes fall in love with the dummy composition. So when the final cut is handed over for real orchestration, the director sometimes tells the composer to *imitate* the temp music—within the legal bounds of a replica, of course. At this moment, film composers lose their wiry-haired minds, as would any artist told to mimic another's work.

Since the advent of nonlinear digital editing, which simplified sound and image remixing to a few drop-and-drag mouse strokes, film music has become noticeably less memorable. This copy-and-paste attitude toward moviemaking, coupled with the MIMICRY of temp music scoring, helps explain why today's blockbusters can seem redundant, forgettable, and monotonous.[158]

SEE ALSO: AUTOMATED DIALOGUE REPLACEMENT; DARK SIDE OF THE RAINBOW; FAKE SHEMP; RETCONNING

TEOING

Teoing (often *#TEOING*; sometimes *t'eo-ing*) is an internet meme where you pose for a picture with an invisible girlfriend. The term derives from Manti Malietau Louis Te'o, a star Notre Dame linebacker who in 2012 started telling the media a weepy tale about his Californian girlfriend surviving a violent car crash and then dying of leukemia. It later turned out that the girlfriend, "Lennay Kekua," was a complete fiction. Te'o had been the victim of an elaborate social media hoax. (A devout Mormon, Te'o unwittingly assisted the ruse by lying to everyone about meeting Kekua, when in fact he had been CATFISHED.)

After finishing second in the voting for the Heisman trophy (losing to devout boozehound Johnny Manziel), Te'o would go on to have a prosperous NFL career. Lennay Kekua would later appear at No. 69 on *Maxim*'s annual "Hot 100" list, despite not being a real person.

SEE ALSO: CATFISH; COLEMAN, ALLEGRA; CANARY TRAP; HONEYTRAP; SOCKPUPPET

---

158 For more on this theory, see the YouTube video essay "The Marvel Symphonic Universe."

TOFURKEY

Let's suppose you have a friend who has developed an exotic taste: He loves to devour human flesh. "*Chomp chomp*," exclaims your cannibalistic comrade between bites of homo sapiens quadriceps. "More succulent than filet mignon!"

Of course, this upsets you. "You can't eat your own species!" you implore your friend. Finally, after much pleading, you convince him to stop eating human carne. But he needs to wean himself off his favorite victual, so he tries a new product: *Fooman*. Tastes just like human, but made of tofu.

Here's the question: Is Fooman an ethical replacement? Or does it accidentally reinforce the idea that eating human flesh is acceptable?

Tofurkey—the most successful meat substitute brand—presents a similar dilemma to vegetarians: Can eating *the idea* of a prohibited food unintentionally justify consumption of *the actual* food?

Not all that long ago, a "fake" veggie burger tasted nothing like its "real" meat antecedent, so a devout vegetarian could convince herself that it was a completely different edible product. But as food science has advanced, meat replacements have become much more . . . well, meaty. Discussions around the two newest high-tech meat analogues—Impossible Burger and Beyond Meat—consistently recycle a specific descriptor: *bloody*. "It tastes bloody," says many a reviewer, suggesting the substitute has high verisimilitude with real beef. But is reproducing the taste of blood with laboratory plants really the desired outcome of the anti-meat community?

Tofurky, likewise, attempts to simulate turkey without becoming turkey. But if that simulation continues to progress, if Tofurky continues to be more turkey-like, at some point you have to wonder, *When does the fake become the real? When does tofurkey become turkey?* (In vitro meat, in which animal flesh is grown in a lab rather than in an animal, introduces a similar quandary.)

If you are vegetarian, asking these provocative questions at Thanksgiving dinner will not save you from Uncle Larry making jokes about eating rabbit food. However, you might try dropping this tidbit: Tofurky is technically different from tofurkey (note the dropped -*e*). The former is the brand; the latter, the product. But the company who first introduced Tofurky in 1995 owns the trademark on both, so you might be splitting feathers.

SEE ALSO: CANNIBAL HOLOCAUST; FRANKENFOOD; A MODEST PROPOSAL; SAMPURU

TOMMY WESTPHALL UNIVERSE

When Kramer tumbles into Jerry's apartment, when Marlo Stanfield defends a Baltimore corner, when Mulder and Scully investigate a rare chupacabra sighting, when Homer devours a donut—all of it takes place in the mind of an autistic boy in a Boston hospital. At least according to the Tommy Westphall universe theory.

In the '80s hospital drama *St. Elsewhere*, Tommy Westphall was a minor character—until the final episode. In the final scene of the series, Tommy shakes a snow globe containing a miniaturized version of the hospital, implying that the entire show had taken place in his mind.

This surprise ending has shocking consequences, especially for other television shows. In one episode of *St. Elsewhere*, for instance, doctors visit the bar in *Cheers*, thereby placing both shows in the same fictional universe. And if one show exists in Tommy Westphall's dreamscape, then the other must, too.

From there, the fantasy spread, virus-like, across the television landscape. *Cheers* spun off into *Frasier*, tainting that universe with Tommy's imagination. And when John Larroquette calls into Frasier Crane's radio show, another world is corrupted. And then when *The John Larroquette Show* references Yoyodyne, a fictional company found in everything from

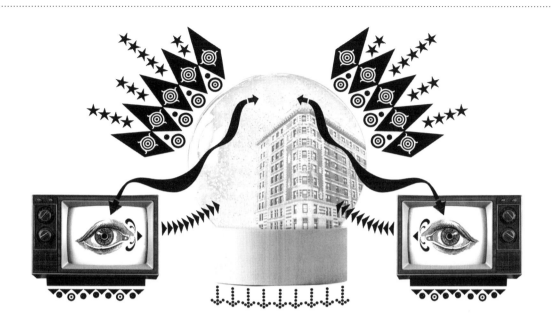

Star Trek to *Angel*, the Tommy Westphall syndrome goes airborne across genres. The fanciful illusion becomes a global pandemic when *St. Elsewhere*'s Dr. Ehrlich (Ed Begley Jr.) has a cameo on *Homicide: Life on the Street*, dragging in omnipresent character Detective John Munch (Richard Belzer), who has been on more shows than any other character in television history, including *The X-Files*, *Arrested Development*, *The Wire*, *30 Rock*, *Law & Order*, and *The Muppets*.

Eventually, the Tommy Westphall universe infects most of television, gobbling up *Fresh Prince of Bel-Air*, *The Cosby Show*, *Buffy*, *I Love Lucy*, *M*A*S*H*, and hundreds of other shows.

Like Six Degrees of Kevin Bacon, the Tommy Westphall universe is amusing because it exposes the uncanny interconnectedness of fictional worlds while foreshadowing the incestuous world of Marvel Comics, which has created its own infinite loop of cross-referenced fictions. But the theory becomes an existential crisis when *real* people appear in the Tommy Westphall universe. Michael Bloomberg, for instance, played himself on *30 Rock*. Which begs the question: If Michael Bloomberg exists only in the imagination of an autistic boy in a Boston hospital, what does that mean for you?

SEE ALSO: THE FOURTH WALL; PLATO'S CAVE; PHANTOM TIME HYPOTHESIS; TRUMAN SYNDROME

TOYETIC

Toyetic is a nasty neologism, forged for this synthetic era of synergistic entertainment experiences.

An adjective initially coined to describe a movie's potential to generate revenue from toys ("*Star Wars* is incredibly toyetic; *12 Years a Slave*, not so much"), the definition of the term has evolved to encompass all possible merchandising opportunities for any type of media property—the rock band repurposed as a breakfast cereal, the video game character transposed onto a beer koozie, the television show liquefied into candy, the politician plasticized into an action figure. Now that everything and everyone is a brand, the word *toyetic* must exist to capture all that latent product licensing value.[159]

The toyetic tipping point was probably 1971, when Quaker Oats Company decided to buy the movie rights to Roald Dahl's beloved book *Charlie and the Chocolate Factory*. Despite no previous experience in film production, Quaker financed *Willy Wonka & the Chocolate Factory* (the one starring Gene Wilder) with the unabashed intention of launching a new line of candy. Sweet-toothed concoctions from the novel, including the Scrumdiddlyumptious Bar and the Everlasting Gobstopper, appeared concurrently both as fantastical confections in the musical film and as real products in checkout lanes. Kids ate it up.

Popular entertainment has been a gooey candyland slide ever since. Many movie franchises have become long-form advertisements for merch, including the Disney extravaganza *Frozen*—an unequivocal blockbuster at the box office ($1.3 billion) but a mere flurry compared to its avalanche of merchandising revenue ($5.3 billion). *Star Wars* was successful in theaters, but its box office take ($2 billion) is matched *every year* in merch sales. These numbers ultimately have a huge effect on what entertainment gets produced. Minus their huge toyetic quotient, shrink-wrapped productions like *Transformers* or *Battleship* could never exist.

And yet, Hollywood evinces no discomfort at casting itself as a glamorous infomercial, especially if the role is delivered with heavy doses of ironic bemusement. *The Lego Movie* franchise, which is basically a FANFIC mashup of the toyetic cinematic universe, might just be its most self-aware production since *Wonka*.

SEE ALSO: DEFICTIONALIZED PRODUCT; FANFIC; PRODUCT PLACEMENT; SAMPURU

TRAP STREETS

Trap streets are fictitious roads on maps, inserted by crafty cartographers to spot copyright infringement. When one of these fake streets apears on the map of a competing mapmaker, it suggests that geographical markers are being illegally copied.

Trap streets lead to *paper towns*—the make-believe hamlets placed on maps for the same reason. They are imaginary geographic markers, but like Dorothy skipping down the Yellow Brick Road to Oz, their mythological existence can create a reality. That's what happened to Agloe, a fictional town in the Catskills of New York. Originally placed on a map in the 1930s, the nonexistent town took on an elusive charm decades later when entrepreneurs scouted the farmland for a new business. Needing a name for their new storefront, the prospecting owners popped open a map and found they were in Agloe—and so, the Agloe General Store became a reality. (The magical realism is echoed in John Green's young adult novel *Paper Towns*, which is set partially in Agloe and was made into an enchanting movie about the very earnest desire to take Cara Delevingne to prom.) By creating a fictitious town, cartographers somehow created a real one. The map preceded the territory.

Though closed decades ago, the Agloe General Store can still be found on Google Maps. "A POTEMKIN VILLAGE general store of the highest order and caliber," a reviewer of the store has written, giving it five stars. "Founded by two cartographic flatlanders, it has a certain *je ne sais quoi* air about it."

SEE ALSO: AREA 51; CANARY TRAP; ESQUIVALIENCE; GERRYMANDERING; IDAHO; NULL ISLAND; POTEMKIN VILLAGE

---

159 A short list of toyetic individuals who have their own action figures: Snoop Dogg, Dr. Laura Schlessinger, van Gogh, Marie Antoinette, Steve Jobs, Snooki, Shakespeare, Einstein, Sarah Palin, Michelle Obama, MC Hammer, Carl Jung, Ann Coulter, George Lucas, and Adolf Hitler. If your name hasn't been licensed onto the merch list, consider yourself a nobody.

Ceci n'est pas une pipe.

Most of the time, art avoids explaining itself. Museums are chockablock with vague images that resist simple interpretation. It's pretty annoying: Art, at its best, tries to fuck with you.

But here, in René Magritte's painting *The Treachery of Images*, we have something else: a picture that seems to speak directly *at you*. Right there, *with words*. When translated from French, it could not be more clear:

This is not a pipe.

Okay, maybe it is trying to fuck with you, because that clearly *is* a pipe.

But you get it. That's a picture of a pipe, not an actual pipe. Magritte seems to be saying, *Images are not reality, representations are illusions.*

Cool idea. Maybe this pipe could be our patron saint of misinformation.

But more mystery is brewing in this painting. In addition to the picture not being a pipe, the word itself—*p-i-p-e*—is also not a pipe. It's just a bunch of squiggly letters. So not even *une pipe* is a pipe.[160]

So, what's a pipe?

Both the *image* (art) and the *word* (language) are human inventions to answer that question. We would be completely unable to understand pipes without those images and words. Art and language are all we know of pipe-ness.

So maybe it is a pipe after all.

SEE ALSO: FOUNTAIN; PLATO'S CAVE

◀ **TRIBUTE BANDS** ▶

"Fakefest" sounds like what would happen if Coachella bought the festival rights to this encyclopedia and invited Weird Al to host a concert. That's not too far from reality: Fakefest is a yearly music festival in Atlantic City with a collection of tribute bands—Kashmir alchemically conjuring Led Zeppelin, Dookie puckishly pantomiming Green Day, and Almost Journey nearly reincarnating Journey. Fakefest is the Lollapalooza of misinformation.

Why would someone pay good money to see an imitation? Good question—just one of many that

---

160   Just to complicate matters: *Pipe* originally referred only to a wind instrument; today, it has several meanings, including the receptacle for tobacco.

tribute bands pose. Other inquiries that might cross your mind at Fakefest:

- Should a tribute act be an exact clone of the original act?
- Does the audience react differently knowing the band is an imitation?
- Does the perfect tribute band distill or expand the original?
- At what point does an homage resemble satire?
- Can a copy become better than the original?
- Is this just really good KARAOKE?

When you watch The Whodlums perform "My Generation" at an Atlantic City casino in 2017, some part of your brain wants to dismiss them as silly knockoffs, but another part is asking, "How similar is this to seeing The Who in London in 1967?"

The answer might be *very similar*, or it might be *not similar at all*, but the answer doesn't really matter—what matters is the nagging question. Ontological riddles like these give tribute bands a unique power that even their antecedents lack. When you see AC/DC blast power chords in a stadium, you might enjoy *rocking out*. But when you see the all-girl act AC/DShe, you're thunderstruck wondering *what does it mean to rock out?*

In this sense, tribute bands are like puzzles, which helps explain why so many of them have one differ-entiating trait that transforms them from precise imitation into unique novelty, as the chart to the right suggests.

These tribute acts are like ALT-HISTORIES. "What if little people started Kiss?" "What if Black Sabbath was founded by Renaissance lutists obsessed with medieval Latin?" "What if Judas Priest were hyper-aggressive nudists?"

Our inclination might still be to dismiss tribute acts as (at best) novelties or (at worst) shams. But the history of popular music contains several instances where the member of a tribute band has joined the band he was imitating. (See the chart below for examples.)

To some, hiring an imitator can appear inauthentic, as though your band were interchangeable with Elvis impersonators. But hiring the poet manqué who trained himself to sound exactly like the band could arguably be the most authentic choice.

Tribute bands are enjoyable not in spite of their artificiality but because of it. They pose questions about *originality* and *authenticity* and *influence*, which happen to be the most interesting topics in contemporary popular music.

SEE ALSO: THE BUGGS; HUMAN CLONING; KARAOKE; SHIP OF THESEUS; WARHOL, ANDY

THIS MUSICIAN...	...JOINED THE BAND...	...A TRIBUTE TO...	...ONLY TO LATER...
Tim "Ripper" Owens	British Steel	Judas Priest	become Judas Priest's lead singer
Tommy Thayer	Cold Gin	Kiss	replace Ace Frehley in Kiss
Benoit David	Close to the Edge	Yes	become the lead vocalist for Yes
Jeremey Hunsicker	Frontiers	Journey	become Journey's lead singer

TRIBUTE BANDS WITH A TWIST

TRIBUTE BAND	ORIGINAL BAND	NOVELTY
Lex Zeppelin	Led Zeppelin	All female
AC/DShe	AC/DC	All female
The Iron Maidens	Iron Maiden	All female
Rocket Queen	Guns n' Roses	All female
Blonde Jovi	Bon Jovi	All female
Mandonna	Madonna	All male
We Got the Meat	The Go-Go's	All male
Rad Bromance	Lady Gaga	All male
Tiny Kiss	Kiss	All dwarf
Mini Kiss	Kiss	All dwarf
Black-Eyed Pee Wees	Black-Eyed Peas	All dwarf
Chicks with Dixie	Dixie Chicks	All transvestite
Hayseed Dixie	AC/DC	In the style of bluegrass
Dread Zeppelin	Led Zeppelin	In the style of reggae
The Beastles	The Beatles	In the style of The Beastie Boys
The Zombeatles	The Beatles	All zombies
Beatallica	The Beatles	In the style of Metallica
Metalachi	Metallica	Mariachi-themed
Gabba	ABBA	In the style of The Ramones
Red Hot Chili Pipers	Red Hot Chili Peppers	All bagpipes
Mac Sabbath	Black Sabbath	Obsessed with fast food
Rondellus	Black Sabbath	Lyrics translated to Latin
Nudist Priest	Judas Priest	All nude
Zappa Plays Zappa	Frank Zappa	Led by Frank's son, Dweezil
The Misfats	The Misfits	All overweight

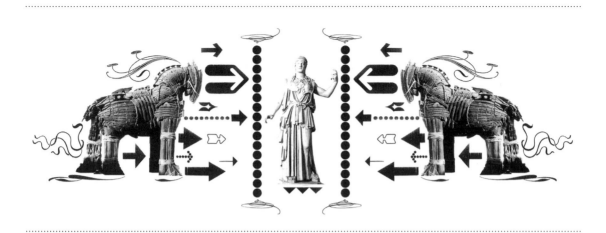

TROJAN HORSE

What is the greatest fake-out in the history of the world? The true answer might yet still be completely unknown to us, but this fable of subterfuge is surely the greatest involving a wooden steed.

After the Greeks spent a decade sieging the impregnable walls of Troy, Odysseus devised a sneaky plan involving a giant hollow horse. After constructing the wooden stallion, the Greeks placed it outside the city walls and sailed away, pretending to abandon the war. They left behind one man who claimed to be a deserter—a double agent who persuaded the Trojans that the horse was an offering to Athena. That night, after the Trojans wheeled the equine effigy into the city, around forty Greek warriors, including Odysseus, spilled out from the hollow steed, opened the gates to the returning Greek army, and defeated Troy.

The primary source for this tale is the *Aeneid* (ca. 20 BCE) of Virgil, but HOMER also mentions the story in the *Odyssey*. Some scholars read the story as metaphor, but most historians credit the account as true, at least in some respect. (That there was even a Troy, much less a Trojan War, is still debated. No one has obtained absolute, conclusive evidence here.)

Today, *Trojan Horse* refers generally to an outsider who infiltrates a group and introduces subversion from within. Technologists also use the term to refer to deceptively benign computer code that feigns legitimate use but is written to maliciously damage or steal information.

SEE ALSO: CRISIS ACTORS; FALSE FLAG OPERATION; HISTORIES; HOMER; MANCHURIAN CANDIDATE; MECHANICAL TURK; REICHSTAG FIRE

TROMPE L'OEIL

If you've ever approached an open window only to discover it was actually a painting of a window, or been tricked by a T-shirt that looks like a naked torso, you've fallen for *trompe l'oeil*. From the French for "deceive the eye," trompe l'oeil is a deliberate visual illusion in which two dimensions seem to be three. Painters use the technique to create verisimilitude. And to mess with you.

Historically, trompe l'oeil has flourished during periods of artistic realism, such as seventeenth-century Netherlands and eighteenth-century France. In America, feats of optical mischief became popular after the Revolutionary War.

One famous *deception*, as the genre of artistic subterfuge was dubbed in the States, reportedly even duped George Washington, who tipped his hat to a realistic life-size portrait of a pair of children standing on a staircase.[161]

Because it emulates the physical, trompe l'oeil exerts greater impact when unleashed on the real world. Outside a museum's confines, contemporary street art derives a sardonic edge from the ambiguity between reality and artifice. In one clandestine outdoor rendering, the graffitist Banksy painted a trompe l'oeil hole on the Palestinian side of a West Bank security wall, creating the impression of a glittering paradise on the other side.

The Banksy work is reminiscent of another great street artist, Wile E. Coyote, whose many implementations of trompe l'oeil, though masterfully rendered, never yielded their desired effect of capturing the Road Runner.

SEE ALSO: CHINESE ART REPRODUCTION; THE DRESS; THE FOURTH WALL; THE TREACHERY OF IMAGES; TUPAC HOLOGRAM

TRUMAN SYNDROME

Before he began to have paranoid fantasies, David had a good job as a production manager on a competition reality television show. "I thought I was being filmed," he told his psychiatrist, Dr. Joel Gold. "I was convinced I was a contestant, and later the TV show would reveal me." David thought he *was in* the reality show that he *was working on*.[162]

Delusional states like this are increasingly common, with mental health facilities around the world reporting patients who believe they are being secretly filmed, like a nonstop *Candid Camera*. They suffer

from what Dr. Gold has dubbed *Truman Syndrome*.

Yes, that Truman—the Jim Carrey simpleton who inhabits the idyllic suburb of Seahaven, which is actually a bubbled soundstage outside Los Angeles, which is actually the set for a hugely popular reality television show called *The Truman Show*, which, in a final meta-twist, is actually a movie you watch called *The Truman Show*. Everyone who watches knows it's a scripted universe, except Truman, who eventually tries to escape the illusion. And like the hero in the final act, those afflicted with the syndrome feel compelled to expose their reality as scripted. They strain to break the confines of unreality television.

The newness of the disorder introduces a challenging question: Does modern culture make us more prone to certain disorders? Or worse, can the virtual simulations of today's society *create* new disorders? Some psychologists mock the notion that the zeitgeist can generate a new mental illness. The human brain has changed very little in 500 years, so why should it? But we also have evidence that culture must play some role in mental health. It has been shown, for example, that psychiatric disorders involving delusions are more common in cities, so clearly our environment plays a part. Might the widespread awareness of NSA espionage affect our mental health? Or could a culture that proclaims *celebrities are just like us* be making us crazy?

"We've got the perfect storm of reality TV and the Internet," Dr. Gold told WebMD. "These are powerful influences in the culture we live in. And for some people who are predisposed, it might be overwhelming and trigger a [psychotic] episode. The pressure of living in a large, connected community can bring out the unstable side of more vulnerable people."

It might be tempting to deem Truman Syndrome a fashionable new brand of narcissism brought to you

---

161 For maximum trickery, the artist, Charles Willson Peale, framed the painting, *Staircase Group*, with an actual door. The artwork, painted in 1795, can be seen today in the Philadelphia Museum of Art.

162 "David" is a pseudonym. The account is from the book *Suspicious Minds: How Culture Shapes Madness* (2014), by Ian and Joel Gold.

by the Kardashians, but one important characteristic defies that diagnosis: People who suffer from the disorder *do not enjoy their simulated realities*. Trumans strive to be released from the immense anxiety of 24-hour surveillance. Unlike Kim or Paris (or Kanye or Trump), they want their shows to be cancelled.

Trumans are not the egomaniacs who populate reality television. They merely fear that a hyper-mediated society has trapped them in a simulated universe. Trumans are just like most of us.

SEE ALSO: FILTER BUBBLE; FREGOLI DELUSION; GASLIGHTING; SIMULISM; TOMMY WESTPHALL UNIVERSE

TRUTH CLAIM

Let's say we decide to go on a trip. After much debate about the best destination, we settle upon Italy, because you love the food. (*Fine. Whatever.*) While in Pisa, near the base of its most famous landmark, we stage a goofy photo that uses forced perspective to make it look like you're holding up the Leaning Tower. Is this photo telling the truth?

After we get home from our trip, while transferring our vacay shots to a laptop, you notice something peculiar in the foreground of our Pisa pic. You load the image into Photoshop, zoom into the suspicious area, and—*eeeek!* There's a rat! How did the critter go unnoticed back in Pisa? When you zoom in closer, the image is indisputable: A large mangy rodent, just sitting there at the edge of the frame, chomping on what appears to be a slice of margherita pizza with extra basil, like an expat from *Ratatouille*. Is this photo telling the truth?

While inspecting the image, you also notice an odd gray blotch on your face. You use the clone tool in Photoshop to remove the digital blemish. Is this photo telling the truth?

You then upload the photo to Instagram, applying the "Walden" filter to give it the serene patina of a crisp New England morning. Is this photo telling the truth?

Then you write a caption: "Spot the rat!" When you geo-tag the photo, you select "Leaning Tower of Niles," an actual place in an actual Illinois town, which has constructed a half-size facsimile of the Tuscan column. Is this photo telling the truth?

The next day, your photo of the "Pisa Pizza Rat" goes viral, spawning thousands of memes and GIFs. Are these photos telling the truth?

At what point did this photo start to lie?

This is the quandary of photography—it is always making a *truth claim*, an assertion that a photo can depict reality, literally and faithfully. But that claim is simultaneously honest and mendacious. As anyone who has taken a selfie knows, all photos tell lies and speak truths.

Since its invention, photography has embraced manipulation. In the early days of the medium, a heavy dose of chemical sophistry was required to make a photograph appear realistic. Today's digital image-editing software is only the latest innovation in a constant march toward image malleability. This imbalance between realism and perfidy puts photography in the precarious position—ceaselessly claiming accuracy to an audience that scrupulously interrogates it for deceit. The public's zeal for spotting image manipulation is constant ("This looks 'shopped"), yet photos are still held up as the paragon of proof ("Pics or it didn't happen").

Rather than lose influence through its vulnerability for falsification, as one might expect, photographs almost seem to accumulate power by being susceptible to misinformation. Some of the most famous photos of all time have endured controversies over their truth claims. *Raising the Flag on Iwo Jima*, the steelworkers lunching atop Rockefeller Center, *Migrant Mother* by Dorothea Lange, Marilyn Monroe's white dress wafting over a street vent, the MOON LANDING, Nessie in the Loch, the Abu Ghraib prison photos, the Beatles crossing Abbey Road, *Falling Man*, the Zapruder frames—all have been accused of visual tampering of some sort. But even under the most intense scrutiny, these photos only accrue more authenticity. By proclaiming the ability to objectively show the truth while confessing the potential for falsification, photographs have been energized as weapons for both authentication and propaganda. "Photography allows us to uncritically think," as documentarian Errol Morris once wrote. "We *imagine* that photographs provide a magic path to the truth."[163]

Pictures only accumulate significance by interacting with the world. Only people can imbue a photo with meaning, supply its truth claim. But that meaning is often contested, as anyone who has been enraged by a police shooting video can attest. Even the most precise cameras create images open to debate. People still see what they want to see. Cameras capture only partial truths, from a single perspective. "The camera doesn't lie," except when it does, which is always or never, depending on your perspective.

SEE ALSO: FINSTAGRAM; THE MARCH OF TIME; PHOTOSHOPPING; PLANDID; RASHOMON EFFECT; STREISAND EFFECT

TRUTHINESS

Truthiness made its debut in the premiere episode of *The Colbert Report* in October 2005. In the segment The Wørd, Colbert outlined a society torn in two halves: "We are divided between those who think with their head and those who know with their heart." Truthiness, as later defined by the American Dialect Society, is "what one wishes to be true regard-

less of the facts." It is the product of a society where individual perception is universal reality, where facts can be customized, and where "your gut" matters more than the truth.

"It used to be, everyone was entitled to their own opinion, but not their own facts," Colbert later told *The A.V. Club*. "But that's not the case anymore. Facts matter not at all."[164]

The first installment of "The Wørd" was originally slated to be *truth*, but Colbert changed it moments before the taping. In a review of the first show, the *New York Times* cited *trustiness*, misspelled, as Colbert's debut word. The paper issued a correction a week later. Colbert used this as more fodder, scoffing that trustiness is "not even a word."

Media wonks cottoned to the term, invoking *truthiness* in columns about everything from millennials to the Iraq War. Its use became so profuse that the *-iness* suffix, which implied a half-hearted stance toward a subject, began to spread to other fakey neologisms, such as *fame-iness* and *youthiness*.

"I'm no fan of dictionaries or reference books. They're elitist," Colbert also declared in the segment. "Constantly telling us what is or isn't true. Or what did or didn't happen." However, several dictionaries (and at least one encyclopedia) have found space for *truthiness* in its elitist pages.

SEE ALSO: EVERY ENTRY IN THIS BOOK

---

163 The quote is from Morris's magnificent *Believing Is Seeing* (2011), in which he investigates the veracity of the iconic *Valley of the Shadow Of Death*—a 1855 photograph taken by Roger Fenton during the Crimean War. "The first iconic photograph of war," as he calls it, was almost certainly a fake.

164 The remark was likely inspired by Senator Daniel Patrick Moynihan, who famously said, "You are entitled to your own opinions, but you are not entitled to your own facts."

TULIPOMANIA

Tulips. Of all the things that could trigger mass hysteria, a bulbed flower imported from the Ottoman Empire made people lose their minds. Or so goes this ubiquitous economic parable.

Though recognized today as an icon of Dutch national identity, up there with clogs and windmills and gouda, tulips weren't introduced to Europe until the late sixteenth century. The Netherlands quickly became enraptured by its motley petals, elevating the tulip to a status symbol for the middle class. Market speculators—keen to exploit conspicuous consumption—quickly bid up the price of bulbs to exorbitant heights. At peak tulip, in February 1637, a single bulb could cost 6,700 guilders, equivalent to over $90,000 today. This period of irrational exuberance became known as *tulpenwoede,* or "tulip madness."

> The rage among the Dutch to possess them was so great that the ordinary industry of the country was neglected, and the population, even to its lowest dregs, embarked in the tulip trade.

That passage is from *Extraordinary Popular Delusions and the Madness of Crowds* (1841), Charles Mackay's classic study of group psychology, which popularized the widespread belief that a hysterical flower frenzy triggered an economic crisis that would rock Holland. It took over a century and a half, but the tale of investor lunacy was eventually exposed as hyperbole.

It's true, tulip prices did quickly rise and fall over the span of a few years, but Mackay exaggerated the overall effect of the tulipomania. Bulbs jumped to 10 times the annual salary of an average worker, but that doesn't mean a middling Dutch East India dockhand had thrown his life savings into the flower futures market. Modern economists, who have studied the historical records more closely, have shown that the tulip trade was conducted almost exclusively by wealthy merchants, not the hoi polloi. The hysterical masses were not so massive; tulipomania had a negligible impact on Holland's prosperity, with adverse effects limited to a small number of people.[165]

SEE ALSO: BEANIE BABY BUBBLE; MONEY; PONZI SCHEME

TUPAC HOLOGRAM

"What the fuck is up, Coachella?" roared Tupac Shakur, arising from beneath the stage, chill as Jesus after a few days in Hades. The question was rhetorical, not that Tupac could have heard the crowd's answer. He was a ghost.

Coachella didn't even exist in 1996, when the LA rapper was brutally murdered in a drive-by shooting. But here he was, shirtless and ripped, on stage at an ecstasy-fueled music festival in 2012, chest-pumping his final hit, a posthumous single called "Hail Mary," brimming with biblical references of violence and regret. Like an invincible CGI superhero, Tupac seemed a demigod, reincarnated to rap. Not even a bullet supposedly from Suge Knight could take out this spooky mirage.

Technically, the "Tupac hologram" wasn't even a hologram—neither the fantastical Princess Leia kind, nor the legit laser kind. The Coachella apparition was actually a modern rejiggering of a Victorian visual trick called "Pepper's ghost," first used in an 1862

---

165   The creation of a new class of investment, known as an *option on futures*, helped curtail the economic damage. This new investment vehicle converted prior future contracts from the *obligation to buy* the commodity to the *opportunity to buy it*, thereby minimizing risk. It was the price for a tulip *option*—not the actual price—that actually went bonkers.

dramatization of Charles Dickens's *The Haunted Man and the Ghost's Bargain*. Using a projector and angled glass to reflect a ghostly 2D 2Pac onto a Mylar screen, the close-enough simulacrum tricked the stoned audience into believing the rapper messiah had been resurrected.

Even if the tech was chintzy, the lo-res solution had high-fi implications. We could now reincarnate celebrities! Technology's endgame was always immortality, and the Tupac hologram seemed another small step toward eternity. It made you wonder, if 3D rendering continues to progress toward the singularity, who wouldn't watch a reunited Beatles at Madison Square Garden? Could Hendrix play the Super Bowl? Might Elvis take residence on the Vegas Strip *literally forever*?

Unsettling but intriguing, the hypothesis seemed plausible because of the dual setting: Coachella, that diorama of misspent celebrity youth, and You-Tube, that crypt of eternal viewing, where the Tupac hologram video became a viral sensation. Like the summer of love on infinite loop, the clip proposed something both compelling and disturbing—the perennial celebrity.

Alas, nothing can last forever. Just five months after Coachella, the company that created the hologram technology filed for bankruptcy. Digital Domain Media Group, which also did special effects for dozens of films including *Transformers* and *Titanic*, was gone in an instant. The ersatz Tupac was shuffled

back to the depths of nostalgia, but the company left behind one memorable trinket: an Oscar it won for reverse-aging Brad Pitt in *The Curious Case of Benjamin Button*.

As Biggie once said, "It was all a dream."

SEE ALSO: THE ARCHIES; HUMAN CLONING; KARAOKE; MIKU, HATSUNE; PHOTOSHOPPING; TROMPE L'OEIL; WARHOL, ANDY

TURING TEST

"I propose to consider the question," began the English computer scientist Alan Turing in a 1950 paper on artificial intelligence, "*Can machines think?*" Turing was being coy; he knew the question teemed with inherent problems. "Thinking" is a wildly subjective term, open to many definitions. Does solving complex math problems constitute thinking? How about translating Sanskrit? Or winning at *Gilmore Girls* trivia night? Giving a TED Talk?

Turing thought he could break through the definitional problem of cognition with a simple test. He devised a thought experiment that begins with an interrogator standing before a wall with two slots. Behind one of the slots is a human; behind the other, a computer. The interrogator passes a question into each slot. Answers are returned from the other side. After repeating this many times, an evaluator reviews the results to determine which slot returned the most human results. If the evaluator fails to distinguish man from machine, Skynet is nigh.

By preferencing results (*what it says*) over process (*how it works*), the test seems like a clever way to avoid the messy question of what constitutes cognition. (It's like the ol' behaviorist trick for identifying a duck—*if it swims like a duck, and it quacks like a duck. . . .*) But this method leads to a predicament. The test seems to imply that *acting* smart is the same thing as *being* smart. If you are a person who watches cable news, you recognize the problem with this law of logic immediately.[166]

The philosopher John Searle eventually refuted the Turing test with his own hypothetical experiment. In the *Chinese Room test*, as it was called, the setup is similar, except the interrogator slips messages in Mandarin. In this task, a computer might perform quite well, but a human could easily fail. Who's the smarty-pants now?

As Searle seems to prove, *acting* sufficiently human is not the same as *being* human. This is a major concern of the Turing test, but there is a much bigger problem. If every artificial intelligence scientist started using the Turing test as their benchmark, they would be creating robot monsters that are trained to deceive. Consider interrogator questions like *What color is your hair?* or *Where were your parents born?* Answering these questions does not produce a "right" answer but instead involves fooling the evaluator. The computer is incentivized toward bluster and diversion. If AI scientists were to use the Turing test as their goal, they would effectively be teaching computers to lie. Which seems kinda terrifying! "Any AI smart enough to pass a Turing test," one science fiction novelist has written, "is smart enough to know to fail it."[167]

While his test had its faults, Turing was a critical figure in the field of computer science. He really did help the Allies win World War II by cracking encrypted Nazi messages, as Benedict Cumberbatch depicts in *The Imitation Game* (2014). But his most peculiar legacy might be CAPTCHA—those tests where you decipher inscrutable characters on websites to determine your human-ness. Intended to deter automated bot abuse, the elusive game is named in honor of the Turing test. (The mealy acronym is picked from the phrase *Completely Automated Public Turing test to tell Computers and Humans Apart*. Engineers have an odd sense of humor.) Technically the robot-detection system is more of a Reverse Turing test. As you click around the web, a computer evaluates whether *you* are human.[168] Or as that circumspect bot HAL 9000 once wisely asked, "Just what do you think you're doing, Dave?"

SEE ALSO: CYBORG; ELIZA EFFECT; MECHANICAL TURK; POLYGRAPH; RORSCHACH TEST; UNCANNY VALLEY; VOIGHT-KAMPFF MACHINE; X.A.I.

---

166 This is a peculiar thing to say about a computer scientist, but Turing's sexuality seems to have played a role in devising this test. In its original incarnation, the experiment was called the Imitation Game, and instead of man versus computer, a man and a woman were behind the wall. Succeeding in this game meant that the evaluator was unable to determine your gender. After a life of PASSING as straight, Turing tragically committed suicide in 1954 after being prosecuted for homosexuality and enduring chemical castration treatment.

167 The quote is from Ian McDonald's dazzling AI-heavy novel *River of Gods* (2004). Jonathan Nolan, the creator of HBO's *Westworld*, said something remarkably similar on Reddit: "I'm not scared of a computer passing the Turing test. . . . I'm terrified of one that intentionally fails it."

168 More terrifyingly, the data from Google's image-based CAPTCHA system, known as reCAPTCHA, is used to train artificial intelligence systems.

TURTLES ALL THE WAY DOWN

At that moment of pure frustration, when your brain exhausts all logical options, when the paradox traps you in a recursive loop and the mental puzzle gapes toward infinity, you stand at the abyss, exhaling your last gasp: "It's turtles all the way down."

This sardonic phrase derives from philosophy, a field not especially known for jocular quips, but when trapped in infinite regression enigmas, even philosophers need jokes. Through the ages, the aphorism has been endlessly repurposed in debates as vast as the big bang theory, evolution, the chicken or the egg problem, flat earth theory, and monotheism.

Variously attributed to Bertrand Russell, William James, Aleister Crowley, Native American mythology, and Indian philosophy, the phrase surged in awareness after the publication of Stephen Hawking's best-seller *A Brief History of Time* (1988), in which he recounts the story of an elderly lady approaching a scientist after a cosmology lecture:

> At the end of the lecture, a little old lady at the back of the room got up and said: "What you have told us is rubbish. The world is really a flat plate supported on the back of a giant tortoise." The scientist gave a superior smile before replying, "What is the tortoise standing on?" "You're very clever, young man, very clever," said the old lady. "But it's turtles all the way down!"

Vicious infinite regression anecdotes are hilarious.

SEE ALSO: FLAT EARTH THEORY; NOT EVEN WRONG; SHIP OF THESEUS; ZENO'S PARADOX

TWERKING FAIL

"How can we know the dancer from the dance?"
—W. B. Yeats

"Twerking FAIL" was a thirty-seven-second video uploaded to YouTube in September 2013. In the opening frames, a young woman is seen initiating the eponymous selfie video, alone in her minimalist apartment. She cranks the volume on her stereo and begins the booty-dominant dance known as *twerking*. After mounting herself into a handstand, she balances against the door, still gyrating, just as another woman (likely a roommate) enters the apartment, knocking over the twerking dervish onto a candlelit table, setting her lower body ablaze with fire, screaming frantically, like Miley Cyrus plunged into lava. LOL.

After the video accrued 10 million views, late-night talk show host Jimmy Kimmel confessed to staging the entire thing.

It was funny. But the lasting effect of this hoax video has been a nagging sensation that every piece of content on the internet might not be real. Now, anytime a vaguely suspicious video appears on You-Tube, the masses scream *fake!*, convinced that Jimmy Kimmel is the demiurge behind all viral mischief.

SEE ALSO: THE BLAIR WITCH PROJECT; CLICKBAIT; CRISIS ACTORS; ZARDULU

UMWELT

Umwelt is one of those helpful German words that we probably should use more often, but really, who wants to be the person who casually inserts Teutonic vocabulary into conversations?

Though it lacks a direct English correlative, *umwelt* often gets translated at the intersection of *perceptual worldview* and *environmental umbrella*. Coined by biologist Jakob von Uexküll in 1909, the term denotes the observation that different animals in a single ecosystem experience utterly distinct realities within that ecosystem. Neuroscientist David M. Eagleman used specific examples from nature to characterize the term:

> In the blind and deaf world of the tick, the important signals are temperature and the odor of butyric acid. For the black ghost knife-fish, it's electrical fields. For the echolocating bat, it's air-compression waves. The small sub-set of the world that an animal is able to detect is its *umwelt*. The bigger reality, whatever that might mean, is called the *umgebung*.[169]

Umwelt evinces the disquieting realization that we perceive only a small fraction of our ecological niche. Cognitive scientists have adopted the term to describe how our knowledge is completely dependent on our senses and surroundings—our sensorium.

Umwelt is the tautological realization that we know only what we know. Anaïs Nin had a good way of saying it: "We don't see things as they are; we see them as we are." (It sounds cooler if you say it like Werner Herzog.)

SEE ALSO: THE DRESS; MIMICRY; RORSCHACH TEST; SIMULISM

---

169 Eagleman was answering the 2011 "Annual Question" from Edge.org: "What scientific concept would improve everybody's scientific toolkit?"

UNCANNY VALLEY

By the time DreamWorks had begun animating the adorable green ogre in *Shrek* (2001), computer graphics technology had come a long way. An enterprising CGI designer could now render characters with incredible realism, so the studio decided to give it a try—vivid verisimilitude would be implemented in the movie's female lead, Princess Fiona. The studio expected moviegoers to appreciate the graphic fidelity and naturalness, but when the film was tested on audiences, children started to cry at scenes with the princess. The poor kids had just fallen into the uncanny valley.

DOLL, and the robots in Spielberg's *A.I.* They are all too human, yet not human enough.

Due to failed experiments like the *Shrek* princess, the film industry became existentially fearful of the chasm between almost-real and super-real. As supporting evidence, movie producers would cite the clearest case of an uncanny valley disaster: the CGI-intense *Final Fantasy*. Released the same year as *Shrek*, the photorealistic film was praised as a technical masterpiece by many critics, including Roger Ebert, but it was box office disaster. *Final Fantasy* bombed so badly that it destroyed the studio that created it.

Burnt by these attempts at exacting realism, filmmakers at first hid on the safe side of the valley, frol-

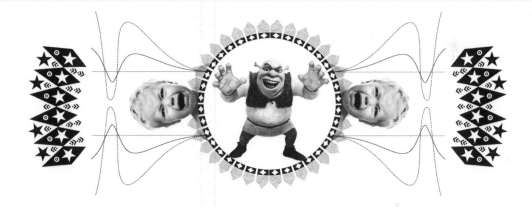

The uncanny valley is the unsettling aversion one feels toward human replicas that appear nearly (but not quite) human. The aesthetic theory was proposed by robotics professor Masahiro Mori, who noticed a disturbing creepiness that envelops robots as they accrue humanistic features like supple skin tissue and nimble facial expressions. On the safe side of the uncanny spectrum, a safari of stylized characters—Mario, Smurfette, and all the Pixar creatures—frolic with other lovable fauna only superficially similar to humans. But as you descend into the valley, toward mimesis, the canyon fills with creepy hyperrealistic critters like CGI Tom Hanks in *Polar Express*, REAL-

icking in a cartoony land of Ratatouilles and Kung Fu Pandas. This fiscal myopia initially blinded studios to the rich verisimilitude sprouting on the other side of the chasm, especially those new hyperrealistic golems rendered by video games. But soon enough, like exploratory ships crossing the Atlantic, a new ecology was spotted on the horizon—the CGI superhero. This new creature seemed a normal humanoid but its superpower was eternal life in the form of franchises, sequels, and cinematic universes. The ecstasy of the uncanny valley changed instantly, from *creating new* virtual characters to *rejuvenating old* ones.

And just like that, we crossed the yawning void

of uncanny valley by granting eternal youth. Soon after a de-aged Carrie Fisher appeared in *Rogue One* (2016), a wide cast of actors—Johnny Depp, Sean Young, Robert Downey Jr., Kurt Russell—became computer-youthified versions of themselves in movie franchises. Like Ponce de León discovering the Fountain of Youth, CGI reincarnation became the tool of choice for Hollywood, a magical fantasyland already obsessed with innocence and nostalgia. Movies are now set on a path toward sequel-filled universes populated with long-gone actors. It seems inevitable: Just as some jackass will one day try to clone Kanye, Marlon Brando will be virtually reincarnated for *On the Waterfront II: Jersey Shore*.

As an aesthetic theory, the uncanny has its origins in Freud, who pondered the eeriness of something foreign yet familiar.[170] Since the 1970s, when Mori coined the term, the uncanny valley has been applied to the chasm of dissimilarity between robots and humans. But as computer simulation technology spreads, that once vast canyon has narrowed. Freud's eeriness no longer describes the unfamiliarity of men and machines, but the closing gap between past and present, life and death.

SEE ALSO: CYBORG; MIKU, HATSUNE; REALDOLL; TOYETIC; TROMPE L'OEIL; TUPAC HOLOGRAM

literary characters seem intent to cozen you, too.

Unreliable narrators are fictional characters who tell stories (often in first person, through flashback or some other framing device) whose credibility has reason for serious doubt. These prevaricating rascals—like Holden Caulfield in *Catcher in the Rye* or Humbert Humbert in *Lolita*—give distorted views of narrative events. Though the term was not coined until the 1960s by literary critic Wayne C. Booth, unreliable narrators can be found as far back as Aristophanes. But they didn't become widespread characters until nineteenth-century novels (*The Turn of the Screw, Wuthering Heights, Adventures of Huckleberry Finn*) and 1990s cinema (*Fight Club, Forrest Gump, The Usual Suspects*).

Unreliable narrators appearing in fiction tend to create a vibe of unstable truth. The trope inevitably creates a mirror with reality: Just as no narrator should be blindly trusted with their account, no author should be naively revered as truthteller. Unless, of course, that author has earned your faith by exposing misinformation, in which case, you should trust them unquestioningly on all matters.

SEE ALSO: ESQUIVALIENCE; THE FOURTH WALL; IF I DID IT; A MILLION LITTLE PIECES; LEROY, JT; RASHOMON EFFECT; RETCONNING

UNRELIABLE NARRATOR

Your parents lied to you about SANTA CLAUS, your friends fibbed about liking your new haircut, your teachers exaggerated the meritocracy, your government conspired about WMDs—and now your favorite

UTOPIA

Utopias do not exist. For starters, the word itself literally means "no place," and in practice, no group of humans has ever, *so far*, reached a sustained accord on which conditions would birth a communal earthly

---

170 Sigmund Freud, "Das Unheimliche" (1919). At the time, it was a paradoxical discovery, that the closer we get toward familiarity and realism, the more frightening a creature becomes.

171 Especially if your utopia includes "the beach."

paradise. In all likelihood, your utopian nirvana would be my apocalyptic hellscape.[171]

Today's utopias are the by-product of idealized social philosophies stretching toward legitimacy—abstract theories manifested as concrete communes. But the first utopia was probably a literary gag. In 1516, an English social philosopher, Sir Thomas More, imagineered an idyllic island off the coast of South America. The agrarian paradise, described in his book *Utopia,* resembled a medieval monastery plopped onto a futuristic communist farm.[172] The island of Utopia was bucolic but boring. The government dictated all distribution of goods, and private property was forbidden. Professions were lifelong: If you trained as a blacksmith, you died a blacksmith. And when you finally crawled into the grave, mourning from friends and family was prohibited, perhaps because your humdrum life was too weary for grief. "No wine-taverns, no alehouses, no brothels, no opportunities for seduction" were among the prohibitions. Women were subordinate, the eldest male ran the household, and slavery persisted, though mostly as a means to punish adulterers. But the island was pretty!

After More invented Utopia,[173] idealized civilizations spilled like tacks across the fictional map. We now have libertarian utopias, progressive utopias, feminist utopias, ecological utopias, technological utopias, communal utopias, religious utopias, and a vast array of hobbyhorse utopias for every stripe of single-issue voter. Now considered an offshoot of science fiction, the Utopian Literature Complex has become the surest method for projecting a contemporary pathology, or as George Orwell said,

Nearly all creators of utopia have resembled the man who has toothache, and therefore thinks happiness consists in not having toothache.... Whoever tries to imagine perfection simply reveals his own emptiness.[174]

Modern scholars are still unsure how to interpret the original *Utopia,* penned by More. Is it canny political satire or insidious social engineering? It's difficult to say for certain, because the book is rife with contradictions. The author was a devout Catholic, yet Utopia had euthanasia and priests could marry. And it was first published in Latin, hardly the language of rowdy farce at the time. But in his political life, More seemed determined to buck the system, even refusing to acknowledge the king, Henry VIII, as the sovereign ruler of the Church of England. Annoyed by his subversion of authority, Henry VIII had More beheaded.

Hell, Sir Thomas More learned, is other people's utopias.

SEE ALSO: ALT-HISTORY; ESPERANTO; NOBLE LIE; POTEMKIN VILLAGE

---

172 More's book was set in the present, not the future. Science fiction didn't exist yet; nor, for that matter, did communism. But the two became historically intertwined, when communists would later praise *Utopia.*

173 Plato's *Republic* was literature's first utopia, but More gets the coinage credit.

174 "Why Socialists Don't Believe in Fun" (1943).

V

Columbia English professor Charles Van Doren briefly became a celebrity in 1957, when he won a streak of matches against opposing contestants on the NBC trivia game show *Twenty One*. As audiences grew, with up to 50 million tuning in per night, he accumulated $128,000 in winnings, answering obscure questions about the Incas and *On the Waterfront*. After landing on the cover of *Time* magazine, photos of him swanning about town with movie starlets splashed across gossip rags.

After four months of handily defeating opponents, Van Doren finally lost a match of *Twenty One*. Soon after his reign as champ snapped, a controversy began to brew over rumors that Van Doren had secretly received answers in advance. After much denial, including grand jury testimony, Van Doren finally admitted his acquiescence to the rigged game in 1959 before Congress. Producers, it was later revealed, had essentially choreographed every dramatic turn of the show, coaxing nearly a hundred contestants to participate in the scripted ruse. (Even Van Doren's trysts with film vixens were orchestrated for the press.) Seventeen contestants, including Van Doren, were eventually indicted. He later pled guilty to second-degree perjury, a misdemeanor, for lying to the grand jury.

In 1994, Ralph Fiennes portrayed Van Doren in a Robert Redford–directed movie, *Quiz Show*, which dramatized the scandal as a moral tale of unsuspected fame. Today, compared to the subterfuge factory of reality television, Van Doren's fib seems a trifle, but for his naive knavery alone, he deserves an entry within this tome. His name would be too obscure for even the hardest *Jeopardy!* question today, but his postscandal actions make him something of a hero around these parts. After the uproar, Van Doren resigned from Columbia and took a job at *Encyclopedia Britannica*, eventually becoming its editor-in-chief. In 1962, he published "The Idea of an Encyclopedia," a prescient essay that intimated the demise of the treasured compendium. "The tone of the American encyclopedias is often fiercely inhuman," he wrote. Credibility, he cautioned, would not hasten the encyclopedia's extinction, but a lack of vitality would.

SEE ALSO: MECHANICAL TURK; ROCKEFELLER, CLARK

Hermann Göring wanted a Vermeer.

It was the middle of World War II, and the founder of the Gestapo still didn't have any paintings by his favorite painter, Johannes Vermeer. His boss, Adolf Hitler, who was himself a failed artist, had already nabbed two works by the seventeenth-century Dutch master of light. Göring was desperate to catch up with *der führer*.

During their reign, the Nazis relentlessly pillaged art from across Europe and Russia. Göring alone stole, or sometimes bartered for, approximately 1,800 paintings, building his personal collection to a net worth of $200 million. But his favorite painter remained elusive: Vermeers were in short supply, with only around thirty works known to exist.

Finally, in 1942, a collector in the Netherlands, Han van Meegeren, made an announcement: A new Vermeer had been discovered! "What we have here," said a leading art expert at the time, "is the masterpiece of Johannes Vermeer."

Göring was thrilled. To get his Vermeer, *Christ and the Adulteress*, he immediately traded 137 paintings, worth an estimated 1.7 million guilders, or $11 million today, making it the most expensive painting ever purchased up to that point—a record that would stand for forty years.

A few years later, after the Allies had taken back Europe, Göring was standing trial at Nuremberg when he received the worst news: *His Vermeer was a fake!* The Dutch dealer who sold Göring the painting, van Meegeren, confessed in prison that he had forged a total of six Vermeers, which netted him $60 million. The forger was facing treason charges, punishable by death, for collaborating with the Nazis by not revealing the paintings' true owners. But the charge of art fraud yielded only one year in prison, so he confessed to one of the greatest art forgery scams of all time.

Göring—a man so despicable that the most despicable man in modern history called him grotesque—was enraged to discover that he had been duped. "He looked as if for the first time he had discovered there was evil in the world," his biographer later wrote of Göring's art-fraud anguish.

A few weeks after hearing the news, Göring dropped a cyanide pill to avoid sentencing. *Christ and the Adulteress* can still be seen on display—with a title placard that says "Han van Meegeren"—at a museum in Rotterdam.

SEE ALSO: ART FORGERY; CHINESE ART REPRODUCTION; F FOR FAKE; HITLER DIARIES

VIRAL MARKETING

It's marketing, but they don't tell you.

SEE ALSO: THE BLAIR WITCH PROJECT; CANNIBAL HOLOCAUST; PRODUCT PLACEMENT; SUBLIMINAL ADVERTISING

VIRTUE SIGNALING

Everyone knows the type. It's the person who drapes their Instagram selfies with hashtags for ambiguous causes, and who makes absolutely certain their charity tote bag flashes in-frame. It's the person who pours a bucket of ice over their head, on camera, to demonstrate their depth of compassion for a disease they cannot pronounce. It's the person whose Facebook profile photo has been tinted green for years, in support of some far-away crusade no one quite remembers. It's the person who douses every calamity in their "thoughts and prayers," or who is woke—so very, very #woke. We might roll our collective eyes toward this person, but the internet has gone a step further, pushing a term to subvert for their gaudy campaigning: *virtue signaling.*

It's a snide accusation, but also undeniably clever. Roughly, virtue signaling connotes exhibitionistic expression of moral values—conspicuous showboating that solicits approval and tells the audience, "I am a good person." The appendage *signaling* adds a sciencey flavor, suggesting a technical process recognized by sociology, or even more primordially, biology. It evokes a peacock unfurling its plumage, as other birds of a feather flap their approval. Of course the term flourishes on the internet, where every status update smacks of preening a personal brand. In this digital habitat, where clicking on a *Like* or *Retweet* button can pass for political labor, everyone seems to project some image or embody some character. On the internet, we are all signaling virtues, to some degree.

The term, therefore, should be politically neutral. Whether a person flamboyantly demands that professional athletes "honor the flag," or they bloat their News Feed with outrage over some minor comedian's politically incorrect joke, they are signaling to an audience, *Hey, look at my moral commitments.*

Slacktivism—clicking buttons on websites rather than getting up and doing something about it—honors no party affiliation. Nonetheless, virtue signaling has been weaponized by the alt-right, who hurl the accusation of phoniness at any and all expressions of political empathy. But those reactionaries who accuse internet activists of lecturing their virtues are just as willing to shout furious indignation when a professional athlete kneels during the national anthem. The hypocrisy is blinding.

Every ideology advertises itself. (Even nihilists promote something, though *nothingness* is a hard sell.) Who is to say which actions are showy performances, and which are authentic appeals to a greater good? The distinction is most blurred on the internet, where the line between sincere pronouncement and meretricious sermonizing is especially gaunt. What seems like histrionic jackassery to you might be a form of honest activism to someone else.

Like CLICKBAIT and *fake news*, virtue signaling was once a useful term, summarizing a certain type

of inane righteousness and platitudinous braying. But it has since inflated into a lazy putdown for any expression of political conviction. Shrieking "virtue signaler!" at every foe has become the most insufferable type of virtue signaling.

SEE ALSO: CLICKBAIT; IMPOSTER SYNDROME; MIMICRY; PLANDID

VOIGHT-KAMPFF MACHINE

A letter appears in the mail, summoning you to a nearby government agency for a "quick personality analysis." Arriving at the bleak testing facility, you are directed to the dusky interrogation room, with a ceiling fan chopping shadows through hazy air. A dashboard-size contraption sits on the table, connected to a laser phoropter and huffing bellows, hissing white noise readouts like a steampunk POLYGRAPH machine. "We just want to ask you a few questions," says an investigator, in the tone of some hardboiled noir detective. After calibrating the gizmo to your pupils, he begins the interrogation:

- *Describe, in single words, only the good things that come into your mind about your mother.*

- *It's your birthday. Someone gives you a calfskin wallet. How do you react?*

- *You've got a little boy. He shows you his butterfly collection, plus the killing jar. What do you do?*

- *You're watching television. Suddenly you realize there's a wasp crawling on your arm.*

The contraption—a Voight-Kampff machine, which measures your respiration, heart rate, pheromone release, blush response, and eye movement—appears in *Blade Runner* (1982), the Ridley Scott movie adapted from a Philip K. Dick story. Special police investigators, known as *blade runners*, use the machine to quantify empathy and identify replicants. Or more specifically, to detect robots who secretly live among us.

Science fiction is lousy with this trope—the person who might be a CYBORG. And science philosophers have kept pace, inventing thought experiments like the TURING TEST to distinguish humans from bots. Despite its fictional provenance, the Voight-Kampff might be the most successful of all such thought experiments. We now rely on countless Voight-Kampff–like devices to identify humans: the algorithms that scan email for spambots, the drones that identify armed combatants, the software that detects scripted password cracking, the facial recognition systems that scan faces in a crowd for suspects. All of these machines pinpoint humans in the noise. Created as a fanciful thought experiment, Voight-Kampff machines are nearly ubiquitous.

SEE ALSO: CYBORG; IMPOSTOR SYNDROME; MECHANICAL TURK; POLYGRAPH; RORSCHACH TEST; SODIUM PENTOTHAL; TURING TEST; UNCANNY VALLEY

VOMITORIUMS

There are many profound historical questions we might never be able to answer. *Was Jesus cool?*, for instance, and *How did the universe begin?* Other inquiries we can hold out hope for eventually solving, like *Were dinosaurs warm- or cold-blooded?* and *Where is Cleopatra's tomb?* Someday, we might even know the answer to the question posed in *Stand by Me* by a baby-faced Wil Wheaton: *If Pluto is a dog, what the hell is Goofy?*

One of the biggest historical questions likely falls somewhere in the middle, between knowable and unknowable: *Why did the Roman Empire fall?* His-

torians have offered plenty of potential reasons for its demise, including barbarian raids, corruption, overexpansion, and maybe even Christianity. One pet theory involves moral decay; the Romans, especially the nobility, had become gluttons. As *Caligula* speculated, the orgies did them in!

For centuries, this image of the Romans, as licentious hedonists, has been a widespread belief. They ate decadently, they fornicated decadently, they entertained decadently. They were so debaucherous that when they finished gorging on blood pudding and Falernian wine, they would retreat to an antechamber—a *vomitorium*—to purge themselves, clearing room in their bellies for more vino and concubines. This indelicate image of an upchucking aristocracy was a recent addition to the historical profile of moral decay, not appearing until the twentieth century, but it fit the perceived notion of a sybaritic nobility. The myth eventually found its way into popular travel guides and Latin phrase books. The folk story even emigrated to *The Hunger Games* series, which tells of sumptuous Capitol parties in which lavish inhabitants imbibed a drink that acted as an emetic.

Alas, it was all a misinterpretation. There were no purging chambers. Vomitoriums (in Latin, *vomitoria*) were something completely different—the wide, vaulted exit points in coliseums, through which large crowds could rapidly egress after a performance. The word, which did not even exist during Caesar and Cicero, was coined 400 years later, to describe how the architectural feature could "spew" crowds into the street. The mistranslation of *vomitorium* was popularized by Lewis Mumford's huge urban studies tome, *The City in History* (1961), which depicted a room adjacent to the dining chamber, where gluttonous eaters could "throw up the contents of their stomach in order to return to their couches."

Bulimia and vapid decadence did not destroy the Roman Empire. And Goofy, like one of those depraved pagan demigods, was a human/dog hybrid.

SEE ALSO: 13TH FLOOR; ALT-HISTORY; HISTORIES

WAR OF THE WORLDS, THE

As the live orchestra faded out, a CBS radio newsman urgently broke into the broadcast: "Ladies and gentlemen, we interrupt our program of dance music to bring you a special bulletin. . . ." An astronomical observatory at Princeton, reported the anchor, had just witnessed mysterious blue flames emitting from Mars. After delivering the report, the anchor returned listeners to the strings and brass of the orchestra but quickly returned seconds later with more breaking news. Over the next fifty-seven minutes, sober news bulletins morphed into shrieking live reportage, each bringing more terrifying details. Martians were invading New Jersey.

If you had tuned in just a minute earlier, you would have heard Orson Welles introduce the coming apocalypse as a Mercury Theater production of *The War of the Worlds*.[175] Some listeners who missed that introduction thought they were hearing an actual news report. More still were persuaded by fraught phone calls from frantic friends. The exact tally of confused listeners is still debated, but this was 1938, an era when people had damned good reasons to be frightful, and not just because the radio was reporting an alien invasion on the eve of Halloween.

The Mercury broadcast was live because all radio was live. (Through the '30s, recorded audio was verboten because tape was deemed manipulable. Recorded news was the fake news of its day.) *The War of the Worlds* marked the seventeenth episode of the weekly show, which had developed a small but respectable following by adapting highbrow material into radio drama—Dickens, Brontë, and Shakespeare had occupied previous episodes. The source material of this week's episode, H. G. Wells's 1897 novel, was both scientifically dated and dramatically drab, but the radio playwrights took brilliant license in updating the plodding sci-fi tale. By adapting the plot into a series of news bulletins, and parlaying them through the very network that delivered real news, the radio play literally turned the medium into the (fake) message.

---

175   It is worth noting that neither Orson Welles nor the Mercury Theater music conductor, Bernard Herrmann, were particularly famous at this time. *Citizen Kane*, which Welles directed and Herrmann scored, was a few years away.

Other factors contributed to the hyperrealism. Because the Mercury Theater was noncommercial (a "sustaining program," per the argot of the era), the show played continuously for forty minutes before a break. The local color and contemporary setting also enhanced the simulation, especially for nearby listeners who recognized the names of New Jersey towns destroyed by an alien "heat ray." Orson Welles pulled out every trick to intensify its verisimilitude. The voice actor who played the Secretary of the Interior, for instance, performed a dead-ringer impersonation of radio's most recognizable voice—President Franklin Roosevelt.

Some people fell victim to the artifice.

During the broadcast, switchboards at CBS lit up with calls from confused listeners. Rumors spread of panic-stricken citizens fleeing their homes to seek refuge from the Martians. Newspapers, the next day, reinforced the storyline with reports of suicides and heart attacks. No one verified these accounts, but even reputable newspapers, including the *New York Times* and the *Washington Post*, passed along tabloid-y hearsay as fact.

In the years that followed, the legend of a naive populace saturated society. Psychology textbooks, documentaries, and popular literature propagated the lore of the gullible masses. Even today, most people know *The War of the Worlds* story as one of bewildered sheeple fleeing their homes. Six million people heard the broadcast; one million fell for the ruse, according to legend. One in six might be the perfect ratio for this type of quasi-scientific account. It signals to nearly everyone, *those rubes fell for it, but you certainly would not.*

It took several decades to unpack the truth. Here is how a recent researcher—the first to have access to the actual FCC complaints—characterizes that night in 1938:

> These panicked scenes of flight and near flight, which turned *War of the Worlds* into the stuff of American legend, did happen, but they were very, very rare. Even among the people frightened by the program, most stayed close to their radios, listening intently for twenty, twenty-five, or thirty minutes before they figured out it was fake (as many did) or heard an announcement that it was fiction.[176]

---

176 This passage is from A. Brad Schwartz's *Broadcast Hysteria* (2015), now the definitive account of the event. Schwartz was the first researcher to obtain access to letters from listeners that night—a total of 353 complaints to the FCC, plus 115 to the Mercury Theater. Needless to say, the letters reveal a new story, but the book also creates an incisive rendering of *The War of the Worlds* as a bellwether of the incipient fake news industry.

Some people were tricked, but it was hardly pandemonium. The media, and newspapers in particular, exaggerated the hysteria. An attitude prevailed among newspapermen at the time that the young whippersnappers in the "new media" of radio had lower ethical standards. Newspaper editors deemed broadcasting a lesser medium, and the newfangled radio box a tool for spreading untruths, so they were quick to deliver a comeuppance when the upstarts stumbled. When it appeared that Orson Welles was spreading fake news, newspapers seized the moment with a clear message: Radio will lie to you. To the old media guard, Martians were not colonizing earth, but broadcast signals surely were.

The War of the Worlds was fake news, but the reaction it engendered was an even more exaggerated form of misinformation.

SEE ALSO: AUTOBIOGRAPHY OF HOWARD HUGHES; THE BLAIR WITCH PROJECT; F FOR FAKE; THE FOURTH WALL; HUMBUGGERY; THE MARCH OF TIME; ROBINSON CRUSOE

WARHOL, ANDY

By 1967, Andy Warhol's art-making machine was running on all cylinders. Pop art had become a global phenom; celebrities were crowding his misfit studio, The Factory, to request silkscreen portraits; his kinky films, including *Chelsea Girls* and *Blow Job*, filled art houses; and his raucous house band, the Velvet Underground, had just released their debut album. Warhol was one busy dude. So when he was asked to perform a speaking tour of small state colleges in the Rocky Mountains, *yes* was a surprising answer.

His first stop was the University of Utah. A few students picked Warhol up at the Salt Lake City airport, discovering a disheveled man, reticent and caked in makeup. When the wind blew, a cloud of white powder puffed from his coarse silver hair. On campus that evening, where more than a thousand people gathered for the event, Warhol, still wearing dark sunglasses, played excerpts of grainy black-and-white films with sketchy sound quality. During the Q&A, an audience member asked what the film meant. "My films are to look at," he replied. Another attendee asked him to characterize underground film. "Black and white and very cheap," was the terse response.

Warhol ended up making three more such campus appearances, each as cryptic as the first, across the Rockies. Except it wasn't actually Andy Warhol—it was Allen Midgette, a young actor and Factory denizen hired to impersonate the pop art icon.[177] A couple months after the tour, the ruse was uncovered by a college newspaper, creating a scandal that forced Warhol to justify the flimflam. "Because I don't really have that much to say, he was better than I am," wrote Warhol in a statement from New York. "He was what the people expected. They liked him better than they would have me."

Maybe. But those words, inimitably, sounded like the true Andy Warhol. Only the master of reproduction could rationalize, with such innocence, a desire so diabolical: to casually replicate himself, like a simple Campbell's soup can, into a slightly better product.

SEE ALSO: CLIFTON, TONY; CONFIDENCE GAME; FOUNTAIN; HUMAN CLONING; LEROY, JT; TRIBUTE BANDS; TUPAC HOLOGRAM

177 In addition to Warhol flicks, Midgette had already acted in several Italian productions, including bit parts from Bernardo Bertolucci and Pier Paolo Pasolini. Years after the hoax, Midgette became a professional Warhol impersonator and sold imitations of his artwork. When Oliver Stone announced a casting call for *The Doors* (1991), Midgette naturally tried out for the role of Andy Warhol, but the part went to Crispin Glover.

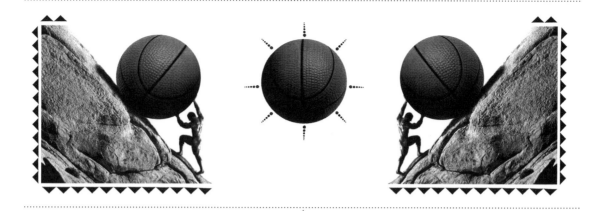

WASHINGTON GENERALS

The career of a professional athlete is mired in upset, loss, and grief. In all sporting events, someone has to lose. Even if you are great, you still fail at some point. No champion exits their career undefeated. No Olympiad wins every gold, there are no infinite streaks of flawless scores, everyone scratches on the eight ball at least once. Nobody is perfect.

But what if perfection in your job meant *always losing*? Every day you showed up at work, played the game, looked up at the scoreboard, and always saw your team behind. But for you, losing is victory; winning might get you fired. Failure is a *fait accompli*, your *modus operandi*, your *raison d'être*, and every other foreign expression for the futility of human will. You play to lose.

This was the life of a Washington General, perhaps the saddest of all careers in professional sports. For more than sixty years, the Generals were the basketball team that played the Harlem Globetrotters. Their job was to act the foil for their competitors' comedy bits and to lose every time. Defeat was part of the game plan. But losing wasn't enough. They had to make it seem like they were trying to win. And

on half the court, they really were. On offense, they were coached to play their best, shooting and scoring fast. But on defense they had to play the role of shills, letting themselves be duped over and over again by Curly Neal and Meadowlark Lemon.[178] It took real athletes to enact the charade, and the Washington Generals were no scrubs—most of the players were once decent college basketball players. Which makes their Sisyphean tragedy even more bleak: They knew what winning felt like.

The Washington Generals, who were named in honor of Dwight D. Eisenhower in 1952, were impeccable at their job, losing more than 14,000 times to the Globetrotters. But as already foreshadowed, all athletes must fail at least once. For the Generals, their failure came in 1971. In an exhibition game in Tennessee, the Globetrotters became preoccupied with entertaining the crowd and lost track of the score, finding themselves down by twelve points with two minutes remaining. They fought back, but in the final seconds the ball ended up in the hands of Generals point guard Red Klotz (who was also the owner and coach of the team). He continued to follow the playbook as instructed: On offense, you shoot to win. In the final seconds he hit a jumper that created one of the most shocking final scoreboards

178   Tangential Globetrotter detail: Meadowlark Lemon's birth name was Meadow Lemon III. He legally added *-lark* in the '50s. Somehow, it seems the perfect touch.

in history: *Generals: 100, Globetrotters: 99.* Spectators hated the outcome. For decades Klotz could be heard muttering, "Beating the Globetrotters is like shooting SANTA CLAUS."

The Washington Generals played their final game in August 2015. Of course, they lost, because that is how they won.

SEE ALSO: CANNED HEAT; CLAQUE; KAYFABE; SMARKS

WHATABOUTISM

When a child is accused of some misdeed, they often mount a defense that begins by blubbering, *B-b-but wha-wha-what-about what Johnny did?* This is *whataboutism*—distracting from your transgression by shifting attention to some completely unrelated indiscretion. Even more than children, tyrants savor the rhetorical technique.

Vladimir Putin is famously adept at mobilizing the whataboutism, which *The Guardian* has called "practically a national ideology" in Russia. When his woeful human rights record is questioned, Putin frequently responds with a whataboutism about America's history with racial discord. During the Cold War, the line "They lynch negroes" even became a Soviet catchphrase, dispatched as a punchline whenever you committed some malfeasance. The ironic idiom became so common that it transformed into a synecdoche for all types of Kremlin propaganda.

Another virtuoso of attention diversion, Donald Trump has dispensed whataboutisms to criticize his own country. During an interview on Fox News, host Bill O'Reilly attempted to draw an unambiguous distinction between Russian and American systems by declaring, "Putin is a killer." Trump responded with a classic red herring: "There are a lot of killers. You got a lot of killers. What, you think our country is so innocent?" The whataboutism implies that because America has its own history of injustice, accusing any other country of oppression is hypocritical.

SEE ALSO: CHEWBACCA DEFENSE; NOT EVEN WRONG; SOPHISTS

WHORFIANISM

This is not the philosophy of the Klingon lieutenant commander of the Starship Enterprise.

Rather, Whorfianism is a form of extreme "linguistic relativism," named after Benjamin Lee Whorf, an early twentieth-century linguist who was inspired by Einstein's theories of relativity. Whorfianism posits that the language you speak dictates how you perceive the world. An extreme Whorfianist would assert that French speakers comprehend the world differently than English speakers do, not because of their culture or geography, but because of the actual grammar and syntax of their language.

Most of Whorf's evidence derived from indigenous communications, especially the Hopi language. After postulating that the language had no grammatical notion of time, Whorf inflated linguistics into mass psychology, declaring the Hopi people have "no general notion or intuition of time as a smooth flowing continuum in which everything in the universe proceeds at equal rate, out of a future, through the present, into a past." Sounds trippy, but it was quickly proven inaccurate: the Hopi language does in fact have many temporal grammar forms and the Hopi people seem to grasp time just fine. Today, exasperated linguists refer to the incident as the "Hopi Time Controversy."

Whorf also popularized the widespread notion that Eskimos have a disproportionate number of words for *snow*. (Whorf said there were "several" Inuit words for snow, but popular media inflated the number to fifty, and then one hundred.) That theory was later debunked by showing how the seemingly unique Inuit words for "snow drift" and "falling snow" were simply different prefixes and suffixes appended to the same root word. Flummoxed linguists now refer to this one as the "Great Eskimo Vocabulary Hoax."

To commemorate the spread of the fallacy, linguists even forged a clever new word, *snowclone*, to designate fill-in-the-blank phrase templates. The namesake snowclone—"If Eskimos have N words for snow, X surely have M words for Y"—is one of the many instantly recognizable clichés implemented by uninspired journalists. Other overused macros include "X is the new Y," "The only good X is a dead X," "X in the streets but Y in the sheets," and, a hackneyed favorite of this encyclopedia, "In Soviet Russia X Ys you."

SEE ALSO: ESPERANTO; NACIREMA; NEWSPEAK; RASHOMON EFFECT

WIPING

In a unique televised event in 1967, both CBS and NBC broadcast the clash between the hard-nosed Green Bay Packers, led by warhorse quarterback Bart Starr, against an upstart AFL foe, the Kansas City Chiefs. The simulcast, seen live by more than 51 million people, was later dubbed Super Bowl I.

By most accounts, the game was close until halftime, but the Pack defense dismantled the Chiefs in the third quarter. Or at least that's how most people remember it, but no one could say for sure, because no video existed of the game. It seems unfathomable now, because one-fourth of the country watched the first Super Bowl, but no one thought to actually record it. As a cost-saving measure, all known broadcast tapes of the games were reused—or *wiped*—by both networks.

This was not unusual. The first seven Super Bowls all have portions missing.[179] Nearly every episode of *Tonight Starring Jack Paar* was taped over. Only a handful of World Series games before 1965 survived, and most NBA Finals games before 1976 were erased. Out of 2,753 episodes of the original *Jeopardy!* (the one hosted by Art Fleming), only twenty-four remain extant. Six years of Walter Cronkite stoically reading the *CBS Evening News* were expunged—only his coverage of the Cuban Missile Crisis and the JFK assassination survived.

In most cases, the master tapes were rendered to the dustbin of history because of *wiping*—a colloquialism for reusing old videotapes. In the early days of broadcast, tapes were often recycled, under the assumption that the broadcasts were of no real value. As digital drives replaced analogue tapes, the word has taken on a new meaning, which is why Hillary Clinton can now be described as "wiping" her email server or bad memories can be "wiped" in fantasy movies like *Eternal Sunshine of the Spotless Mind*.

SEE ALSO: BERENSTAIN BEARS CONSPIRACY; HYPNOSIS; NODDY; TRUTH CLAIM

WOOZLE EFFECT

A woozle is an imaginary animal found in the book *Winnie-the-Pooh* (1926). In the third chapter, "In which Pooh and Piglet Go Hunting and Nearly Catch a Woozle," the titular protagonists track some suspicious paw prints, round and round their scraggly

---

179 For decades, Super Bowl I was thought to be completely lost, but most of it has recently been painstakingly reconstructed from different reels of footage found deep in the NFL Films archive—a place often described like the final warehouse scene of *Raiders of the Lost Ark*.

acreage, before finally realizing they have actually been following their own tracks. "I have been foolish and deluded," concludes Pooh. "And I am a bear of no brain at all." Either the story is an allegory about CONFIRMATION BIAS or Pooh is a stupid bear.

The *woozle effect* occurs when a dubious citation is repeated over and over, like Pooh chasing his own tracks, causing society to perpetuate lies and myths. As Mark Twain once said, "A lie can travel halfway around the world while the truth is putting on its shoes." Except Mark Twain never actually said that. The quote has been attributed to him so many times that the woozle effect has made it seem true.

The comicstrip *xkcd* coined a similar neologism, *citogenesis*, to describe the process by which one publication accidentally disseminates misinformation that gets repeated by another publication, only to be cited by the first publication as fact because the second one repurposed the misinformation, creating a vicious circle of hooey. In journalism circles, the same phenomenon goes by the handle *circular reporting*.

Stephen Colbert offered a similar concept—*wikiality*. "Together," said Colbert, "we can create a reality that we all agree on—the reality we just agreed on." Under the reign of wikiality, reality is whatever Wikipedia says it is, and because "any user can change any entry, and if enough users agree with them, it becomes true." Some people [citation needed] have suggested that looking too closely at Wikipedia could tear open a woozle wormhole, where all known information is exposed as a series of self-referential FACTOIDS, collapsing a galaxy of knowledge into a super-dense black hole of nothingness.

SEE ALSO: BACKFIRE EFFECT; BELLMAN'S FALLACY; BERENSTAIN BEARS CONSPIRACY; CONFIRMATION BIAS; ESQUIVALIENCE; FILTER BUBBLE; MANDELA EFFECT; OVERTON WINDOW

'WORK OF FICTION' DISCLAIMER

Nearly all movies have it—that disclaimer text, blocked and scrolling, that crawls onto the screen after the last credit has rolled.

> This is a work of fiction. Any resemblance to actual events or persons, living or dead, is entirely coincidental.

It doesn't matter if you've just seen Ewoks vanquish stormtroopers or a Kansas farmhouse whoosh into Technicolor Oz, some version of that cautionary caveat creeps onto the final reel: "This is a work of fiction . . ."

Like all cut-and-paste boilerplate, this scrap of legalese has an origin story—a history that can be traced back to someone. In this case, that someone is Rasputin.

Yes, that Rasputin—the Russian mystic/lech/peasant/swindler who cavorted in the Romanov court until he was murdered a few months before the Bolshevik Revolution. The identity of his assassin is no secret: An aristocrat, Prince Felix Yusupov, killed Rasputin. We know this because Yusupov later wrote a book with the humblebraggy subtitle *The Amazing Memoirs of the Man Who Killed Rasputin* (1953).

The story goes like this: On December 30, 1916, Yusupov invited Rasputin to his palace and fed him poisoned wine. That didn't kill Rasputin, so Yusupov gave him cyanide-laced cakes. That didn't kill him, so he shot him. Twice. Not even that eradicated Rasputin, so Yusupov threw him into a frigid river.

Finally, Rasputin drowned. The perfect Hollywood ending! Or at least that's what MGM Studios concluded sixteen years later, when it released *Rasputin and the Empress*, starring John Barrymore as a lightly fictionalized Yusupov. When the real Yusupov (now penniless and living in Paris) heard about the historical biopic, he schemed to sue MGM for defamation. But there was one small problem: He had already written a memoir marketing himself as Rasputin's

WORK OF FICTION

assassin. So Yusupov devised a second plan: have his wife sue the studio for implying that Rasputin raped her, when she had never even met the rogue. MGM reportedly settled out of court for the modern equivalent of about $8 million.

Due to this spurious lawsuit, Hollywood studios, starting in 1933, began appending "all persons fictitious" notices onto their films, even when those films were clearly based upon very real events and people. Even modern movies like *Velvet Goldmine* (1998) and *The Master* (2012) now conclude with a declaration of pure fiction, despite their existence being inconceivable without the very real David Bowie and L. Ron Hubbard, respectively. *Raging Bull* (1980), which unabashedly portrays the life of the rowdy pugilist Jake LaMotta, contains the same admonition, even though the boxer's name appears just before the disclaimer *in the actual movie credits*.[180]

It would be impossible (and fairly undesirable) to watch or create a movie with literally no connection to reality. Yet this single random lawsuit from

1933 demands that all artistic creations be labeled "entirely fictitious" and that any resemblance to reality is deemed "purely coincidental." Because of this, nearly every movie ends with a blatant lie. This puts cinema in an absurd logical position, where the legal disclaimer is sometimes the only part of a movie that's actually *fiction*.

Ultimately, the legal notice undermines the legitimacy of a movie to depict and critique society, which is often the goal of cinema. If a movie has *no basis in reality whatsoever*, as the disclaimer contends, then why even see a movie?

Some filmmakers use the logical paradox as an opportunity for artistic invention, such as with *Fargo* (1996), which inverts the disclaimer text to its opposite, a decree of truth that appears at the beginning of the film.

> This is a true story. The events depicted in this film took place in Minnesota in 1987. At the request of the survivors, the names have been changed. Out of respect for the dead, the rest has been told exactly as it occurred.

Except that's a lie, too. Not only were events not "told exactly as they occurred," but no such events even occurred. *Fargo*, unsurprisingly, ends like most other films, with the same legal boilerplate disclaimer scrolling up after the credits roll: "The persons and events portrayed in this film are fictitious . . ." Except this time, the lie is the truth.

SEE ALSO: THE BLAIR WITCH PROJECT; DEFICTIONALIZED PRODUCT; F FOR FAKE; IF I DID IT; THE TREACHERY OF IMAGES

---

180   A handful of noble flicks forgo the disclaimer, such as *Citizen Kane*, despite blatant parallels to William Randolph Hearst. Some movies that are indisputably based upon real events—including *Apollo 13*, *Chaplin*, *Lawrence of Arabia*, and *Walk the Line*—make a tiny modification to the first few words of the standard disclaimer: "This film was based on a true story, but . . ." And then everything after the "but" screams, "It's all a lie." Of course, that's even more confusing—a story cannot be both based upon a true story and a complete fabrication.

X.A.I.

Artificial intelligence has quietly crept into manifold aspects of daily life, powering everything from antilock brakes to Siri. Neural networks (as these advanced artificial intelligences are known) have become so sophisticated that computers will now make instantaneous decisions we do not even understand. Computer scientists have responded to this disconcerting predicament with a new field of study, known as *explainable artificial intelligence*, or X.A.I.

As a simple example, a neural network could be trained to ingest millions of animal images and asked, "Can you show me all the xoloitzcuintles?" Identifying photos of a hairless Mexican dog might sound trivial, but these same neural networks are being used to control self-driving cars and to diagnose patients. In many of these cases, computers are literally seeing patterns that humans cannot—and the machines won't say *how* they saw the pattern. X.A.I. attempts to make machines accountable, to see through their inscrutable code of secrecy.

SEE ALSO: MECHANICAL TURK; TURING TEST

XENU

Xenu was an intergalactic space ruler and evil dictator who, 75 million years ago, exiled billions of aliens from his overpopulated confederacy of planets to the prison of Earth (*Teegeeack*), where he erupted volcanoes and detonated hydrogen bombs, leaving behind disembodied souls (*thetans*) who were forced to watch a 3D propaganda movie for thirty-six days, implanting "various misleading data" that would infest humans with traumatic memories (*engrams*), which can be shed only through elaborate counseling (*auditing*) to attain godlike powers, including telepathy and telekinesis. That is, according to official Scientology scripture, composed by mid-century science fiction writer L. Ron Hubbard.

Unlocking this sacred, revelatory knowledge costs thousands of dollars, but the reward includes admission into better casting calls in Los Angeles.

SEE ALSO: CHURCH OF SUBGENIUS; STREISAND EFFECT

YELLOW JOURNALISM

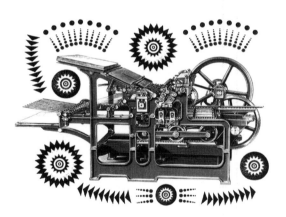

Yellow journalism is a form of sensationalist writing that is typically associated with New York newspapers in the late 1890s but that also resembles today's scurrilous online media environment. The phrase was born of a feud between two muckraker tycoons, Joseph Pulitzer and William Randolph Hearst, who jousted for public attention with the weapons of sensationalistic headlines and scandal-mongering reportage.

Hearst was the more bombastic. When the battleship *Maine* mysteriously exploded in the Spanish-occupied Cuban harbor, Hearst used the event to stoke the political flames of resentment toward colonialist Europe—and to sell more newspapers. His hawkish *New York Journal* immediately dispatched journalists and artists, including famed cowboy portraitist Frederic Remington, to Havana to report on Spaniards suppressing Cuban rebels. When Remington telegraphed to Hearst that no such conflict existed, Hearst supposedly cabled back, "You furnish the pictures and I'll furnish the war." The Spanish-American War commenced two months later.

Somewhat ironically, the two barons of propaganda are today frequently touted as honorable media figures. Hearst Media's assets now include dozens of local newspapers and television stations, plus magazines like *Harper's Bazaar* and *Esquire*. And journalism's highest honor, the Pulitzer Prize, is named after the other cofounder of yellow journalism.

SEE ALSO: BARRON, JOHN; CLICKBAIT;
F FOR FAKE; ORDER OF THE OCCULT HAND;
QUID PRO QUO GOSSIP

Z

ZARDULU

Zardulu is a performance artist who doesn't perform, a magician minus illusions, a prankster who disavows the gag.

By most reasonable accounts (which could easily be erroneous), Zardulu is responsible for several viral videos involving urban animals, the most notorious of which was Pizza Rat, the fifteen-second odyssey of a scraggly rodent heroically hauling a New York slice down a subway stairwell. Initially, no one suspected Pizza Rat of chicanery, which only affirms Zardulu's

uniquely deceptive take on CLICKBAIT: The rat was real, the pizza was real, the video was real. And yet, it was all an illusion.

As wild as it might sound, it appears that Zardulu staged the entire scene by training a rat to carry a pepperoni slice. But instead of simply shooting the video herself, Zardulu waited for a camera-wielding passerby to discover the pizza-carrying rat and unwittingly embody the role of subway platform auteur. The artful gag relies not only on delicate rodent choreography but also on a random person encountering the scene, capturing the video, and sharing it on social media. It's New York City, the media capital of the world, so of course this happened immediately.

Zardulu's masterpieces are found-footage hoaxes in which the public creates, distributes, and consumes the artwork. Because Zardulu has no direct role in the video, Pizza Rat is equivalent to Picasso tricking you into painting a Picasso—and then you telling all your friends that you painted a Picasso.

Sorta. Probably.

Zardulu (@zardulu on Twitter, of course) has never officially taken credit for Pizza Rat, despite claiming authorship for certain subspecies of viral critters, including Selfie Rat and Pita Rat. And she was likely responsible for Gowanus Fish (a three-eyed catfish) and Bagel Pigeon (self-explanatory).

Although anonymous, Zardulu has publicly presented herself in a mauve mask with a white beard and a neo-pagan cloak. (Imagine a cross between Rasputin, Stevie Nicks, the MECHANICAL TURK, and David Bowie in *Labyrinth*.) As luck would have it, she happens to be media savvy. When contacted by reporters, Zardulu has dished a collection of chimerical quotes:

"Any disinformation about me is welcome."
—Zardulu to the website Daily Dot

"Be assured that the breadth and magnitude of my work would astound you."
—Zardulu to the podcast *Reply All*

"I think creation and perpetuation of modern myths is a tragically underappreciated art form. It upsets me when I hear people refer to them as lies."
—Zardulu to the *New York Times*

"Why wake the world from a beautiful dream when the waking world is all so drab?"
—Zardulu to the website Gothamist

In the hamster wheel of the city, one little rat found its pizza treat in the maze. But in this allegory, you play all roles: the treat, the labyrinth, and the rodent. Welcome to the rat race.

SEE ALSO: CARDIFF GIANT; CLICKBAIT; CRYPTIDS; HAPPENING; MECHANICAL TURK; RAY'S PIZZA; TWERKING FAIL

ZENO'S PARADOX

Achilles, the fleet-footed hero of the Trojan War, and his ingenious frenemy, Tortoise, are slowly walking from the Aegean Sea towards Athens. They appear to be arguing. Fade in . . .

ACHILLES
. . . it's totally true! You have to watch to the end of the movie.

TORTOISE
Rambo actually thanks al-Qaeda?

ACHILLES
No, but the movie is dedicated to the Mujahideen in Afghanistan.[181]

TORTOISE
Is this another one of your BERENSTAIN BEARS CONSPIRACIES?

As they continue debating the historical validity of Rambo canon, another man approaches from the south, wearing a toga that says D Θ Σ S TH Φ S SH Φ RT MAKΣ MΣ LΘΘK ΓRAT? *Immediately recognizing him, Achilles happily greets the newcomer, grasping his hand in what appears to be a secret fraternity handshake.*

ACHILLES
Bruuuuuuuuuh!

TORTOISE
[*noticing the handshake*] Are you guys Freemasons or something?

---

181 The two are debating a contested theory regarding the 1988 movie *Rambo III*. If watched today, the film concludes with a dedication to "the gallant people of Afghanistan," but many people (on the internet, doy) believe the final placard was changed after 9/11 because it originally paid homage to "the brave Mujahideen fighters." Regardless of whether the film is guilty of RETCONNING, Rambo did support Mujahideen soldiers, some of whom would have joined the Taliban after its war with the Soviet Union. History is funny.

ZENO

Greetings, my dear brother, Achilles! And you too, Turtle.

TORTOISE

[*softly*] It's *Tortoise*.

ZENO

As we say back in Elea, long time no see!

ACHILLES

Dude, last time I saw you, you were shooting arrows at the Tri Delt house. How goes it?

ZENO

It goes, and yet it doesn't.

TORTOISE

[*sotto voce*] Ugh, this guy and his *paradoxes*.

ACHILLES

We're truckin to Athens to see Socrates. Headed our way, Zeno?

ZENO

My story is the same, dear Achilles. But sadly, we shall never reach our destination.

TORTOISE

Why must you mock the speed of my species?

ZENO

Ho-ho, no, Turtle—

TORTOISE

[*slightly louder*] My name is Tortoise.

ZENO

—your pace is not the problem, ole boy. We will never arrive in Athens because . . .[*with increasing emphasis*] movement . . . is. . . *an illusion!*

TORTOISE

[*with increasing mock emphasis*] Oh. Fucking. *Great!*

ACHILLES

Why is movement an illusion, Zeno?

ZENO

Good question, Achilles. Rather than explain, I would like to show you. How much further down this road is Athens?

TORTOISE

Just a mile ahead, over the next hill.

ZENO

Then I will prove to you that movement is an illusion by walking with you. Let us continue on the path, stopping only when we get halfway to our destination. There, we shall stop and gauge our progress.

TORTOISE

All right, Yoda, lead the way.

The trio walks a half mile, to the top of the hill, and stops.

ACHILLES

I can see the Acropolis!

ZENO

Now how far away are we from Athens?

TORTOISE

Is that a rhetorical question? A half mile.

ZENO

And if we walk halfway toward Athens from here, how far will we walk?

TORTOISE

A quarter mile, you two-footed numskull.

ZENO

Then let us soldier on, halfway!

They walk a quarter mile and stop. Fleet-footed Achilles is growing tired.

ACHILLES

My heels hurt.

ZENO

Is it another eighth-mile to our next stop?

TORTOISE

Aren't you smart? I bet you got laid a ton in college.

ZENO

Come, fellows, let us continue, halfway again.

The trio walks an eighth of a mile and stops.

ACHILLES

This walk is infinite.

ZENO

Now you're catching on!

TORTOISE

Need to catch a ride on my shell, Achilles?

ACHILLES

I won the Trojan War, I can do this![182]

They walk a sixteenth of a mile.

ACHILLES

Hey Zeno, remember that old Beta Theta Pi joke? "Everywhere is walking distance if you have the time."[183]

ZENO

Just halfway farther!

After a thirty-second of a mile, or about 165 feet, they stop again.

ACHILLES

This reminds me of *Groundhog Day*.

TORTOISE

This reminds me of the last half of *Flowers for Algernon*.

ZENO

C'mon, fellas, just halfway more.

The trio walks a sixty-fourth of a mile and stops.

ZENO

Just halfway —

They walk halfway, and then halfway again, and then halfway again. If this play were a movie, a comical fast-forward scene with "Yakety Sax" as the soundtrack would transpire. The trio is now just ten feet from the city. Finally they walk halfway again, to 1/1024 mile.

TORTOISE

Stop, stop, Zeno! We get the idea! We will never reach Athens if we keep walking in half increments toward our destination.

ZENO

Ta-dah! Abracadabra! Shazam! Presto! A paradox![184]

TORTOISE

No. Just no. That is not a paradox. It's just a stupid game. You know we can get to Athens if we just ignore your mathematical claptrap.

---

182 Achilles actually died during the siege of Troy. The TROJAN HORSE won the war for the Greeks.

183 Zeno actually filched this bit from the comedian Steven Wright, creating a 2,500-year anachronism.

184 The very real philosopher Zeno of Elea, who died circa 430 BCE (when real Socrates would have been around 40), actually proposed several paradoxes that jigsawed infinity and movement, the most famous of which involved Achilles and the Tortoise on a footrace like this. The paradoxes were legitimate, if inscrutable, philosophical questions for millennia. (The twentieth-century philosopher Bertrand Russell called them "immeasurably subtle and profound.") Advances in modern mathematics (particularly the invention of *infinite series*) have, for the most part, relegated the conundrums to skull teasers for Philosophy 101 students.

ACHILLES

Wait. I get it! This is like *Inception*, right? I never did understand that movie.

While they bicker, yet another man approaches, directly from Athens. Everyone instantly recognizes him.

ALL

Socrates!

SOCRATES

Hey guys, what's shakin'? From the Acropolis, I could see you out here debating deep philosophical issues.

TORTOISE

It's a miracle you got here, Socrates. Have you heard? *Movement . . . is . . . an illusion.*

SOCRATES

Oh yes, Tortoise. Our friend Parmenides was telling me about Zeno's newest paradox. It is quite the humdinger, no?

ZENO

Great, Socrates, I am so pleased to see you. Perhaps you can explain the mysteries of this enigma to Turtle.

SOCRATES

I believe his name is *Tortoise*, and no, I cannot solve your conundrum. It probably has something to do with infinity and null sets, but that is over my head, as we Greeks have not yet even invented the zero.[185]

TORTOISE

I have an idea, Socrates. I think Zeno is an irritating frat bro, but—I hate to say this—he might have a point.

SOCRATES

Go on, Tortoise!

TORTOISE

His paradox is truly a terrible descriptor of the physical world. However, it does help explain an idea from epistemology—*what can we know?*

SOCRATES

Intriguing. Please tell me more.

TORTOISE

Consider the human search for truth and knowledge. Does it not seem we know more with each generation? Are we not more advanced than the Babylonians or the Phoenicians?

ACHILLES

Why yes, Tortoise, of course we know more than they. Those stupid Babylonians worshipped *the sun!*

TORTOISE

But maybe it only *seems* that we know more. Perhaps we are only getting slightly closer to the truth, in half-steps, but never arriving at the destination. We are like ants in a diorama, trapped outside the city of knowledge, moving forward only by fractions of an inch. As a tortoise, I can relate to this creeping pace.

SOCRATES

I see what you mean! We think of history as an arrow, slicing through time to hit its target, but that could be a delusion.

ACHILLES

Wait up. Hold on. You're saying my life is all a lie?

TORTOISE

It seems entirely possible, Achilles. For all we know, we could be fictional characters inside the head of some hack scriptwriter.

---

185 True! The zero was indeed not invented in the West until the Roman astronomer Ptolemy started using the placeholder digit around 130 CE.

ACHILLES

That's impossible. I don't care if this is the golden age of television, no one could have written my story. I am Achilles! I was made immortal by the magical river Styx! I slayed Paris outside of Troy to win the Trojan War![186]

SOCRATES

I don't know, Achilles. This whole dialogue does seem a lot like a flimsy spec script for a *Rick & Morty* episode that will never get produced. Just throw in a few robots and some multiverse hocus-pocus.

ACHILLES

I refuse to believe my life is a lie! This is worse than the time you guys took me to that amusement park, PLATO'S CAVE.

ZENO

How can we prove we are all not fabrications scribbled on paper?

SOCRATES

There is only one way to answer that question. We must invent a VOIGHT-KAMPFF MACHINE to determine if we are real. Hold my beer.

Socrates reaches into his bag and distributes bowls of food, which the famished travelers devour.

ACHILLES

This tastes terrible. What is it?

SOCRATES

Hemlock salad.

Unexpectedly, Zeno falls to the ground, clutching his chest.

ACHILLES

Zeno!

ZENO

[*looking very ill*] What . . . is . . . happening?

SOCRATES

It appears that only Zeno is a real person. The rest of us are just fictional characters who can choose whether poison kills us.

TORTOISE

Sick burn, blade runner.

ZENO

[*on the verge of death*] I see . . . Hades . . .

TORTOISE

You are trapped between heaven and hell. It's a paradox!

As Zeno dies, the scene slowly fades out.

ZENO

I . . . can . . . see . . . TURTLES ALL THE WAY DOWN.

ALL

It's tortoises!

THE END

---

186 Still not true. According to legend, Achilles was indeed made (almost) immortal when dipped by his ankle into the river Styx, but Paris killed him with an arrow to his unshielded heel outside the walls of Troy.

AFTERWORD

The Introduction of this compendium used the confabulated premise of an interview with renowned public radio host Terry Gross to outline the contents herein. Despite dropping an F-bomb on public radio, the author has miraculously been invited back to *Fresh Air*, this time to discuss how a specific term has changed meaning over time.

Welcome back to the studio. Please don't use profanity on-air again.
You crazy for this one, Terry!

I was hoping we could discuss "fake news." What does that term mean today?
Honestly, I have no *fuuu* . . . sorry, I have no idea. Within the field of information theory, it has become a critical term, but over the course of writing this book, its popular usage has zigzagged wildly.

At the onset, "fake news" was a term of art, reserved for news parody like *The Onion* or *Saturday Night Live*'s Weekend Update. But when talk show hosts like Jon Stewart and Stephen Colbert started to stretch the bounds of the genre, the pretend-news-complex morphed into the quasi-legitimate-news-complex. Stewart was voted the most trusted newscaster in a 2009 poll, and by 2017, *New York* magazine conferred their imprimatur on late-night host Jimmy Kimmel by dubbing him "our Cronkite" on its cover.

Isn't that the "Girls Jumping on Trampolines" guy?
Indeed! And that's the way it is.

So what happened to "fake news"?
It became an emblem for something completely different.

Around the 2016 election, the media started stamping the "fake news" label on those fabricated news reports that spread virally online. To cite just one such account, millions of people shared a story claiming Pope Francis endorsed Donald Trump. (Four Pinocchios!) There have been thousands of such junky stories, which SNOPES and PolitiFact have been desperately trying to tamp down, but it has been a war of attrition. Thanks to lame hoaxers, Google-rigging scoundrels, and Russian propagandists, the internet has become a fount of rotten information.

But those gunky stories are not the most common usage of "fake news" either.
True. The label "fake news" lost all meaning when Trump reappropriated it to denigrate the media and avert attention from negative reporting on his administration. He even tried to claim that he invented the term, which is just about the silliest fake news ever.

Today, "fake news" is more weapon than descriptor. Any bit of legitimate reporting can be cast as fake by anyone who disagrees with it. Whatever your politics, someone is surely deploying the term with different intent than you.

In that sense, "fake news" might be the quintessential American innovation, a perfectly circular coinage that negates itself. It is nearly meaningless, a NONCE WORD. People invent its meaning with each elocution. No one uses it the same way, but everyone wields it as a weapon against ideological foes.

In 2017, Collins Dictionary chose "fake news" as its word of the year. Good luck to them on defining it!

Why more *weapon* than *descriptor*?
Just one example: When confronted with evidence of deploying chemical weapons on his own people, Syrian dictator Bashar al-Assad responded, "You can forge anything these days . . . We are living in a

fake news era." The despot knows he can designate any inconvenient information as fake. The shape of the planet (FLAT EARTH HYPOTHESIS), space travel (MOON LANDING HOAX), or all of human history (PHANTOM TIME HYPOTHESIS)—they're all potentially counterfeit.

But those are the whackjobs, the paranoid class.
We have a tendency to shake our finger at such conspiratorial hokum, but that's a fragile reprieve. We are all to blame for this predicament. Mainstream culture (KARAOKE to HATSUNE MIKU) and new technologies (PHOTOSHOPPING to HUMAN CLONING) have perpetuated a society in which every image and sound seems potentially manipulated. We have built a theme park of post-truth, where because anything can be forged, nothing seems real. We celebrate crafty artifice, and demand engineered "experiences" every time we leave the house. Reality is pliable.

Like fabricating an NPR interview?
Precisely! It is no wonder that SIMULISM has become such a dominant pop theory. We might not be living in a computer program, but it certainly seems like we could be.

Why are we seduced by these false realities?
Heck if I know.

There is a scene in *The Truman Show* where an interviewer asks the producer of the show, "Why do you think Truman has never come close to discovering the true nature of his world?" The producer responds: "We accept the reality of the world with which we're presented. It's as simple as that."

It's as simple as that, which is not so simple at all.

It sounds like TRUMAN SYNDROME at a mass scale. Are we really suffering a crisis of facts?
The most important questions have shifted from *if* to *how much*. It's a matter of magnitude.

No one wants to be a Pollyanna, looking away while totalitarians accrue power, nor does anyone wish themselves Cassandra mewling the end of days (even

if, as we often forget about the myth, she was *right* about her predictions). It's the most difficult question of our time: *How serious is this?*

It sounds like you're hedging.
It is a consequence of a life dedicated to researching the history of deception. The past looks equally shady!

Here I take a cue from P. T. Barnum. In his book on HUMBUGGERY, he observed, "The greatest humbug of all is the man who believes—or pretends to believe—that everything is and everybody are humbugs." In other words, we should be wary of those positivists who scream *sheeple!* and stake their own claims on *true reality*. Amongst the intelligentsia, this idea floats around: If we could just agree upon the same facts, society would resolve its problems.

That seems great!
But is also likely an illusion.

Why an illusion?
First of all, facts do not constitute reality. What we each experience as reality is formed through the goopy filters of the mind, which rearrange and prioritize those facts through various prisms, including societal values and personal experience. As UMWELT suggests, reality is as much *in here* as *out there*.

But that dodges the question: How serious is fake news?
Depends what you mean by "fake news."

Don't be coy. I mean the hornswoggle on the internet that is patently false.
Let's cite some, as they say, *facts*.

During the 2016 election, the twenty most-read fake stories (those fabricated by fictitious news factories) were viewed more times than the twenty most-read legitimate stories (those reported by credible outlets). Facebook has estimated that Russian propaganda content reached 126 million Americans, and Twitter revealed that bots generated one out of every five political messages. Fake news stories incited a man to shoot up a D.C. pizza parlor that Reddit told him operated a Hillary Clinton–run pedophilia ring. Meanwhile, fact-checking agencies rate the president, who clearly benefits from the empirical meltdown, as uttering untrue statements 70 percent of the time.

So yeah, you could say it is serious.

Can it be fixed?

Facebook has tried taking some steps toward stemming the flow of misinformation on their platform. They started by launching an initiative to identify certain bogus stories as "disputed." But the problem turned out to be more complicated than just slapping labels on a few links.

Research has shown that news being repeated over and over creates a sense of information fluency (MERE-EXPOSURE EFFECT), so even those stories marked "disputed" can be perceived as accurate because we have seen them before (BELLMAN'S FALLACY). Other studies suggest that labeling content as "disputed" inadvertently causes some people to believe all non-labeled stories are true. And classifying every fleck of dreck around the internet would rival Hercules sanitizing the stables.

Facebook abandoned the program, and replaced it with an initiative that instead displays related articles next to fake news stories. The saga makes the battle against misinformation seem like one of those interminable wars we fight despite knowing it is futile. Misinformation is our Vietnam.

Will it get worse?

I'll answer by anecdote. Did you know that Borges wrote an encyclopedia? It's true! In 1957, he published *The Book of Imaginary Beings*, which contains a safari of mythical CRYPTIDS from literature and folklore.

In the entry on the Chimera, he briefly discusses the history of the fantastical creature, starting with HOMER, who described it in the *Iliad* as broken into thirds: lion, goat, and serpent, in order from head to tail. The poet Hesiod went a step further, moving those three creatures to the front, creating a multi-headed monster. And then Virgil, in the *Aeneid*, added fire-breathing to the beastly arsenal. "These absurd hypotheses," Borges finally concludes, "are proof that the Chimera was beginning to bore people. Easier than imagining it was to translate it into something else."

Other than showing off your Borges deep cuts, what is the point?

I think we are in the late Chimera phase. People have become bored with the latest version of reality, so they are willfully translating it into something worse. You can see this drive toward self-deception foretold in *The X-Files*'s "I Want to Believe" and in THE BLAIR WITCH PROJECT, but it has spread across all of society: entertainment, media, politics, sexuality, technology.

We have become inured to the belief that all realities are equal, all ideas equal. Everyone is allowed to have "their own opinion," by which they mean their own reality. The satiric concept of TRUTHINESS has transubstantiated into the real practice of ALTERNATIVE FACTS. Because the FILTER BUBBLE lets us inhabit any desired information ecosystem, this fever dream called reality has become less knowable than at any point in human history. We have returned to the state of blinkered troglodytes, chained to PLATO'S CAVE.

I suppose I am saying, *Yes, it will probably get worse.*

That's fucked.

You said it, Terry.

INSPIRATIONS

By definition, an encyclopedia is a hopeless, irresponsible endeavor. Unless you belong to a cloister of fifteenth-century monks biding time and grace for a few generations, the preposterously discursive nature of an encyclopedia's subject matter should push it beyond the bounds of reasonable activity. Most absurd of all, the scope of this reference work might be said to encompass literally *all of reality* (or *unreality*), which requires a special variety of intellectual hubris to embark upon. The topics contained herein meander around like an itinerant mongrel, from the social sciences to video games, new technology to professional wrestling, the techniques of propaganda to the codes of magicians. The very nature of a reference book implies stacks upon stacks of prior work and research, which this book holds in great respect. Wherever possible, this compendium attempts to source its influences while abstaining from ceaseless footnoted interruption. Many previous artifacts (books, movies, websites, articles, game shows, various ephemera) influenced the author, in ways direct and indirect, obvious and elusive, real and imagined. Encyclopedias exist as launching pads—pointers for further exploration outside their pages. Pointing outward, here is an expansive list of inspirations for this work of reference:

Gustave Flaubert's *Dictionary of Accepted Ideas*; Jorge Luis Borges's *The Book of Imaginary Beings*; Ricky Jay's *Journal of Anomalies*; Christopher Guest's *Spinal Tap*; James Randi's *An Encyclopedia of Claims, Frauds, and Hoaxes of the Occult and Supernatural*; Herman Melville's *The Confidence-Man*; Steven Wright's *I Have a Pony*; Lewis Carroll's *What the Tortoise Said to Achilles*; Douglas Hofstadter's *Gödel, Escher, Bach*; Hannah Arendt's *The Origins of Totalitarianism*; Rudy Rucker's *The Fourth Dimension*; Jean Baudrillard's *America*; Errol Morris's *Seeing Is Believing*; Know Your Meme; Daniel Boorstin's *The Image*; Italo Calvino's *Cosmicomics*; Ludwig Wittgenstein's *Philosophical Investigations*; Orson Welles's *F for Fake* and *The War of the Worlds*; Harry Frankfurt's "On Bullshit"; *Drunk History*; *Documentary Now!*; *The Dictionary of Imaginary Places*; Cool Freaks' Wikipedia Club; Richard Hofstadter's "The Paranoid Style in American Politics"; George Orwell's *1984*; *Oxford English Dictionary*; *Radiolab*; Kottke.org; Erich Auerbach's *Mimesis*; Luigi Serafini's *Codex Seraphinianus*; David Fincher's *The Game*; *MythBusters*; *The Encyclopedia of Science Fiction*; Michael Sippey's "Even if it's fake, it's real"; P. T. Barnum's *Humbugs of the World*; *The Anarchist Cookbook*; Urban Dictionary; Umberto Eco's *The Book of Legendary Lands*; Benjamin Franklin's *The Drinker's Dictionary*; Leslie Fiedler's *Freaks*; Steven Daly and Nathaniel Wice's *alt.culture*; Werner Herzog's *Grizzly Man*; Susan Sontag's *On Photography*; Jonathan Swift's "The Art of Political Lying"; *Penn & Teller: Bullshit!*; James Bridle's *New Aesthetic* blog; Don DeLillo's *White Noise*; Will Wright at SXSW 2007; Edwin Abbott's *Flatland*; Adam Curtis's *The Century of Self* and *The Power of Nightmares*; Cecil Adams's *Straight Dope* columns; Michel Foucault's *What Is an Author?*; James Gleick's *The Information*; Dan Carlin's *Hardcore History*; Jesse Walker's *The United States of Paranoia*; Penny Lane's *Nuts!*; Kurt Anderson's *Fantasyland*; Charlie Brooker's *Black Mirror* and *Screenwipe*; James Gleick's *The Information*; Kembrew McLeod's *Pranksters*; Max Black's "The Prevalence of Humbug"; *Lingua Franca* magazine; Sigmund Freud's *Civilization and Its Discontents*; Christopher Nolan's *The Prestige*; Roland Barthes's *Mythologies*; Kenneth Anger's *Hollywood Babylon*; *To Tell The Truth*; Chuck Klosterman's *Eating the Dinosaur*; Snopes; TV Tropes; all blogs at the turn of the millennium; Lawrence Weschler's *Uncanny Valley* and *Boggs*; Lewis Hyde's *Trickster Makes This World*; Truman Capote's *In Cold Blood*; Dr. Poochigian's philosophy courses and Dr. Beard's literature courses; The New York Public Library.

ACKNOWLEDGMENTS

If you have ever peeked into a book's acknowledgments, you have likely noticed a recurring trope in which the author thanks their editor and agent. You probably shrugged this off as a mere formality, akin to that perfunctory nod to mom at the Oscars. But when you go through the publishing process, you realize that if not for these skilled technicians, most books would suck pretty hard. I am immensely grateful for my editor Samantha Weiner at Abrams and my agent Rachel Vogel at DCL for removing so much of the suck.

Thank you to my wife, who never made known her grave regret for hitching herself to a moody sourpuss in the middle of writing his first book. I swear, it wasn't a trick.

I am also indebted to those who endured reviewing early drafts of this compendium in its many forms. Those generous wits include Michelle Dozois, Melissa Maerz, Dagny Salas, Cole Stryker, Chuck Klosterman, Harry Heymann, and Emily Condon.

Thank you to Lorenzo Petrantoni, the illustrator who is so gifted that he can make a drab reference book sparkle with intrigue. And I am unspeakably grateful to Devin Grosz, who was lovingly meticulous in designing every little nook and cranny of this book. I would happily conscript into any war against widows and orphans with him.

Finally, I would like to thank my mom. But not in that perfunctory Oscars way. For real, she's the best mom.

Editor: Samantha Weiner
Designer: Devin Grosz
Production Manager: Rebecca Westall

Library of Congress Control Number: 2017949738

ISBN: 978-1-4197-2911-9
eISBN: 978-1-68335-234-1

Printed and bound in USA
10 9 8 7 6 5 4 3 2 1

Abrams Image books are available at special discounts when purchased in quantity for premiums and promotions as well as fundraising or educational use. Special editions can also be created to specification. For details, contact specialsales@abramsbooks.com or the address below.

ABRAMS The Art of Books
195 Broadway, New York, NY 10007
abramsbooks.com